P9-DUJ-932

DATE DUE

MR 1 0			
MY 3 0 96			
DE 1 7 05			

Tracking America's Economy

Second Edition

Tracking America's Economy

Second Edition

NORMAN FRUMKIN

M. E. SHARPE, INC.
ARMONK, NEW YORK
LONDON, ENGLAND

Available in the United Kingdom and Europe from M. E. Sharpe, Publishers,
3 Henrietta Street, London WC2E 8LU.

Library of Congress Cataloging-in-Publication Data

Frumkin, Norman.
Tracking America's economy / by Norman Frumkin. — 2nd ed.
p. cm.
Includes bibliographical references and index.
ISBN 1-56324-002-5 (cloth)
ISBN 1-56324-003-3 (paper)
1. Economic forecasting—United States.
2. Economic indicators—United States.
3. United States—Economic policy—1981–
I. Title.
HC106.8.F78   1992
338.5′44′0973—dc20
91-38370
CIP

Printed in the United States of America
The paper used in this publication meets the minimum
requirements of American National Standard for
Information Sciences—Permanence of Paper for
Printed Library Materials, ANSI Z 39.48-1984.

MV   10   9   8   7   6   5   4   3   2   1

To Sarah, Jacob, and Samuel

In memory of Anne Frances Frumkin and Joseph Harry Frumkin

CONTENTS

TABLES

FIGURES

ABBREVIATIONS

BEA	Bureau of Economic Analysis
BLS	Bureau of Labor Statistics
CCAdj	Capital consumption adjustment
CPI	Consumer price index
CPI-U	Consumer price index based on spending patterns of urban consumers
CPI-W	Consumer price index based on spending patterns of wage and clerical workers
CPS	Current Population Survey
CURs	Capacity utilization rates
FOMC	Federal Open Market Committee
FR	Federal Reserve
GAO	General Accounting Office
GDP	Gross domestic product
GNP	Gross national product
IPI	Industrial production index
IVA	Inventory valuation adjustment
LCLg	Leading, coincident, and lagging indexes
NABE	National Association of Business Economists
NBER	National Bureau of Economic Research
OMB	Office of Management and Budget
OPEC	Organization of Petroleum Exporting Countries
OTA	Office of Technology Assessment
PPP	Purchasing power parity
SNA	System of National Accounts
SPI	Service production index
ULC	Unit labor costs
UR	Unemployment rate

PREFACE

This second edition of *Tracking America's Economy,* like the first, attempts to help students and the general public interpret trends in the major statistical indicators of the U.S. economy. Bridging theory and practice, it explains the significance of the basic economic indicators, details their cyclical and longer-term movements since World War II, analyzes their relationship to each other and to broader developments in the domestic and international economies, and discusses their implications for economic policy. Written in everyday language with easily understood tables and figures, the book is intended for classroom teaching, self-study, or reference.

The second edition updates, refines, and augments the analyses and discussions of the first edition. This enhancement includes the measurement, analytic, and policy aspects of the indicators, as well as institutional factors that affect the indicators, such as the independence and accountability of the Federal Reserve system, the national economic goals of the Full Employment and Balanced Growth Act of 1978, and the effectiveness of the unemployment insurance system. In addition, the second edition has several new features of recent important economic topics. These include:

- New sections on investment and saving, the federal budget deficit, the international dimensions of the U.S. economy, interest rates, and the leading index system.
- New chapter on economic forecasting.
- Review questions at the end of every chapter.
- Epilogue on the production of economic statistics.

The book introduces the reader to the basic elements of macroeconomics: economic growth, employment, inflation, and finance. These complex subjects generate considerable disagreement among economists, who apply a wide variety of theories to interpret the same data differently. To some, the American economy in the early 1990s is sound and requires a continuation or only minor modification of the economic policies of the 1980s, while others believe the economy is faltering and needs fundamentally different economic policies.

These varying views reflect the difficulty of identifying true cause-and-effect relationships when considering issues such as the impact of the federal government budget deficit and the foreign trade deficit on the economic well-being of the nation, or the causes of the deficits in the first place. The conflicts also indicate the role of the philosophic premises economists use. For example, whether an economist is politically liberal or conservative colors the analysis, in some cases obviously and in others not so transparently.

With such disagreement among specialists, how is the public to know whose economic advice is most credible? Unfortunately this book cannot definitively answer this question. Just as in many other aspects of life, nonspecialists must listen to conflicting expert testimony in court suits, conflicting medical advice from doctors, and conflicting claims by producers of food, cars, and other products, and ultimately make their own decision. This book provides households, businesses, unions, investors, elected officials, and voters with a more rational basis for making decisions based on perceptions of the economy. I also hope it helps some journalists to become more astute in reporting economic news, and some students in economics courses to understand and apply the theories better.

The idea for this book came from a course on interpreting economic trends which I give at the Graduate School, U.S. Department of Agriculture. In preparing for the course, I found there is no suitable single volume on the topic and decided to write one. Both editions of the book have benefited considerably from the thoughtful and perceptive questions and discussions by class members who work in a variety of fields in both the private and public sectors.

Richard Bartel, editor of *Challenge,* encouraged me to write this second edition. It has been a pleasure to work with him, and I deeply appreciate his support.

Several persons provided important comments on drafts of the book. I thank these people for their insights, but ultimately I take sole responsibility for the book's contents. Edward Steinberg commented on the entire second edition. His acuity and insight were invaluable. Others to whom I am grateful for reviewing various sections of the book are: William Alterman, Christopher Bach, Alvin Bauman, Barry Beckman, John Berry, Carol Carson, Elinor Champion, Carol Corrado, Edward Cowan, Dennis Cox, Edwin Dean, Jerry Donahoe, Faye Duchin, Joseph Duncan, Clark Edwards, Seth Elan, Maria Eli, David Findley, Paul Flaim, Sarah Frumkin, Gary Gillum, John Gorman, Thomas Holloway, Jeanette Honsa, Michael Horrigan, Patrick Jackman, Marshall Kaplan, Zoltan Kenessey, Ronald Kutscher, Stephen McNees, Ralph Monaco, Robert Parker, Richard Raddock, Gerald Schluter, Benjamin Slatin, James Stock, Milo Sunderhauf, Robert Villanueva, Stephen Wandner, George Werking, and Obie Whichard. I also had helpful discussions on statistical methodology with Lee Abramson and David Hirschberg and on international comparisons with Arthur Neef. The staff of M. E. Sharpe did an outstanding job of transforming a complex manuscript into the published book: Angela Piliouras was the project editor for most of the preparation of the book; Lynn Frede-Tripicco was the project editor in the last phase of the work; Laura Cohn was the copyeditor; Carol Johnson was the typesetter.

I was again fortunate to have Jody Foster as style editor. With extraordinary perception, she simplified involved topics and brought a freshness and clarity to the overall presentation and the writing.

In the excitement of completing the first edition, I neglected to note the contributions of those closest to me, my sons. Samuel Frumkin taught me how to use the computer, and Jacob Frumkin gave me the idea of including advice to the analyst on interpreting each indicator at the end of each section. I continued to benefit from their long-lasting help in working on this second edition.

Revising the book has been like revisiting a favorite place. It has been all the more satisfying being done in the company of my wife, Sarah.

Tracking America's Economy

Second Edition

INTRODUCTION

Data on the state of the U.S. economy abound. With what some may call information overload, federal agencies publish statistics for the most recent month or quarter on economic growth, employment and inflation, and finance. Trade associations, research organizations, and international institutions add to this data base with their own indicators on particular sectors of the economy.

These indicators are typically historical and descriptive, although they also include forecasts such as Census Bureau surveys of business plans for investment in plant and equipment, Federal Reserve target ranges for the money supply, and projections of the federal budget by Congress and the president. They are reported in the newspapers and on radio and television, with economists and politicians offering interpretations of the most recent trends and their implications for future economic activity.

Yet after all these assessments, which sometimes vary considerably, the question remains: What do these economic indicators mean? This book cannot answer that question, but it can give the reader a framework for assimilating the vast array of economic data, or at least a basis for asking relevant questions and evaluating the answers. Depending on interest and background, the reader will become more self-sufficient in conducting independent economic analyses, deciding which experts give the most credible explanations, or recognizing when another opinion is needed.

Why would members of the general public want a better understanding of economic indicators? At a pragmatic level, some household activities and business activities, such as buying a house or investing funds, are influenced by the overall economy, and more understanding of the economy will help the reader to anticipate some of the fluctuations that could affect these decisions. Knowledge of economic trends may also be helpful in assessing statements made by candidates for public office. And, more generally, the economy is so much in the news that some people simply have an intellectual interest in learning more about it.

GUIDING PRINCIPLES OF THE BOOK

The book is shaped by three principles: information is presented as clearly as possible for the reader, the basic concepts behind the indicators are related to their behavior, and past experience is used to forecast the future.

Clarity

When I was in elementary school, the principal would come into the classroom from time to time to observe the teaching. He invariably took over from the teacher who was in the middle of a history, arithmetic, spelling, or geography lesson. I had mixed feelings about the principal's presence. He was initially intimidating, and I felt uneasy for the teacher, who seemed to be getting on-the-job training. But as the principal continued, I enjoyed it because he was a superb teacher and I felt I learned a lot from him. At some point, he would ask the class a question. If a student said, "I know it, but I can't explain it," he replied, "If you can't explain it, you don't know it."

I have long believed this man hit on one of those basic truths of life. Even though many questions cannot be answered definitively and others are problematic, a clear presentation always aids in the search for better answers. Thus, I have strived to provide the reader with simple, clear explanations for economic phenomena. This is not always an easy task. In economics, for example, the significance of unemployment and inflation levels, or of investment and saving, is easier to explain than the relationships between these factors. Yet, even the simpler meanings are not always straightforward. Nevertheless, I have reduced the complex phenomena to clear and simple concepts that a reader at the college level or the equivalent in independent reading and life experience can apprehend. I admit this clarity is achieved at some loss in subtlety, but this loss is justified.

Concepts and Behavior of the Indicator

Just as you can drive a car without knowing what is under the hood, and in many cases be just as good a driver as someone who understands the engine, you can also analyze the movement of economic indicators without knowing much about how the indicators are defined or how the data are obtained. But this lack of knowledge about the concepts behind the indicators can lead to superficial and misleading interpretations. Therefore, this book analyzes the estimating methodology as well as the historical trends for each indicator. This "under the hood" approach helps the reader understand how the conceptual aspects of an indicator affect its behavior.

Past Experience and Forecasting

Forecasts of economic activity are made largely by projecting past trends. Using historical experience to forecast the future is problematic in two ways, however. First, the past itself is uneven with some periods above the long-term average and others below the average. The forecasting challenge is to discern if the current period is above, below, or similar to the long-term average. Second, structural factors such as markets, technology, labor-management relations, and worldwide competition change over time, sometimes quite rapidly, and a mechanical extrapolation of the past that does not take such changes into account will produce an unrealistic forecast. Making such forecasts can be likened to driving a car while looking at the rear view mirror. You get a better view of where you have been than where you are going. Thus, the analysis of each indicator includes general advice on how to deal with the challenges of applying past experience to future forecasts.

NATURE OF THE BOOK

The book focuses on understanding the U.S. economy's strengths and weaknesses, as well as its probable future direction, by applying the concepts and statistics of macroeconomics. Macroeconomics is the branch of economics that focuses on the overall economy's performance in terms of economic growth, business cycles, unemployment and inflation, and on methods for improving the performance.[1] Macroeconomic indicators trace the ups and downs of overall economic activity in the expansion and recession stages of business cycles. They also portray longer-term trends in the growth rate over several business cycles. While the book emphasizes cyclical movements of the macro indicators, it puts them in the context of economic theory and longer-run trends.

For example, in considering goals for an acceptable level of unemployment, the book examines how and why the definition of full or high employment has changed since the end of World War II. In economic theory, when unemployment falls below certain levels, unemployment and inflation develop an inverse relationship—as unemployment decreases, inflation increases and vice versa. This relationship in turn leads to a trade-off between the two, which is central to much of the political debate on appropriate economic policies. Economists disagree on the timing and extent of the trade-off—when and to what degree a reduction in unemployment should be balanced against a rise in inflation, or a reduction in inflation against a rise in unemployment. Examination of these relationships in turn points up how well economic theories conform to experience.

MACRO VS. MICRO ANALYSIS

The indicators in the book are at the *macro* level. The macro level summarizes into broad totals the activities of all households, businesses, state and local governments, and the federal government. For example, spending by households for food, housing, and other items is encompassed into a single figure for all households in all income groups. By contrast, the *micro* level focuses on individual decisions; micro analysis of consumer spending distinguishes differential spending and saving rates for low-, middle-, and high-income households.

However, the distinction is more than one of separate and consolidated units. At the micro level, the decisions by individual households, businesses, and governments to spend, save, and invest result from buyers and sellers in the market-place agreeing or disagreeing on the price and quantity of the time to be sold. At the macro level, these marketplace transactions are reflected in and affected by overall trends in economic aggregates such as employment, income, and inflation. There also is interaction between the two, as micro decisions to buy and sell depend partly on how buyers and sellers think the macro environment will affect them.

Figure 1 highlights the micro-macro factors influencing the purchase of a house. Basic questions asked by prospective homeowners are: Can I make the monthly payments without being strapped? Is this a good time to buy in terms of the overall economy? Analysts resort to macro indicators to summarize the activities of individual decision units at the mirco level because economic methodology is not sufficiently advanced to quantitatively bridge the effect of micro decisions on overall macro trends.

ECONOMIC INTERPRETATION
IS NOT AN EXACT SCIENCE

Despite the fund of available information, the continuing expert analyses of trends in the private and public sectors, and advances in economic theory and analytic techniques, the beginning student and others with limited exposure to the field should realize that analysis and forecasting of economic activity are not an exact science. Although fairly refined measures of economic activity have been available since the 1940s, the major economic events of recent years—the slow economic growth and high inflation (stagnation) of the 1970s and the deep recession of 1981–82, continued growth during the rest of the 1980s accompanied by lower but still high inflation, loss of jobs to foreign producers, and no progress in reducing poverty—were not anticipated by economists.

Interpreting economic data is closer to an art than a science for several reasons. First, in order to be available quickly, the indicators are based on preliminary data; subsequent revisions, based on more complete and accurate information, may give a different picture of current trends. Moreover, because the relationships between the factors affecting the economy are complex, interpretations are heavily colored by the most recent movement in the indicators. Experts frequently revise their forecasts as the latest wiggles in the gross national product, unemployment rate, or consumer price index diverge from their expectations of where the economy is heading. The speed with which forecasts of economic growth, employment, and inflation are outdated indicates the complexity of the subject.

Second, the signals of current and future economic activity given by the indicators will not always seem consistent—for example, rising federal deficits and falling interests rates, or lower unemployment and lower inflation. This may be due to relationships that are not fully understood, such as those among the

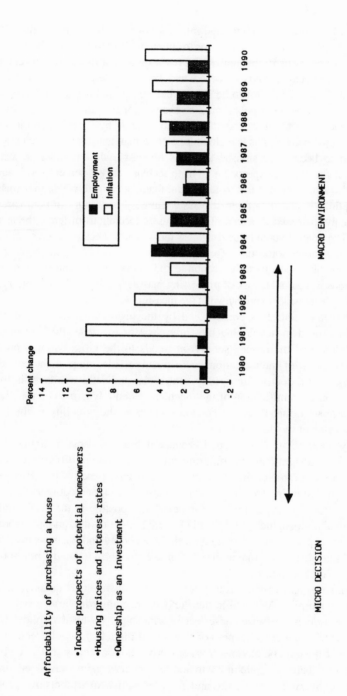

Figure 1. **Micro-Macro Interrelationships**

money markets, unemployment, and inflation; or to technical problems with the data, which will result in revisions; or to inherent shortcomings in the data, such as changes in an industry that make a survey's sample of firms unrepresentative.

Third, interpretation tends to be colored by the difference between what the analyst expects the indicator to be shortly before it is published compared to the actual indicator when it is published. For example, if the analyst expects the gross national product for the most recent quarter to increase by 3 percent and it actually increases only 2 percent, this is a gloomier picture than anticipated, which may lead the analyst to become pessimistic and thus forecast a slower future growth rate. However, if the analyst expects the GNP to increase only 1 percent and it actually increases by 2 percent, this is a rosier picture than anticipated, which may make the analyst optimistic and thus forecast a faster future growth rate. In both cases, the GNP actually increased 2 percent. But because expectations differed, the analyses differed. The analyst should guard against this reaction because it gives too much weight to the earlier conjecture of what the indicator would be. The preparation of weekly, monthly, and quarterly economic indicators by government and private organizations is a complex task of processing masses of data, and it is a problematic exercise for the outsider to predict what the measure will be.

Fourth, interpretation is complicated by the historical instability of certain relationships used in developing the forecasts (for example, the impact of the federal deficit and the money supply on trends in the gross national product). The tentativeness of interpretation has a positive side, since it moderates any tendencies toward doctrinaire rigidity. But it also indicates weakness in the understanding and quantification of the mechanisms and dynamic changes, both at home and abroad, that drive the economy (such as the volatility in the foreign exchange value of the dollar).

Finally, interpretation is clouded because political and psychological factors that may have a significant bearing on economic trends are difficult to quantify and are subject to rapid change. Examples are the emergence of the Organization of Petroleum Exporting Countries as an effective cartel, perceptions of our international responsibilities and our resultant defense posture in the post–Cold War era, political philosophies affecting the federal budget deficit, and inflationary or deflationary expectations affecting household spending and business investment. Factors like these have major effects on the economy, but do not show up explicitly in the indicators.

In summary, as in many aspects of life, it is difficult to quantify ultimate causes in economics. As noted in the Preface, specialists in various fields differ among themselves on cause-and-effect relationships. Baseball provides a good example of the inherent weakness of theoretical models. It would seem that the player's worth would be obvious from objective, bottom-line statistics on batting averages, runs-batted-in, pitching win and loss records, games saved, etc. Indeed, there is a proliferation of statistics and complex statistical artifacts that probe the bottom-line figures to better understand what they mean. For example, the "runs created" measure has sixteen factors, eleven in the numerator and five in the denominator.[2] Despite these complex formulas, however, analysts remain unable to define the fundamental aspects of superior player performance. Thus, ultimate causes remain elusive in America's favorite pastime, despite the considerable quantification in every game, and even though millions of fans analyze every game. How much more elusive, then, is the economy that is driven by tangible and intangible factors in the United States and all over the world, most of which cannot be quantified.

Given the limits of human understanding, perhaps the best we can do is develop theoretical models that conform to our understanding of economic phenomena and use these models to conduct analyses until they are shown to be untenable or are superseded by improved models.

OUTLINE OF THE BOOK

The first two chapters provide background material for the subsequent discussion of the specific economic indicators. Chapter 1 addresses the implications of monthly and quarterly wiggles in the indicators due to data revisions and seasonality, the uses of index numbers, and the macroeconomic effect of the underground economy. Chapter 2 focuses on the determination of cyclical expansions and recessions, business cycles since the nineteenth century, depressions and cyclical analyses, and the role of fiscal and monetary policies in moderating the extremes of expansions and recessions.

Chapters 3 through 8 cover the economic indicators that represent the main forces associated with trends in economic growth, employment, inflation, and financial markets. These are the gross national product; industrial production and capacity utilization; unemployment, employment, and productivity; the consumer price index; money supply and interest rates; and leading, coincident, and lagging indexes. These chapters highlight the key factors driving the indicators and suggest which items to consider when interpreting trends in the data; advice to the analyst is highlighted in italics. Each chapter has two parts: a methodological section with the definitions, estimation, and limitation of the indicators (Part A); and an analytic section on their relationships and significance over the post–World War II business cycles (Part B). Readers with some background in the methodological aspects may wish to move directly to Part B.

The last two chapters look at basic issues in the use and provision of economic indicators. Chapter 9 discusses macroeconomic forecasting as a subject in its own right: this includes alternative forecasting methodologies; short-term, medium-term, and long-term forecasts and their uses; the accuracy of forecasts; and the effect of forecasts on future economic trends. Chapter 10 addresses the content and accuracy of economic statistics produced by federal agencies in the context of concerns that they have not kept pace with the increasing complexity of the economy and the consequent efforts to remedy certain deficiencies.

NOTE ON DATA SOURCES

All tables and figures in the book are based on information available as of April/May 1991 except for a few tables that include data which became available in the summer of 1991. The statistics are from primary data sources, published monthly: the *Survey of Current Business* of the Bureau of Economic Analysis in the U.S. Department of Commerce; the *Monthly Labor Review* of the Bureau of Labor Statistics in the U.S. Department of Labor; and the *Federal Reserve Bulletin* of the Federal Reserve Board. Most of the data from these sources relevant to the book are compiled monthly in a handy form in *Economic Indicators*, prepared by the U.S. Council of Economic Advisers for the Joint Economic Committee of Congress. The annual *Economic Report of the President* provides excellent appendix tables of historical data. All of these publications are sold by the U.S. Government Printing Office. Single copies of the *Economic Report of the President* are available free from the Executive Office of the President.

REVIEW QUESTIONS

• Microeconomics represents the real world and macroeconomics is an artifact. Explain.
• Why does economic interpretation combine the properties of an art and a science?

NOTES

1. Sherman J. Maisel, *Macroeconomics: Theories and Policies* (W. W. Norton & Company: 1982), pp. 3–4.
2. The formula for runs created is:

Numerator =   Hits + Walks + Hit by Pitch –Caught Stealing
      –Grounded into Double Plays x Total Bases
      + 0.26 x (Hit by Pitch + Unintentional Walks)
      + 0.52 x Sacrifice Hits + Sacrifice Hits
      + Sacrifice Flies

Denominator =   At Bats + Walks + Hit by Pitch
      + Sacrifice Hits + Sacrifice Flies

See Gerald Eskenazi, "Baseball Statistics: How Much Is Enough?" *New York Times*, April 30, 1990, pp. C1, C16.

1
COMMON PROBLEMS AFFECTING
THE INDICATORS

At the outset, beginning students and others with a limited background should familiarize themselves with several technical problems generally inherent in economic indicators, which may affect their interpretation at particular times. While the nonspecialist typically does not get into the details, it is important to be aware of these factors and how they can distort the picture of the economy given by the indicators. The most problematic factors are data revisions, seasonality, index numbers, and the underground economy. This chapter provides a generic topical discussion of these factors; they will also be referred to in chapters on the individual indicators.

REVISIONS

The statistics on production, unemployment, prices, money supply, etc., published month after month, sometimes have a decided upward, downward, or sideways trend over several months. While this may reflect actual events in the marketplace for which no explanations have yet become evident, it may also result from problems with data accuracy. In some of these cases, the preliminary information will be revised. These revisions sometimes change the pattern of the earlier information—for example, an indicator that had portrayed a robust economy could turn out to indicate a sagging one, and vice versa.

There are several reasons why the preliminary data may be inadequate. The most common reason is erroneous survey information. Many indicators are based on information collected from households, businesses, or governments responding to surveys. Often, early erroneous reports from some respondents must be corrected, or reports not received in time for the publishing deadline must be included later. Errors in survey data can be particularly troublesome when the problem respondents, such as large companies, account for an important share of the survey.

Monthly and quarterly economic indicators are often revised in several stages on a regular schedule, although the frequency varies among indicators. As increasing amounts of more accurate and detailed data become available, revisions are made in the succeeding months or quarter, in the following year or years, and in some cases every five or ten years. Revisions based on a comprehensive set of data that will undergo no further improvements are called "benchmarks," and are the most accurate and detailed data available. Benchmark figures include survey data from the most representative samples of survey respondents, improved methodologies for statistical estimating, and new definitions for components of the indicator. They require a lengthy computation and usually occur at intervals of five or more years (although a major one on employment is done every year). Due to their necessarily delayed presentation, analysts use benchmark figures to revise theoretical relationships of one indicator to another rather than for policymaking or interpreting the current movement of the indicators.

Some indicators like the gross national product are revised for historical periods both before and after the most recent benchmarks, while others like the consumer price index are revised only for periods after the most recent benchmark. These variations reflect judgments about the most effective presentation for each indicator. The judgments are made by weighing such factors as the need to have consistent data over time, the availability and accuracy of comparable data, the additional data processing costs to make the more extensive revisions, and the issue of whether history should be "rewritten" by including factors that previously were not considered in economic analysis and policymaking. Ideally, historical data before the benchmark period should be revised. When they are not, the data series has a break that makes the earlier years inconsistent with the later years. Such inconsistencies should be considered when analyzing long-term trends.

Because of wiggles in marketplace activity and revisions that become available shortly after the preliminary data are released, it is important not to be swayed by the most recent blip in the indicators. A trend of at least two quarters should be identified before determining that a significant change is occurring. There have been instances however, when even this amount of time does not preclude being misled by recent trends. For example, the gross national product growth rate for the last three quarters of 1989 was revised significantly downward in the annual GNP revisions published in July 1990, which was also the eve of the recession of 1990–91 (see tabulation below). Had policymakers been aware early in 1990 of this much weaker trend in economic growth, they may have adopted policies to stimulate growth in the six months preceding the onset of the recession in place of the neutral economic policies (neither stimulative nor restraining) actually in existence.

Real GNP Annual Growth Rate: 1989
(percent)

	Initial estimates (prior to July 1990)	Revised estimates (July 1990)
2nd quarter	2.5	1.6
3rd quarter	3.0	1.7
4th quarter	1.1	0.3

Revisions play a fundamental role in the leading, coincident, and lagging indexes that are used to forecast economic activity. Generally, the preliminary data that are available when forecasts are prepared give only limited advance signs that the economy is heading for a recession, while clear signals of an impending recession are more apparent in the revised data that became available in later years (although the timing of when the recession will occur is uncertain). There is no difference between the preliminary and revised data in signaling a recovery from the recession.

Some indicators are published with numerical ranges of error due to sampling of survey respondents or revision of preliminary data (e.g., there may be an expected error in the data in 19 out of 20 cases of plus or minus 3 percent). In such cases, one should allow for a lower and upper range of the figure in assessing trends over time. When the error range is larger than the movement in the currency indicator (say, the error is plus or minus 3 percent and the monthly movement in the indicator is only 1 percent), the single-period movement is highly tentative. If such small movements cumulate in one direction over several periods, that trend is more significant. For example, an unemployment rate change of 0.1 percent in one month is not statistically significant because it is within the range of likely sampling error. But if the unemployment rate rises or falls by 0.1 percent in the same direction for two or more months, the cumulative change is significant.

SEASONALITY

Economic activity is bumpy from day to day, month to month, and quarter to quarter. Even when cyclical movements continue in the same direction over several periods (rising during an expansion or declining during a recession), there are daily deviations as households, businesses, and governments speed up or slow down their rate of spending. These short-term fits and starts stem from various sources: the intrinsic tempo of economic life with its bursts and lulls in activity followed by a return to the routine pace; quick response to changes or perceived changes in the economic environment; single-event shocks such as hurricanes, earthquakes, oil spills, and strikes; and repetitive seasonal variations during the year resulting from such factors as school vacations, holidays, Christmas shopping, heavier construction during the warmer months, automobile plant shutdowns for model year changes during the summer, and the payment of annual individual income taxes in the first four months of the year.

Adjustments for single-event shocks like hurricanes are made on an ad hoc basis depending on whether the organization providing the data considers the shock to have abnormally affected economic activity and whether the organization has resources available to make the adjustment. But for short-term analysis of movements in the monthly and quarterly economic indicators, eliminating recurring seasonal variations is desirable. "Seasonally adjusted" data suppress

Figure 2. **Seasonal Patterns of Retail Sales: 1990**

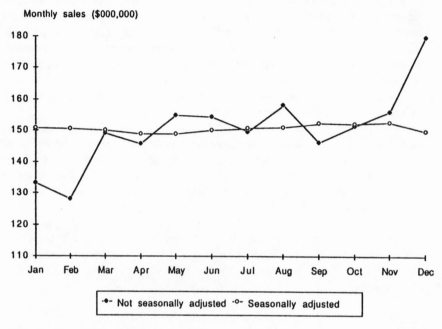

Monthly sales ($000,000)

-•- Not seasonally adjusted -○- Seasonally adjusted

Note: Based on Bureau of the Census data.

the effect of normally expected short-term increases or decreases during certain times of the year. The "smoothed" data reduce the chance of misleading movements in the indicator by neutralizing the effect of certain temporary and predictable changes.

Estimates of seasonal adjustment are based on the economic experience of previous years. When consistent seasonal patterns for particular months (or quarters in the case of quarterly data) indicate on average that the indicator is a certain amount higher or lower, or is the same as the monthly (quarterly) average based on the entire year, then the indicator is adjusted accordingly that month. For example, if sales of women's shoes typically are 5 percent below the monthly average for the year in January and 7 percent above the monthly average for the year in April, actual January sales are increased by 5 percent and actual April sales are reduced by 7 percent.

Figure 2 shows total retail sales of all products in 1990 both "seasonally adjusted" and "not seasonally adjusted." Seasonally adjusted sales are far less volatile than the actual, not seasonally adjusted sales. Thus, given the normal buying patterns before and after Christmas, actual sales are much higher in

December and much lower in January and February than the seasonally adjusted sales figures reveal.

Sophisticated techniques are used to seasonally adjust economic data. The procedures are too technical to detail here, but the following techniques illustrate the general method:

• At least seven to ten years of historical experience are used to develop seasonal factors.

• Seasonal patterns of recent years receive greater weight than those in earlier years.

• Revisions of the last few years' seasonal factors are made every year, with data for the most recent year replacing the data for the first year in the series. That is, a rolling fixed period of years is used. For example, in a series of fifteen years of data from 1976–90, the series becomes 1977–91 when 1991 data become available.

• Extreme values of the indicator in particular months or quarters, such as those due to a strike or flood, are downweighted or excluded as aberrations.

• An increasing number of data series have adopted a "concurrent adjustment" method which uses actual data from the most recent period to develop seasonal factors for the most recent month.

• In some cases, the trend of seasonal factors in previous years is projected one year ahead for use in the current year. For example, during 1991 seasonal factors are available only through 1990. In order to apply seasonal factors to the current data in 1991 that are considered appropriate for 1991, a forecast is made of the expected 1991 seasonal factors.

Regardless of the technique used, seasonally adjusted economic indicators are a statistical artifact that cannot entirely deal with seasonal phenomena. Although seasonal data are based on the average experience of past years, seasonal variations may be atypical in any particular year. For example, the winter may be colder or warmer than normal, or automobile model year changeovers may be more or less extensive than average in a particular year. On the other hand, movements that appear to be merely seasonal, such as a decline in business from December to January, may in fact reflect an actual deterioration in the health of the economy that will only become apparent when the data of subsequent months appear. These possibilities should be examined in analyzing monthly or quarterly movements of the indicator.

The majority of economic data are seasonally adjusted, but some are not. The reasons for no seasonal adjustment vary: the monthly or quarterly data may be too erratic to establish a seasonal pattern; in the case of new data series, there may be insufficient historical experience; or the organization providing the data may not think a seasonal pattern is relevant. When an indicator is not seasonally adjusted, one indirect means of understanding the seasonally adjusted movement is to compare percent changes between the current period (month or quarter) and the same period (month or quarter) of a year earlier for several consecutive periods. While this indirect approach provides a broad magnitude of the current seasonally adjusted movement, it cannot indicate cyclical turning points. The result also may be misleading if differences in the calendar are significant from year to year. For example, in one year, March could have more weekends than in the next year; this fact could affect the amount of business activity in the month.

INDEX NUMBERS

Some economic indicators are shown as index numbers, which state the figure for the current period as a percentage of a base period that is established as 100. For example, if the base period is 1987 (1987 = 100) and the figure for the current month is 142, then the indicator shows a 42 percent increase since 1987; if the current figure is 88, the series has decreased by 12 percent since 1987. Examples of index indicators that are discussed in later chapters include the industrial production index and the consumer price index.

The base period of an indicator may represent a single year, such as the industrial production index where 1987 = 100, or a few consecutive years, such as the consumer price index of 1982–84 = 100. The base period is selected according to when the most recent comprehensive and detailed survey data are available: for example, the base period for the gross national product is the year of the most recent economic census, while the base period for the consumer price index is the period of the most recent consumer expenditure survey. Although it is desirable for the base period to be one when the economy is relatively balanced with no excesses of high unemployment or high inflation, in practice the availability of data governs the selection of the base period.

Index numbers are a convenient way to combine a wide range of items into a single figure to show their overall relative change. Indexes are calculated by multiplying each item's importance in the base period by the percent change in the item's value since the base period; the sum of the products of all the items is the index for the current period. The combination of several items in an overall index also causes a problem, however, because the relative importance of the various items in the index will have changed since the base period. For example, see the discussion of production indexes in Chapter 4 and of price indexes in Chapter 6.

Some index number indicators are based on the same fixed proportions of items that add up to 100 in the base period. Other index numbers allow these proportions to change with actual production or consumption: some items increase in use and others become less important because of changes in buyer preferences, competition from substitute products, etc. Because individual items in the index change at different rates over time (e.g., housing costs may rise faster than food prices in the consumer price index), the overall index will show different rates of change depending on whether the base-period or current-period proportions are used. This "product mix" problem has been a long-standing issue in the construction of index numbers.

For example, in the case of price indexes, one that maintains the same relative *quantities* of the various items purchased as in the base period will show a higher rate of price increase (or lower rate of decline) than when the index represents the actual items bought in each period. This occurs because buyers switch to cheaper substitute products or to substitutes that have had more slowly rising prices, and to new products primarily after the new product price declines. Analogously, a production index that holds the relative *prices* of the various items produced constant at their base-period relationship shows a higher rate of production growth (or lower rate of decline) than when the index represents the actual prices paid in each period, again because the introductory high price of a new product usually declines with the growth in production.

There is no right or wrong way to construct index numbers. Usually the choice of which period proportions to use is based on a judgment concerning the use of the index. For example, when the goal is to measure price change for the same items over time, the base-period proportions of the items purchased are held constant. But when the interest is in measuring price change for actual items purchased over time, the proportions of items purchased are changed in every period to reflect actual buying patterns. In most cases the government develops only one index, typically using base-period proportions, and the user has no estimate of the rate of change using alternative proportions. When there are alternative period calculations, such as those provided in the price measures developed from estimates of the gross national product, the user can regard the alternative figures as reflecting the upper and lower ranges in the analysis. This is a way of handling the dilemma of shifting proportions, as distinguished from an expected error range associated with the sampling and revision problems discussed above.

THE UNDERGROUND ECONOMY

The "underground economy" refers to income, derived from both legal and illegal activities, that is not reported or is understated on tax returns and surveys. Consequently, in addition to raising the budget deficit, the underground economy creates problems in using various statistics to measure economic trends and to assess the trends for economic policy. Legal sources of income include employment, investments, and income-support programs that are consistent with national and state laws. Illegal income is typically associated with street drugs, unauthorized gambling and prostitution, theft, fraud, and many other activities as noted below.

Economic indicators typically do not reflect illegal activity, either because it is excluded from the definitions used or because, as a matter of reality, it is unlikely to be reported on tax returns and surveys. However, the income generated from illegal activity affects many indicators as the money is spent for legitimate purposes. (This exclusion of illegal activity should be remembered when making economic comparisons with countries in which certain activities are not banned.)

Two different methodologies are used to estimate the underground economy. One uses "direct" measurements—for example, studies of compliance with the income tax laws in reporting business incomes. The "indirect" approach uses information that suggests attempts to hide income, such as the tendency to use cash rather than checks in business transactions. The direct approach is more appealing methodologically, although it involves considerable estimating. Government estimates are based on the direct method and are lower than private estimates, which are more likely to be based on the indirect technique. Richard Porter and Amanda Bayer question the indirect approach that uses currency data on methodological grounds and conclude that the indirect approach does not provide reliable estimates of underground activity.[1]

Clearly, the level of activity in the underground economy will affect the analytic relationships used in economic forecasts, such as the economic growth deemed necessary to maintain a steady unemployment rate or to reduce unemployment by specific amounts. However, since underground activities are not reflected in surveys, tax returns, applications for income maintenance payments, and other documents used to develop economic indicators, official statistics understate the actual level of economic activity and overstate unemployment.

In recent years, private and government estimates of the underground economy range from 5 to 33 percent of the gross national product.[2] Some observers have also concluded that the underground economy has been growing faster than what is shown by the published indicators, which suggests that the official indicators are giving increasingly misleading information.[3] If the economy is in fact substantially stronger than the indicators suggest, fiscal and monetary policies (discussed in Chapter 2) based on the indicators will tend to be more expansionary than they would be otherwise, and possibly inflationary, because they assume a larger pool of unemployed workers than actually exists.

Government estimates of the underground economy are relatively recent, so there are limited official figures on which to base an assessment of its impact on the indicators over time. In 1985, the Bureau of Economic Analysis in the U.S. Department of Commerce published the 1977 benchmark revisions of GNP data that incorporate adjustments for misreporting of income on income tax returns (in addition to previously incorporated adjustments based on Internal Revenue Service audits and other studies of taxpayer compliance). These revisions increased the GNP for 1984 by $44 billion, or 1 percent.[4]

This 1 percent revision of the GNP cannot be viewed as an accurate representation of the underground economy. As noted above, most estimates put the underground economy at 5 to 33 percent. The large difference between the tax-data revisions to the GNP and estimates of the underground economy as a percentage of the GNP results from three factors. *First,* large adjustments had previously been made for misreporting on tax returns used in estimating the GNP. *Second*, tax data revisions apply only to those elements of tax returns that are used in estimating the GNP. In some cases, other data sources avoid tax return misreporting: Household surveys provide accurate estimates of consumer spending even though the seller may not report the transaction; and business taxpayers report certain payments, like wages, interest, and dividends more accurately than the recipients. In other cases, some elements of tax returns such as capital gains are excluded from the GNP by definition. The overall effect is that tax data are used for only about 5 percent of the GNP estimates on the product side and 55 percent of GNP estimates on the income side (the GNP is discussed in Chapter 3). *Third*, illegal activities are excluded from the GNP by definition. In practice, a small fraction of illegal activities is probably represented in the GNP because they are mixed with statistics on legitimate activity; this can occur when illegal activities are financially laundered as legal activities and therefore appear on tax returns or when stolen goods are fenced and sold in legitimate stores.

In general, there may be a tendency to exaggerate the potential importance of illegal activities for the GNP. Because the GNP is a measure of production, much illegal activity probably does not qualify for inclusion in the GNP even if good data were available. The redistribution of goods already produced or of other forms of wealth, such as stolen money, has little practical significance on the GNP, although redistributions between persons and businesses (for example, from shoplifting) may slightly affect estimates of personal and business saving.

Other major economic indicators that are affected by the underground economy are employment and unemployment statistics (discussed in Chapter 5). Respondents to household surveys on employment and unemployment may report they are not working, when in fact they do have jobs, either in legal or illegal activities. The effect of this misreporting, which is probably most serious among those whose sole job is in the underground economy and among undocumented alien workers, is to lower the employment and raise the unemployment measures.

In a review of the literature on the problem in 1984, the Bureau of Labor Statistics in the U.S. Department of Labor concluded that there are no sound estimates of the effect of the underground economy on the unemployment rate. The BLS did not estimate the effect of misreporting on the official labor force figures, but they questioned the validity of other analysts' estimates, such as that the 1978 official unemployment rate was overstated by 1.5 percentage points.[5] Their analysis of the household survey data did not substantiate the claims of a significant effect on the unemployment rate.

The effects of the underground economy on the federal budget deficit, however, are substantial. Internal Revenue Service estimates of unpaid individual and corporate income taxes associated with legal economic activities (due to unreported and underreported income, overstated deductions and exemptions, calculation errors, and other factors) range from $83 to $94 billion for tax year 1987.[6] Based on details regarding the unreported and underreported income, deductions, exemptions, and other factors on individual tax returns (no such detail is available for corporate tax returns), about $60 billion of these unpaid taxes are directly related to unreported and underreported income. Thus, the underground economy's "legal" portion alone accounted for about 40 percent of the $150 billion federal budget deficit in 1987. (In the above discussion of tax data used in estimating the GNP, the relevant figures for the underground economy are unreported and underreported income, which of course are much higher than the unpaid taxes on that income.)

Unpaid taxes associated with unreported and underreported income rose from $69 billion in 1981 to $96 billion in 1986, and then declined to $83 billion in 1987 following the Tax Reform Act of 1986. However, the IRS projects this legal-sector income tax gap will rise to $110–$127 billion by 1992.

The illegal portion of the underground economy also increases the budget deficit. Illegal activities are taxable, but the taxes are obviously very difficult to collect. The IRS occasionally estimates unpaid taxes on illegal activities for drugs, gambling, and prostitution. The most recent figure for this tax loss is $9 billion in 1981, up from $3 billion in 1976 and $6 billion in 1979.[7] In 1983 Abt Associates conducted a study of other illegal activities for the IRS, which estimated the dollar value of various types of theft (personal, household, employee, shoplifting, and cargo), robbery and burglary from business, arson, bank embezzlement, currency counterfeiting, cigarette smuggling, and government program fraud.[8] However, these data have not been assembled into comprehensive figures on the tax loss associated with them. Moreover, this study did not include other illegal activities such as various types of fraud (insurance, consumer, mail, check, and credit card), customs violations, loansharking, business embezzlement, bribery, securities theft and counterfeiting, computer crime, alcohol and petroleum excise tax evasion, theft of pension assets, and illegal firearms trading. A simple listing of the myriad types of illegal activities suggests why indirect estimates of the underground economy, which are based on transactions conducted in cash, represent such a large percentage of the GNP.

The underground economy is a problematic factor in economic analysis. Edgar Feige, a long-time student of the underground economy, believes that it has become larger relative to the observed economy over time, and that as a result current economic indicators distort economic analyses.[9] For example, he suggests that the deterioration in recent decades in the Phillips curve trade-off between inflation and unemployment (discussed in Chapter 6) is at least partially due to faulty data associated with the underground economy. Feige thus advocates improving the data rather than modifying the theory.

Unfortunately, incorporating the effects of the underground economy in economic indicators is exceptionally difficult. While the significance of the underground economy is undeniable, the wisdom of using the current, unreliable methods of incorporating underground activities in the data (such as using indirect estimates) is debatable. The underground economy is a disturbing problem that refuses to go away and adds one more uncertainty to interpreting the movements of economic indicators.

REVIEW QUESTIONS

• In analyzing current economic trends, what is the best way to deal with upcoming data revisions?

• If monthly or quarterly data are not seasonally adjusted, "seasonal" comparisons are sometimes made between the current month or quarter and the corresponding year-earlier period. What are the limitations of this approach?

• Index numbers are a convenient way to summarize masses of data, but they also have an inherent "product mix" problem. What is the problem?

• Why is the underground economy an issue in analyzing economic data?

NOTES

1. Richard D. Porter and Amanda S. Bayer, "A Monetary Perspective on Underground Economic Activity in the United States," *Federal Reserve Bulletin,* March 1984; and Richard D. Porter and Amanda S. Bayer, "Monetary Perspective on Underground Economic Activity in the United States," in Edgar L. Feige, ed., *The underground economies: Tax evasion and information distortion* (Cambridge University Press: 1989).

2. Carol S. Carson, "The Underground Economy: An Introduction," *Survey of Current Business,* May 1984, Table 3, p. 33.

3. Ibid., Table 4, p. 34.

4. For a discussion of the methodology used in estimating the misreported income, see Robert P. Parker, "Improved Adjustments for Misreporting of Tax Return Information Used to Estimate the National Income and Product Accounts," *Survey of Current Business,* June 1984.

5. Richard J. McDonald, "The 'underground economy' and BLS statistical data," *Monthly Labor Review,* January 1984.

6. Internal Revenue Service, U.S. Department of the Treasury, *Income Tax Compliance Research: Net Tax Gap and Remittance Gap Estimates,* Publication 1415, April 1990.

7. Internal Revenue Service, U.S. Department of the Treasury, *Income Tax Compliance Research: Estimates for 1973–1981,* July 1983.

8. Abt Associates Inc., *Unreported Taxable Income from Selected Illegal Activities,* March 31, 1983. This report was prepared for the Internal Revenue Service, and the IRS printed it in September 1984.

9. Edgar L. Feige, "The meaning and measurement of the underground economy," in Edgar L. Feige, ed., *The underground economies* (Cambridge University Press: 1989).

2
BUSINESS CYCLES, ECONOMIC
INDICATORS, AND ECONOMIC POLICIES

Business cycles are the recurring rises and falls in the overall economy as reflected in production, employment, profits, and prices. They are associated with capitalistic societies in which production, employment, prices, wages, etc., are largely determined in the private sector marketplace. Business cycles reflect the inability of this marketplace to accommodate smoothly such factors as new technologies, changing needs for occupational skills, shifting markets for new and substitute products, uncertainties and risks in business investments, intensified worldwide competition, and shortages and gluts created by wars harvests, and cartels. Economists have offered various theories on the causes of business cycles in the past and they continue to disagree on the causes today. Ultimately, the theories are tested empirically through the behavior of economic indicators.[1]

Theoretically, business cycles do not occur in socialist countries with centrally planned economies, as the information underlying the plan and the plan's implementation are assumed to anticipate and smoothly accommodate the main dynamic changes. In practice, the rapid changes characteristic of business cycles seem to be less of a problem for centrally planned economies. However, such economies do not encourage basic changes in production technologies, cater to shifting consumer preferences for substitute and new products, or avoid bad harvests. Until the mid-1970s, these rigidities in the socialist system did not result in lower long-term economic growth rates (i.e., trends in production that span the shorter-term business cycles) in these countries as compared with the more fluid capitalistic economies. But during 1976–90, growth was slower in the socialist economies of the Soviet Union and Eastern Europe than in the market economies, according to worldwide estimates of real gross national product compiled by U.S. and international organizations.[2] Moreover, the long-standing inefficiencies of centralized planning and the continuing low productivity and poor living conditions in socialist economies ultimately were underlying factors causing the political and economic upheavals in the Soviet Union and Eastern Europe during 1989–91. By the end of 1991, this culminated in the disintegration of the Soviet Union as an entity and the emergence of the Commonwealth of Independent States with profoundly different political and economic foundations.

The overall thrust of the American economy fits the capitalist model even though the U.S. government provides public services and intervenes in the econ-

22

omy in other ways, and though there are monopolistic aspects in the private sector that are insulated from fully competitive markets. While the American economy has changed considerably over the past two centuries because of new technologies and the growing population, business cycles are not new. They have occurred repeatedly in the nineteenth and twentieth centuries.

The rising phase of a business cycle is typically referred to as expansion, and the falling phase as recession. Although business cycle analysis focuses on the overall economy, it recognizes that particular sectors may be moving against the overall trend—a smokestack industry may not participate in the prosperity of a general expansion, for example, or a growth industry may be insulated from a general recession.

DESIGNATION OF RECESSIONS
AND EXPANSIONS

What is a recession? Generally speaking, we know there is a recession when we see slack business activity and high unemployment (sometimes aggravated by anomalously high inflation). But there also is an observable measure of a recession period. By common agreement in the economics profession, the National Bureau of Economic Research, Inc. (a private, nonprofit organization, abbreviated as NBER), officially designates such periods.

Under the auspices of the NBER, a committee of economists with diverse views on economic policies determines the beginning and ending points of recessions and expansions by assessing the preponderant direction of a wide range of indicators. The NBER has established a reputation for objectivity, and its designations are accepted by many liberal and conservative economists and politicians.

The advantage of having a nongovernmental body such as the NBER designate recessions and expansions is clear. It reduces the possibility that the administration in office will politicize the designations to put its own policies in the most favorable light, or even revise designations for previous periods to make the opposition party look worse.

The NBER designates a recession as beginning in the month in which the overall direction of several economic indicators turns downward; similarly, an expansion is designated as beginning in the month in which the overall direction turns upward.[3] While various numerical tests are applied to the indicators to assess their direction, ultimately the decision is based on the judgment of the NBER committee. For example, a recession is generally defined as occurring when the real gross national product (i.e., the GNP in constant dollars) declines for two quarters in a row. However, this is not a fixed rule, and the NBER considers a variety of monthly and quarterly data before making a designation, including the GNP in current and constant dollars, business sales, bank debits outside New York City, the industrial production index, the unemployment rate, nonfarm employment and hours worked, and personal income. In fact, as noted by Edward Renshaw, if the two-quarter real GNP rule were the criterion, no short recessions would have been recorded in 1960 and 1980, and the 1973–75 recession, which is shown as beginning at the end of 1973, would appear as beginning a year later at the end of 1974.[4]

A notable exception to the typical designations occurred after World War II. In 1946 the real GNP declined by 19 percent, which was larger than any annual decline in the depression years of the 1930s. The sharp drop was due entirely to the demobilization and concomitant plunge in defense outlays. In contrast, the private sector and civilian government components of the GNP rose during the demobilization, and so 1946 was not considered a recession year.

A few terms relating to the designation of recessions and expansions should be noted. A "growth recession" occurs when overall production and unemployment rates are both rising. Production in such cases is not keeping pace with the ranks of young people just out of school or labor force re-entrants with job experience.

While expansion is the general term for the upward phase of the cycle, the upturn immediately following a recession is often referred to as "recovery." When overall activity in the recovery exceeds the highest levels attained before the recession, this higher-growth period is called expansion. A comparable designation in the downward phase is the transition from recession to contraction. The immediate downturn is called recession; if overall activity falls below the lowest level of the previous recession, the depressed period may be called "contraction." However, economic literature gives little attention to contraction. It has not occurred since the depression of the early 1930s except for the decline in 1981–82, which by the "coincident" measure in the system of leading, coincident, and lagging indexes (see Chapter 8) fell below the low point of the 1980 recession. Expansion is typical of the United States' long-term growing economy. Figure 3 depicts these phases of the business cycle from 1973 to early 1991.

The high point of an expansion before it turns downward to recession is called the "peak," and the low point of a recession before it turns upward to recovery is the "trough." A complete cycle is composed of both the expansion and recession phases and is typically viewed from the peak of one expansion to the peak of the following expansion. This way of looking at the cycle emphasizes the long-term growth of the economy independent of short-term cyclical movements, although for some analyses it may be useful to measure the cycle from the trough of one recession to the trough of the next recession.

All told, as indicated in Table 1, in the nine business cycles since World War II, the average expansion was 50 months and the average recession was 11 months (excluding the recession that began in the summer of 1990 and was still in progress in the spring of 1991). For the seven peacetime cycles (excluding the Korean and Vietnam wars), the average expansion was 43 months and the average recession 11 months. Thus, since World War II, the average expansion has lasted about 4 to 4½ times longer than the average recession. These durations

Figure 3. Stages of the Business Cycle in Relation to the Composite Coincident Index of Economic Activity: 1973–91

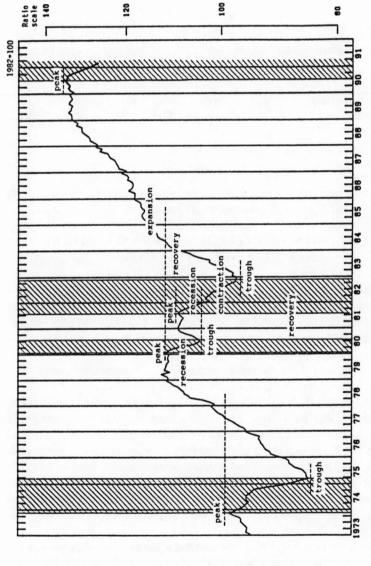

Note: Based on Bureau of Economic Analysis data. Lined bars are downturn periods. The author designated the recovery, expansion, recession, and contraction stages. The recession of 1990-91 was in progress in the Spring of 1991 (when the manuscript was completed).

Table 1

Average Duration of U.S. Business Cycles (in months)

	Expansion	Recession
All Cycles		
1854–1919 (16 cycles)	27	22
1919–1945 (6 cycles)	35	18
1945–1990 (9 cycles)	50	11
Peacetime Cycles		
1854–1919 (14 cycles)	24	22
1919–1945 (5 cycles)	26	20
1945–1990 (7 cycles)	43	11

Source: *Survey of Current Business*, April 1991, p. C-25.

are an improvement over the experience of the previous century, when the length of recessions was closer to the length of expansions.

CHANGING CHARACTERISTICS OF BUSINESS CYCLES SINCE THE NINETEENTH CENTURY

The duration of expansions and recessions is a direct indicator of the economy's performance. The longer the expansion and the shorter the recession, the better off people are. Longer expansions and shorter recessions mean steadier and perhaps even higher rates of long-term economic growth, as well as lower and shorter terms of unemployment.

In assessing how the durations of expansions and recessions change over time, peacetime cycles are the best indicator since peacetime economic activity excludes the temporary but significant stimulus of wartime military production. Table 1 shows that on average peacetime expansions became progressively longer and peacetime recessions progressively shorter over the 146-year period from 1854 to 1990. But most of this improvement occurred after World War II. During 1854–1919, expansions and recessions were almost equally long (24 months for expansions and 22 months for recessions); during 1919–45, expansions were 6 months longer than recessions (26 months and 20 months, respectively); and during 1945–90, expansions were 32 months longer than recessions (43 and 11 months, respectively).

In the author's view, there are two major and related reasons the economy has performed better since World War II. First, Keynesian economics fostered a greater understanding of the economy as well as more widespread recognition of the importance of government budgets. The government's more active role in influencing the economy resulted from this triumph of Keynesianism over the classical belief that full employment would occur automatically. The Keynesian perspective was in turn critiqued and refined by several developments: the importance given by monetarists to the money supply and the greater attention to interest rates as key factors determining economic activity; the Phillips curve analysis of the tradeoff between unemployment and inflation; and the rational expectations theory that the market adjusts to and frustrates government intervention in the economy.

The second reason the economy has done better is that this greater understanding is applied to economic policies. Thus, the federal government activity stabilizes the economy through fiscal policies. The active role of the government was encouraged by the Employment Act of 1946, which established the goals for maximum employment and purchasing power. This was heightened by the monetary policy change of 1951 (i.e., the Treasury Department-Federal Reserve accord), which allowed the Federal Reserve to pursue interest rate policies to benefit the economy independent of their effect on the interest rates of government securities used in financing the federal debt. (Fiscal and monetary policies are discussed in the section entitled Economic Policies.)

Other factors contributing to the economy's performance include the cushioning effect of unemployment insurance and other income maintenance programs that provide a floor during recessions; bank deposit insurance and actions taken by the federal government and the Federal Reserve to prevent a widespread financial collapse of failing banks; and the increasing sophistication of companies in using greater amounts of economic information to balance sales and production. This last factor may also result in better inventory control and thus moderate production fluctuation.

Christina Romer has challenged the impression given by the official statistics that the economy since World War II has become more stable.[5] She argues that statistics on unemployment, the gross national product, and industrial production are misleading because the underlying data on which they are based changed considerably after World War II. The prewar statistics use far more fragmentary and less reliable underlying data than the postwar statistics. When historical statistics are reconstructed to simulate a consistent methodology over the prewar and postwar periods, Romer's argument continues, the prewar economy appears to be similar to the postwar economy in terms of the severity of economic declines during recessions and the volatility of yearly changes in the rate of output and unemployment as measured by yearly deviations from long-term trends. Whatever the merits of Romer's argument, her reconstructed measures do not refute the assertion that the relative duration of expansions and recessions has improved. Because the methodology does not alter the dates for the turning points of business cycles, the reconstructed statistics do not refute the conventional measures that indicate an improvement over time toward longer expansions and shorter recessions.

Moreover, the methodology Romer uses to reconstruct the historical statistics is itself rough, since it adds no new basic data but uses statistical procedures that assume similar cyclical behavior in the labor force and in production in the prewar and postwar economies. While this criticism does not necessarily negate the thrust of Romer's argument regarding the severity of recessions and year-to-year volatility, it explains why the challenge does not affect the conventional view that expansions have become longer and recessions shorter. Ultimately, however, regardless of limitations with the methodology of the reconstructed statistics, Romer's challenge points up the tentativeness of analyzing economic data over long time periods and drawing conclusions about them.

DEPRESSIONS AND CYCLICAL ANALYSIS

A depression is a collapse of the economy such as last occurred during the 1930s. It involves a general breakdown of economic life affecting people in all economic strata, including mass unemployment, widespread loss of assets such as homes and life savings, the disappearance of established businesses through bankruptcy, and an overall undermining of the financial system through failures of the banking and securities industries. A depression is far more devastating than a recession. For example, the unemployment rate in the 1930s reached about 25 percent, compared to peaks of 9 percent and 11 percent during the severe recessions of 1973–75 and 1981–82, respectively.

Fortunately, depressions do not occur as frequently as recessions. Over the past two hundred years, Ravi Batra estimates they have occurred in either thirty-year or sixty-year intervals.[6] He details similarities between the 1920s and 1980s that make us vulnerable to a depression, and concludes we are inexorably headed for a depression during 1990–96 (a recession started in 1990 and was in progress in the spring of 1991 when this manuscript was completed).[7] The similarities he finds are the growing concentration of wealth among the richest in the population, a Republican presidency that is pro-business and anti-labor, low money-supply growth, low inflation, deregulation, a high rate of business mergers, and considerable stock market speculation. Batra believes the similarities are more important than the differences, such as low interest rates in the 1920s but high interest rates in the 1980s, government budget surpluses in the 1920s but government deficits in the 1980s, and foreign trade surpluses in the 1920s but foreign trade deficits in the 1980s. These differences actually show the 1920s in a more favorable light than the 1980s, since current hopes for achieving lower budget and foreign trade deficits and lower interest rates are unlikely to be fulfilled. At any rate, their presence in the 1920s was not enough to prevent the depression. Batra also downplays the effect of major changes in economic and political regimes of the 1980s, such as the much greater role of government budgets; the existence of unemployment insurance, social security, bank deposit insurance, and stock market regulation; and far more active and sophisticated Federal Reserve roles in influencing the economy. Hopefully, today's government will be more successful in staving off the snowballing effect of slides in production and employment and in limiting the spread of a financial collapse due to bank failures.

Batra's prediction of a depression in the 1990s is cited here to illustrate the problematic judgments that underlie such prognostications. In the first place, Batra precisely pinpoints the onset of the future depression in the first quarter of 1990 although his book was only published in 1987; given the uncertainty of even annual forecasts three years into the future, quarterly forecasts three years ahead are simply unrealistic. More importantly, as noted above, the forecast is based on selective analogies between the 1920s and the 1980s that stress the similarities but dismiss the differences between the two periods. The forecast also assumes a fixed regularity in human affairs that is too mechanistic. According to the thirty-year theory, another depression should have occurred in the 1960s, which was thirty years after the 1930s. But because a depression did not occur in the 1960s, the alternative sixty-year period between depressions is deemed certain to result in a depression in the 1990s. Batra's estimates of repetitive thirty- and sixty-year spans between depressions are based on far more exactness than the rough data of the nineteenth century merit. In his view, each generation is active for approximately thirty years. If a generation recalls the consequences of the previous generation's mistakes, it may avoid repeating the mistakes. However, the passing of another thirty years will dull people's recall. Thus, if the children do not repeat the parents' mistakes, the grandchildren are certain to do so, and so depressions must occur in either thirty- or sixty-year cycles. This deterministic interpretation of human behavior, although presented in a rigid psychological mold, probably has an element of truth in it. The question is whether today's generation has in fact forgotten the lessons of the 1930s.

ECONOMIC POLICIES

The federal government and the Federal Reserve attempt through fiscal and monetary policies to moderate cyclical fluctuations and maintain steady long-term economic growth. Fiscal policy refers to guidance of federal spending and tax rates by the president and Congress, while monetary policy is guidance of the money supply, bank reserves, and interest rates by the Federal Reserve.

This section centers on fiscal and monetary policies because they are the main instruments used in influencing the economy. From time to time they are supplemented with incomes policies, which are either voluntary wage–price guidelines or mandatory wage–price controls. Incomes policies diverge from the complete market determination of prices and wages, and they are instituted only when it is thought that fiscal and monetary policies are too blunt to have the desired effect in curbing inflationary behavior at the micro level by business and labor unions. They are resorted to as a temporary device to break the inflationary psychology engendered when wages and prices spiral upward with no end in sight, and when it is believed that a recession and high unemployment caused by restrictive fiscal and monetary policies are too high a price to pay for breaking the inflationary behavior. Mandatory price and wage controls were used in World War II, part of the Korean War (1950–51), and part of the Vietnam War (1971–73); voluntary price–wage guidelines were used in 1962–65 and 1978–79. Economists debate their effectiveness; some say they distort price and profit relationships among products and result in higher inflation after they are removed, while others say they hold inflation below what it would have been, without undue interference with market determined wages and prices, so long as they are temporary. Because of their sporadic use, incomes policies are not analyzed in this book. But if they are used in the future, the analyst will have to take them into account in assessing economic trends.

Although there is considerable sophistication in analyzing the effect of fiscal and monetary policies, the causes of and remedies for business cycles are complex, and the application of such policies is in part quantitative but also includes considerable judgment. Fiscal and monetary policies must take many factors into account: purely economic considerations such as balancing sales, production, employment, investment, prices, and interest rates; and political and other influences such as wars, harvests, consumer and business optimism and pessimism, international tensions, cartels, and protectionism.

Interpreting economic indicators requires an understanding of the way fiscal and monetary policies react with each other. It should be kept in mind that fiscal policy is enacted through federal spending and taxes, which do not exist solely to influence the economy. Government spending is first aimed at meeting needs that society feels are best satisfied by the public sector, and taxation aims to finance that spending consistent with concepts of ability to pay, equity, and efficient collection. By contrast, monetary policies, which are adopted and modified throughout the year by the Federal Reserve, aim solely at influencing the economy's level of activity through money-supply manipulation and credit availability. Hence, fiscal policy is derived as a secondary agenda while monetary policy's primary purpose is to influence the economy. In addition, fiscal policy is not as flexible as monetary policy, because spending and tax changes require a lengthier legislative process than do changes in monetary policy, which can be made on a relatively current basis. Thus, while fiscal and monetary policies are both important, monetary policies are easier to implement.

Perhaps the major achievement of these policy tools is that no recession since World War II has degenerated into a cataclysm such as the depression of the 1930s.[8] In addition, the Kennedy-Johnson period from 1961–68 plus most of 1969 totaled nine years without a recession, and the Reagan–Bush period from the end of 1982 to mid-1990 totaled eight years without a recession. By historical standards, these are very long time spans. These successes have fueled the hope that fiscal and monetary policies can maintain steady growth without recession or inflation, although both periods were tarnished by large military spending increases that bolstered production and employment (in the 1960s for the Vietnam War and in the 1980s for the Cold War). The hope was first dashed by recessions and inflation in the 1970s and early 1980s. And another recession began in mid-1990 that was in progress in the spring of 1991 at the time of this writing. In an analysis of the factors underlying cyclical fluctuations, Alan Garner and Richard Wurtz conclude that while recessions are less frequent and severe since World War II, the business cycle will likely continue to be part of the economic landscape.[9] Thus, the challenge remains: maintaining steady, recession-free growth, low unemployment, and little or no inflation in peacetime.

REVIEW QUESTIONS

• How does the United States depoliticize the determination of when a recession begins and ends?

• Can the designation of when a recession begins be objective if no fixed formulas are used for determining the onset of a recession?

• Since the end of World War II, the economy has been healthier than it was in the prewar period, according to generally accepted data. But this improved performance has been questioned on statistical grounds. What is a lesson of this challenge?

• Are analogies between the 1920s and the 1980s persuasive for predicting a depression in the 1990s?

• Why is fiscal policy clumsier to carry out than monetary policy?

NOTES

1. For a critique of business cycle theories prominent in the 1980s, see Ernst A. Boehm, "Understanding Business Cycles Today: A Critical Review of Theory and Fact," in Philip A. Klein, ed., *Analyzing Modern Business Cycles: Essays Honoring Geoffrey H. Moore* (M. E. Sharpe: 1990).

2. Council of Economic Advisers, *Economic Report of the President,* February 1991, Table B-110, p. 411.

3. For a discussion of the methodology, see Geoffrey H. Moore, *Business Cycles, Inflation and Forecasting,* second edition, National Bureau of Economic Research Studies in Business Cycles, no. 24 (Ballinger Publishing: 1983), pp. 3–9.

4. Edward Renshaw, "On Measuring Economic Recessions," *Challenge,* March/April 1991, pp. 58–59.

5. See Christina D. Romer, "Spurious Volatility in Historical Unemployment Data," *Journal of Political Economy,* February 1986; and Christina D. Romer, "Is the Stabilization of the Postwar Economy a Figment of the Data?" *American Economic Review,* June 1986. See also Christina D. Romer, "New Estimates of Prewar Gross National Product and Unemployment"; David R. Weir, "The Reliability of Historical Macroeconomic Data for Comparing Cyclical Stability"; and Stanley Lebergott, "Discussion"; all in *Journal of Economic History,* June 1986. The articles by Weir and Lebergott are rejoinders to Romer.

6. Ravi Batra, *The Great Depression of 1990* (Simon & Schuster: 1987), Chapter 6.

7. Ibid., Chapter 7.

8. Besides fiscal and monetary policies, additional factors in preventing a depression are unemployment insurance and other income maintenance programs that provide a floor during recessions, bank deposit insurance, active government intervention to stem a widespread financial collapse of failing banks, and perhaps more sophisticated inventory controls by business. The above section, Changing Characteristics of Business Cycles, cites these factors as also contributing to longer expansions and shorter recessions since World War II.

9. C. Alan Garner and Richard E. Wurtz, "Is the Business Cycle Disappearing?" *Economic Review,* Federal Reserve Bank of Kansas City, May/June 1990.

3
GROSS NATIONAL PRODUCT

As a system of accounts recording income and spending in both the domestic and international sectors of the economy, the gross national product (GNP) is the most important and comprehensive macroeconomic indicator for assessing the overall state of the American economy. The GNP accounts operate as an integrated construct for tracking trends in economic growth and inflation and for analyzing the effects of past fiscal, monetary, and incomes policies on the economy. As such, the GNP also provides the best basis for developing economic projections based on assumed fiscal, monetary, and incomes policies and for anticipating the likely impact of potential changes in those policies. The GNP estimates are developed quarterly by the Bureau of Economic Analysis in the U.S. Department of Commerce.

The analyses in this chapter are based on GNP data before the quinquennial benchmark GNP revision was published in December 1991. After the revision, the gross domestic product (GDP) is featured as the primary measure of U.S. production, although the GNP measure will continue to be published. Differences between GNP and GDP for the United States are small; the distinctions are discussed below and are also depicted in the figures. The revised statistics are based on modified definitions and classifications, more detailed and accurate data, new estimating procedures, and a shift in base-year prices from 1982 to 1987. These led to slightly lower long-term growth rates from those previously published, but they do not change the thrust of the analyses presented here. The revised lower growth rates are summarized below.

PART A: ESTIMATING METHODOLOGY

Demand (Markets) and Supply (Costs)

The GNP summarizes in a single number the nation's total economic output valued in dollars. It is derived by organizing the various sectors of the economy—the household, business, government, and international sectors—into a system of spending and income accounts. These are referred to as the "national income and product accounts," "national economic accounts," or simply the "national accounts."

The summary GNP figure consolidates spending and its counterpart income

Table 2

GNP and Major Components: 1989

	Product Side			Income Side	
	$ billions	percent		$ billions	percent
Gross National Product	5,200.8	100.0	Gross National Product	5,200.8	100.0
Personal Consumption Expenditures	3,450.1	66.3	Compensation of Employees	3,079.0	59.2
			Wages and salaries	2,573.2	49.5
Durable goods	474.6	9.1	Supplements	505.8	9.7
Nondurable goods	1,130.0	21.7	Proprietors' Income[c]	379.3	7.3
Services	1,845.5	35.5	Farm	48.6	0.9
Gross Private Domestic Investment	771.2	14.8	Nonfarm	330.7	6.4
			Rental Income	8.2	0.2
Nonresidential[a]	511.9	9.8	Corporate Profits	311.6	6.0
Residential[b]	231.0	4.4	Net Interest	445.1	8.6
Inventory change	28.3	0.5	Indirect Business Taxes and Nontax Liability[d]	414.0	8.0
Net Exports	−46.1	−0.9			
Exports	626.2	12.0			
Imports	−672.3	−12.9	Capital Consumption Allowances[e]	554.4	10.7
Government Purchases	1,025.6	19.7	Business Transfers, Government Subsidies, and Government Enterprises	26.1	0.5
Federal	400.0	7.7			
State and local	625.6	12.0	Statistical Discrepancy	−17.0	−0.3

Source: Bureau of Economic Analysis, U.S. Department of Commerce, *Survey of Current Business,* July 1990.

Note: Detail may not add up to totals due to rounding.

[a] Business plant and equipment.

[b] Mainly new housing construction.

[c] Profits of unincorporated business.

[d] Mainly sales and property taxes.

[e] Mainly depreciation allowances.

flows to represent the nation's output from two perspectives, the differing components of demand and supply. The *demand* concept (known as the "product side") refers to the end-use markets for goods and services produced in the United States. It appears in the national accounts as sales of these items (plus inventory accumulation or depletion) to households, businesses, governments, and foreigners. The *supply* concept (known as the "income side") refers to the costs involved in producing these goods and services. It is shown in the accounts as workers' wages, business profits, interest payments, depreciation allowances for business plant and equipment, and sales and property taxes.[1]

Table 2 below shows the product and income sides of the GNP in 1989 and their major components. The total value of goods and services produced in 1989 was $5.2 trillion. The figures indicate the dominance of consumer expenditures on the product side (66 percent of the GNP) and employee compensation on the income side (59 percent of the GNP). However, as will become apparent, these and the other components move at different rates over the business cycle, and these variations affect overall GNP growth rates.

Meaning of Production

The GNP is constructed on a "value-added" basis. This means that as goods pass through the various stages of production—from raw materials to semifinished goods to final products—only the value that is added in each stage is counted for GNP purposes. If goods and services purchased from other businesses for use in production were included, their value would be endlessly recounted. The value-added method counts only the total resources used in producing the final item, as represented in the wage, profit, and other income-side components, and the final markets of the product side. This prevents double counting of items on either the product or income side of the GNP accounts.

Another key point in defining production is that the GNP excludes capital gains and losses in the sale of securities, land, and used goods. These are considered valuation changes in the transfer of assets, and while they may have effects on future production, they do not change output at the time of the transfer. However, brokerage charges associated with these transactions are in the GNP because the broker's service is current production.

The GNP measures production in terms of dollar costs, without making any value judgments on the differential worth to society of the activities measured. Equal weight is given to purchases of goods and services for everyday living, investment for future production, and public services—food, housing, machinery, inventories, education, defense, etc., are all valued strictly in dollar terms. Similarly, the labor and capital resources necessary to produce this output are measured strictly in dollar amounts as workers' wages and business profits. This objective measure of the nation's output may be contrasted to measures that could account for the nation's "welfare" or "well-being" by assigning a positive or negative value to activities based not only on their marketplace value but also on their intrinsic worth.

A GNP that accounted for welfare would measure the nonmaterial effects of activities by deducting from production for "bad" items and adding for "good" items. Such a computation would assign greater value to industrial activity that protects the environment than equally productive activity that harms the environment. Similarly, defense spending that deters war would be valued more highly than defense spending that results in destructive or war-provoking actions, although in practice such a distinction would be very difficult to make. A GNP that took welfare into account would also include the value of many "products" currently not valued in dollar terms, such as the increased leisure time resulting from shorter work weeks, the greater security resulting from improved police protection, and the unpaid labor services of homemakers, parents, and volunteers. Such a GNP measure would also evaluate consumer goods like autos, furniture, and appliances differently to incorporate the value of their services over the years of their useful life, as well as the actual dollar amount involved in producing the goods which is included in the traditional GNP measure. In the 1970s, the Bureau of Economic Analysis began to develop estimates of such items that economists could use to modify the traditional GNP measures, but the project was discontinued for lack of funding. (By contrast, some nonmarket activities are included as "imputed" estimates in the GNP. The main one is the rental value of owner-occupied housing, and second in importance are the services provided by financial intermediaries without payment. These imputed terms currently account for 9 percent of the GNP.)

The UN System of National Accounts: Contrasts with the United States

The United Nations has developed definitions of the GNP, and particularly of the gross domestic product (GDP), that differ slightly from those used by the United States.[2] (The GDP differs from the GNP in the treatment of profits and investment income of international activities of U.S. businesses and individuals abroad and of foreign investment in the United States, as well as of the wages of U.S. workers abroad and of foreign workers in the United States. See discussion below under Selected Technical Topics: Alternative Summary Measures.) The UN definitions, which are part of the System of National Accounts (SNA), provide a uniform basis for comparing the GDP levels, distribution of the GDP components, and GDP growth rates of different nations.

In 1989, the SNA-based figure showed a U.S. GDP that was three-fifths of one percent less than the U.S.-based figure. This difference results from the differing treatment that the two accounting systems accord three major items: (1) Federal, state, and local government nonmilitary spending for structures and equipment: the SNA treats such spending as capital investments that also increase GDP in subsequent years through depreciation while the United States treats such spending solely as current outlays in the year the money is spent. (2) Imputed financial charges to individuals and governments for banking services for which there is no explicit fee: the SNA treats such charges as offsetting entries that do not affect the total GDP while the United States counts them as increasing the total GDP. (3) Federal government pensions of government workers: the SNA counts these when the benefits are paid by the pension fund while

Table 3

Comparison of Annual Percentage Change in Constant-Dollar U.S. GDP, SNA vs. U.S. Definitions: 1981–89

	SNA	U.S.	Difference in percentage points (U.S. minus SNA)
1981	2.3	2.0	−0.3
1982	−2.6	−2.5	0.1
1983	3.9	3.7	−0.2
1984	7.2	7.0	−0.2
1985	3.8	3.6	−0.2
1986	3.2	2.9	−0.3
1987	3.5	3.6	0.1
1988	4.5	4.4	−0.1
1989	2.8	2.5	−0.3

the United States counts them when the federal government makes the employer contribution to the pension fund; because benefits paid have exceeded employer contributions in recent years, the SNA-based figure for this component has recently been consistently higher than the U.S.-based figure. There are other differences between the SNA and the U.S. definitions that affect the distribution of the GDP components (such as government services, types of income, and saving) but not the actual amount of the total GDP.

Table 3 shows the annual differential growth rates of real GDP between the SNA and U.S. definitions from 1981 to 1989. The U.S. definition shows slower growth ranging from 0.1 to 0.3 percentage points in seven of the nine years; and the U.S. definition has faster growth of 0.1 percentage point in the other two years. While the U.S. definitions tend to show a slightly slower growth rate, the differential is well within the margin of error of the GDP measures and also is too small to affect economic policymaking significantly.

Except for the United States, most countries with market economies use SNA definitions to measure the GDP, and most nations with centrally planned economies are variously working on adapting their accounting systems to the SNA. Such nations typically measure the GDP according to a materials product concept, based on socialist theory, which excludes certain services such as housing, health, education, and transport of persons (although transport of goods is included). The materials product figures are typically adapted in abbreviated fashion by using statistical factors to convert the materials product to the SNA. However, at least one country, Hungary, is known to be preparing detailed SNA tables.

The United States plans to follow the SNA definitions in the future for two reasons. First, the ongoing globalization of the U.S. economy has increasingly highlighted the need for internationally comparable data in economic analysis and policymaking. In addition, the SNA definitions provide a more comprehensive framework for integrating the national accounts with the Federal Reserve Board's flow of funds and balance sheets on the U.S. economy. Thus, the United States plans to consider adoption of the SNA definitions in the mid-1990s following their expected revision by the UN in the early 1990s.

Real GNP and Inflation

GNP in constant dollars, also referred to as "real GNP," reflects the growth in the *quantity* of economic activity abstracted from price increases or decreases. (Such price effects are included in the GNP in current dollars, also known as "nominal GNP.")[3] As of this writing, real GNP uses 1982 as its base year (after the GNP benchmark revision published at the end of 1991, real GNP uses 1987 as its base year). Thus, for any given period since, the real GNP figures have no real significance in absolute terms; however, precisely because they measure economic activity abstracted from price changes, real GNP figures are quite significant as measures of the *rate of change* in quarterly or yearly GNP movements. Thus, real GNP figures are used for economic analyses such as comparing GNP to employment to estimate labor productivity (see Chapter 5) or comparing income to population to assess trends in living conditions.

The real GNP figures also yield measures of price change. There are three variants of these indexes of inflation (rising prices) and deflation (falling prices). The first is the "implicit price deflator," derived by dividing current-dollar GNP by constant-dollar GNP. The deflator reflects continuing shifts in tastes and spending patterns because it accounts for actual spending as new or substitute products replace old ones and as consumers choose between higher- and lower-priced products or between items with slow or rapid price increases. Thus, the deflator's measure of price change includes price movements of the individual items as well as the effect of the changing mix of items bought.

The "fixed-weighted price index" is a second kind of inflation index. This index keeps spending patterns, i.e., "price weights," constant for *all* years, using the spending patterns in the most recent benchmark year as the guide. New weights are introduced with the new GNP benchmark estimates that are calculated every five years, but with lags of about three to thirteen years. Thus, it assumes no shifts in product spending until the new benchmark is completed. To illustrate, the spending patterns for the fixed-weighted price index from 1977 through 1991 were based on the 1977 and 1982 experience; and at the end of 1991 the index was revised to reflect the 1982 and 1987 experience. This time lag in the fixed-weighted price index can be limiting. For example, product substitutions due to the big increases in oil prices following the 1973 oil embargo by the Organization of Petroleum Exporting Countries were not reflected in the structure of the fixed-weighted price index until 1985. The advantage of the fixed-weighted index, however, is that it allows the user to see clearly what inflation changes occurred due simply to price changes and not product substitution. This is particularly relevant for periods of a decade or so. But it is highly questionable to use the fixed-weighted price index for long-run analyses over several decades because the premise of no change in price weights over such long time spans is unrealistic.

A third kind of index is the "chain price index," which maintains constant expenditure patterns between each quarter or year—for example, the first- to the second-quarter price change refers to expenditure patterns in the first quarter, and the second-to-third quarter price change refers to the expenditure patterns in the second quarter. Thus, this index represents expenditure patterns somewhere between the continually moving ones in the implicit price deflator and the constant ones in the fixed-weighted price index, but it is closer in nature to the deflator.

These alternative price indexes highlight the classic index number problem of a shifting product mix (in this case, expenditure patterns). As noted in Chapter 1, choosing one index as superior is difficult. The most useful approach for about the most recent ten-year period is to treat them as providing a range of lower and upper bounds for the actual inflation occurring in the everyday world. The implicit price deflator is the most relevant measure for analyses of price trends over several decades.

The GNP price measures indirectly affect real GNP growth rates because of their role in the GNP benchmark revisions that are done about every six years. With each new benchmark, real GNP for all past years is recalculated according to the new base period. For example, in the benchmark revision that was completed in 1985, the price index base year was changed from 1972 = 100 to 1982 = 100; therefore, all real GNP figures back to 1929 were revised to reflect 1982 = 100. As Edward Steinberg pointed out, this revision resulted in a striking shift in the apparent pattern of net exports of goods and services during the 1960s.[4] In all years of the 1960s, the current-dollar net exports were positive—that is, exports exceeded imports. Before the revision, the constant-dollar measure in 1972 dollars was also positive for all years during the decade. However, after the revision, the constant-dollar net exports in 1982 dollars were negative in most years of the 1960s—that is, imports exceeded exports. This apparent reversal, due simply to changing the base year, is a statistical fluke that distorts long-term analyses of trends in real net exports and real GNP. Allan Young notes that the problem of changing the base year in measuring real GNP has worsened since the 1970s, and a shift from 1982 to 1987 price weights lowers the annual growth rate during 1983–88 by 0.3 percentage point.[5] The GNP benchmark revision published in December 1991 includes alternative measures of real GNP based on more sophisticated index number techniques to prevent distortions of this kind. The revised benchmark data showed a slightly lower growth rate than previously published. Over the 1977–90 period, average annual growth rates of real GNP and real gross domestic product were both revised downward from 2.7 to 2.5 percent. The 0.2 percentage point decline primarily was due to the shift in the base period from 1982 to 1987 prices.

In addition to the problem of shifting base period proportions, price indexes are beleaguered by the problem of accounting adequately for changes in the goods and services being priced that affect their value. These indexes purport to measure price changes that result solely from a price increase or decrease, not one from changes in the quality or specifications of the item. For example, if a loaf of bread increases in price without a change in quality or size, that is a price increase for purposes of GNP measurement. But if the loaf increases in size equivalent to the price increase, there is no price change for GNP measurement. Or if the price of the bread is unchanged but the loaf is now larger or contains a nutritious new ingredient, a price decrease will be registered.

Price measurement issues are discussed more fully in Chapter 6, which treats the consumer price index. They are noted here simply to indicate that price measurement is an imprecise concept.

Government Budgets

The GNP measurement of government *purchases* of goods and services is less inclusive than that of *expenditures* in federal, state, and local official budgets. Government purchases include outlays for goods, services, and construction bought from the private sector and wages paid to government workers. They exclude transfer payments to individuals for Social Security and other income maintenance programs, federal grants to state and local governments and state grants to local governments, interest on government debt, foreign economic aid, and government loans less repayments—all of which are included as spending in official government budgets.

The spending generated by the items not included in government purchases is included in the GNP markets that use the money to buy goods and services. For example, Social Security and other income maintenance payments when spent become consumer expenditures; state and local government spending of federal grants appears in state and local purchases; foreign spending of economic aid appears in net exports; and interest payments on government debt and government loans and subsidies appear in the spending by the recipients of these funds in the domestic and foreign components of the GNP. Thus, while these transfer-type items are excluded from government purchases in the GNP, they are accounted for in the other sectors.

Nevertheless, the exclusion of these items from the GNP's accounting of the government sector limits one's view of the economic impact of government. For example, in fiscal year 1989, federal purchases in the GNP of $399 billion represented only 35 percent of all the outlays in the official federal budget. One way to more fully analyze the economic impact of government in the GNP framework is to use supplementary data in the national accounts on government statistical budgets which include total expenditures and receipts. These are similar to the official budgets, but are modified to make them more useful for estimating the effects of expenditures, receipts, and the budget surplus or deficit on economic activity.

Besides definitional differences, such as distinctions in coverage of government loans, land purchases, contributions to government-employee retirement funds, and spending and receipts in U.S. possessions outside the fifty states and the District of Columbia, the two budgets—the GNP national accounts statistical measure and the official budget—differ in terms of timing. While both are calculated essentially on a cash basis, which counts spending when government checks are issued and receipts when taxpayer checks are received, the cash concept has some exceptions. These occur mostly in the statistical budget. The federal official budget, which the Office of Management and Budget prepares semiannually, has only one exception to the cash basis: since interest payments on the public debt are accounted for on an accrual basis, they are recorded when the interest liability is incurred. The federal statistical budget, on the other hand, which the Bureau of Economic Analysis (the BEA) prepares quarterly as part of the national accounts (the GNP framework), diverges from the cash basis for several items: interest payments on the public debt are on an accrual basis (similar to the official budget); spending for large defense items like airplanes, missiles, and ships are recorded when the items are delivered to the government; and business income taxes are recorded when the tax liability is incurred (i.e., on an accrual basis). For state and local governments, national totals of the official budgets are not published. However, two statistical budgets are prepared that encompass all state and local governments in a national total, one annually by the Bureau of the Census and the other quarterly by the BEA as part of the national accounts (the GNP framework). The Census budget is completely on a cash basis. The BEA budget diverges from the cash concept in two aspects, both similar to the exceptions in the federal statistical budget: interest payments on the public debt and business income taxes on an accrual basis.

The GNP accounting method is more useful for economic purposes because, in general, production is geared closer to deliveries than to payments, and investment decisions are shaped by advance indication of profits after taxes. Statistical budgets in the GNP framework are used in fiscal and monetary policymaking, where the overall impact of expenditures, receipts, and the surplus or deficit are of major concern. By contrast, official budgets generally are linked to planning expenditures for individual programs and agencies in the appropriation process and in changing tax rates through legislation.

Because of the two methods of accounting, the national accounts deficit usually is less (or the surplus is more) than the official budget deficit (or surplus). Table 4 shows that for 1985–90, the national accounts deficit differed by no more than 15 percent from the official budget deficit, except for 1990 when the

Table 4

Federal Budget Deficit (in billions of dollars)

1 Fiscal year	2 Official budget	3 Statistical national accounts budget	4 Difference (national accounts minus official)	5 Difference as a percent of official figure (4)/(2) x 100
1985	$-212.3	$-185.5	$26.8	-13%
1986	-221.2	-212.8	8.4	-4
1987	-149.7	-160.7	-11.0	7
1988	-155.1	-144.1	11.0	-7
1989	-153.4	-130.3	23.1	-15
1990	-220.4	-158.2	62.2	-28

Source: Joint Economic Committee of Congress, *Economic Indicators,* February 1991, pp. 32 and 34.

difference was 28 percent. In all years except 1987, the statistical deficit was less than the official deficit. For practical purposes, most economic analyses and projections are based on the national accounts budget, and if necessary for the analysis they are then modified for known or expected special transactions to assess their impact on particular programs such as defense or agriculture.

Selected Technical Topics

This section addresses several technical aspects of the GNP relevant to interpreting trends: alternative summary measures, seasonally adjusted annual rates, error ranges, the statistical discrepancy, net exports, and valuation adjustments.

Alternative Summary Measures

In addition to the GNP, other summary measures of the national accounts are available to better reflect special circumstances in the domestic or international economies. These measures are final sales, final sales to domestic purchasers, gross domestic product, and command GNP. Another alternative GNP measure, GNP on the income side, is discussed in the Statistical Discrepancy section below.

Final sales are the GNP excluding inventory change. In the GNP, an inventory increase is added to final sales and an inventory decrease is deducted from final sales. Inventory movements arise from differences between production and sales—inventories increase when production is larger than sales, and they decrease when sales are greater than production. Businesses augment or cut back on their stock of goods based on their perceptions of future sales and prices, or because of unexpected market developments such as substantially greater-than-anticipated rises or falls in sales, in which case the subsequent inventory depletion or accumulation is referred to as "unplanned." The unplanned changes may in turn generate deliberate actions to bring inventories into a desired balance with sales. Short-term inventory movements can be important signals that production may increase because inventories are low in relation to sales, or that production may decrease because inventories are relatively high.

It is also informative to assess the economy's performance independent of inventory movements by focusing on the strength of demand in all GNP markets as evidenced in sales. For example, if sales are level or falling but production is adding to inventories, the overall GNP growth rate may be deceptively high. Or if sales are increasing and inventories are being depleted because of production bottlenecks, the GNP growth rate may understate the economy's underlying strength. The purpose of the final sales measure is to capture this underlying strength in demand.

Final sales to domestic purchases are final sales minus exports and plus imports, which measures underlying demand (excluding inventory movements) in the domestic economy. By excluding exports, it abstracts from foreign demand for American production, and by including imports, it recognizes an American domestic demand that is not being met by American industry.

Gross domestic product is the GNP adjusted to exclude the effect of profits from foreign investments and of foreign workers' wages. It focuses on economic activity within the geographic boundaries of the fifty states and the District of Columbia. In contrast, the GNP treats multinational corporations' profits according to the nationality of the company's ownership, and foreign workers' wages according to the nationality of the worker. In the GNP, profits from foreign operations of U.S.-owned companies are included as business income and treated as exports on the product side, while profits from operations in the United States of foreign-owned companies are excluded from business income and treated as imports; analogously, wages of U.S. workers abroad are included as an export and wages of foreign workers in the United States are included as an import. For some analyses of the American economy, however, the level of economic activity occurring in the geographic United States, regardless of the nationality of companies and workers, is most significant. While profits of a multinational company with affiliates in several countries accrue to the parent company in the home country and thus affect the company's business decisions on investment and operations worldwide, the profits are in fact generated from production and employment in particular countries. Similarly, while foreign workers send some of their wage income to relatives in their home country, they also spend money in the nation where they are working. Thus, to focus on the geographical aspect of these activities, GDP excludes profits of U.S.-owned companies earned from foreign operations and wages of U.S. workers employed abroad, and includes profits of foreign-owned companies from their U.S. operations and wages of foreign workers employed in the United States. This reverses the treatment in the GNP.

Command GNP is a shortened version of "Command over Goods and Services, GNP Basis." It expresses the notion that as prices for exported and imported items diverge and substantially change the terms of trade (the ratio of export prices to import prices), the conventional deflation of exports and imports by their respective price trends affects real GNP growth rates by giving foreigners a higher or lower claim on U.S. production.

This impact results from the accounting need to subtract imports from exports for the net export component of the GNP (see later section on net exports). This is done to offset the inclusion of imports in the other product-side GNP components of consumer expenditures, investment, and government purchases. If imports were not subtracted from exports, the product and income sides of the GNP would not balance, because income-side wages and profits do not exist for imports.

The impact occurs when important internationally traded items such as petroleum have relatively large price changes. For example, for some years in the 1970s and in 1980, when the price of imported oil rose very sharply, constant-dollar imports were much lower than current-dollar imports. This in turn raised constant-dollar net exports (because net exports are exports minus imports) and therefore real GNP. This suggested that Americans had a greater supply from which to "command" goods and services because of the higher import prices. This is an anomaly of the accounting need to deduct imports, because higher import prices *lower* the availability of goods and services for consumption. Analogously, the oil price decline from 1981 to 1986 falsely suggests a lower command of goods and services over that period in the conventional GNP.

Command GNP handles such problems by changing the deflation procedure of net exports. The conventional GNP method deflates exports and imports separately by export and import prices, and then subtracts constant-dollar imports from constant-dollar exports. Command GNP deflates net exports in a single step, using import prices as the only deflator (export prices as the single deflator would yield similar results). This device tends to moderate anomalies produced by the accounting need to subtract imports in the net export component.

Seasonally Adjusted Annual Rate

The GNP is estimated quarterly, but the figure for each quarter is published as if the activity in the quarter were at an annual rate. This facilitates comparison of the economy's current volume with past and projected annual levels. Two measures are involved in this concept: the first is the GNP absolute level for the quarter at an annual rate, and the second is the percentage change in this level from the previous quarter at an annual rate.

The GNP level is the sum of the seasonally adjusted data for the three months of the quarter, multiplied by four to raise it to an annual level. For example, for the first quarter of the year, the seasonally adjusted data for January, February, and March are summed, and the total is multiplied by four. The resulting figure is the quarterly GNP at a seasonally adjusted annual rate. Because the quarter includes activity for three months, the monthly economy can be declining (or rising) even if the quarter is rising (or falling).

To derive an annual percentage rate of change in the current-quarter GNP from the preceding quarter, the relative change for the present quarter is *compounded* to represent an annual rate. The procedure is to raise the rate of growth or decline in the current quarter to the fourth power, subtract 1.0, and multiply by 100, as follows:

$$\left(\frac{\text{Seasonally adjusted annual GNP (current quarter)}}{\text{Seasonally adjusted annual GNP (previous quarter)}} \right)^4 - 1.0 \times 100$$

Percentage changes from quarter to quarter or year to year are published for all GNP components except inventory change and net exports because these components of the GNP can be either positive or negative, and a percentage change is not defined between two periods that do not have the same sign. To avoid confusion, however, the BEA reports only measures of economic activity that can be calculated on a regular basis. Thus, percentage changes for exports and imports are published separately.

Error Range

The preliminary GNP estimates published shortly after each quarter are tentative, as is evident from the size of the revisions made as more complete and accurate information becomes available. Experience with these revisions has shown that, in 9 cases out of 10, their likely effect on seasonally adjusted annual growth rates for quarterly real GNP is in the ranges indicated in Table 5. Thus, when real GNP for the fourth quarter of 1990 was first reported to have declined at an annual rate of 2.1 percent, the chances were 9 out of 10 that the final figure would fall somewhere between −3.2 to −0.1 percent. There is also a tendency for revisions, which incorporate new and additional data, to raise growth rates or lower the rate of decline.

The table shows two sets of revision ranges. One set focuses on the revisions that occur on a current basis, that is, the revisions that are made between the advance and preliminary GNP published 25 and 55 days after the quarter and the final GNP published 85 days after the quarter. The other set focuses on the subsequent revisions of these three early estimates based on the annual revision that is prepared every July and on the still later five-year benchmark GNP revisions.

Table 5

Probable Revisions to Quarterly Real GNP Annual Growth Rates
(percentage points)

Publication schedule of initial GNP estimates for the same quarter	Average without regard to sign (plus or minus)	Range
Advance to final	0.7	−1.1 to 2.0
Preliminary to final	0.4	−0.8 to 0.9
Advance to latest	1.8	−2.8 to 4.1
Preliminary to latest	1.7	−3.2 to 4.1
Final to latest	1.8	−2.7 to 3.6

Source: Bureau of Economic Analysis, U.S. Department of Commerce, GNP press release, October 30, 1990.

Note: Based on 9 of 10 revisions during 1976 to 1987.

Advance: 25 days after the quarter

Preliminary: 55 days after the quarter

Final: 85 days after the quarter

Latest: Most recent annual and five-year benchmark revisions

Both sets of revisions in Table 5 are sizable, but as would be expected, those associated with the annual and five-year benchmark revisions are greater than those between the GNP published 25 days and 85 days after the quarter. The table indicates that growth rate revisions typically have a probable range that is larger than the growth rate itself, which over the years averages about 3 percent.

However, policymakers responsible for setting fiscal and monetary policies to influence the economy clearly cannot apply such high revision ranges in their analyses of the current rate of economic growth. Moreover, to be timely, economic policymakers must respond to trends based on the early GNP figures before the annual and five-year benchmark revisions become available. For current policy analysis, then, a more workable measure of revision range is the average without regard to sign (also shown in Table 5). These figures, which combine the revision ranges into a single number and thus moderate the extremes appearing in the actual ranges, indicate notably lower error ranges of approximately plus or minus 0.5 percentage point between the 25-day and 85-day estimates, and plus or minus 1.8 percentage points between the three early estimates and the annual and five-year benchmark revisions.

In contrast to the quite high error ranges associated with the revisions, the average without regard to sign provides at least a workable error range. However, in actuality, whether one uses the actual revision ranges or the average without regard to sign, the error range for revisions to the GNP is quite high, which underscores the need to observe the trend for at least two consecutive quarters before using it as a basis for changing economic policies. But even current trends of three consecutive quarters can be misleading for economic policy analysis, as occurred in 1989–90 (see Chapter 1 under Revisions). In general, one should also wait for the final estimate eighty-five days after the most recent quarter before concluding that the numbers reflect the actual circumstances of the quarter. *The overall lesson is that no single GNP figure should be interpreted to indicate a new trend or validate an existing one, but rather should be viewed in the context of trends for previous quarters to determine whether a change is occurring.*

Statistical Discrepancy

Conceptually, the product and income sides of the GNP measure in grand total the same output. In practice, limitations in the underlying data mean that the totals are rarely equal. The data are obtained from a variety of surveys, tax records, and other sources that have varying comparability with the GNP concepts. They also have varying degrees of accuracy, because the survey samples are not necessarily representative and the respondents may provide erroneous information.

The difference between the totals on the product and income sides is the *net* effect of these inconsistencies and inaccuracies, and is referred to as the "statistical discrepancy." The discrepancy is not systematic from quarter to quarter, as different data problems are always occurring. By convention, the discrepancy is calculated as the product side minus the income side, and it appears on the income side. In some cases the deficiencies are offsetting, which results in the statistic discrepancy's being smaller than if the *gross* deficiencies were added without regard to their upward or downward direction.

From the user's perspective, the discrepancy allows alternative GNP growth rates to be calculated from the product- and income-side information. These upper and lower bounds recognize that, due to data shortcomings, neither the product nor income side is inherently more accurate and that "reality" is more a range than a precise number. (This is similar to the approach suggested previously for the alternative price indexes.)

For analytic purposes, the user should be aware that a noticeable change in the discrepancy could affect the growth rate. For example, in a $5 trillion GNP, a $10 billion discrepancy is 0.2 percent and a $30 billion discrepancy is 0.6 percent of the GNP. If the GNP on the product side grows at a rate of 3 percent for two quarters in a row, and the discrepancy increases from $10 billion to $30 billion in the two quarters, the alternative growth rate for the second quarter will become 2.6 percent, which—while not startling, as will be seen later—approaches the range where unemployment rises.

Net Exports

Net exports of goods and services are the GNP component that represents U.S. transactions with other countries. It is derived by subtracting imports from exports. The net concept is necessary to keep the product and income sides of the GNP accounts in balance, due to the special situation of imports.

Because imports are produced abroad, their production does not generate wages and profits in the United States, and thus no income-side payments are associated with their production. However, imported items do appear on the product side as households, businesses, and governments buy the imported goods and services. If nothing was done to offset purchases in the consumption, investment, and government components on the product side, that side would be higher than the income side. Therefore, imports are deducted from exports in the net export component to neutralize their inclusion in the other product-side components.

The deduction of imports, however, causes the net export component to appear as a deceptively small share of the GNP. In 1989, for example, net exports were -$46 billion ($626 billion of exports minus $672 billion of imports), or a deficit of 1 percent of the GNP. This relatively small net figure masks the much higher actual economic impact of exports and imports separately, as exports were 12 percent and imports were 13 percent of the GNP in 1989.

While net exports give an overall view of the differential effort of exports and imports and of money flows between the United States and other countries (and can be important for foreign-exchange values and U.S. monetary policies), exports and imports taken separately are more relevant for assessing the impact of international trade on American production and prices. Exports and imports affect and are affected by employment and inflation in the United States, American competitiveness in international markets, the value of the dollar, and the pace of the American and world economies.

Valuation Adjustments for Inventories and Depreciation

Special adjustments are made for the effect of price movements on the change in business inventories and on depreciation allowances for equipment and structures as conventionally reported by companies. These adjustments are particularly important during periods of high inflation and when depreciation allowances in the tax laws differ substantially from the use of capital facilities in business practice over their economic lifetime.

In both cases, the purpose of the adjustments is to reflect the *replacement cost* of inventories and capital facilities based on prices when they are used up, as distinct from prices at the time the inventories and capital facilities were acquired (their historical cost). Doing so eliminates the effect of valuation gains and losses on inventories due to price increases and decreases of goods since they were acquired. And for capital facilities, the adjustment provides a truer picture of the actual costs of replacing outmoded or inefficient plant and equipment as compared with the depreciation deductions allowed in income tax laws.

The *inventory valuation adjustment* (IVA) appears in the change in business inventories on the product side and in business profits on the income side of the

GNP. During periods of rising prices, the IVA is negative to offset valuation profits when goods are sold; when prices are falling the IVA is positive to offset the valuation losses. Since prices generally are rising, the IVA is typically negative, although the amounts vary considerably depending on the inflation rate. For example, after sinking to –$51 billion in 1979 and –$50 billion in 1980, the IVA moved toward zero and became positive, reaching +$11 billion in 1986, and then turned negative in the –$12–28 billion range during 1987–90. These trends mirrored changes in the inflation rate, which declined during the early part of the 1980s and increased in the latter part of the decade. (The figures cited here refer to the IVA on the product side. The product- and income-side estimates of the IVA differ because they are derived from different data sources. The levels are of the same general magnitude, although the product side usually is greater, and the year-to-year movements are almost always the same.) Because inventories are continually replenished and sold at current prices, the IVA provides a more realistic assessment of actual inventory buildups and depletions and of business profits.

The *capital consumption adjustment* (CCAdj) affects the income side of the GNP accounts and appears as offsetting items to business profits and capital consumption allowances (mainly depreciation). The CCAdj reflects that the actual usage of capital facilities by business (known as economic depreciation) differs from the depreciation based on tax law provisions (known as tax depreciation). While tax depreciation is based on statutorily defined schedules, economic depreciation is based on the actual service lives of various types of equipment and structures as indicated by industry surveys conducted in the 1970s by the U.S. Department of the Treasury and by information collected from regulatory agencies; moreover, economic depreciation is based on straight-line rather than accelerated depreciation over the life of the capital item because of the lack of data on the declining productivity of capital items over time.

The CCAdj is affected mainly by the tax laws and to a lesser extent by inflation. When the tax laws allow accelerated depreciation schedules, which permit businesses to recoup the original cost of capital facilities faster than businesses actually use them up, the CCAdj appears as a positive item in business profits and a negative item in capital consumption allowances. When prices of capital goods are rising and thus raising the cost of new capital facilities, the CCAdj is deducted from profits and added to capital consumption allowances. The opposite occurs when the tax laws require slower depreciation rates than those at which business tends to use up capital facilities or when capital goods prices are falling. The CCAdj tends to be smaller when the tax laws have few investment incentives or disincentives in their own right, and larger when tax-generated investment incentives and disincentives are great. Thus, the smaller the CCAdj is, the closer the depreciation assumptions of the tax laws are to economic reality.

The CCAdj has changed considerably in recent years as a result of the Economic Recovery Tax Act of 1981 (which greatly accelerated depreciation tax deductions by shortening the "tax life" of capital facilities), the slowdown of inflation during the early 1980s, and the less accelerated depreciation tax deductions in the Tax Reform Act of 1986. The CCAdj for corporations and nonfarm businesses increased from –$18 billion in 1980 to a peak of +$91 billion in 1985 and 1986, and then declined to +$35 billion in 1990. While the CCAdj does not affect total GNP, it does affect the distribution between profits and depreciation. Because profits are an important element driving future investment in capital facilities, shifts of these magnitudes can significantly affect plant and equipment investment. (The CCAdj for unincorporated farm businesses and rental income of persons reflects changes in the capital goods inflation rate, but does not reflect differentials between tax law depreciation and actual business practice in accounting for capital costs. This occurs because: (a) data problems in the case of unincorporated farm businesses and rental property income limit the use of tax return information; and (b) rental income is mainly composed of "rent" for owner-occupied dwellings that is imputed as if it were a cash payment to a landlord, but for which no depreciation is taken on the individual income tax return.)

PART B: ANALYSIS OF TRENDS

This portion of the chapter covers the main patterns taken by American business cycles from the 1945–48 expansion to the recession beginning in 1990 (which was in progress in the spring of 1991 when this was written) and highlights the major factors driving these trends. This period represents a major change from the depression of the 1930s and World War II both in the nature of the economy and the tools available for moderating business cycles. These postwar cycles are assessed from two perspectives: (a) a "top-down" view based on the total GNP and alternative summary GNP measures; and (b) a "building-block" approach focusing on the household, business, government, and internation components. A last section focuses on trends in investment and saving in the GNP framework.

There have been nine expansions and nine recessions since World War II, as measured from the expansion of 1945–48 to the recession that began in the summer of 1990. There was a recession from February to October 1945, but because it was so closely linked to the war and the demobilization, it is not included in this analysis. The subsequent expansion from 1945 to 1948 was affected by the pent-up demand from the steadily growing incomes and deferred purchases of wartime, and thus the war had an important, although indirect, effect. Therefore, the 1948–49 recession was the first postwar cyclical movement that was sufficiently removed from the war not to have been affected by the war's aftermath.

The turning point used here to mark the peak of expansions and the trough of recessions is the change in direction of the real GNP. The real GNP turning point is used as a standard to allow a consistent analysis of movements among the GNP components. The components may fall in the same quarter or the quarter immediately before or after the turning point designated by the National Bureau

Table 6

Duration of Expansions and Recessions Based on Real GNP Beginning and Ending Quarters

Expansions		Recessions	
	Duration (quarters)		Duration (quarters)
1945:4–48:4[a]	13	1949:1–49:4	4
1950:1–53:2	14	1953:3–54:2	4
1954:3–57:3	13	1957:4–58:1	2
1958:2–60:1	8	1960:2–60:4	3
1961:1–69:3	35	1969:4–70:4	5
1971:1–73:4	12	1974:1–75:1	5
1975:2–80:1	20	1980:2–80:2	1
1980:3–81:3	5	1981:4–82:3	4
1982:4–90:3	32	1990:4–[b]	

Note: The beginning and ending quarters are shown after the colon of each year.

[a]Quarterly real GNP data are not available before 1947. Use of 1945:4 as the starting point of the 1945–48 expansion follows the designation by the National Bureau of Economic Research of November 1945 as the beginning of the expansion (see text).

[b]The recession that began in 1990 was in progress in the spring of 1991 when this was written.

of Economic Research, which is specified as a particular month (see Chapter 2 under "Designation of Recessions and Expansions").

Table 6 shows the beginning and ending quarters for the postwar business cycles used in this analysis. For expansions, the first date is the quarter the economy turned up from the previous recession and the second date is the last quarter (peak) of the expansion before the economy turned down into the next recession. For recessions, the first date is the quarter when the economy turned down and the second date is the last quarter (trough) of the recession. For example, the 1950–53 expansion lasted from the first quarter of 1950 to the second quarter of 1953, and the subsequent recession lasted from the third quarter of 1953 to the second quarter of 1954.

As noted in Chapter 2, in the postwar period expansions averaged 4 years in peacetime and 4½ years including wartime cycles, and recessions averaged one year in both cases. However, the duration of individual cycles varies widely around these averages. The expansion of the 1960s lasted nine years, and the expansion of the 1980s lasted eight years. Still, the duration of the expansions was far more varied during 1970–90 than in the 1950s; this change in part probably reflects the growing internationalization of the economy, which makes it more vulnerable to economic events around the world and thus subject to greater variability.

Comparison of Real GNP and Other Summary Measures

This section concentrates on the postwar cyclical movements of the GNP and other summary GNP measures. To put these cyclical movements in a longer-run context, it first briefly highlights postwar trends in economic growth. Economic growth in relation to unemployment is discussed in Chapter 5.

Long-term Trends

Over the twentieth century as a whole, average annual economic growth rose from 2.6 percent during 1909–48 to 3.3 percent during 1948–89. Thus, economic growth accelerated in the second half of the twentieth century. The second half was more peaceful, as World Wars I and II occurred in the first half of the century, and real GNP growth was slow for several years after both wars were over. The second half of the century also did not have an economic collapse like the depression of the 1930s. These patterns suggest an improved economic climate in the twentieth century after World War II, but such long-term comparisons are inherently tentative because the increasing accuracy of GNP measures over time limits the statistical comparability of the two forty-year periods (see Chapter 2, Changing Characteristics of Business Cycles since the Nineteenth Century). In particular, there is little documentation of the statistical methodology used in developing the GNP estimates from 1909 to 1928; they were prepared by private researchers outside of the BEA, although the BEA publishes them in the historical five-year GNP benchmark publications.

Long-term trends in real GNP that span several business cycles show distinct shifts in the annual growth rate from 1948 to 1989. The average for the entire period is 3.3 percent. As indicated below, rates in the 1950s and 1960s were increasingly above the long-term average, while the 1970s and the 1980s had much slower rates of growth than average.[6]

The slowdown in the growth rate during 1969–89 was accompanied by the greater variability (previously noted) in the duration of expansions, while the rapid growth of the 1960s occurred during an exceptionally long expansion. A theoretical case could be made that fewer or possibly more uniform cyclical fluctuations result in faster economic growth or vice versa. Looking more closely

---

Annual Average Growth in Real GNP

1948–59	3.6%
1959–69	4.1
1969–79	2.8
1979–89	2.6
1909–48	2.6
1948–89	3.3
1909–89	2.9

Figure 4a. **Business Cycle Movements of Real GNP, Final Sales, and Final Sales to Domestic Purchasers: Expansions**

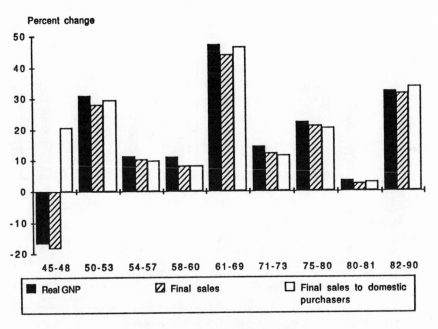

Note: Based on Bureau of Economic Analysis data in 1982 dollars.

at the second half of the twentieth century, however, the evidence on the growth-cyclical relationship during 1948–89 is inconclusive. While the highest growth rate occurred during the expansion of the 1960s, which is the longest since World War II, the growth rate of the 1980s, which included the second longest postwar expansion, was below that of the 1950s.

Cyclical Movements

The cyclical analyses discussed below focus on the entire period for each expansion and recession. Changes within each expansion and recession period are not shown. For example, in the 1983–90 expansion, the *increase* in the federal budget deficit was a major stimulus to economic growth until 1987, while the *reduction* in the foreign trade deficit propelled economic growth during 1987–90.

Figures 4a, 4b, 4c, and 4d summarize the movements of real GNP and the other summary GNP measures over the postwar business cycles. Final sales (GNP excluding inventory change) and final sales to domestic purchasers (final sales including imports and excluding exports) are the only alternative summary GNP measures that diverged substantially from the real GNP. Figures 4a and 4c

Figure 4b. **Business Cycle Movements of Real GNP, GDP, Command GNP, and GNP Minus Statistical Discrepancy: Expansions**

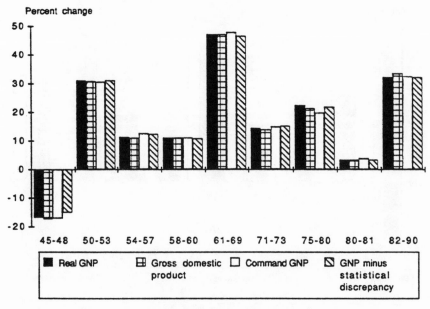

Note: Based on Bureau of Economic Analysis data in 1982 dollars.

show that real GNP is more volatile than final sales; GNP rose in expansions and declined in recessions more sharply than final sales. During expansions, the GNP typically increased by 1 to 3 percentage points more than final sales and final sales to domestic purchasers; in recessions, GNP typically fell by 1 to 2 percentage points more than both final sales categories. (In the recession of 1949, 1960, and 1969–70, both final sales categories actually increased.)

Figures 4b and 4d show that other GNP measures—gross domestic product (GNP adjusted for foreign earnings of multinational companies), command GNP (GNP modified by the import deflator to deflate the net export component), and GNP less the statistical discrepancy—are not significantly different from those of real GNP. They indicate that the differences are typically less than 0.5 of a percentage point. There were only a few instances when they differed by 1 to 1.5 percentage points. These instances occurred during the expansions of 1945–48 (GNP minus the statistical discrepancy), 1954–57 (command GNP), 1975–80 (gross domestic product and command GNP), and 1982–90 (gross domestic product), as well as during the recessions of 1949 (GNP minus the statistical discrepancy) and 1974–75 (command GNP). In general, these comparisons indicate that differential movements between the GNP and the alternative measures

Figure 4c. **Business Cycle Movements of Real GNP, Final Sales, and Final Sales to Domestic Purchasers: Recessions**

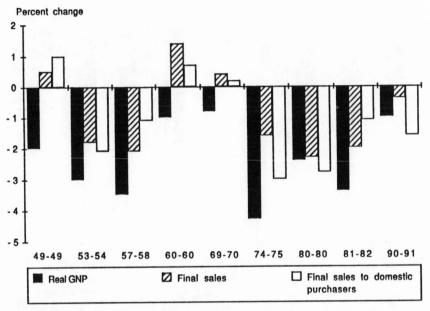

Note: Based on Bureau of Economic Analysis data in 1982 dollars. Recession of 1990-91 in progress in spring of 1991.

are of analytic interest for short-term movements of one to two years rather than for movements over several years.

Differences between GNP and final sales reflect the working off of "unplanned" inventory accumulations in recessions due to the unexpected decline in sales from the previous expansion. During expansions inventories are replenished, although usually at a slower rate than the increase in sales; but as the expansion matures and sales begin to slow down, inventories are likely to become higher than businesses wish to maintain for normal sales and production levels.

This pattern points up the importance of watching final sales during an expansion. When final sales slow down, businesses are likely to retrench from ordering new goods. Even though the greater impact of excessive inventories occurs mainly in recessions, the problem emerges in the latter part of expansions when sales become sluggish and retailers and manufacturers cut back on orders. Thus, the challenge is recognizing the emerging inventory excess.

Inventory shortages may also affect the rate of growth. Sometimes during expansions when businesses can use more goods than their suppliers can furnish because the demand exceeds the suppliers' productive capacity, inventory short-

Figure 4d. **Business Cycle Movements of Real GNP, GDP, Command GNP, and GNP Minus Statistical Discrepancy: Recessions**

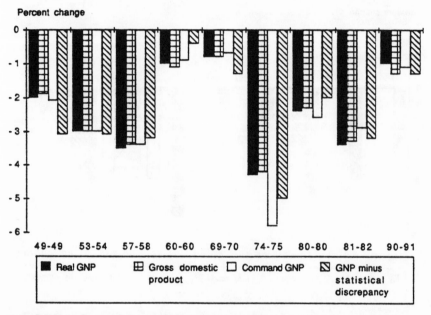

Note: Based on Bureau of Economic Analysis data in 1982 dollars. Recession of 1990-91 in progress in spring of 1991.

ages may temporarily reduce the growth rate; however, unless the shortages are severe enough to cause much higher prices (as in the case of some raw materials and oil the 1970s), they do not have the significant cyclical impact that excessive inventories do.

Although inventories are only one element of business cycles, better inventory planning probably could moderate the steepness and duration of recessions. Reports in the press indicate that some businesses are deliberately working with smaller inventories since the 1980s by applying the just-in-time concept of Japanese companies. As seen in Figure 5, ratios of nonfarm inventories to final sales in constant dollars (the number of months inventories would last at current sales rates) indicate that inventories in relation to sales declined during 1985–90, although they were still above the levels of the 1950s and 1960s.

In addition to the long-standing volatility of inventories, an important factor affecting GNP movements in recent years has been the greater inroads made by foreign goods in U.S. markets. This is apparent in the domestic demand concept of final sales to domestic purchasers. For example, from 1989:3 to 1990:3, a period of slow economic growth, real final sales increased by only 1.5 percent

Figure 5. **Turnover of Nonfarm Inventories: Inventory/Final Sales Ratio**

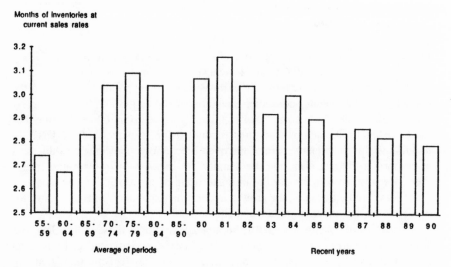

Note: Based on Bureau of Economic Analysis data for the fourth quarter of the year in 1982 dollars.

and final sales to domestic purchasers increased at the still slower rate of 1.0 percent. Thus, domestic demand in the year preceding the onset of the recession gives an even weaker picture of the U.S. economy than does the conventional GNP treatment of the foreign sector. The slowdown actually began in 1989:2, which was one year before the recession; the growth rates of the alternative GNP measures did not vary significantly over this period.

Overall, these similarities between real GNP and the alternative summary measures tend to confirm the GNP movements over the complete business cycle, although for shorter periods of about one year the other measures sometimes give a slightly different picture, which bears watching.

As noted at the beginning of the chapter, the gross domestic product is featured as the primary measure of output starting at the end of 1991. The GDP is most relevant for countries in which foreign investments (by the home country abroad and by foreigners in the home country) are a major factor in the nation's economy. While foreign investments are important in certain U.S. industries, overall they are not dominant. However, in the future both foreign investment in the United States and American investment abroad will be encouraged by several factors: the belief by American business that the dollar remains substantially overvalued compared to other nations' currencies (even after the sharp decline from 1985 to 1987), the continuance of worldwide tariffs and other import barriers, the threat of new protectionism by regional trading blocs such as the European community single market, and America's need to be more competitive in export markets.

Consumer Expenditures

In simple terms, the ultimate purpose of economic activity is to provide for the needs of the population at as high a level as possible, and consumer purchases of goods and services are the most direct measure of living conditions. Among the main GNP components, consumer spending is the largest. This spending by households for necessities and luxuries typically ranges from 62 to 65 percent of the GNP; in 1989, such expenditures accounted for 66 percent of the GNP. In addition to this prominent share of the overall economy, consumer spending has an important indirect effect on the demand for investment in plant and equipment. Because consumers are the ultimate users of most of the goods and services provided by business, the growth in consumer spending leads to outlays for modernizing and expanding plant and equipment.

The cycles of consumer spending are not as extreme as those of the GNP as a whole, particularly during recessions. For example, as indicated in Figures 6a and 6b, in five of the nine recessions since World War II, consumer spending rose while real GNP declined. Consumer spending declined by smaller percentages than the GNP in three recessions; in two of them (1957–58 and 1974–75) the consumer spending decline was under 1 percent and the differential with GNP was substantial. The one exception was the recession of 1990–91, when consumer spending declined slightly more than GNP. During the nine postwar expansions, consumer spending increased less rapidly than the real GNP in seven cases. In these instances the differentials were at most 2 percentage points, except for the 1950–53 expansion, which had a large government spending increase for the Korean War. In only two postwar expansions did consumer spending increase faster than the GNP: in 1945–48, government spending dropped precipitously because of the military retrenchment following the war resulting in a decline in the GNP, and in 1954–57 the differential was 2 percentage points. Generally, the differential movements between consumer spending and GNP are more noticeable during recessions than in expansions. *In view of these less extreme cyclical movements and the overall importance of consumer spending, the analyst when monitoring economic trends should closely observe consumer spending as a major item both for maintaining growth during expansions and for moderating the decline in recessions.*

Consumer Spending Components—
Volatility of Durable Goods

Consumer expenditures comprise three broad categories: durable goods, nondurable goods, and services. Durable goods are items intended to last three or more

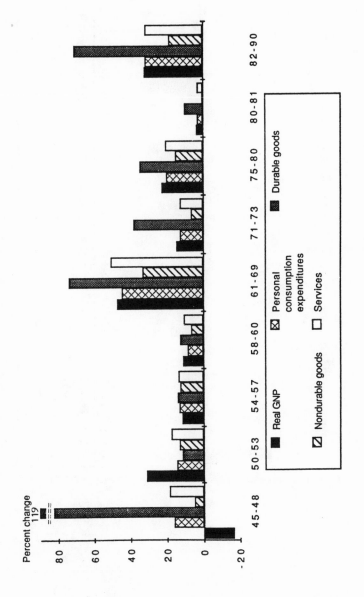

Figure 6a. Business Cycle Movements of Real GNP and Consumer Expenditures: Expansions

Note: Based on Bureau of Economic Analysis data in 1982 dollars.

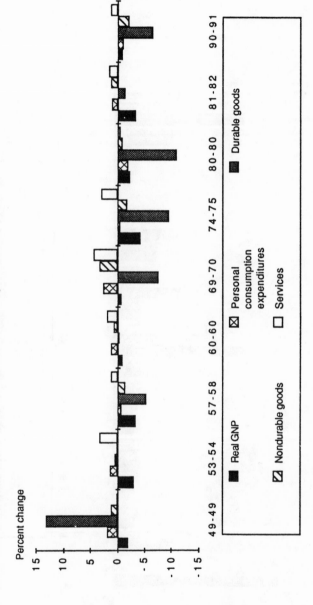

Figure 6b. **Business Cycle Movements of Real GNP and Consumer Expenditures: Recessions**

Note: Based on Bureau of Economic Analysis data in 1982 dollars. Recession of 1990-91 in progress in spring of 1991.

years, such as cars, furniture, and household appliances. Nondurable goods, such as food, clothing, and gasoline, last less than three years. Services are non-commodity items such as housing rent (including both tenant rentals and non-market imputed rent for owner-occupied housing),[7] utilities, public transportation, private education, medical care, and recreation.

These main categories of consumer spending have noticeably different cyclical and longer-term movements. Durable goods account for the smallest share of consumer outlays, ranging from 12 to 15 percent of the total. But because of the longer life of these items, it is easier for households to defer purchasing them when economic conditions, such as unemployment or inflation, are adverse. Thus, while spending for durable goods is much smaller than that for nondurables and services, durable goods outlays are far more volatile over the business cycle.

Figures 6a and 6b indicate this volatility in both the expansion and recession phases of the business cycle. In eight of the nine expansions, durable goods spending increased more rapidly than did spending for nondurables and services. The differentials between durables and the other categories are also substantially larger starting in the 1960s, with durables increasing two to four times faster than nondurables and services during these more recent expansions. As for recessions, durable goods spending declined in every postwar downturn except 1949 and 1953–54, nondurable goods purchases declined in four of the nine recessions, and purchases of services increased in all recessions except 1980. In cases when both durable and nondurable goods spending declined, the durable goods decline was much steeper. For example, in the 1974–75 recession, durable goods declined by 9.5 percent compared with 2 percent for nondurables, and in the 1990–91 recession, the durable and nondurable declines were 7 and 2 percent respectively.

The tendency for consumer spending to be consistently less cyclical than the rest of the GNP results from two offsetting patterns: (a) the long-term shift from nondurables to the more cyclically insulated services (from 1948 to 1989, nondurable goods dropped from 55 to 33 percent of all consumer spending, while services increased from 32 to 53 percent), and (b) the increasingly volatility in durable goods spending since the 1960s. *However, although these patterns were offsetting in the past, they may not be so in the future, particularly if there is a slowdown or end to the shift to services. Thus, the analyst should monitor these components to determine if a change is occurring in the less cyclical nature of consumer spending.*

Key Factors Affecting Consumer Spending

Consumer decisions to spend are affected by two broad considerations. One is the macroeconomic environment of employment and inflation; the other is the individual consumer's purchasing power as reflected in household income, loans, existing savings, and other wealth.

Macroeconomic Environment

Employment and price trends weigh heavily in the timing and types of consumer spending. Households in which the primary worker or workers are currently employed with little likelihood of being unemployed are among the best candidates to spend in the near future, both for necessities and deferrable items. By contrast, households in which workers are employed but expect to be unemployed, or in which they are unemployed with low expectations of finding a job, are likely to curtail spending sharply for deferrable items, such as a new car, clothing, or recreation, while maintaining or somewhat reducing outlays for necessities. These households are far more constrained, both by a currently limited income and by the need to save money for future spending, than are households with more secure job situations.

Consumer spending decisions are also affected by current and anticipated inflation. Ideally, consumers time their purchases to buy at the lowest price. For deferrable items, if prices are rising rapidly and inflation is expected to continue at a high rate, consumers are likely to feel it is better to buy immediately. If prices are rising now but are expected to decline without a certain period, consumers may defer some purchases. In addition to affecting timing, prices can also affect the overall amount of spending depending on relative prices between necessities and deferrable items. For example, a sharp rise in gasoline prices may curtail spending for other items. Or if deferrable items (say, television sets) drop sharply in price, spending for these items may increase.

Two private organizations conduct surveys to track the combined effects of these employment and inflation factors on consumer attitudes toward spending: The University of Michigan's Survey Research Center publishes a "consumer sentiment index," and The Conference Board publishes a "consumer confidence index." These indexes have been advance indicators of the turning points of business cycles, turning down before a general recession sets in and turning up before a general recovery begins. However, as in the case of all such indexes giving advance signals, they should be viewed as giving general notions of future trends rather than specific forecasts, since their timing varies from cycle to cycle and they sometimes give false signals (see Chapter 8 on leading and lagging indexes). *These indexes provide the basic information on the macro environmental influences on consumers' spending decisions, but in using them for specific situations, the analyst should examine how well they performed in predicting consumer spending in the most recent six to twelve months.*

Consumer Purchasing Power

Consumer purchasing power refers to consumers' capability to finance spending. It encompasses personal income from wages and all other sources, consumer installment credit loans, existing household savings in bank deposits, financial assets (money market accounts, stocks and bonds, etc.), and less liquid assets (such as real estate). All of these sources may be used to finance current consumer spending and repay consumer debt by liquidating savings and other assets or by using these assets as collateral for further loans. Because the end result of using all these financing sources is reflected in personal income, spending, and saving, this discussion and the following section on personal saving integrate them in the framework of personal income and saving.

Personal income is primarily income received by households, before the payment of income taxes, from wages and fringe benefits, profits from self-employment, rent, interest, dividends, Social Security benefits, unemployment insurance, food stamps, and other income maintenance programs. (Social security taxes paid by employees and employers are excluded from personal income.) It also includes operating expenses of nonprofit organizations, and investment income of life insurance companies, noninsured pension funds, private nonprofit organizations, and trust funds. In recent years, the investment income components have accounted for 4.5 percent of personal income

Personal income is dominated by wages and fringe benefits (these represented 64 percent of personal income in 1989). It thus increases steadily during expansions and times of rising employment, but increases more slowly or declines in recessions. Figures 7a and 7b show that the less extreme cyclical movement of personal income compared with the GNP is most apparent in recessions. This in part reflects the exclusion of the highly cyclical corporate profits from personal income. It also results from the stabilizing effect of unemployment insurance, even though the benefit payments to unemployed workers account for a relatively small share of personal income. For example, in the 1981–82 recession, unemployment insurance rose from $15 billion in the third quarter of 1981 to $26 billion in the third quarter of 1982, or from 0.6 to 1 percent of personal income in those periods (in the fourth quarter of 1982, when the real GNP turned up, unemployment insurance rose to its peak of $32 billion or 1.2 percent of personal income). These relatively small shares, together with the exclusion of corporate profits from personal income, were enough during the recession to soften the decline of 3.4 percent in the real GNP to a decline of 0.9 percent in real personal income. The decline during the 1980s in the proportion of laid-off workers that receive unemployment benefits is discussed in Chapter 5.

An important factor influencing the availability of personal income for spending is taxation. The measure of after-tax income is *disposable* personal income, which is income after the payment of income, estate, and gift taxes, and miscellaneous fines and penalty taxes (as noted, Social Security taxes paid by the employee and employer are excluded from personal income). It thus represents the actual purchasing power available to consumers from current income. These taxes (which exclude sales and property taxes) are dominated by income taxes; for example, federal, state, and local income taxes in 1989 were 84 percent of all personal taxes collected by all three levels of government, while federal income

Figure 7a. **Business Cycle Movements of Real GNP, Personal Income, and Disposable Personal Income: Expansions**

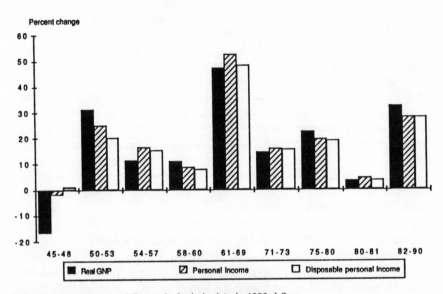

Note: Based on Bureau of Economic Analysis data in 1982 dollars.

taxes accounted for 69 percent of all personal taxes. All told, the personal taxes of $659 billion in 1989 were 15 percent of the $4.4 trillion personal income. Theoretically, disposable personal income is more stable than income before taxes because of the progressive income tax (a main attribute of federal income taxes). Under the progressive income tax, higher proportions of income are paid as taxes as income increases; conversely, as income declines, relatively lower proportions are paid in taxes. This progressivity should result in less income after taxes being available during expansions and more being available during recessions, thus tending to restrain income and spending growth during expansions so as to moderate economic growth and inflation, and to shore up income and spending during recessions so as to stimulate growth and employment.

The conceptual greater cyclical stability of disposable personal income compared with personal income is borne out in practice, although more clearly in expansions than in recessions. Figure 7a indicates that in seven of the nine postwar expansions, real disposable personal income increased relatively less than personal income. The two exceptions are the 1945–48 and the 1982–90 expansions. In 1945–48, the sharp drop in defense spending caused a decline in personal income, but the concomitant reduction in tax rates led to an increase in disposable income. In 1982–90, the similar increase in disposable income is attributable to the reduction in income tax rates, the slowdown in inflation, and

Figure 7b. **Business Cycle Movements of Real GNP, Personal Income, and Disposable Personal Income: Recessions**

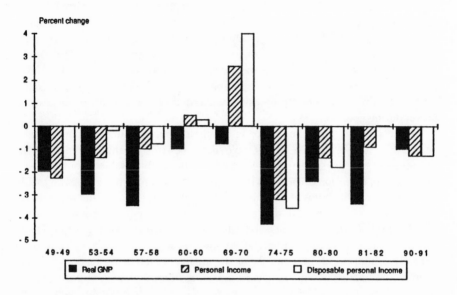

Note: Based on Bureau of Economic Analysis data in 1982 dollars. Recession of 1990–91 in progress in spring of 1991.

income tax inflation indexing discussed below.

During recessions, disposable income showed less extreme cyclical movements than personal income in five of the nine cases (Figure 7b). Disposable income declined less than personal income in three of the nine downturns; in one recession, disposable income increased more than personal income, and in another, disposable income was unchanged while personal income declined. In two cases when disposable income fell more than personal income, the recessions of 1974–75 and 1980, the greater fall in disposable income probably was due to the high inflation of those periods; by pushing individual incomes into higher tax brackets, inflation more than offset the falling incomes from higher unemployment. Disposable income increased less than personal income in the recession of 1960. Both income measures declined the same amount in the recession of 1990–91.

The Economic Recovery Tax Act of 1981 contained a provision to index individual income taxes for inflation. This provision first went into effect for 1985 incomes and is likely to affect further the cyclical behavior of after-tax income. The indexing provision limits the extent to which wage increases lift individuals into higher tax brackets. The higher tax bracket will only apply when, after deducting wage increases equivalent to the percentage increase in inflation according to the consumer price index, the remaining increase in income is sufficient to put the individual in the higher bracket. For recessions accompanied by high inflation, the indexing probably will prevent disposable income from declining more than personal income, such as occurred in the 1974–75 and 1980 downturns; this will increase the likelihood that disposable income will cushion the decline in consumer purchasing power in recessions, although this was not apparent in the recession of 1990–91 (as noted above). On the other hand, during expansions the indexing is likely to lessen the differential growth rates between personal and disposable income, thus decreasing the inflation-related stabilizing effect of progressive income taxes on consumer purchasing power during upturns.

To recapitulate, the major factor in stabilizing personal income during business cycles is the increase in unemployment benefits during recessions. The federal income tax system also gives some stability to disposable income, particularly during recessions. The indexing of income taxes for inflation starting with 1985 incomes probably will have different effects on this stabilizing property of income taxes, enhancing it during recessions and lessening it during expansions, thus modifying effects of the tax laws that existed before indexing began. Any subsequent major changes in federal tax laws, such as tax reform or actions to reduce the budget deficit, could have still different stabilizing or destabilizing features for macroeconomic policy. *In assessing future trends in disposable personal income, the analyst should allow for the effect of inflation indexing on after-tax income as well as any new tax legislation that could affect trends in disposable income over the business cycle. The assessment should also include the effect of changes in the generosity of the unemployment insurance system with respect to eligibility criteria and the amount and duration of benefit payments (see Chapter 5).*

Personal Saving

Personal saving is what is left of disposable income after all personal outlays.[8] Personal outlays consist mainly of consumer spending for goods and services (97.1 percent in 1989), but also include interest on loans paid by consumers to business (2.9 percent) and net personal payments by U.S. households to foreigners (less than 0.1 percent). Because personal outlays are financed by personal income plus other sources of consumer purchasing power available from installment credit, existing savings, and loans obtained on real estate and other financial assets, personal saving is affected by the use of credit, existing savings, and sale of existing assets as well as by current personal income. For items bought on credit, their total value is included as spending when the purchase is made; and in later periods, repayments of the principal of the loan are included as saving. In addition, while personal outlays exclude household purchases of homes and investments such as stocks, bonds, money market instruments, and real estate, personal saving includes the equity in these housing and investment transactions

Figure 8a. **Personal Saving Rate: 1948–90**

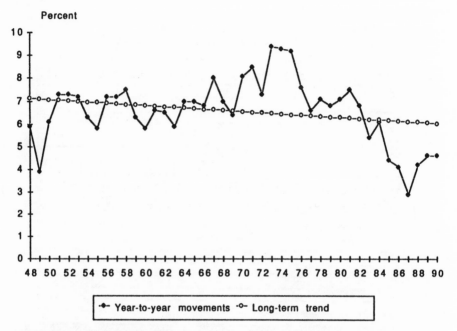

Note: Based on Bureau of Economic Analysis data. Personal saving as a percent of disposable personal income.

if they are financed from current income. However, these items are not included in saving to the extent that they are financed by selling homes or other assets to other households or by interpersonal gifts (e.g., from parents to children).

The saving rate measures actual saving as a percentage of disposable personal income.[9] Figure 8a shows a gradual decline in the long-run saving rate during 1948–90 from approximately 7 to 6 percent (downward-sloping diamond line). The main deviations from this trend occurred during the early 1970s when the rate was 8 to 9 percent and in the late 1980s when it was 3 to 4.5 percent. These variations in the saving rate result in substantially different spending rates for the same income level. For example, in 1989 the saving rate was 4.6 percent and real consumer expenditures (consumer spending in constant dollars) increased by 1.9 percent. Assuming the same levels of income and inflation, if the saving rate had been 7 percent, real consumer spending would have decreased by approximately 0.5 percent, thus resulting in negligible economic growth for the year.

Intuitively, a low saving rate is associated with high spending, and a high saving rate with low spending. Thus, low saving would be expected during expansions and high saving during recessions, except for very deep recessions in which a precipitous drop in income results in small saving or even dissaving (by

Figure 8b. Quarterly Personal Saving Rate: 1948–90

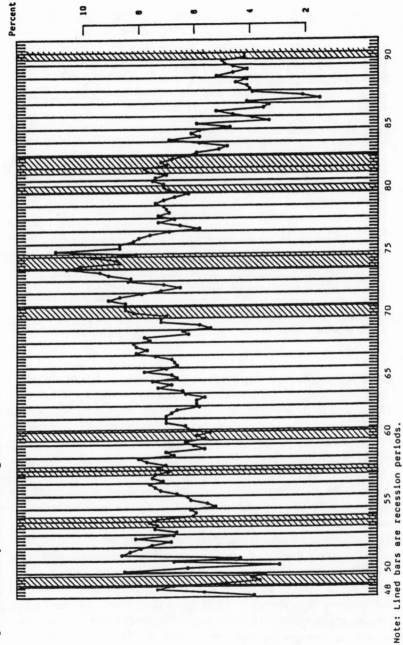

Note: Lined bars are recession periods.

requiring the use of existing assets to maintain minimum living needs).

In practice, the average saving rate differs slightly during expansions and recessions—6.5 percent in expansions and 7.5 percent in recessions (the average saving rate for all years during 1948–89 is 6.6 percent). But these long-term averages mask noticeable and unpredictable year-to-year changes during the same phase of economic expansion (Figure 8a). Because recessions since World War II have lasted no more than 1¼ years, there is no year-to-year experience of the behavior of saving rates during economic downturns. (The far more volatile quarter-to-quarter changes in saving rates defy explanation, as apparent from Figure 8b.) *In projecting saving rates to anticipate consumer spending, the analyst should develop saving rates that appear appropriate for that phase of the cycle. These projections require considerable judgment regarding consumer behavior, including the tendency to use consumer installment credit, because consumer behavior over the years has not displayed the repetitive patterns that are essential for developing quantitative relationships.*

Consumer Installment Credit

Because the debt burden from existing consumer credit may significantly affect consumer spending, this section focuses explicitly on consumer installment credit. Data on consumer installment credit provided by the Federal Reserve Board encompass loans to households by banks, credit companies, and retail stores in which there is the option to repay in two or more monthly payments. Consumer installment credit includes credit for purchases of automobiles, the range of goods and services that can be charged on credit cards, home improvements, mobile homes, and personal cash loans. It excludes home mortgages, but because of classification problems in the reporting from lending organizations, in practice the data include some consumer loans backed by housing equity as well as consumer loans used for business purposes. The extent of this inclusion is not known, but it is considered relatively small according to a 1990 Federal Reserve Board study.[10]

An overall measure of consumer debt burden is the ratio of consumer installment credit to personal income. As the ratio increases, consumers will retrench in spending because of an unwillingness to take on additional debt and/or because lenders, noting the higher debt burdens and associated increase in loan defaults, will become stricter in extending credit to consumers. It is difficult to infer from postwar experience, however, at what level the ratio begins to have a retrenching effect. Generally, consumers cut back spending because they are concerned about declining incomes due either to an ongoing recession and unemployment or fears of a possible future recession; thus, it is quite difficult to isolate the point at which debt burden, independent of the state of the economy, can be expected to discourage consumer purchases.

Figure 9 shows that consumer installment credit outstanding as a percentage

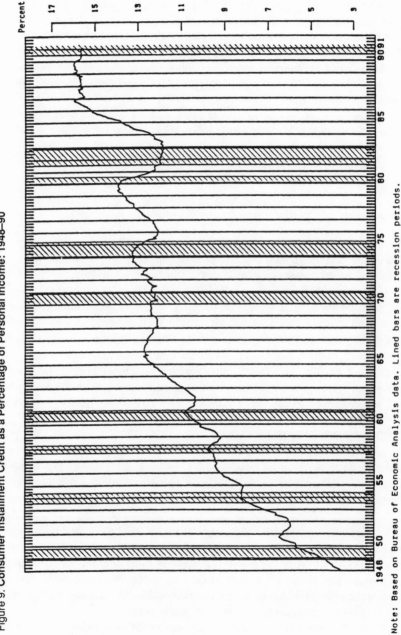

Figure 9. Consumer Installment Credit as a Percentage of Personal Income: 1948–90

Note: Based on Bureau of Economic Analysis data. Lined bars are recession periods.

of personal income rose substantially over the postwar period, from 4 percent in 1948 to a peak of 16 percent in 1986; it subsequently leveled off and in 1990 dipped below 16 percent.[11] Most of the rise occurred by the mid-1960s. The increase from 1948–65 resulted variously from the pent-up demands from World War II, growth of household formation, greater willingness of consumers and lenders to finance spending with credit, and a tendency to lengthen the period for repaying consumer loans.

Since the mid-1960s, there has been a slower and less consistent upward movement. For example, in the last half of the 1960s—associated with the substantial buildup of the Vietnam War, continuation of the expansion of the early 1960s, and the onset of more rapid inflation—the ratio declined; consumers may have felt it was desirable to build up their liquid assets of savings deposits and savings bonds (i.e., those assets that are readily transferable into money without the loss of capital value). The opposite behavior occurred in the expansion of the late 1970s when inflation was very high (the consumer price index rose 9 percent in 1978 and over 13 percent in 1979): consumers increased their debt burden to 14 percent in 1979 (the pre-1986 peak). This increase reflected the inflationary expectations of the time, as concern that prices would continue to rise rapidly caused consumers to increase their current purchases to avoid buying at much higher future prices. The data in this period even understated the credit expansion, as the sharp rise in housing prices led to the additional use of mortgage credit to finance consumer purchases, but as noted previously, mortgages are not included in the consumer credit data.[12]

Subsequently, the debt burden declined from 1980 to 1982, which included two recessions and one very limited expansion. In the subsequent expansion through the third quarter of 1990, the ratio rose to 16 percent in 1986 and then remained at that level through 1989 before declining below 16 percent during 1990.

The leveling off of the debt burden ratio in the late 1980s reflects two trends: a decline in automobile purchases and a shift in consumer borrowing patterns due to changes in the tax laws affecting consumer loans. The number of automobiles purchased fell from 11.4 million in 1986 to 9.9 million in 1989. Because automotive installment credit accounts for a significant share of all consumer credit (41 percent in December 1989), decreased automobile purchases have had a weighty impact on additions to consumer credit. In addition, the Tax Reform Act of 1986 began to phase out income tax deductions for interest on consumer loans over the 1987–90 period, with the deduction to be completely eliminated by 1991. In response, some consumers have shifted their financing of purchases from installment credit to automotive leasing and home equity loans. Since interest on car loans is no longer deductible, it is now often cheaper to lease a car than to buy it with an auto loan; alternatively, since interest payments on home equity loans remain deductible as part of the mortgage, such loans have become an increasingly attractive way to finance purchases. Existing home equity loans by all banks added 7 percent to outstanding consumer credit in December 1989, 1 percentage point higher than in December 1988. (Data on home equity loans were first collected in 1987 for large banks only.) However, consumer credit data includes neither automotive leasing nor home equity loans. Thus, the leveling off of consumer debt burden as measured by installment credit as a percentage of personal income is in part a statistical illusion.

The ratio of consumer credit to personal income is classified as one of the major lagging indicators, turning down after a general recession sets in and up after a general recovery begins (see Chapter 8). Yet a review of the postwar trends makes it difficult to establish if there is some point where the debt burden becomes excessive. The problem is partly the nature of the consumer credit data, which are limited to the total amount of credit without distinguishing for persons in different income categories where differential debt burdens could be significant. In addition, there are no data on scheduled monthly principal and interest payments, which would be a more meaningful measure in terms of income. It is also complicated by the fact that some decisions to buy are made independently of debt burden and thus affect debt rather than debt affecting purchases.

From the lender's viewpoint, of course, a main factor in determining whether to make a consumer loan is the creditworthiness of the borrower. Information on the overall risk of nonpayment of existing consumer loans is available in the American Bankers Association's data on consumer loan delinquency rates. The delinquency rate is a good predictor of likely changes in the financial standards that banks apply in determining whether to lend money to households, with rising delinquency rates making it more difficult to obtain a loan and falling rates making it easier. The delinquency rate is a leading indicator in that it turns up before a general recession begins and turns down before the subsequent recovery. However, it is quite volatile, and thus it is often difficult to establish the directional trend of a current period.

The consumer debt burden can affect consumer spending, although determining when debt is excessive, and is thus likely to lead to a slowdown or retrenchment of borrowing and spending, is very difficult. *In making these assessments, the analyst should monitor trends in the consumer sentiment and confidence indexes noted previously under Macroeconomic Environment. The delinquency rate in the repayment of existing consumer loans should also be considered.*

Private Investment

Of all GNP components, private investment expenditures for business plant and equipment, residential construction, and inventory change have the most extreme cyclical movements. Private investment increases more rapidly in expansions and decreases more rapidly in recessions than other GNP components. This volatility is the main cause of cyclical fluctuations in overall economic activity.

This section focuses on plant and equipment investment and residential con-

Figure 10a. **Business Cycle Movements of Real GNP and Private Nonresidential Fixed Investment: Expansions**

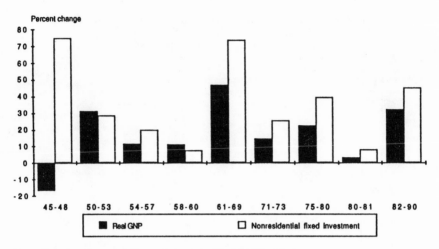

Note: Based on Bureau of Economic Analysis data in 1982 dollars.

struction; inventory change was discussed in the comparisons of real GNP and final sales movements.

Plant and Equipment

Business investment in plant and equipment provides the industrial capacity to produce goods and services for household, business, government, and export markets. It covers all construction (building and nonbuilding), machinery, and other capital equipment used to expand, replace, and modernize capital facilities, as well as first-time investments in new businesses. It encompasses capital spending in all private profit and nonprofit organizations, nonfarm and farm. Plant investment includes factory, office, retail, and warehouse buildings, electric-power and telephone-transmission structures, and oil- and gas-well drilling; machine tools, trucks, computers, and office furniture are examples of equipment. Investment expenditures depreciate over the life span of each item and thus become an annual cost of production, which appears as depreciation allowances in business income tax returns. Plant and equipment investment is referred to as "nonresidential fixed investment" in the GNP, with separate categories for plant (structures) and equipment.

The share of plant and equipment investment in the GNP during 1950–89 rose gradually from an average of 9.6 percent in the 1950s to 10.7 percent in the

Figure 10b. **Business Cycle Movements of Real GNP and Private Nonresidential Fixed Investment: Recessions**

Percent change

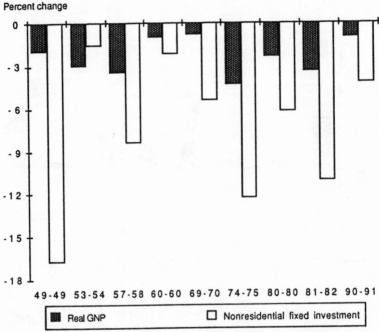

Note: Based on Bureau of Economic Analysis data in 1982 dollars. Recession of 1990-91 in progress in spring of 1991.

1980s, although the average dropped to 10.0 percent during 1986–89.

Figures 10a and 10b show the postwar cyclical movements of real GNP and plant and equipment investment. These indicate that plant and equipment spending increased more rapidly than the GNP in seven of the nine expansions, and declined more rapidly than the GNP in eight of the nine recessions. The differential movements between plant and equipment and GNP were substantial. In expansions, plant and equipment outlays typically increased 60 to 75 percent faster than GNP, exceptions being the 1980–81 expansion, when the differential was 135 percent, and the 1982–90 expansion when it was 40 percent. In recessions, plant and equipment investment most commonly fell by two to three times the rate of decline in the GNP, the notable exceptions being the still greater decline of plant and equipment investment in the 1949, 1969–70, and 1990–91 recessions. Clearly, while the long-term average trend of plant and equipment investment relative to GNP has been rising, plant and equipment has shown considerable cyclical fluctuation.

The sharp cyclical patterns arise because such investment is deferrable and it

Figure 11. **Plant and Equipment Investment as a Percentage of GNP: 1950s–1980s**

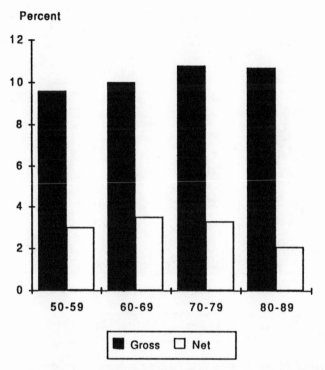

Percent

Note: Based on Bureau of Economic Analysis data in current dollars.

is difficult to anticipate demand for goods and services produced with these capital facilities. Investment is deferrable because businesses often can "make do" with existing facilities, although doing so may result in profits below their potential: the facilities are less efficient than more modern technology would allow and are unable to meet sudden surges in demand. The difficulty of anticipating demand results in waves of optimism and pessimism, which in turn lead to substantial additions of capital facilities during expansions, only to be followed by overcapacity in recessions and accompanying deep cutbacks in investment outlays. The Dun & Bradstreet Corporation publishes quarterly measures of business optimism based on surveys of executives' expectations for sales and profits. Plant and equipment investment is also affected by the usage of existing capital facilities (see capacity utilization rates in Chapter 4).

In addition to these cyclical movements, plant and equipment investment strongly affects long-term productivity improvements. (Productivity is discussed in Chapter 5.)

Figure 12. **Plant Investment as a Percentage of GNP: 1950s–1980s**

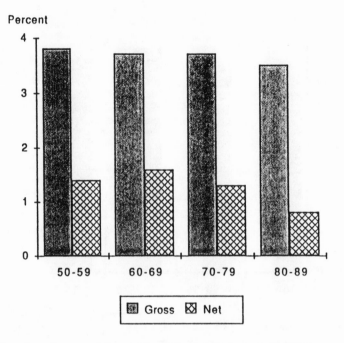

Note: Based on Bureau of Economic Analysis data in current dollars.

Gross vs. Net Investment

Gross investment refers to investment in new facilities for producing goods and services, while net investment represents the increment that the new facilities add to the stock of existing plant and equipment after depreciation on the existing plant and equipment has been deducted. Figure 11 shows that during the 1980s, net investment as a percentage of the GNP markedly declined compared to gross investment. While the gross investment proportion was practically identical from the 1970s to the 1980s (10.8 to 10.7 percent), the net investment proportion fell from 3.3 in the 1970s to 2.1 percent in the 1980s. Net investment during the 1980s declined in both the plant and the equipment components (Figures 12 and 13). The sharpest decline occurred in net equipment, reversing the upward trend of the 1960s and 1970s. Net plant continued and accelerated the drop that began in the 1970s.

In part, the net-investment decline during the 1980s reflects the shift to service industries, which use more labor and fewer capital facilities than manufac-

Figure 13. **Equipment Investment as a Percentage of GNP: 1950s–1980s**

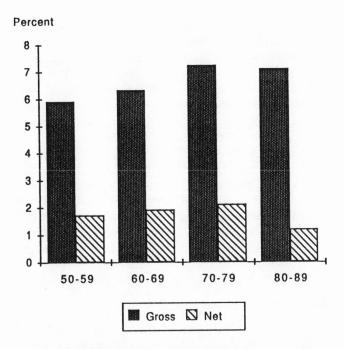

Percent

Note: Based on Bureau of Economic Analysis data in current dollars.

turing. But the nature of plant and equipment investment also seemed to change in the 1980s. Although gross investment declined slightly from the 1970s, it was still higher than in the 1950s and 1960s. The distinction in the gross and net investment trends suggests that businesses are using a shorter time horizon when planning their investment commitments. They are continuing to build new plants but at a slower rate. Plants represent the ultimate in long-term commitment because of their high costs and long durability. Some of the plant decline probably reflects long-term technological developments that allow more use to be made of existing space. But the acceleration of this decline during the 1980s indicates that plant investment was dissuaded by something other than this. The sharp decline in net-equipment purchases during the 1980s is similarly striking, since equipment investment had actually risen continuously in the previous decades. While part of the net-equipment decline probably reflects many businesses' computer purchases which are sometimes replaced in a few years with more powerful models, the magnitude of the equipment decline also suggests businesses are purchasing less equipment with a longer payoff period.

Statistically, estimating depreciation charges is an imperfect procedure, and small changes associated with differential movements probably fall within the margin of error of the data. But the magnitude of the decline in net investment relative to the GNP suggests that the decline is not simply due to statistical error.[13]

The net-investment decline indicates U.S. industry's loss of competitiveness in world markets. During the nineteenth century, the situation was similar. Foreign investment was negative, with imports exceeding exports, and foreigners acquired more U.S. assets than Americans acquired abroad. However, as Benjamin Friedman notes, money obtained from the sale of stocks and bonds to foreigners during the nineteenth century was used for financing plant and equipment investments in U.S. enterprise, which was important in building canals, railroads, steel factories, and the broad industrial base of the nation.[14] In contrast, foreign money coming into the United States during the 1980s was used primarily to acquire existing real or financial assets such as government securities, corporate stock, and real estate. Moreover, the money obtained from the sale of these assets did not result in a burst of new plant and equipment investment by the U.S. recipients. While some foreign companies, notably in the automotive industry, have invested in plant and equipment for production in the United States, this is a drop in the bucket compared to the total investment decline by U.S.-owned and foreign-owned companies. (The plant and equipment data include investments in the United States by both domestic and foreign companies.)

Profits and Investment in Plant and Equipment

Because the basic purpose of business is to make a profit, current and anticipated profits largely determine the pace of plant and equipment investment. Anticipated profits are the incentive to invest in capital facilities, while past and current profits are an important source of funds for the investment.

Profits are sales less costs. They reflect both the demand for a company's products and its ability to meet the demand at efficient costs. If profits are rising, business tends to be optimistic that markets for its products will grow; it is thus encouraged to invest in new facilities to meet those markets. In contrast, during periods of declining profits and shrinking markets there is little urgency to expand productive capacity, and more of the new investment is limited to replacing and modernizing existing facilities in order to lower production costs.

Profits provide financing for plant and equipment investment in two ways. First, as internally generated funds from company operations, profits provide money to buy the capital facilities. Second, a business's profits are a key factor for lenders' and investors' decisions to provide external funds through bank loans, debt instruments (e.g., bonds), and equity capital (e.g., stock).

Like spending for plant and equipment, business profits show more extreme cyclical movements than the overall economy. The similar although not identical cyclical patterns of investment and profits are consistent with their strong theoretical relationship.

Business profits as reported in the national accounts represent the combined

Figure 14a. **Business Cycle Movements of National Income and Business Profits: Expansions**

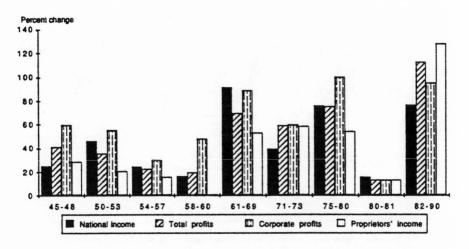

Note: Based on Bureau of Economic Analysis data in current dollars.

income of corporations and unincorporated business (proprietors' income) before the payment of income taxes and including the valuation adjustments for inventories and capital consumption. Figures 14a and 14b show the patterns of business profits and national income (employee compensation, rental income, proprietors' income, corporate profits, and net interest) over the postwar business cycles in current dollars (see note 27 for use of national income rather than the GNP). Business profits increased more rapidly than national income in only four of the nine expansions. Profits decreased more rapidly than national income in all nine of the postwar downturns (national income increased in four recessions and profits decreased in all nine recessions). The differential movements between profits and national income were much larger in recessions than in expansions— profits fell several multiples more rapidly than national income in recessions, while profits increased less than one multiple more than national income.

These differential patterns are associated with the long-term decline in profits as a proportion of national income, from 31 percent in 1950 to 16 percent in 1989; in the 1980s, this share fluctuated in a range of 13 to 17 percent. In relation to other components of the national income, most of the decline in profits is related to increasing shares of employee compensation (primarily from the rapidly growing fringe benefits, as distinct from money wages) through the 1960s, and of interest in the 1970s and 1980s. The long-term relative decline in profits is difficult to explain, other than to state that business as a whole did not pass along costs into

Figure 14b. **Business Cycle Movements of National Income and Business Profits: Recessions**

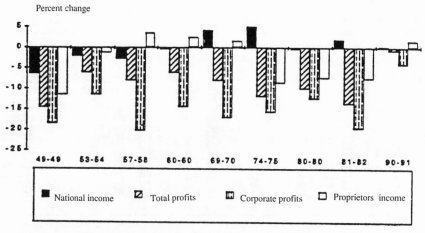

Note: Based on Bureau of Economic Analysis data in current dollars. Recession of 1990-91 in progress in spring of 1991.

higher prices sufficiently to maintain profit margins, apparently because demand for its goods and services was not considered strong enough to sustain the higher prices. Other explanations, such as that profits in the earlier years were too high or that business feared government antitrust actions or price controls if prices were increased to maintain the earlier profit margins, are difficult to substantiate.

However, as discussed in the following section on depreciation, the long-term relative decline in profits is not apparent when depreciation allowances on existing plant and equipment investment are added to profits. Because internally generated funds are the sum of profits and depreciation allowances, it is more useful to consider the effects of both in assessing long-run incentives for plant and equipment investment.

Impact of Taxes and Depreciation on Investment

Funding for plant and equipment investment is available from profits and depreciation allowances generated by company sales and investments (internal sources), and from outside lenders and investors (external sources). Because internally generated funds are the basis of a company's economic well-being, as well as the underlying incentive for lenders and investors to provide external funds, this discussion concentrates on internal funding.

Profits after the payment of business income taxes plus tax deductible depreciation allowances on existing plant and equipment make up the funds available from internal sources for distribution to company owners and for further spending on plant and equipment investment, inventories, and other operational needs. This internal funding is called cash flow; a refined version referring to corporations is "net cash flow," which is undistributed profits (profits after the payment of income taxes and distributions of dividends to owners) plus depreciation allowances, including inventory valuation and capital consumption adjustments (an alternative version of net cash flow excludes the inventory valuation adjustment).

Depreciation allowances for the wear and tear and obsolescence of plant and equipment are deducted as a cost in figuring how much is due in business income taxes.[15] Depreciation rises steadily over the years, even in recessions, because it reflects the *cumulative* investments of previous periods—a gradually increasing total, regardless of whether all facilities are used in a particular period. Since depreciation also accounts for the preponderant share of cash flow (87 percent of corporate cash flow in 1989), the cyclical movements of cash flow are less extreme than those for profits. For example, during the 1981–82 recession, undistributed corporate profits declined by 46 percent while net cash flow *increased* by 1 percent; and in the expansion during the 1982–90, undistributed profits increased by 14 percent compared with a cash flow increase of 50 percent. Thus, in addition to providing funds for the long-term replacement of older capital facilities, depreciation allowances are a particularly important source of financing for plant and equipment investment in recessions.

Since World War II, corporate net cash flow as a share of the GNP has fluctuated in a narrow range of 7 to 9 percent. This stability resulted from offsetting effects of the rising importance of depreciation allowances and the declining share of profits. The relative increase in depreciation is due to the increasingly faster write-offs of capital facilities allowed over the postwar period (until the slower write-offs adopted in the Tax Reform Act of 1986), and to the tendency for an increasing share of investment to be in shorter-lived equipment, which has faster write-offs than structures.

As noted in Part A of this chapter under Valuation Adjustments for Inventories and Depreciation, an adjustment is made both for the difference between depreciation costs allowed to be deducted from income for tax payment and the depreciation estimated as the economic life of the asset (which is longer than the tax life), and for the effect that changing prices of capital goods have on the cost of replacing plant and equipment. This capital consumption adjustment (CCAdj) has changed considerably in recent years, mainly as a result of the more rapid depreciation allowed in the Economic Recovery Tax Act of 1981, and to a very limited extent as a result of the slowdown in inflation. For example, the corporate capital consumption adjustment went from –$17 billion in 1980 to $60 billion in 1985, a shift of $77 billion over five years. Based on an income tax rate of 46 percent on corporate profits, corporations had $35 billion more available in purchasing power after the payment of income taxes in 1985, basically because of the faster depreciation.

By contrast, because of the slower depreciation write-offs in the Tax Reform

Act of 1986, the corporate CCAdj declined from $60 billion in 1985 to $26 billion in 1989, for a reduction of $34 billion. The smaller CCAdj resulting from the 1986 Tax Act means that the slower depreciation write-offs used in calculating income tax liabilities are closer to actual lifetime use of capital facilities by industry. However, the tax laws are still not neutral in terms of investment incentives. The positive CCAdj in 1989 indicates a faster write-off for taxes than industry practice and thus a positive tax stimulus to investment. (A CCAdj of zero would reflect a neutral tax depreciation schedule.) Based on the lower corporate tax rate of 34 percent adopted in the 1986 Tax Act, corporations paid $12 billion more in taxes in 1989 because of the slower write-offs (at the previous tax rate of 46 percent, corporations would have paid $16 billion more in taxes). Thus, the CCAdj is important in assessing the impact of tax laws and inflation on the financing capacity of business cash flow.

How has the business income tax cut resulting from faster depreciation write-offs of plant and equipment in the Economic Recovery Tax Act of 1981, as modified by the partial business tax increases in the Tax Equity and Fiscal Responsibility Act of 1982, affected plant and equipment investment? Studies have given conflicting results. Leonard Sahling and M. Akhtar concluded in an econometric macro analysis that about 20 percent of the rise in spending for producers' durable equipment from 1982 (fourth quarter) to 1984 (third quarter) resulted from the tax legislation of the early 1980s; the study also found that lower interest rates accounted for about 15 percent of the 1982–84 investment increase, and that the remaining 55 percent was attributable to economic growth and all other factors.[16]

However, a micro analysis of the investment behavior from 1981 to 1983 of 238 nonfinancial corporations from a sample of the *Fortune* 500 and from other identifying information on large companies by Robert McIntyre and Dean Tipps found that there was no relationship between tax rates and investment in plant and equipment.[17] In that study, the fifty lowest-taxed companies reduced their capital investment by 22 percent, while the fifty highest-taxed companies increased their investment by 33 percent from 1981 to 1983. The study also indicated that lower-taxed companies increased dividends more than higher-taxed companies, an indication that tax reductions were used more for investor income than for plowing back into plant and equipment investment.

Barry Bosworth's study of the effect of the business tax cuts on the components of plant and equipment investment concluded there was no relation between the size of the tax cuts and investment in particular items.[18] Thus, while 93 percent of the increase in equipment investment from 1979 to 1984 was in office equipment and business automobiles, the 1981 tax laws increased the tax rate on computers (office equipment), and decreased only slightly the taxes on automobiles. In the case of plant, moreover, while commercial buildings (offices, stores, warehouses) were given the same tax cuts as industrial buildings (factories), spending from 1979 to 1984 increased for commercial buildings and decreased for industrial buildings. The study indicated that in assessing the effect of costs on investment, the tax cuts were outweighed by several factors: the relative decline in capital goods prices compared with other prices, returns on alternative investments (opportunity costs), and differences in the resale value of particular assets (for example, the greater resale value of commercial buildings than industrial buildings).

On balance, although their conclusions on the importance of tax cuts vary significantly, these studies of tax incentives in the first half of the 1980s indicate that taxes are secondary in driving plant and equipment investment. Generally, the macro assessment suggested that the tax cuts had a greater effect on investment than the micro and detailed component analyses found.

In assessing business profits for their relation to plant and equipment investment, the analyst should consider any substantial shifts in business income tax laws for their effect on plant and equipment investment. While taxes do not appear to have a major affect on capital investment, they may influence particular types of investment in certain periods.

Future Indicators of Investment Spending

In contrast to the effects of the underlying factors—economic growth, profits, and cash flows—on plant and equipment spending, other economic indicators focus on actions taken by business early in the investment process. This section notes the main characteristics of these indicators and gives guidelines for monitoring their movements for clues to future investment trends. They are discussed in the sequence they have in the investment process: capital appropriations for investment spending, nonresidential construction contracts and capital goods orders, and projections of plant and equipment spending.

CAPITAL APPROPRIATIONS FOR MANUFACTURING INVESTMENT: In large companies, intentions to invest in plant and equipment become more specific when capital budget funds are appropriated. Capital appropriations are the *earliest* indicator of business sentiment for future capital spending.

The Conference Board provides the only regularly reported information on companies' capital appropriations. It obtains quarterly survey data from the nation's one thousand largest manufacturing corporations, which had approximately 75 percent of all manufacturing corporations' assets in 1985. In recent years, investment by all manufacturing companies accounted for close to 40 percent of plant and equipment spending in all nonfarm industries. Thus, capital appropriations by the companies surveyed represent about 30 percent of all private nonfarm capital investment spending. The capital appropriations data are available about two months after the quarter in which the decision to appropriate the funds was made.

Capital appropriations pay for all or part of an investment project, but they do not indicate when the spending will occur. They are not necessarily commitments for actual spending, as they can be deferred or canceled depending on business conditions and perceptions of the future; in addition, the spending patterns vary among individual projects depending on the lead times required for their completion. As a result, trends in appropriations reveal manufacturers' confidence in the growth prospects for their products, but they do not estimate planned spending over time.

There are two main series on appropriations, one on the backlog of cumulated appropriations from previous periods that have not yet been spent or canceled, and the other on newly approved appropriations in the current quarter. The backlog is the basic source of future spending. The new appropriations indicate the effect that the most recent patterns of business confidence (in terms of initiating new investment projects) have on increasing or lowering the backlog.

Capital appropriations data are a guide to business perceptions of growth prospects in an important segment of the economy, but they cover only about 30 percent of all nonagricultural investment in plant and equipment. *The analyst should use the capital appropriations information as a qualitative indicator of manufacturers' intentions to invest in plant and equipment. Because some investment projects included in the appropriations data are postponed or canceled, and others have long lead times, appropriations are best used as only one factor in assessing future trends in capital investment spending.*

CONTRACTS AND ORDERS FOR PLANT AND EQUIPMENT: The second stage in the investment process is the decision to start the acquisition of capital facilities. This results in the commitment of funds to begin work on the investment project, which in turn will result in spending (payments) for the work done. The commitment of funds in construction contracts and equipment orders is a firmer action than the appropriation of capital funds, as a construction contract or equipment order is subject to less chance of postponement or cancellation. Monthly data on the commitment of funds for plant are derived from contract award information on nonresidential construction of the McGraw-Hill Information Systems Company; monthly data on new equipment orders received by nondefense capital goods manufacturers are based on surveys by the Bureau of the Census in the U.S. Department of Commerce. The two series are shown separately and also are combined into one, in current and constant dollars, in the *Survey of Current Business.*

A few basic differences between the data on construction contracts and equipment orders on the one hand, and plant and equipment spending on the other, should be kept in mind. First, the contract and order data (as in the case of capital appropriations) are for part or all of an investment project, but they do not specify when the spending for the project will occur. This is particularly pertinent for large-scale projects with lead times of more than one year. Second, the order data do not give precise coverage of equipment purchases by American business because the orders exclude U.S. imports of machinery and other capital goods that are part of investment spending, while they include U.S. exports that are not part of investment spending in the United States. Third, while the combined contract and order data in constant dollars constitute one of the major leading indicators of overall economic activity (see Chapter 8), the indicator is subject to sharp monthly movements and must be observed for about six-month periods to tell whether its direction is increasing, decreasing, or holding steady.

The data on construction contracts and equipment orders denote a key point in the investment process when financial commitments are made to proceed with plant and equipment projects. The data are a relatively reliable indicator of the willingness of business to proceed with capital investment projects. *Nonetheless, in using the data to anticipate the trend of plant and equipment spending, the analyst should treat them as broad orders of magnitude because they are limited by the absence of a time span over which the contracts and orders are spent, inconsistencies between plant and equipment spending for exports and imports, and by month-to-month gyrations.*

PROJECTIONS OF PLANT AND EQUIPMENT EXPENDITURES: Business spending for plant and equipment in the GNP, referred to as nonresidential fixed investment, is based on data from the Census Bureau's monthly surveys of the value of construction and manufacturers' shipments of equipment. It is analogous to, but not completely consistent with, investment data obtained from a quarterly survey by the Census Bureau of businesses' actual and planned expenditures on plant and equipment. Because the expenditure survey provides quarterly and one-year projections of plant and equipment outlays as well as actual spending in past periods, its data are particularly useful for anticipating investment trends. In studies over the past decade, the investment projections in this survey were more accurate than those in similar surveys conducted in the private sector or in projections developed from large-scale econometric models.[19]

Differences between the GNP investment and the survey estimates for plant and equipment reflect variations in the industries covered and timing of the measures.[20] For example, farm investment and outlays for drilling oil and gas wells are both included in the GNP and excluded from the survey data; additionally, the GNP measures investment as occurring when the construction work is done and when the manufacturer ships the equipment, while the survey measures investment as occurring when the payments are made for these purchases, which tends to be after the work is done.

Even when the two investment series are adjusted to make them comparable, their movements over time are not always consistent. For example, after the series were made conceptually comparable, GNP investment in 1982 increased by 4.6 percent and the survey investment increased by 5.6 percent; in 1983, GNP investment increased by 3.4 percent while the survey investment *decreased* by 6.7 percent. Thus, the relationship of the series changed significantly between the two years. This pattern of year-to-year variability also occurred in previous years.

Using business investment plans, the plant and equipment survey projects investment at various times during the year for one and two quarters ahead and for one year ahead. Based on several years' experience in which the projections were systemically higher or lower than the actual figures, the survey data are adjusted to correct for systematic biases. Over 1955–83, the average difference between actual and projected spending, without regard to whether the projection was lower or higher than the actual, ranged from 2 to 3 percent.[21] As expected, the projections are less accurate the further out they extend in time:

Average Difference between Actual and Projected Plant and Equipment Investment

One quarter ahead:	1.8%
Two quarters ahead:	2.6%
One year ahead:	3.0%

The long-term averages are suggestive of the accuracy in particular years, although occasionally the differential was substantially higher. For example, in the yearly projections, differences greater than 5 percent occurred only in 1958 and 1982.

The survey of plant and equipment expenditures is useful for projecting expected business investment outlays in the GNP, if it is tempered by other information on future investment, such as profits, capital appropriations, and nonresidential construction contracts and nondefense equipment orders.

Residential Construction

The residential construction component of private investment covers the value of new construction of privately owned single-family and multifamily housing units, mobile homes, dormitories and other group quarters, as well as additions, alterations, and major replacements to them. Construction of new housing dominates the category of private residential fixed investment in the GNP (65 percent in 1989), which also includes real estate commissions on the sale of new and existing housing, furniture and other consumer durables provided in furnished apartments, and the net purchase of existing residential structures between the private and public sectors. After reviewing overall trends based on residential fixed investment, this section will focus on the construction of new housing units—single-family homes (including townhouses), apartments, and mobile homes.

Residential fixed investment has not grown as fast as the rest of the economy over the long run. For example, from 1950 to 1989, real GNP increased by 242 percent while residential investment increased 116 percent. Thus, residential investment as a proportion of the GNP declined from 5 to 6 percent in the 1950s to 4 to 5 percent in the 1980s. This long-term relative decline reflects the slowdown in population growth, from increases of over 28 million in the 1950s, to 23 million in the 1970s, to 21 million in the 1980s.

Figure 15a. **Business Cycle Movements of Real GNP and Residential Fixed Investment: Expansions**

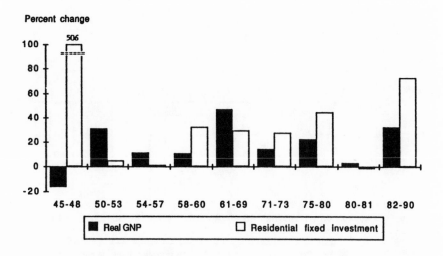

Note: Based on Bureau of Economic Analysis data in 1982 dollars.

Although the residential investment share of the GNP is small compared with other components, it has secondary and cyclical impacts that are not apparent from size alone. The secondary impacts result from the tendency for the purchase of a new home to generate additional spending on household appliances, furniture, and other consumer durables. The cyclical impact has two aspects. In terms of timing, the number of housing starts, building permits issued by local governments for housing, and the value of residential fixed investment in constant dollars are all classified as leading indicators of the overall economy—turning up in a recession before the expansion begins and turning down in an expansion before a recession begins. However, in terms of the size of the increases and decreases in spending for residential fixed investment over the business cycle, there is no clear evidence that residential construction stabilizes or destabilizes the overall economy. Figures 15a and 15b show that residential investment increased faster than real GNP in five of the nine postwar expansions, and decreased more than real GNP in five of the nine postwar recessions.

Factors Affecting New Housing Demand

The market for new housing construction is driven by *long-term* national and geographic demographic trends and—to a much smaller extent—by the replacement of substandard housing and housing destroyed by fire and flood. It is also

Figure 15b. **Business Cycle Movements of Real GNP and Residential Fixed Investment: Recessions**

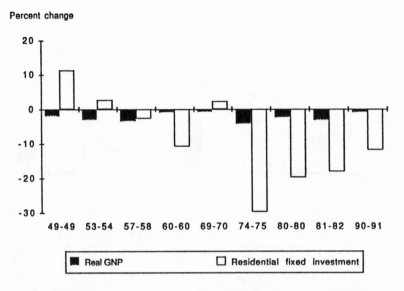

Note: Based on Bureau of Economic Analysis data in 1982 dollars. Recession of 1990–91 in progress in spring of 1991.

driven by *short-term* cyclical movements of economic growth, inflation, and interest rates. These influences on the value of new construction, along with the effect of shifts in the average size and cost of housing units, are discussed below. Figure 16a shows that housing starts were more volatile during the 1970s and 1980s than during the previous two decades. Figure 16b indicates that privately owned housing accounts for practically all new housing units, and that the building of new publicly owned housing was virtually eliminated during the 1980s (only 2,200 public housing units were built in 1987, and after that year the Census Bureau no longer published data for them).

LONG-TERM FACTORS: The typical annual construction of new housing units (the number of single-family homes, townhouses, and dwelling units in apartment buildings) has averaged about 1.5 million over the postwar period. It has generally ranged from 1.1 to 2 million (the peak was 2.4 million in 1972). As noted below, new housing construction declined in the 1980s and is expected to be lower still in the 1990s.

Future demographic trends are mainly determined by the age distribution of the existing population, birth rates, and migration from foreign countries. These in turn are affected by attitudes toward marriage and family size and by political conditions abroad.

Figure 16a. **Private Housing Starts: 1950–90**

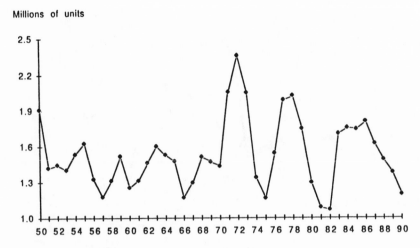

Note: Nonfarm and farm since 1959; nonfarm before 1959.

The demand for new housing is mainly related to trends in the number of new households (a household includes a family, a single person living alone, or unrelated individuals sharing a house or apartment). Subsidiary factors affecting demand are the replacement of housing lost to demolition, fire, or flood, and the purchase of vacation and other second homes. Harvard University's Joint Center for Housing Studies projects an increase of 1.15 million households annually in the 1990s.[22] This projection reflects a continuing trend of lower annual increases from 1.7 million in the 1970s to 1.3 million in the 1980s. Based on these projections, new housing construction and purchases of mobile homes will decline in the 1990s. For example, the Joint Center has forecast average annual construction of 1.3 million new housing units in the 1990s—down from 1.8 million in the 1970s and 1.5 million in the 1980s—and annual purchases of 200,000 mobile homes in the 1990s, down from 250,000 in the 1980s.[23] These projections seem reasonable unless there are major, unanticipated geographic shifts of the population within the United States, or significant changes in the formation of new households that affect housing construction independent of national population increases.

Another long-term factor affecting housing demand is the replacement or rehabilitation of housing that has major structural, heating, plumbing, or other physical defects. Of the 91 million housing units occupied in 1987, 1.2 million had "severe" physical problems with plumbing, heating, electricity, upkeep, or hallways, and 5.2 million had "moderate" physical problems, according to the American Housing Survey conducted by the Bureau of the Census for the U.S.

Figure 16b. **Total Housing Starts: 1959–90**

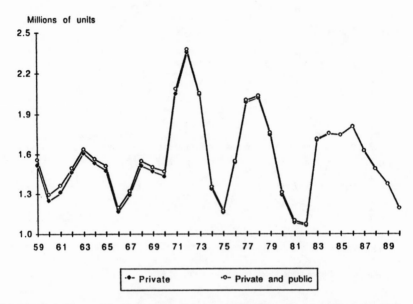

Note: Based on Bureau of the Census data. Data for public housing units not published after 1987.

Department of Housing and Urban Development. But projecting the number of these units that will be replaced or rehabilitated is problematic. The construction of new publicly owned housing has dwindled from an annual average of about 30,000 housing units in the 1960s to 15,000 units in the 1970s to a mere 2,000 units in 1986 and 1987, and data collection on the construction of public housing units had virtually ceased by the end of the 1980s because the construction was minuscule. The low-income tax credit for new and remodeled housing has in a minor way substituted for new public housing, but it only scratches the surface in providing adequate housing for low-income people. While a gradual upgrading of the housing stock occurs as households in various income groups move to better housing when they can afford it, such effects are difficult to quantify. Over the long run this trickling down may improve housing quality for low-income groups, but in practice this is a very slow process for which there are no adequate indicators.

SHORT-TERM FACTORS: While housing demand from year to year reflects the long-term underlying demand noted above, it also fluctuates in the short term. These movements reflect the effects of business cycle expansions and recessions on employment, inflation, and interest rates. In expansions, as employment and incomes rise, more households have sufficient income to qualify for mortgage loans to buy housing or to rent costlier new apartments, both of which stimulate new construc-

Figure 17. **Mortgage Interest Rates vs. Private Housing Starts: 1967–90**

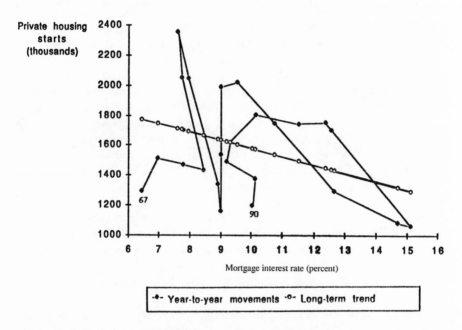

Note: **Based on Federal Housing Finance Board and Bureau of the Census data.**

tion. This increase in purchasing power is partially offset during expansions by higher inflation and mortgage interest rates and the resultant higher cost of housing, but the net effect is increased housing demand and construction. The opposite occurs in recessions when falling employment lessens the demand for housing, although this decline during recessions is similarly tempered by reduced inflation and interest rates as well as the accompanying slower rise or decline in housing costs.

Figure 17 shows the relationship between mortgage interest rates and private housing starts over the 1967–90 period. The interest rate data reflect the annual average rate charged on mortgages for new single-family homes (interest rates for new multifamily housing have similar movements). Private housing starts refer to the beginning of construction of privately owned new single-family homes, townhouses, and multifamily apartment buildings including condominiums and cooperatives, with each single-family home and each separate apartment within apartment buildings counted as one housing start.

For each year, the point at which the mortgage interest rate on the horizontal scale intersects housing starts on the vertical scale is plotted as a black diamond. The long-term average is represented by the line of white diamonds that slants downward to the right, indicating that interest rates and housing starts typically move in opposite directions (i.e., they have an inverse relationship). Such inverse relationships are to be expected, since higher interest rates make housing more expensive and thus depress housing purchases. The wide dispersion of individual years above and below the average line makes clear, however, that the relationship between interest rates and housing starts is unpredictable on a short-term year-to-year basis. The correlation coefficient for the two variables, interest rates and housing starts, is only −.37. (A correlation coefficient measures the similarity of the movements of two statistical variables; a perfectly direct relationship is represented by a correlation coefficient of 1, and a perfectly inverse relationship is represented by a coefficient of −1.) If the correlation in this figure were perfect, all points for all years would fall on the long-term average line.[24]

The disparity from the average is even greater when the line connecting two points slopes upward to the right, as it did from 1984 to 1988 (see Figure 17). Such a line indicates that both variables moved in the same direction during this period, so that interest rate increases were associated with increased housing starts, and vice versa for decreases. Thus, although historically interest rates have an important effect on the cyclical movements of housing starts, the relationship did not hold for most of the 1980s. Indeed, during 1983–90, the correlation coefficient was a positive .5, contradicting both the expected negative relationship and the prior statistical experience.

George Kahn and Randall Pozdena attribute the lessened influence of interest rates in the 1980s to three recent structural changes and innovations in financial markets: (1) banks were allowed to set their own interest rates on deposits as a result of the Depository Institutions Deregulation and Monetary Control Act of 1980; (2) secondary mortgage markets continued to develop; and (3) adjustable rate mortgages were introduced. John Ryding argues that the first factor, the lifting of the interest rate ceiling, is most responsible for the breakdown in the traditional relationship between interest rates and housing starts.[25] At any rate, the sum effect of these financial changes is that banks no longer discriminate against investing in housing mortgages during periods of credit restraint, which accounts for the lessened influence of interest rates on housing starts.

The experience of the 1980s raises a question about the role of interest rates for the 1990s, but it does not diminish their general importance in household decisions on whether and when to buy a home. The role of interest rates, however, is always moderated by other economic factors, particularly in the short term. In addition to interest rates, factors such as real GNP, employment, and housing prices are important determinants of short-term demand for new housing. Kenneth Stiltner and David Barton have shown that the influence of these factors, which is not apparent from simple comparisons to housing starts, appears quite robust when analyzed jointly with interest rates in econometric models.[26] Clearly, the housing demand cannot be explained thoroughly without complex economic analysis.

In anticipating the future demand for housing, the analyst should consider both long-term factors, such as national demographics and the general level of housing standards, as well as short-term cyclical influences, such as employment, personal income, interest rates, and housing prices. Unless substantial changes are expected in the long-term factors, such as sizable changes in geographic migration and household formation or in government programs to replace substandard housing, the long-run demand is largely determined by current population and household trends. Short-term cyclical forecasts are more difficult because of the complex interrelationships among determinants of housing demand.

Government Spending and Finances

The money governments spend to satisfy civilian and defense needs comes from taxes, user charges, and borrowing. Because government spending and taxation puts money in and takes money out of the income stream, government budgets are central to economic policies for fostering economic growth, high employment, and low inflation. This section focuses on how fiscal policy can use government budgets to moderate the extremes of business cycle expansions and recessions. It does not address other important ways that government budgets affect the economy, such as the redistribution of income between low- and high-income people, the effects of defense spending on employment and prices, the incentive effects of tax laws, and so forth. These aspects affect economic growth, but they are difficult to quantify in terms of the overall impact of government budgets on the economy.

Public spending by federal, state, and local governments for education, health, police, income maintenance, transportation, national defense, and all other government functions in 1989 totaled $1.8 trillion, or 34 percent of the GNP. The role of government in the economy had expanded considerably until the 1980s, rising from 21 percent of the GNP in 1950 to 33 percent in 1980. The federal government accounted for 67 percent of government spending while state and local governments accounted for 33 percent in 1989. Over the postwar period in general, the federal proportion has ranged from 65 to 70 percent, moving toward the lower end during expansions and the higher end during recessions, with no long-term upward or downward movement.

As noted in Part A of this chapter under Government Budgets, the measure used for government "purchases" in the GNP is lower than government "spending" in the official budget figures. This difference is due to the fact that the GNP treats government transfer payments (e.g., Social Security and unemployment insurance benefit payments, and interest) and federal grants to state and local governments as being spent by the recipients rather than by the governments providing the funds. Thus, Social Security and unemployment benefit payments enter the GNP only when they appear as consumer expenditures, while federal grants to state and local governments only appear as spending by state and local governments.

The category of "government purchases" in the GNP, then, is limited to government spending for wages of government workers and purchases from private industry of materials, equipment, and services. Government purchases accounted for 20 percent of the GNP in 1989. While this figure is substantially lower than the above-noted 34 percent share for all government spending including transfer payments, it is still the second largest component of the GNP, surpassed only by consumer expenditures. However, although the GNP's measure of government purchases provides a consistent accounting method to avoid double-counting of spending, the concept is limited for assessing the total impact of government spending on the economy. Therefore, this section focuses on government budgets, which include all spending and the financing of the spending.

Government as a Cyclical Stabilizer

Use of the federal budget for influencing the economy—in other words, fiscal policy—is secondary to the main purpose of government spending and taxation, which is to provide for the nation's needs and to finance the spending programs in the most equitable and efficient manner. Still, one of the main attributes of government budgets, and in particular the federal budget, is using overall spending and taxation levels to restrain economic growth and inflation in business cycle expansions and to stimulate growth and employment in recessions (see the Economic Policies section in Chapter 2).

Government budgets function in two ways that affect expansions and recessions. The first is through "automatic stabilizers." This term refers to the built-in institutionalized aspects of government budgets that cause government spending and tax collections, without any direct intervention of new government programs, to move in the opposite direction or in less extreme patterns than trends in the overall economy. For example, the inherent nature of unemployment insurance is to put more money in the income stream in recessions than in expansions. Budget outlays for unemployment insurance rise in recessions and drop in expansions. The progressive income tax removes proportionately more income from households in expansions and less in recessions. Thus, these stabilizers automatically move consumer purchasing power in the direction desired in recessions and expansions.

The second way government budgets affect the economy is through their use as an analytic fiscal policy tool. The federal budget's basic posture may be assessed by the size of its surplus or deficit (receipts less expenditures) independent of whether the economy is in an expansion or recession, based on hypothetical budgets that focus on whether the budget inherently stimulates or restrains overall economic activity. These hypothetical budgets are referred to as the "cyclically adjusted budget" or the "high-employment budget," depending on the statistical measures used to develop them. Experience with each of these budget functions over the postwar business cycles is discussed below.

Stabilizing Effect of Government Budgets

How well have government budgets performed as automatic stabilizers? One way of assessing their performance was covered in the earlier discussion of consumer purchasing power in the Consumer Expenditures section. That review of the postwar cyclical trends in personal income and disposable personal income indicated that unemployment insurance payments were more important than the progressive income tax in shoring up income in recessions, and that income taxes were more effective in moderating income increases in expansions than in cushioning income decreases in recessions. This section takes a broader approach and assesses the automatic stabilizing aspect of government budgets by analyzing the extent to which all government spending and taxation puts money in or takes money out of the income stream over business cycles.

A budget surplus (receipts exceeding spending) results in the government taking money out of the income stream, while a budget deficit (spending exceeding receipts) puts money into the income stream. Figures 18a and 18b show this experience for all governments, federal, state, and local, in the postwar business cycles. In relating government budgets to the overall economy, the figures depict the change in the budget surplus or deficit for each expansion (from trough to peak) and for each recession (from peak to trough) in relation to the average national income in the period.[27] If the budget surplus increases or the deficit decreases, the change is positive; and if the deficit increases or the surplus decreases, the change is negative. *Thus, this analysis focuses on the direction of the change of the surplus or deficit during the expansion or recession, not whether the budget is in surplus or deficit.*

The federal, state, and local budgets typically restrained income growth in expansions and boosted incomes in recessions, which fits the concept of the stabilizing role. The budgets moved in the stabilizing direction in eight of the nine expansions (it was neutral in 1950–53) and in eight of the nine recessions (the exception was 1990–91).

The impact of the surplus and deficit shifts in relation to national income in expansions showed the federal budget having a more stabilizing role in six expansions. In the expansions of 1950–53, 1975–80, and 1980–81, the state and local budgets were more stabilizing. In recessions, the federal budget was far more stabilizing than the state and local budgets, except for 1953–54 and 1990–91.

These patterns reflect the combined effects of the level of economic activity, changes in tax laws, and the inflation rate on tax receipts and spending. The general stabilizing movements of both the federal and the state and local budgets result from different patterns of spending and tax receipts. At both levels, expenditures continually increase in expansions and recessions. However, in recessions federal revenues decrease and state and local revenues increase. Federal revenue falls in recessions because of the greater reliance on income taxes as a source of revenue. High unemployment and low business profits cause tax collections to

Figure 18a. **Change in Government Budgets toward a Surplus (+) or Deficit (–) as a Percentage of National Income: Expansions**

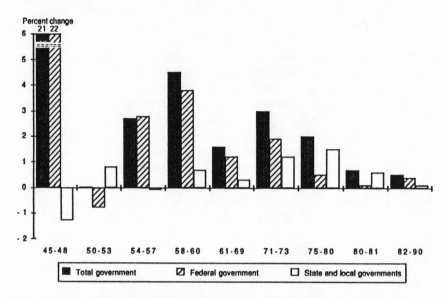

Note: Based on Bureau of Economic Analysis data in current dollars.

drop. This decrease is enlarged by the progressivity in the federal income tax, in which proportionately lower taxes are paid as income decreases. By contrast, a much greater share of state and local tax collections comes from sales and property taxes, which are not as cyclically sensitive as income taxes. For example, in 1989, the personal income tax accounted for 43 percent of federal budget receipts and only 14 percent of state and local budget receipts. In addition, because unemployment insurance benefit payments are part of the federal budget but are not included in state and local budgets, they raise federal but not state and local outlays in recessions, which heightens the stabilizing impact of the federal government in recessions (unemployment insurance is a joint federal-state program, but unemployment taxes paid by employers are held in a federal trust fund and thus are counted as receipts in the federal budget).

The opposite effect occurs in expansions, when federal tax receipts increase more than spending. This was only marginal in the 1982–90 expansion, however, because of the sharp drop in tax rates under the new tax laws. The stabilizing patterns of state and local budgets result from the effects of cyclical changes in both spending and tax receipts, as neither spending nor tax receipts appear to have a dominant cyclical role.

The overall result for the combined budgets of all governments—federal, state, and local—is that the government sector was a stabilizing factor in postwar

Figure 18b. **Change in Government Budgets Toward a Surplus (+) or Deficit (–) as a Percentage of National Income: Recessions**

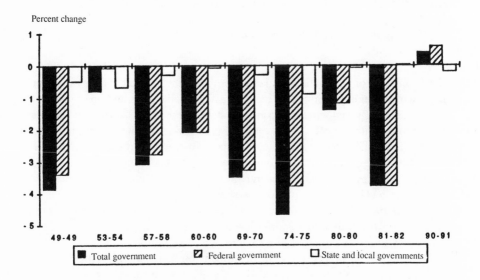

Note: Based on Bureau of Economic Analysis data in current dollars.
Recession of 1990-91 in progress in spring of 1991.

business cycles. As noted above, the government sector moved in the direction of a budget surplus in eight of the nine expansions and the budgets moved in the direction of a deficit in eight of the nine recessions. The federal budget has had a greater influence than state and local budgets on the total government sector in the expansions except for 1950–53, 1975–80, and 1980–81, and in all the recessions except 1953–54; this tendency would be expected because the federal government accounted for 65–70 percent of all government spending over the postwar period. However, it is noteworthy that in two of the three most recent expansions and in the most recent recession, state and local governments' budgets have had a greater cyclical stabilizing role in the overall economy (the federal budget was actually destabilizing in the 1990–91 recession).

The experience of the automatic stabilizing effect of government budgets over the postwar business cycles suggests the following:

1. While the federal budget generally has a more dominant cyclical role than the aggregate of all state and local government budgets, the growing cyclical importance of state and local budgets in the most recent expansions suggests that the analyst should give more attention to the total government sector in future expansions.

2. Unless state and local governments shift a much greater share of their tax collections to an income tax system, their budgets are not likely to have significantly different impacts on stabilizing the economy in future recessions.

The Federal Budget in a Growing Economy: A Fiscal Policy Tool

The discussion of automatic stabilizers focused on the variable effects of government budgets in expansions and recessions. Tax collections and unemployment insurance benefit payments in expansions increase the budget surplus or decrease the deficit, while the effect in recessions is to lower the budget surplus or increase the deficit. These automatic movements in the budget surplus and deficit stem from the *effect of the economy on the budget.* The modified income flows from this process then tend to moderate the extremes of high economic growth in expansions and low or negative economic growth in recessions.

The federal government's role in the economy may also be assessed from a fiscal policy perspective not appropriate to state and local governments.[28] When viewed as an *active influence that drives the economy rather than reacting to it,* the federal budget becomes a tool for influencing the economy. To do so, analysts develop hypothetical budgets for obtaining high economic growth consistent with a low or nonaccelerating inflation rate. These hypothetical budgets abstract from short-term cyclical shifts in budget surpluses and deficits to postulate the size of the surplus or deficit that would occur in a steadily growing economy in which there were no cyclical expansions or recessions. They are used as a basis for analyzing the inherent posture of current and future budgets as a stimulus or restraint on economic growth (in terms of the money they put into or take out of the income stream). The analyses center on the budget implications of government spending programs that are not tied to the cyclical ups and downs of the economy and of tax laws that specify the tax rates and the income, wealth, sales, or other items to be taxed.

Economic theory about how best to balance rapid economic growth and low or nonaccelerating inflation has evolved over the years. In the 1960s a "fully employed" economy (defined as 3 to 4 percent unemployment) was regarded as desirable, and "full employment surplus" budgets were developed and used as a fiscal policy tool. Because the budget surplus generated from such high employment was found to be a "fiscal drag" on economic growth, it was a basic rationale for the tax cuts of the early 1960s. During the 1970s the model was moderated to the "high employment" budget, which raised the minimum unemployment rate believed consistent with low inflation to 5 to 6 percent. The spiraling inflation of the 1970s modified the model further. The "cyclically adjusted budget" of the 1980s specified a minimum unemployment rate of 6 percent.

The main difference among these various budgets lies in the measurement of the high economic growth rate. The full or high employment budgets refer to what the GNP and federal budget receipts and expenditures would be at unemployment rates associated with full or high employment, such as unemployment ranging from 3 to 6 percent.[29] These measures are used to develop a "potential GNP" that would occur at the assumed full or high employment levels. But quantifying the optimal relationship between employment and economic growth is difficult. The economic growth requirements of the assumed unemployment rate tended to rise over the years until the 1980s, when the growth requirements declined (this is discussed further in Chapter 5).

The cyclically adjusted budget assumes a relatively steady growth rate that is uninterrupted by cyclical fluctuations.[30] The measure currently published in the *Survey of Current Business* is based on the GNP trend at a 6 percent unemployment rate. It provides an appropriate tool for assessing budget surpluses and deficits according to the stage of the business cycle. The specific unemployment rate is also suitable for setting fiscal policy guidelines if the unemployment rate is considered a goal for economic growth, in contrast to an alternative cyclically adjusted budget based on actual trends in economic growth.[31]

Table 7 shows the federal budget deficit for the actual budget and the cyclically adjusted budget as a percentage of GNP and the unemployment rate during the 1980s. The actual deficit peaked at 5.2 percent of the GNP in 1983 and subsequently declined to 2.5 percent in 1989, compared to the cyclically adjusted deficit, which peaked at 4.3 percent of the GNP in 1986 and declined to 3.2 percent in 1989. In relation to the GNP, the actual budget deficit was more than twice as large as the cyclically adjusted deficit during 1981–83. This differential diminished during 1984–87, and by 1988 and 1989 the actual budget deficit was smaller than the cyclically adjusted deficit. These patterns parallel the differential movement between the actual unemployment rate and a constant 6 percent unemployment rate during the 1980s.

Thus, the two measures give different pictures of how the budget deficit affected economic growth in the 1980s, although both measures show the deficit was a stimulus. However, the actual budget shows a much faster buildup and subsequent slowdown of the stimulus, and at the end of the 1980s the deficit appears less stimulative than in the cyclically adjusted budget. On the other hand, the cyclically adjusted budget more accurately portrays the effect of the tax and spending policy changes during the decade (i.e., the tax cuts of the Economic Recovery Tax Act of 1981 as modified by the Tax Equity and Fiscal Responsibility Act of 1982 and the Deficit Reduction Act of 1984, the Balanced Budget and Emergency Deficit Control Act of 1985 as amended by the Gramm-Rudman-Hollings Act in 1987, the Tax Reform Act of 1986, and the Omnibus Budget Reconciliation Act of 1990) because it holds the rate of economic growth relatively steady by relying on the 6 percent unemployment rate, which is not affected by yearly changes in the growth rate due to cyclical factors.

While some economists maintain that large deficits do not affect interest

Table 7

Alternative Measures of Federal Budget Deficits Based on National Income and Product Accounts

	Actual deficit as percentage of GNP	Cyclically adjusted deficit as percentage of GNP* (6% unemployment)	Unemployment rate (percent)
1980	2.2	1.3	7.0
1981	2.1	0.8	7.5
1982	4.6	1.7	9.5
1983	5.2	2.6	9.5
1984	4.5	3.5	7.4
1985	4.9	4.2	7.1
1986	4.9	4.3	6.9
1987	3.6	3.4	6.1
1988	3.0	3.5	5.4
1989	2.5	3.2	5.2

Sources: Survey of Current Business, August 1990, August 1989, August 1987, and March 1986; and *Economic Report of the President,* February 1991.

Notes: Budget deficits are based on the statistical budgets in the national income and product accounts as distinct from the official budget. Differences between the two budgets are discussed in Part A of this chapter under Government Budgets.

*The GNP for the cyclically adjusted deficit is the long-term trend GNP based on an unemployment rate of 6 percent.

rates, others indicate they do raise rates for two reasons: (a) the large demand the deficits create for borrowed funds to finance them raises rates, and (b) lenders perceive the large deficits as meaning that inflation is not under control and consequently charge higher rates to ensure that the purchasing power of the loans is maintained when they are repaid.[32]

A corollary of the persistently higher budget deficits is that they cumulate to a considerable increase in the federal government's debt, which may affect business investment. Debt represents government borrowing through short-term and long-term interest-bearing obligations, such as notes, bonds, and mortgages, mainly to finance past and current budget deficits, and secondarily in anticipation of future spending, such as capital construction projects of state and local governments. Because the refunding requirements of the debt provide investment opportunities in U.S. securities that have no risk attached, they may lead to redirecting investment activity toward government debt instruments and away from business investment, such as in plant and equipment and new ventures. Frank de Leeuw and Thomas Holloway discuss this "crowding out" effect of government borrowing.[33]

Federal Budget Deficit Reduction Plans

The large increases in federal budget deficits and debt that emerged in the 1970s and worsened considerably in the 1980s are perceived as a major national problem. Figures 19 and 20 show the patterns of deficits and debt as a percentage of the GNP during 1950–90. During the forty-year period, the budget typically had a deficit (the last annual surplus was in 1969), but the deficits were persistently much greater in the 1980s than in the earlier decades (Figure 19). Both total debt and debt held by the public declined in the 1950s and 1960s, leveled off in the 1970s, and rose in the 1980s (Figure 20). Debt held by the public is confined to government securities owned by individuals, businesses, pension funds, and foreigners, while total debt also includes debt held by government funds including trust funds, such as those for Social Security and unemployment insurance, and public enterprise "federal" funds, such as those for the Postal Service and nuclear waste. Federal debt held by the public is considered more relevant for interest rates because it directly affects credit markets, while government funds invested in debt securities (which are included in total debt) are internal to the government and thus do not directly affect credit markets and interest rates.

In response to concern about the persistence of large deficits, Congress and the president have made two major efforts to reduce it. In 1985, the Gramm-Rudman-Hollings Act (amended in 1987) established annual targets for specified deficit reductions that would reduce the deficit to zero over a five-year period by requiring overall spending cuts to meet the deficit reduction targets. The Gramm-Rudman-Hollings Act has failed in its overall objective, although it probably has held the deficit below what it would have been without it. One of the major reasons for its failure is that the rule for setting the deficit reductions targets is based on a forecast of the deficit in the coming year, rather than on the actual deficit in the current or past year. Thus, the forecasts assume rates of economic growth, unemployment, inflation, and interest rates that will generate sufficient tax revenues and hold down spending to meet the deficit targets for the coming year. Because the forecasts have been unrealistically optimistic, the targeted reductions have not been achieved. While the past performance of the economy keeps the forecasts within some realistic bounds, the mechanism allowed Congress and the president continually to evade the responsibility of raising taxes and/or reducing spending but still to comply with the law.

In 1990, Congress and the president addressed the deficit problem again in the Omnibus Budget Reconciliation Act. This act specified reductions in the deficit, which it figured to cumulate to $490 billion during 1991–95 based on legislated spending cuts and tax increases, and on assumed improved performance of the economy. The $490 billion figure is misleading, however. It represents a cumulative reduction over the five years that counts a reduction in one year in all succeeding years as well. For example, the $40 billion reduction scheduled for 1991 is counted again with the new reductions in 1992–95, the $37 billion

Figure 19. **Federal Budget Surplus (+) or Deficit (–) as a Percentage of GNP: 1950–90**

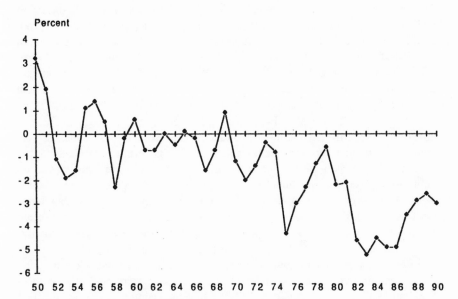

Note: Based on Bureau of Economic Analysis data in current dollars.
Budget data are on national accounts basis.

reduction in 1992 is counted again with the new reductions in 1993–95, and so on. This cumulative rendering is useful for budget accounting, but the total it produces is much greater than the sum of the incremental reductions that are scheduled for each year. The unduplicated cumulative reduction obtained by summing the annual incremental reductions in the deficit over 1991–95 is $143 billion. While $143 billion is less than the total 1990 deficit of $220 billion, according to the five-year plan this reduction will lead to a budget surplus of $78 billion in 1995. Such are the mysteries of budget accounting.

Table 8 summarizes the economic projections in this five-year deficit reduction plan. They envision substantially improved economic performance compared to 1989 and 1990 in terms of faster growth, less inflation, and lower interest rates. If the economy falls short of these projections, the deficit reductions will also fall short. While the projections include a recession in the early 1990s, it is a fairly limited one (unemployment is projected to peak at 6.4 percent in 1992). If a prolonged and severe recession were to occur, the deficit reductions would probably be delayed or suspended entirely in order to counter spending declines in the private sector of the economy.

Thus, the success of the legislated spending cuts and tax increases depends on the overall performance of the economy. For example, while a lower deficit

Figure 20. **Total Federal Debt and Federal Debt Held by Public as a Percentage of GNP: 1950–90**

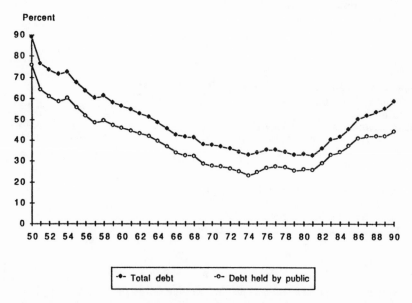

Percent

Note: Based on Department of the Treasury and Bureau of Economic Analysis data in current dollars.

resulting from spending cuts and tax increases should bolster economic growth through its effect on lower interest rates, in case of a recession the lower deficit could in fact aggravate the downturn by reducing public and private spending. On balance, Congress's and the president's efforts will probably make an inroad into the deficit, but because of the optimistic economic projections underlying the plan and possible future legislative changes to the five-year spending cuts and tax increases adopted in 1990, more legislation will probably be required to reduce the deficit substantially.

The following considerations are suggested for assessing the impact of the large federal budget deficits on the economy:

1. *The analyst should be alert to signs in credit markets when changes in the competing demands for funds between private industry and the federal government raise or lower interest rates, or for signs that lenders view the inflationary implications of high deficits differently in periods of slow or rapid economic growth.*

2. *In monitoring the progress of efforts to reduce the federal budget deficit,*

Table 8

Economic Assumptions of the Five-year Federal Deficit Reduction Plan: Omnibus Budget Reconciliation Act of 1990 (percent)

	Actual 1989	Estimated 1990	Projected 1991–95 (annual rate)
Real GNP (4th quarter to 4th quarter)	1.8[a]	0.7	3.3
GNP implicit price deflator (4th quarter to 4th quarter)	3.7[b]	5.2	3.4
Unemployment rate (calendar year)	5.2	5.6	5.7
Ten-year Treasury notes (calendar year)	8.5	8.7	6.5
Domestic crude oil price to refiners per barrel (calendar year)	$17.88	$21.15	$22.49

Source: Executive Office of the President, "Budget Summit Agreement," September 30, 1990.

[a]Incorrectly noted in the source as 1.6 percent.

[b]Incorrectly noted in the source as 3.8 percent.

the analyst should identify reductions attributable to spending cuts and tax increases as distinct from reductions attributable to the performance of the economy in order to highlight the strong and weak links in the deficit reduction process. While determining the separate impact of two such broad and interconnected factors necessarily requires some guesswork, the resulting estimations will provide a better basis for assessing the likely outcome of the current deficit reduction plan as well as new actions proposed or taken in the future.

3. The refunding of considerable amounts of risk-free U.S. debt stemming from the cumulative federal budget deficits could lead to some diversion of investment funds away from new plant and equipment or business ventures, which could lower economic growth rates. *The tendency for such diversion would not necessarily be evident from data on actual investment trends, but in assessing the impact of the federal debt on the economy, the analyst should monitor credit markets for evidence of significant amounts of such diversion.*

Exports and Imports

Foreign trade in goods and services and income on foreign investments have become increasingly important in the American economy. The internationalization of the economy has also made it more subject to economic and political developments in other countries. As a proportion of the GNP, exports of goods, services, and income averaged 10 percent and imports averaged 13 percent during 1985–89. This was 70 percent higher than the share for exports and close to twice the share of imports in the early 1960s. In dollar volume, exports and imports are both larger than consumer spending for durable goods, residential construction, and plant and equipment investment.

There have also been shifts among the goods, services, and income components of exports and imports, reflecting changes in the competitive position of American business. Goods are agricultural, mineral, and manufactured products; services include travel, transportation, insurance, telecommunications, and other business services; and income includes profits and interest on foreign investments. Goods make up the bulk of foreign trade, accounting for 60 percent of exports and 68 percent of imports in 1989.

Long-term trends in export/import shares indicate the inroads made by foreign businesses in trade in goods. The export trends indicate that American business increasingly is investing abroad to take advantage of the lower production costs and to comply with requirements in some countries that certain items be produced locally (domestic-content laws). Despite this increasing U.S. investment abroad, while goods declined from 63 percent of all exports in the early 1960s to 59 percent in 1985–89, income from investment abroad also declined from 15 percent of all exports in the early 1960s to 13 percent in 1985–89. The import trends show an increasing share of goods, rising from 64 percent of imports in the early 1960s to 70 percent in 1985–89. Yet, this increase was accompanied by a rise in profits from investment in the United States, from 4 percent of all imports in the early 1960s to 11 percent in 1985–89. These trends reflect the tendency of foreign business to invest in the United States because of the large markets and, more recently, because of the possibility of higher import barriers, such as tariffs and quotas, resulting from American projectionist sentiment.

As noted in Part A of this chapter under Net Exports, exports and imports are recorded in the GNP as a net figure, exports minus imports. This results in a very small number, ranging from about –1 to +1 percent of the GNP, the sign depending on whether exports are larger or smaller than imports. This bookkeeping technique to avoid double counting in the GNP does not indicate the importance of foreign trade in the economy. On the other hand, the net figure is relevant for assessing America's competitive position in the world economy, the foreign exchange value of the dollar, and possibly the extent of protectionist sentiment. These factors in turn have a significant effect on exports and imports.

Several versions of international transactions are in the "current account" of balance of payments data, which are similar but not identical to the figures on exports and imports of goods and services in the GNP. The main differences are the treatment of gold, capital gains and losses of affiliates of U.S. and foreign countries, U.S. government interest payments to foreigners, U.S. territories and Puerto Rico, and money sent to relatives. In addition, international transactions in the balance of payments cover "capital" movements for foreign investments, money flows in payment for the current account exports and imports, and government reserve assets of gold and assets with international monetary organizations. While the capital movements are not directly part of the GNP, they record economic activity that affects the foreign exchange value of the dollar (which in turn affects exports and imports as discussed below), and thus indirectly affect the GNP.

A problem with the balance of payments data in recent years has been the large difference between the sum of the current account exports, imports, and foreign investments on the one hand, and the recording of the money flows to finance these transactions on the other. Conceptually these are identical. The difference is referred to as the statistical discrepancy. The discrepancy rose to $64 billion in 1990, a startling increase over the $18 billion in 1989. Christopher Bach notes that this increase in unrecorded inflows of foreign capital to the United States conflicts with the drop in recorded foreign flows to the United States.[34] The size of the statistical discrepancy has been disconcerting since the late 1970s, but the jump in 1990 magnifies the problem for economic analysis. More accurate reporting of these transactions could affect the picture of some international aspects of the American economy (such as that discussed below with respect to "Balance of Payments Deficits and External Debt") and would allow more reliable analysis of trends in money and investment flows between the United States and other nations.

Demand for Exports and Imports

The volume of exports and imports is determined by three general economic factors: economic activity at home (for imports) and abroad (for exports), relative prices for competing U.S. and foreign goods and services, and the foreign exchange value of the dollar (which reflects relative prices of currencies). The ways in which these factors work is summarized below. In addition, exports and imports are affected by the quality of U.S. and foreign goods and services and other nonprice factors, including tariffs, quotas, and nontariff barriers such as domestic-content laws requiring that imported goods contain minimum proportions of domestically produced items.

Directional Impact of Factors Affecting Foreign Trade Volume

Demand Factor	Exports	Imports
Economic activity abroad	Higher activity, higher exports	—
Economic activity in U.S.	—	Higher activity, higher imports
U.S. prices relative to foreign prices	Higher U.S. prices, lower exports	Higher U.S. prices, higher imports,
Value of the dollar	Higher dollar, lower exports	Higher dollar, higher imports

The relationship of exports and imports to American business cycles is more tenuous than that of the other GNP components because of factors outside the United States that affect foreign trade. For example, economic activity and prices in the United States are not always paralleled in other countries, and the value of the dollar is affected by factors only partially influenced by American actions, such as interest rate differentials between the United States and other countries or political stability abroad.[35]

Figures 21a and 21b show exports and imports in relation to real GNP over the postwar business cycles. In the expansions, both exports and imports typically increased faster than the GNP, which is consistent with the long-term growing importance of foreign trade noted earlier. In the recessions, exports showed no general pattern, increasing in five cases and decreasing in four cases, while imports decreased in seven of the nine cases. This tendency of imports to follow business cycle movements more closely than exports reflects the stronger link of imports to economic activity in the United States.

Relative Importance of Demand Factors

In assessing the importance of the three general factors driving exports and imports—economic activity at home and abroad, relative prices in the United States and foreign countries, and the value of the dollar—it should be noted that some relationships among these factors are difficult to quantify. For example, while exports are directly related to economic activity abroad, they also indirectly reflect economic activity at home: when business is booming in the United States, American companies may be less aggressive in marketing exports, while in recessions they may be more aggressive. Similarly, prices and exchange rates affect each other; thus, an anticipated high rate of inflation in a country may reduce the value of its currency.

Other considerations that affect the demand relationships include the "globalization of production," the "Leontief Paradox," and the "terms of trade." The following gives highlights of their characteristics and the available measures of their impacts.

GLOBALIZATION OF PRODUCTION: The globalization of production refers to a manufacturing trend that became prominent in the mid-1980s when some companies whose basic ownership and operations are in one country establish production plants in foreign countries. Examples are when U.S. automakers (for example, General Motors) produce cars in Brazil and when Japanese automakers (for example, Toyota) produce cars in the United States. American cars produced in Brazil are not a U.S. export, and Japanese cars produced in the United States are not a U.S. import. But the components and parts for these cars that are produced in the company's home country are part of foreign trade—the parts and components produced in the United States and incorporated in the cars made in

Figure 21a. **Business Cycle Movements of Real GNP, Exports, and Imports: Expansions**

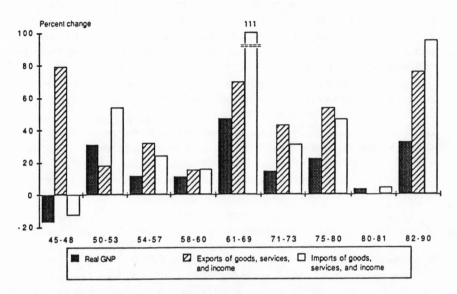

Note: Based on Bureau of Economic Analysis data in 1982 dollars.

Brazil are a U.S. export, and the parts and components produced in Japan and incorporated in the cars made in the United States are a U.S. import. Also, the profits attributable to these companies' foreign operations are incorporated in the income components of the balance of payments, with profits of U.S. companies in Brazil a U.S. export (inflow of income to the United States from Brazil), and profits of Japanese companies in the United States a U.S. import (outflow of income from the United States to Japan).

The globalization of production is relatively small in terms of the overall economy. Foreign companies operating in the United States accounted for 4.3 percent of the "all-U.S.-business gross product" in 1987.[36] After rising from 2.3 percent in 1977 to 4.2 percent in 1981, this proportion remained constant through 1987. This figure is significantly different among industries, however; while foreign companies accounted for only 1 to 2.5 percent of services, real estate, and retail trade, they represented 7 to 10.5 percent of wholesale trade, nonbank finance, and manufacturing in 1987.

Most of the value of the output of the foreign companies is produced in the United States (referred to as "local content"), although the importation of foreign-made parts and components is not negligible. Of the total sales of U.S.-produced products by these companies, 81 percent of their production cost in 1987 was attributable to goods and services purchased from U.S. business and work done

Figure 21b. **Business Cycle Movements of Real GNP, Exports, and Imports: Recessions**

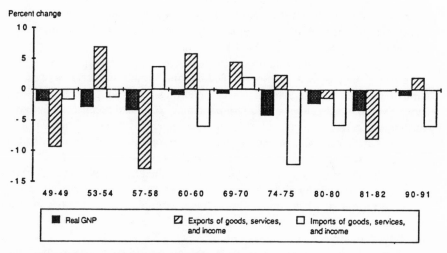

Note: Based on Bureau of Economic Analysis data in 1982 dollars.
Recession of 1990-91 in progress in spring of 1991.

at U.S. installations. In manufacturing, the local content share varied from 65 percent in motor vehicles to 94 percent in chemicals. Employment in these foreign companies followed a similar pattern as the gross product. For example, as a proportion of employment in all U.S. businesses, foreign companies accounted for 3.7 percent in 1987 and 4.1 percent in 1988.[37] Not included in these measures, however, is that most of the top jobs in a foreign-owned company are held by foreign nationals rather than by U.S. citizens.

Changes in the globalization of production occur slowly over time. Thus, these data are more relevant for projections of the economy that cover several years rather than projections of one to two years. For example, James Orr estimates that the influx of foreign investment in U.S. manufacturing industries in the latter half of the 1980s will reduce the foreign trade deficit in goods by roughly $25 billion in the mid- to late-1990s. This is the net effect of a $15 billion increase in exports due to the transfer of technology or other competitive advantages obtained from foreign ownership and a $10 billion decrease in imports due to the displacement of imports from the parent companies of the foreign owners or other foreign suppliers. The expected $25 billion deficit reduction compares to the total foreign trade deficit in goods of $109 billion in 1990 noted below. Analogous projections of the effect of U.S. investment in manufacturing industries abroad, which have the opposite effect of raising the trade deficit, are not available.[38]

LEONTIEF PARADOX: Wassily Leontief, the creator of input–output analysis, observed in accordance with economic theory that in order to have the most efficient specialization of output in the world economy, an advanced industrial country such as the United States should import labor-intensive products and export capital-intensive ones. Paradoxically, however, he found that on average the United States has not adhered to this model.

Leontief's paradox is based on statistical procedures he developed to calculate the effect on employment of exported and imported goods and services (agricultural, mineral, and manufactured products and transportation, banking, services, etc.), given the technologies used in producing exports and competitive imports (materials, services, labor, and plant and equipment). Leontief's method is to estimate whether a dollar of exports generates more or less employment than is displaced by a dollar of competitive imports. (Competitive imports refers to imported products that are also produced in the United States, even though some buyers may not consider all U.S. products as equal substitutes for foreign goods, particularly in luxury categories of cars, liquor, crystal, and so on; noncompetitive imports are those such as coffee and diamonds, which are available only from other countries.)

Leontief determined exports' and imports' relative effects on employment and investment by dividing the ratio of plant and equipment to labor (capital-labor ratio) used in producing competitive imports by the capital-labor ratio used in producing exports. When the quotient is greater than one, it signifies that a dollar of exports creates more employment and less investment than would be required to produce a dollar of imports; when the quotient is less than one, a dollar of exports creates less employment but requires more investment than a dollar of imports.

Faye Duchin estimates that the quotient for the years 1963 to 2000 is greater than one for the entire period (Table 9). Thus, the employment generated by each dollar of exports has been and is expected to be greater (at least until the year 2000) than the employment lost by each dollar of imports. This finding contradicts the general expectation that, because the U.S. economy is highly mechanized, exports will generate less employment than is displaced by imports. Thus, even though the analysis ignores secondary benefits of foreign trade (such as the tendency of imports to increase competition and thus to lower prices and improve the quality of goods and services, or the tendency of exports to bolster the American economy by providing larger markets for U.S. goods), it still provides a justification for a policy of free trade rather than protectionism based on the objective of promoting employment.

However, statistical limitations seriously restrict the extent to which analysts or policymakers should rely on these data. First, Table 9 compares the employment effects of investing one dollar in exports or imports; however, when imports are in reality much greater than exports, as they were in the 1980s and early 1990s, competitive imports will in fact displace more jobs than exports create. Second, the trend of the figures in Table 9 is generally downward, falling from

Table 9

**Capital-Labor Ratio for Competitive Imports Divided
by Capital-Labor Ratio for Exports**

	Quotient
1963	1.31
1967	1.20
1972	1.13
1977	1.33
1990 (estimated)	1.09
2000 (projected)	1.09

Source: Faye Duchin, "Technological Change and International Trade," *Economic Systems Research* (New York University Institute for Economic Analysis), vol. 2, no. 1, 1990.

1.31 in 1963 to 1.09 in 1990, with the year 2000 projected to continue at the 1990 level. Although there is a puzzling break in the trend in 1977, the general movement suggests that the differential of the labor-generating properties of exports over imports has been declining. Third, the data requirements underlying this analysis are enormous, and considerable estimating is necessary to fill data gaps. Finally, as noted above, competitive imports have a definitional problem. It remains questionable whether products such as a Rolls Royce or Waterford crystal should be classified as competitive imports. Overall, although the figures should only be regarded as broad approximations, the approach provides a blunt tool for assessing foreign trade's employment effects and investment requirements.

TERMS OF TRADE: The relative movements of export and import prices are tracked by the terms of trade, which is defined as the ratio of the price of exports (numerator) to the price of imports (denominator). The terms of trade affect the difference between the dollar levels of exports and imports, and thus the trade surplus (i.e., when exports exceed imports) or the trade deficit (i.e., when imports exceed exports). When the terms of trade are rising (export prices rising more or falling less than import prices), export receipts are proportionately greater than import payments for the same quantity of exports and imports, which results in a greater trade surplus or a lower trade deficit. And when the terms of trade are declining (export prices falling or rising less than import prices), the price relationships foster a higher trade deficit or a lower trade surplus.

The terms of trade are only a first approximation of the effect of price movements on the dollar value of exports and imports because they do not include the effects of price movements on quantities sold; for example, higher export prices may result in a lower volume of export sales, and therefore the dollar export receipts may not increase as much as the prices and could even decline if the drop in sales is more than the increase in prices. In addition, measures of the terms of trade before 1984 are suspect because price information then was based on "unit value indexes." Unit value indexes are affected by shifts in purchases of different quality merchandise in the same category, and thus do not reflect price movements for the same product; for example, a shift in imports from lower-priced to higher-priced cars raises the import unit value index even though the price of both models is unchanged. These limitations should be kept in mind when analyzing trends of the terms of trade.

Figure 22 shows two measures of the terms of trade from 1984 to 1990 based on import and export price indexes prepared by the Bureau of Labor Statistics. The terms of trade declined from 1984 to 1987 (particularly during 1985–87), and then were relatively stable from 1987 to 1990. These movements are similar both for "all exports and all imports" and for "all exports and all imports excluding fuel imports," although the measure that excludes imported fuels declined more in the early period (fuel imports are excluded to avoid the distorting effect of the volatile crude oil prices). These movements reflect that from 1984 to 1987 fuel import prices decreased while all other import prices increased, but from 1987 to 1990 fuel import prices rose slightly more than other import prices. Overall, the terms of trade added to the trade deficit from 1984 to 1987 and reduced the trade deficit slightly from 1987 to 1990.

In a study of long-term trends in the terms of trade for the United States and other nations, Norman Fieleke found that the terms of trade generally have cyclical movements rather than prolonged upward or downward trends.[39] He also found that countries whose exports and imports are diversified among many products have less yearly variation in the terms of trade than countries whose foreign trade is concentrated in a few products, since price movements tend to be offsetting when there are many products. Due to the limitations noted above regarding foreign trade price information derived from unit value indexes, these findings should be considered tentative. However, they suggest that the United States is not likely to have a prolonged advantage or disadvantage from movements in the terms of trade and that the United States is likely to experience less yearly variation in the terms of trade than countries that produce a small number of products.

ECONOMIC ACTIVITY AND PRICES: Several studies comparing the effect of economic activity (such as real gross domestic product) and prices on exports and imports have indicated that economic activity is two to four times as important as prices for periods up to one year, and that this differential is significantly lessened although not eliminated for longer periods.[40] Because these relationships are based on several studies that use varied estimating techniques, they are not fully consistent, and thus suggest magnitudes rather than specific numbers.

Figure 22. **Terms of Trade for Commodities, Export Price Index Divided by Import Price Index: 1984–90**

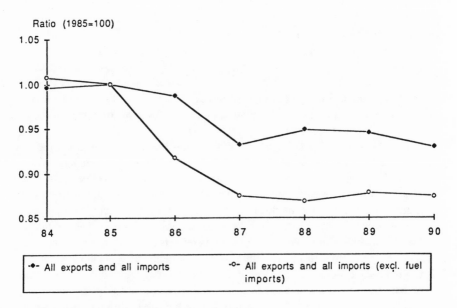

Note: Based on Bureau of Labor Statistics data.

VALUE OF THE DOLLAR: Changes in the value of the dollar affect relative prices between the United States and other countries. Thus, changes in the dollar have the same relative importance to economic activity as was noted above for prices. However, changes in prices and in the value of the dollar do not always show the same movements. Prices are affected by other factors, including the desire of businesses to maintain or increase market shares in export markets, the effect of price changes on profit margins, and the willingness of sellers to allow prices to be dictated by fluctuations in the value of the dollar. One method for calculating the extent that changes in the dollar affect export and import prices is the "passthrough rate," which estimates the percentage of an increase (or decrease) in the dollar that is passed through to change the prices of exports and imports. For example, if the dollar declines by 20 percent, and prices of U.S. exports (in foreign currency terms) decline by 15 percent, the passthrough is 75 percent (15 divided by 20). Analogously, if foreign currencies appreciate (on average) by 20 percent against the dollar, and prices of U.S. imports rise by 10 percent, the passthrough is 50 percent (10 divided by 20).

Passthrough experience can be calculated from information provided in the U.S. import and export price indexes prepared by the Bureau of Labor Statistics.

Table 10 shows passthrough estimates for two periods: March 1985 to December 1988 when the dollar was declining, and December 1988 to September 1990 when the dollar showed no pronounced upward or downward trend. Figures on the value of the dollar for exports differ from those on imports, because the dollar exchange rate is calculated by weighting the currencies of various countries based on the volume of U.S. export and import trade with them. Thus, the Japanese yen is weighted more heavily in the import exchange rate than in the export exchange rate, since U.S. exports to Japan are much less than U.S. imports from Japan. The passthrough estimates are based on the total of all commodity exports and on imports excluding fuels in order to abstract from the sharp fluctuations in oil prices that can distort the analysis.

From March 1985 to December 1988, when the dollar was declining, the passthrough for exports was 73 percent and the passthrough for imports was 58 percent. Thus, U.S. exporters passed through 73 percent of the decline in the dollar into lower foreign prices, while foreign exporters partially compensated for the decline in the dollar by raising dollar prices to offset only 58 percent of the appreciation of their home currency. William Alterman suggests that the greater passthrough of the dollar decline in exports than in imports reflects two tendencies.[41] One is that businesses generally are more willing to pass through price declines when their home currency is depreciating because the lower price abroad allows them to compete better in export markets without lowering prices in their home currency on products sold domestically. The second is that, as a result of differences in management philosophy, foreign companies may be less willing than U.S. companies to allow their export prices to be driven by exchange rate fluctuations.

From December 1988 to September 1990, when the dollar was relatively stable, the passthrough concept was not operative. Prices of U.S. exports were virtually unchanged (prices increased 0.2 percent while the dollar declined 2.2 percent). A price increase in the face of a dollar decline defies the passthrough concept, but these small magnitudes are too close to the margin of error to allow any conclusions to be drawn from such fine distinctions. Similarly, while prices of imports rose much more than would be implied by a complete passthrough of the dollar decline (prices increased 1.4 percent while the dollar declined 0.7 percent), the magnitudes involved are too small to be significant. The lesson of this period is that the passthrough analysis is not relevant during periods when there is little change in the value of the dollar.

According to one widely cited theory, over the long run the value of the dollar is established according to the concept of *purchasing power parity* (PPP). This theory starts with a hypothesized period in which the American and other economies are considered to be in balance, with relatively little excess in unemployment, inflation, and foreign trade balances. The prices of goods and services in the United States and other countries, which are reflected in the value of the dollar in relation to currencies of those countries during this "equilibrium" period, are used as the base from which to calculate future price changes. As

Table 10

Price Passthroughs of Exchange Rate Changes: 1985–90 (percent)

Exports (all commodities)	Foreign currency price	Dollar exchange rate	Passthrough
March 1985–Dec. 1988	–21.7	–29.7	73
Dec. 1988–Sept. 1990	0.2	–2.2	Not applicable

Imports (all commodities excluding fuels)	Dollar price	Dollar exchange rate	Passthrough
March 1985–Dec. 1988	30.9	53.2	58
Dec. 1988–Sept. 1990	1.4	–0.7	Not applicable

Source: Based on data from Bureau of Labor Statistics, U.S. Import and Export Price Indexes.

subsequent price movements in the United States diverge (for example, U.S. prices rise faster than prices in England), the value of the dollar would fall proportionate to the relative rise of American prices in order to maintain the PPP of the base period between the dollar and the pound.

Despite the appeal of the theory, foreign currency values do not typically move in accord with the PPP concept because (a) it is difficult to determine the base period when economies were in balance, and (b) the base period may become obsolete due to productivity changes, investment opportunities, resource supplies (such as North Sea oil), interest rates, and political stability. Hence, the PPP concept is difficult to apply to economic events, particularly during periods when international economic relationships change substantially.[42]

The PPP is measured by the real exchange rate of the dollar. The real exchange rate is the nominal rate, which is the familiar one used in actual transactions, adjusted for price changes in the United States and other nations. Thus, the real exchange rate represents the value of the dollar in terms of the constant-dollar costs of U.S. exports and imports. Both the nominal and real measures of the value of the dollar are based on combining the dollar exchange rates for several nations into a single figure by weighting the export and import trade volumes of the United States and the other nations. The theoretical PPP concept works perfectly if the real value of the dollar is constant over time.[43]

Figure 23 shows Federal Reserve Board measures of the nominal and real value of the dollar from 1973 to 1990. Both have fluctuated widely and in similar patterns. Thus, the real exchange rate has not been constant, as posited by the PPP theory. The relatively close correspondence between the nominal and real exchange rates means that price inflation in the United States and other nations tends to be similar. The Morgan Guaranty Trust Company of New York and the Federal Reserve Bank of Dallas prepare alternative measures of the

Figure 23. **Value of the U.S. Dollar: 1973–90**

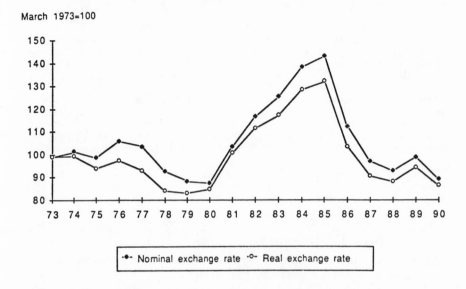

March 1973=100

Note: Based on Federal Reserve Board data. Real=nominal adjusted for consumer price changes in U. S. and abroad.

nominal and real value of the dollar based on including different countries' currencies and weighting the export and import trade volumes differently. However, these measures also show a real exchange rate that fluctuates considerably and in patterns similar to those of the nominal and real rates.

Thus, the PPP theory does not hold up empirically and is of little value in determining if the dollar is "overvalued" and likely to depreciate, or if it is "undervalued" and due to appreciate.

BALANCE OF PAYMENTS DEFICITS AND EXTERNAL DEBT: When exports of goods, services, and income on foreign investments exceed imports, the balance of payments is in a surplus, and when imports exceed exports, the balance of payments is in a deficit. Figure 24 shows the balance of payments for the total of all international transactions and the main components from 1960 to 1990. The total balance was in surplus from 1960 to 1982 except for 1977 and 1978, but then declined sharply to reach a deficit of $148 billion in 1987; subsequently, the deficit shrank to $78 billion by 1990. These trends were driven by those of the goods component, which as noted previously makes up the dominant portion of the balance of payments. The goods component first showed deterio-

Figure 24. **Balance of Payments and Components, Surplus (+) and Deficit (–): 1960–90**

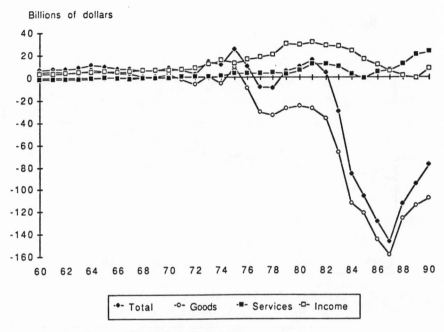

Note: Based on Bureau of Economic Analysis data.

ration in the early 1970s, several years before the total balance declined; after sinking to $160 billion in 1987, the goods deficit was reduced to $109 billion by 1990. After showing continual small deficits during 1960–70, the services component has been in surplus during the 1970s and 1980s; noticeable increases since the mid-1980s left the surplus at $23 billion in 1990. In sharp contrast to these patterns, the long-term trend of the income component had been one of gradually rising surpluses, which peaked at $31 billion in 1981; subsequently, the income surplus declined through the rest of the 1980s to a deficit of –$1 billion in 1989, and then rebounded to $8 billion in 1990.

Figure 25a shows the United States' international investment position. As a result of the balance of payments deficits of the 1980s, foreigners for the first time since before World War I have greater claims on the United States than the United States has on assets abroad. From a peak net creditor position of $141 billion in 1981, the United States declined to its first net debtor status of $2 billion in 1984, and this deficit mushroomed to $664 billion by 1989. The increased net debt reflects the greater increases in foreign-owned assets in the United States compared to the increases in U.S.-owned assets abroad.

Figure 25b shows alternative methods of how the investment position is mea-

Figure 25a. **U.S. International Investment Position Using Historical-Cost Valuation:
1973–89**

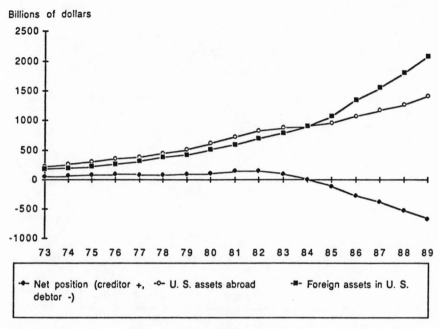

Billions of dollars

Note: Based on Bureau of Economic Analysis data.

sured. These were developed to better reflect the valuation of direct investment
(investments which represent a 10 percent or more ownership of the voting
securities of a company) and to make the direct investment valuation comparable
to the portfolio investment valuation of stocks (investments representing less
than a 10 percent ownership) and bonds.[44] Specifically, estimates of the investment position in Figure 25a are based on the traditional valuation of direct
investment in historical-costs—i.e., prices at which tangible assets of plant and
equipment and land were actually purchased. The alternative measures are in
current-costs and market value. Current-costs measure tangible assets in the
prices of replacing them in the current period. Market value measures tangible
assets by indexes of stock market prices of companies, and thus also includes the
market value of intangible assets such as patents, trademarks, management, and
name recognition (intangible assets are not included in the historical-cost and
current-cost methods). While the current-costs and market value estimates show
lower debt levels than the historical-cost method in Figure 25a, the alternative measures show the same deterioration in the balance of payments and the change to a
debtor nation in the 1980s. Beginning in 1991, the official investment position of the

Figure 25b. **Net International Investment Position Using Alternative Valuation Methods: 1982–89**

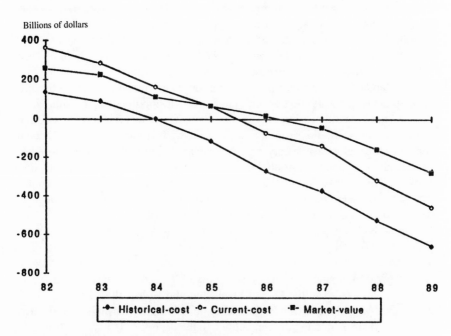

Billions of dollars

Legend: -◆- Historical-cost -○- Current-cost -■- Market-value

Note: Based on Bureau of Economic Analysis data.

U.S. for the total of all direct and portfolio investments is represented by the alternative methods of current-cost and market value. However, the distribution of the direct investment component of the investment position by industry and country is only available on the historical-cost basis. Because most other countries still base their direct investment positions on historical-costs, the historical-cost estimates provide a rough comparison of the direct investment position with other countries.

Typically, the deterioration in the U.S. balance of payments and the international investment position in the 1980s is attributed to four main developments. First, during the 1980s the U.S. economy grew faster than most other industrialized nations, which raised U.S. imports relative to exports. (Only Japan's economy grew faster, but this growth did not lead to significantly higher imports from the United States due to nontariff barriers associated with government procurement, wholesale and retail trade distribution, and technical product standards that discriminate against foreign products in Japan.) Second, during the first half of the 1980s the value of the dollar increased sharply due to high interest rates in the United States (relative to those elsewhere) which accompanied heavy government borrowing to finance the large federal deficits. These higher interest rates attracted foreign funds that in turn drove up the value of the dollar and made U.S. products more expensive in world markets; consequently, U.S. exports increased less than imports. Third, the influx of foreign funds attracted by these higher interest rates also caused greater income payments to foreigners on their investments in the United States. Finally, Asian industrializing nations with wage rates much lower than those in the United States were increasingly competitive in the 1980s and made significant inroads in American markets.

The standard prescription for reversing the deterioration is to undo the four developments of the 1980s that are blamed for causing the decline—that is, the United States should substantially reduce its federal government budget deficit, foreign nations should promote faster growth in their economies through stimulative fiscal and monetary policies, Japan should reduce its nontariff barriers, and the Asian industrializing nations should pay higher wages to their workers. This simple formula has several difficulties, however. First, of course, these changes seem unlikely to occur any time soon. But even if they did, they would merely encourage a U.S. resurgence, not guarantee it.

The problem with the prescribed changes is that they ignore the fact that the 1980s developments reflect a new economic environment that has a life of its own. An economy is not like a driver in a car who, having taken a wrong turn, can simply turn around and drive back to the right road. The loss of markets by American companies in the United States and abroad has altered the economic landscape. Moreover, in hindsight the trend toward increasingly competitive foreign markets is of long duration. Although the decline in U.S. competitiveness accelerated rapidly during the 1980s, the decline actually appears to have begun in the early 1970s when the trade deficit in goods first emerged.

Thus, although the changes mentioned above would no doubt be conducive to a U.S. resurgence, they will not make the foreign competition go away. New foreign companies on the scene will continue to compete by moderating price increases and developing new and improved products to maintain and increase their share of world markets. To make a comeback, American companies must compete in terms of price, quality, and product specifications. Reviving the role of the United States in the world economy will require long-run commitments by American businesses to regain the prestige of U.S.-made products, including investing in new production facilities regardless of fluctuations in the value of the dollar in the 1990s.

What is the problem with chronic balance of payments deficits and growing debt to other nations? Imports and foreign investments in the United States are not intrinsically bad. In fact, they improve living conditions by competing with American industry through lower prices and higher quality products. However, a problem does emerge when deficits and debt are large. Since balance of payments deficits signify a loss of production and employment in the United States, large deficits suggest that improvements to living conditions from increased foreign competition will be outweighed by the loss of wage and profit income due to the lower economic activity in the United States. While there are no quantitative measures of when deficits are "large," a problem appears indicated when American-made products for some items are difficult to find or when American products are, or are perceived to be, inferior. That has been the case in the 1980s and it is likely to continue at least into the early 1990s.

The large and growing debt owed to foreigners adversely affects U.S. well-being in three ways. First, it results in a net outflow of U.S. interest and profits payments to other nations to finance the debt. This outflow reduces domestic business income available to invest in plant and equipment in U.S. industry, ultimately lowering living conditions in the United States. Second, a large foreign debt lessens U.S. control over its economic affairs because the need to manage the debt burden constrains Federal Reserve actions in guiding the domestic economy. The Federal Reserve typically makes decisions to tighten credit and raise interest rates, or loosen credit and lower interest rates, in response to the state of the domestic economy. However, credit and interest rates also have complex relationships to the value of the dollar. Thus, when foreign debt is large, Federal Reserve Board decisions become complicated by concerns about how proposed actions may have unwanted effects on the balance of payments deficit and the amount of foreign debt. Third, as incisively stated by Benjamin Friedman, the debt lowers respect for the United States abroad and ultimately will lead to a loss of leadership in world political affairs.[45]

* * *

In anticipating the importance of exports and imports in the American domestic economy, the analyst should focus on four broad issues:

1. For periods up to one year, greater weight should be given to changes in economic activity (for example, real gross domestic product) than to relative prices at home and abroad for their effect on the volume of export and import trade, given similar percent changes in economic activity and prices. Over longer periods, although economic activity is still more important, relative prices merit greater attention. If there is a large change in relative prices, such as one resulting from a sizable depreciation in the value of the dollar, the price effect could be larger than changes in economic activity.

2. Changes in the size of the annual federal government budget deficit and in the ownership of the federal debt by foreigners should be monitored to determine the influence of foreign holdings of the federal debt on the value of the dollar. Generally, when foreigners buy greater amounts of federal bonds and other debt securities, the value of the dollar tends to rise, and when they buy lesser amounts or are a net seller of government securities, the value of the dollar tends to fall.

3. When the value of the dollar changes, calculating the passthrough of changes on export and import prices is a useful analytic method for assessing the extent to which U.S. exporters plan to maintain their market shares in foreign countries and foreign exporters to the United States plan to maintain their shares of the U.S. market.

4. The actions of U.S. industry in competing for world markets should be monitored from anecdotal reports in newspapers and the trade press for clues about the likelihood of future improvements in the balance of payments.

Investment and Saving

High rates of investment and saving foster better living conditions at home and greater prestige for the United States abroad. Because investment and saving as a percentage of GNP declined during the 1980s, many economists have advocated that the nation consume less and save more in order to raise investment in plant and equipment. This view assumes that economic policies aimed at raising the saving rate will lead to more investment, which in turn will boost the sluggish productivity growth, raise the nation's living standard, and improve U.S. competitiveness in world markets during the 1990s (see Chapter 5 for the discussion of productivity).[46] (In this context, investment is defined as expenditures for new plant and equipment; if it were defined to include company buyouts, junk bonds, etc., there was no shortfall of investment during the 1980s.)

Investment and saving are frequently treated as being theoretically equivalent in analyses of the national economy. This tendency reflects the stylized definitions that equate the saving and investment components in the GNP accounting system, as well as the common-sense notion that investment cannot occur without saving. However, the link between saving and investment is not as simple as sometimes portrayed. Investment and saving decisions are made by different actors and for different reasons. While investment cannot occur without saving, not all saving is used for investment. In theoretical constructs, however, investment and saving are made equivalent through the interest rate, a mechanism that brings the two into equilibrium.

This section analyzes four aspects of investment and saving: (1) the accounting equivalence of investment and saving; (2) the theory and dynamics of the investment–saving relationship; (3) trends in investment and saving from the 1950s through the 1980s; and (4) implications of the investment and saving decline.

Accounting Equivalence of Investment and Saving

The conventional method of equating investment to saving is through the national income and product account approach. It is based on the following syllogism:

Gross national production = Gross national income
Production = Consumption* + Investment
Income = Consumption* + Saving
Therefore: Investment = Saving

---

*Consumption has a broad definition in this instance.
Thus, C = consumer spending + government spending + exports.
This definition implicitly includes imports, since imported finished
goods as well as imported materials used in production are
represented in the consumer, government, and export figures.

By centering on investment spending and saving flows out of current production, however, this syllogism obscures the relationship's true nature. To understand better how investment equals saving, it is useful to think of their functional roles as assets for increasing future production and income. Thus, the sum totals of investment and saving are equivalent because they are counterparts of a balance sheet. Investment represents the acquisition of assets to generate future income, and saving represents the forgoing of current consumption to allow acquisition of assets. Because investment and saving have specific meanings in this context which differ somewhat from normal usage, the terms are defined here to help clarify the concept.

National saving is the accumulation during the accounting period of certain assets by households, businesses, and government through the excess of income over expenditures. Saving represents private saving by households and businesses as well as government saving (or dissaving when budgets are in deficit) by federal, state, and local governments. Although government saving is a component of national saving, government saving affects the investment–saving equivalence only by increasing or decreasing the private assets available for private investment; as noted below, no components of government spending are defined as investment. *Household saving* is disposable personal income that is not spent on goods, services, interest payments on loans, or net personal transfers to foreigners. It includes the change in equity ownership of securities and real estate. *Business saving* is undistributed corporate profits (retained earnings after dividend payments to stockholders and corporate income taxes), plus depreciation charges of both corporations and unincorporated business. By including depreciation allowances, business saving represents the broad measure of business cash flow. (Income of unincorporated business and corporate dividends paid to individuals are included in the household saving component defined above.) *Government saving* represents the difference between government revenues and spending. Saving occurs when the budget is in a surplus, and dissaving occurs when there is a deficit. A government budget deficit reduces national saving because it is financed from the private saving of households, businesses, and foreigners. Specifically, government deficits absorb some private saving when households and businesses purchase government bonds and other debt securities, which reduces the private saving available for financing private investment.

National investment represents gross private domestic investment and net foreign investment. By definition, there is no government investment, because government-owned capital facilities (housing, schools, roads, equipment, etc.) are not separated into capital budgets and depreciated over time as capital facilities are by private business.[47] (Implications of excluding government spending as investment are discussed below.) *Gross private domestic investment* covers business inventories and capital outlays for new housing and plant and equipment before depreciation of existing facilities is deducted. The data represent all investments in the United States by both U.S.-owned business and foreign-owned business, but they exclude financial investments like stocks and bonds (as noted above, equity ownership of stocks and bonds is defined as saving), purchases of existing housing and plant and equipment facilities (such purchases transfer national assets but do not increase them), and business spending for research, development, education, and training (returns on such outlays have been difficult to estimate). *Net foreign investment* represents the excess of exports of goods, services, and income over imports, minus interest paid by the government to foreigners and transfer payments to foreigners from persons and government. When net foreign investment is positive, U.S. residents acquire more foreign assets than foreigners acquire U.S. assets. When it is negative, foreigners acquire more U.S. assets than U.S. residents acquire foreign assets, which results in net foreign disinvestment. Foreign disinvestment reduces national investment because it reduces U.S. net ownership of assets.

Table 11 summarizes the main components of saving and investment in 1989. Gross saving of $691.5 billion is the net effect resulting from $779.3 billion in private saving minus $87.8 billion for the budget deficit (dissaving) of federal, state, and local governments combined (the government deficit is the net result of a deficit for the federal government and a surplus for the aggregate of state and local governments). Of the $779.3 billion in private saving, business depreciation allowances comprise the dominant portion accounting for 71 percent; personal saving is 22 percent, and undistributed corporate profits is 7 percent. The gross investment of $674.4 billion is the net effect of $771.2 billion of domestic investment minus $96.8 billion for the deficit in net foreign investment. Of the $771.2 billion in private investment, plant and equipment investment is dominant, accounting for 66 percent; residential construction is 30 percent, and inventory change is 4 percent. Of the $96.8 billion deficit in net foreign investment, the excess of imports over exports of goods, services, and income is the largest item, accounting for 48 percent, interest paid by the government is 37 percent, and transfer payments are 15 percent.

The difference between gross investment and gross saving is represented by the statistical discrepancy in the GNP. As noted in Part A of this chapter, the statistical discrepancy is defined as the difference between the product and in-

Table 11

Gross Saving and Investment: 1989

	Billions of dollars
Gross Saving	**691.5**
Private saving	**779.3**
Personal saving	171.8
Undistributed corporate profits	53.0
Corporate depreciation allowances	346.4
Noncorporate depreciation allowances	208.0
Government surplus or deficit (–)	**–87.8**
Federal	–134.3
State and local	46.4
Gross Investment	**674.4**
Gross private domestic investment	**771.2**
New plant and equipment	511.9
New residential construction	231.0
Change in business inventories	28.3
Net foreign investment	**–96.8**
Exports less imports of goods, services, and income	–46.1
Transfer payments from persons and government	–14.8
Interest paid by government to foreigners	–36.0
Statistical discrepancy*	**–17.0**

Source: Bureau of Economic Analysis, U.S. Department of Commerce, *Survey of Current Business,* July 1990.

*The entire statistical discrepancy in the GNP appears in the saving and investment data. See text.

come sides of the GNP, which results from inaccuracies and inconsistencies in the various data sources. The saving and investment measure include the entire statistical discrepancy because the measure encompasses those elements among the product and income sides of the household, business, government, and foreign sectors of the GNP for which the underlying data are derived from unrelated data sources, and thus contain the sum total of the statistical inaccuracies and inconsistencies.

Theory and Dynamics of the Investment–Saving Relationship

In economic theory, a distinction is made between *actual* and *planned* investment and saving. The equivalence discussed above refers to actual investment and saving, that is, after the fact. Planned investment and planned saving are not necessarily equal, because investors and savers are mostly different parties with differing motivations. Thus, before the actual transactions occur, investors may plan to acquire assets that cost more than savers plan to accumulate, or vice versa.

Not all households and businesses invest their savings equally. Some invest the total amount of their savings, while others invest only a portion. The accumulation of assets by some households and businesses is used by others to finance their investments in real assets. The investment–saving equivalence occurs after a myriad of intermediate transactions by lenders, borrowers, and savers in the financial system. For example, banks create deposits when they extend loans to households and businesses, households and businesses purchase commercial paper and bonds which provide direct loans to business, and companies raise new equity capital by selling new corporate stock. Businesses invest only some of the borrowed and equity funds in new housing construction, plant and equipment, and inventories. Other funds may be used for household purchases of goods and services and business payments for operating expenses.

To understand how new saving generated from production in a quarter, year, or other period is equivalent to investment in the same period, recall the identity equations in the beginning of this section. Current production not consumed by households, government, a ıd exports must be absorbed by business investment because investment is the only other outlet for the production. The buildup or depletion of inventories is the accounting balance wheel that makes investment always equal to saving. For example, suppose spending for housing construction and plant and equipment is strong and exports exceed imports, but domestic production does not keep pace with this investment growth. The result will be that investments use up more goods than are produced, which will reduce the inventory level in the previous period by the equivalent amount. In contrast, suppose spending for housing construction and plant and equipment is weak and imports exceed exports, but domestic production is not scaled back to the slower pace of these investments. Then the investments will use up fewer goods than are produced and thus raise inventories by the equivalent amount.[48] In this process, inventory movements on the "product side" of the GNP also have a myriad of counterpart movements on the "income side" of the GNP, as personal, business, and government incomes directly reflect changes in production.

Trends from the 1950s through the 1980s

Figures 26 and 27 show gross saving and gross investment as a percentage of GNP for each of the four decades from the 1950s through the 1980s. They indicate the same pattern: relative stability from the 1950s through the 1970s, followed by a noticeable decline during the 1980s. Typically, the decline started in the 1970s, but broadened to more components and accelerated sharply in the 1980s. Except for business saving, the levels in the 1980s were lower than in the preceding three decades.

Gross saving (Figure 26) rose from 16 percent of the GNP in the 1950s to 17 percent in the 1970s, and then declined to 14 percent in the 1980s. Personal saving accounted for approximately 55 percent and the increase in the federal

Figure 26. **Gross Saving as a Percentage of GNP: 1950s–1980s**

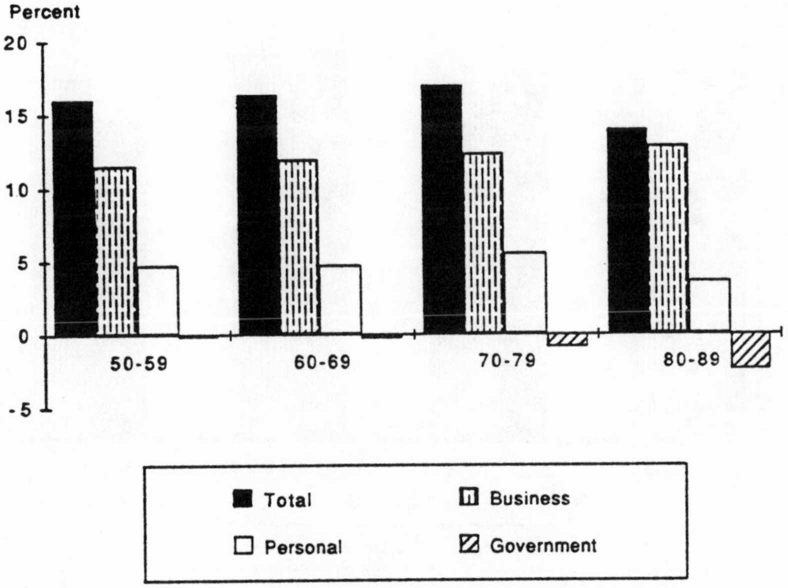

Note: Based on Bureau of Economic Analysis data in current dollars.

government deficit for 45 percent of the 3 percentage point decline in the 1980s; business saving increased during the decade. The only advance indication of the 1980s decline is the 0.6 percentage point increase in the government deficit during the 1970s.

Gross investment (Figure 27) rose from 16 percent of the GNP in the 1950s to 17 percent in the 1970s, and declined to 14 percent in the 1980s. Domestic investment accounted for one-third and net foreign investment for two-thirds of the 3 percentage point decline; foreign investment was actually negative during the 1980s, for the first time since before World War I. The only advance sign of this decline in gross investment was the 0.4 percentage point fall in foreign investment during the 1970s; domestic investment rose 1.1 percentage point in the 1970s.

Implications of the Investment and Saving Decline

Analysis

The relative decline of investment and saving during the 1980s reversed the upward trends of the previous two decades. This reversal occurred despite the

Figure 27. **Gross Investment as a Percentage of GNP: 1950s–1980s**

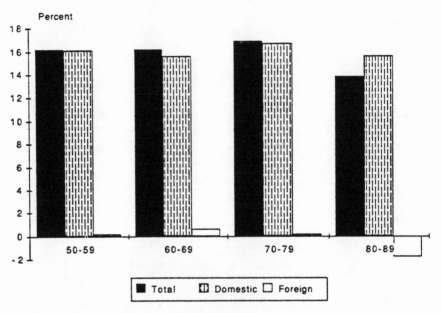

Note: Based on Bureau of Economic Analysis data in current dollars.

fact that the federal government directly acted to promote more investment and saving. Under the general rubric of "get the government off the backs of the people," President Reagan attempted to raise productivity and economic growth and lower inflation by reducing income taxes ("supply-side economics"), reducing regulatory standards in implementing social legislation ("regulatory relief"), and relaxing enforcement of the antitrust laws. Personal and business income tax rates were reduced far more in the early 1980s than in previous tax cuts. Executive agency regulations that spell out the specifics for administering the laws lessened business responsibility relating to environmental protection; consumer protection against harmful food, drugs, and other products; and worker health, safety, and pensions. This deregulatory program considerably expanded the regulatory reviews instituted by presidents Ford and Carter by (a) requiring that all regulations issued by government agencies be approved by the Office of Management and Budget (OMB), and (b) basing the OMB oversight on a net benefit analysis of differentials between benefits and costs of the regulations. William Niskanen, a member of the president's Council of Economic Advisers from 1981 to 1985 and a supporter of the deregulatory program, concludes that the net benefit criterion was often at odds with the legislation underlying the regulations, and therefore the net benefit criterion could not withstand challenges in court.

The laws needed to be changed to achieve the goals of the deregulatory program, but they were not changed because of political opposition in Congress.[49] The federal government also lessened antitrust enforcement against monopolistic practices and took a benign view of the surge in business mergers and takeovers due to junk bond financing. The antitrust program began to concentrate on collusion to fix prices but to relax enforcement of company acquisitions and other practices that may substantially lessen competition or tend to create a monopoly.[50] In a critique of the philosophy and implementation of the deregulatory program, Susan Tolchin and Martin Tolchin conclude that use of cost–benefit analysis in the program is not appropriate for many of the social and economic issues involved in regulations.[51]

In 1990, President Bush reinvigorated the deregulatory program by establishing the President's Council on Competitiveness, which is chaired by the vice-president and composed of the attorney general, secretary of the Treasury, secretary of Commerce, director of the Office of Management and Budget, White House chief of staff, and chairman of the Council of Economic Advisers.[52] The council reviews selected regulations that agencies submit to the OMB for approval, and its cabinet-level status puts more pressure on individual agency heads (than the OMB alone can do) to lower government standards for the environment, drugs, labor, telecommunications, etc., below what the agency considers desirable. This is a sequel to the Presidential Task Force on Regulatory Relief of the early 1980s which the then Vice President Bush chaired.

The intent of these policies in regard to investment was to unleash entrepreneurial vitality and thus increase plant and equipment investment by raising profit incentives both before and after the payment of income taxes. Gross profits (before the payment of income taxes) were expected to rise in the relaxed regulatory environment because of (a) lower business spending and responsibility for worker, environmental, and consumer protections, and (b) fewer restrictions on antitrust restraints of trade, junk bond financing, and use of savings and loan deposits. Net profits (after the payment of income taxes) were fostered by lowering income taxes, which allowed business to retain a higher share of gross profits, although this gain was partially offset by the Tax Reform Act of 1986.

In regard to saving, the intent of these policies was to give households an incentive to save a greater proportion of their income by reducing taxes on both job and property income. With respect to job earnings, the idea was that workers would work harder and longer to raise their wages and salaries and thus have more income to save from. With respect to property earnings, the idea was that households would save more of their income in order to increase their property holdings and thus receive more income from interest, dividends, and rent. But despite the tax incentives as well as the higher interest rates, the saving rate declined.

The policy question is: Why were the prognostications that more investment and saving would result from lower income taxes and the relaxed regulatory environment wrong? The answer is threefold. First, the presumed effect of taxes and regulations on entrepreneurial and worker activity was greatly overstated. Most people who work need a current income, and the wealthy who do not need a current income but work anyway usually do so for feelings of self-worth. In either case, the effect of taxes on work behavior seems marginal. Similarly, the lower taxes and the relaxed worker, environmental, and consumer regulations have not translated into any demonstrable signs of invigorating American business. On the contrary, as noted below, the government policy of allowing unusual financial manipulations in corporate takeovers and buyouts has diverted corporate funds and executive energy into the transfer of assets while failing to raise productivity or plant and equipment investment. In short, the expected behavior modification did not materialize because it was premised on the mistaken notion that taxes and regulations in the United States significantly affect American worker effort and American entrepreneurial vitality.

Second, the sharp tax rate decline in part negatively affected investment because of the resulting interest rate increases. David Stockman, director of the Office of Management and Budget from 1981 to 1985, concludes that lowering taxes without making commensurate reductions in federal spending led to a large increase in the annual federal budget deficit, which required the federal government to increase substantially its borrowing from private savers.[53] The government borrowing resulted in higher market interest rates and higher real interest rates (market interest rate minus the inflation rate) than would otherwise have occurred (see Chapter 7 under Money Supply and Interest Rates). The abnormally high interest rates, which were below the extraordinarily high market rates of the late 1970s and early 1980s but higher than the real interest rates of those periods, did not stimulate higher saving. The high interest rates directly discouraged plant and equipment investment because they increased the cost of borrowing. And they indirectly reduced plant and equipment investment when they harmed the international competitiveness of U.S. business. Thus, the high U.S. interest rates relative to those in other countries attracted foreign savings into the United States, which led to a sharp rise in the value of the dollar (see previous section on Exports and Imports). The inflated value of the dollar led to overpriced exports and underpriced imports and thus reduced the demand for U.S. products. The end result was that U.S. production and therefore U.S. plant and equipment investment were reduced.

Third, in this environment of high interest rates that discouraged borrowing for investment and of the overvalued dollar that depressed U.S. production and investment, executives increasingly spent their time on financial activities like corporate mergers and takeovers in the world of junk bonds and leveraged buyouts, as well as subsequent divestitures of some previous acquisitions, rather than on improving company products and competitiveness through investments in plant and equipment and spending for research and development. Indeed, some people in the investment banking industry went so far as to manipulate the securities markets, a practice that the courts have since found illegal and that has led to prison sentences. These financial manipulations transfer assets from one group to another while substantially raising the debt of the reorganized companies. Walter Adams and James Brock say this process provided a quick way to make money for corporate raiders, investment bankers, and lawyers, as well as for some existing stockholders, but did not add to the industrial base of the nation.[54] In an analysis of mergers in manufacturing industries during the 1960s and early 1970s, David Ravenscraft and F. Scherer conclude that these mergers led to a net loss of productivity for the nation's economy. They also note that although they did not analyze the merger movement of the 1980s, there are sufficient similarities between the two periods to suggest that their conclusions may also be relevant for the 1980s.[55]

The greater debt resulting from the leveraged buyouts appears also to have affected company investment and employment. Richard Cantor concludes from a study of companies with high and low levels of debt that companies with high debt tend to have more volatile investment and employment.[56] This occurs because the need to make interest payments on the high debt makes these companies more tentative than low-debt companies about expanding their operations when business is weak and the cash flow from internally generated funds of profits and depreciation declines.

Some of these mergers and takeovers undoubtedly improved the efficiency of individual companies. In some companies, the resulting reorganizations led to a desirable trimming of fat through downsizing. Moreover, some studies of the 1980s, such as those by Frank Lichtenberg and by Paul Healy, Krishna Palepu, and Richard Ruback, found overall benefits to the economy from the 1980s mergers.[57] However, the jury is still out on the question of what effect these mergers had on productivity. The macroeconomic indicators for the period show no robust increase in plant and equipment investment or productivity, but they do show a distinct decline in the United States' international competitiveness during the 1980s. In the author's judgment, the overriding result has been a more fragile debt structure that leaves many American businesses more vulnerable to bankruptcy during a recession. In the case of an economic slump, an outbreak of massive bankruptcies will have a snowball effect, sharply intensifying the decline. Recent analyses by Benjamin Friedman and James O'Leary conclude that the extraordinarily high debt of American business places the country at a greater risk of a major economic decline.[58]

Future Policies

The lag in investment and saving and the accompanying decline in U.S. competitiveness are insidious. They are gradually slowing the economic growth rate in the United States and eroding both the U.S. living standard and the nation's prestige and leadership in the world community. Unfortunately, the gradual nature of the deterioration tends to obscure the danger. Without a dramatic crisis to call attention to the problem, a concentrated effort to upgrade the nation's industrial capability is hard to energize. Government and business more typically focus on the challenge of stabilizing the cyclical fluctuations of expansions and recessions to maintain a steadier rate of long-term economic growth. But the consequences of the decline in U.S. competitiveness are serious and suggest the nation should begin to spend more energy addressing this problem. An agenda to reverse the decline in competitiveness will have to take a longer view of the nation's economic strength in three major areas: (1) the macroeconomic environment of the federal budget deficit and high interest rates; (2) the microeconomic behavior of some business enterprises that concentrate exclusively on short-term profits; and (3) the current system of national accounting which excludes certain types of government spending as investment.

The huge federal budget deficits of recent years have driven interest rates significantly higher than their historic norm and have hindered government spending for needed investments in housing and education. To reduce the deficit, some combination of higher taxes and lower spending will be necessary. The higher taxes should be progressive in accord with political principles of equity and the ability to pay, but should not stultify individual initiative and incentive. These goals may be accomplished either through the income tax or through a progressive consumption tax that encourages household saving.[59] As noted earlier in the section entitled Government Spending and Finances, the five-year deficit reduction plan adopted in 1990 is a beginning in this effort. However, significant progress in reducing the deficit is not likely unless candidates for president and Congress emerge who can convince the voters of middle America that the deficit is their problem and that it is in their own interest to pay higher taxes and reduce government spending. Such spending reductions will be more palatable politically if they occur in favorite programs of conservatives as well as liberals.[60]

Second, reversing the decline in U.S. competitiveness will require some changes in the microeconomic behavior of businesses. The recent fights for control of American businesses have lead to a preoccupation with short-term profits in the operations of many companies. This effect is particularly apparent in the corporate takeovers and buyouts noted above. Highly publicized cases have made most people aware of the most blatant abuses, such as insider trading. Several states, including Indiana, Ohio, Delaware, Massachusetts, and Pennsylvania, have passed laws restricting attempts to gain control of companies incorporated in their states. However, stronger federal laws regulating the governance and financing of public corporations may be required to address the national dimensions of the takeover problem on a uniform basis. Such laws should maintain the free sale of corporate stock but at the same time eliminate the financial manipulation and corporate debt that result from takeover and buyout fights and that impede a longer view of company investments in plant and equipment and spending for research and development.

Third, a longer view of the nation's needs also needs to be incorporated into our budgeting and accounting systems. Currently, some government expenditures, such as for education and transportation, are treated as outlays but in fact represent investment that generates long-term improvements in productivity. Various analysts disagree, however, about the extent to which public investment increases productivity.[61] A capital budget that redefines such expenditures as investment would have two significant accounting results. First, because all revenues remain in the current budget but the figure for spending is decreased, the current deficit would be reduced (or the surplus increased); second, because the government deficit is treated as dissaving, which is deducted from private saving, the redefinition would also significantly raise national saving.

Robert Eisner has developed such a capital budget for the federal budget by removing government investment spending from the current budget and placing it in a newly created capital budget that includes spending for capital facilities for pollution control (including federal grants to states and localities for this purpose), and all other federal spending for construction, equipment, research and development, and education and training.[62] He concludes that in 1984 the federal deficit was equal to federal investment so that, except for depreciation charges for these investments, there was no deficit.

Some state governments currently use a capital budget, which allows them to conform with state constitutional requirements that the budget be balanced. If adopted by the federal government, the capital budget would bring the federal budget into line with business accounting practices. Businesses typically depreciate plant and equipment assets and deduct them in increments from taxable income over the lifetime of the asset (although businesses do not capitalize outlays for research and development and employee training since they are treated as current expense items on income tax returns).

Despite the theoretical advantages of the capital budget, however, adopting one in the near future would be risky. As Barry Bosworth notes, unscrupulous politicians could make revenues falsely appear in balance with expenditures by defining a broad spectrum of government programs as investment even though appropriate financing has not been provided.[63] Business enterprises are disciplined by the need to make a profit or face bankruptcy, and no accounting technique can disguise which is the reality for long. The federal government, however, is not subject to this discipline because it can always borrow from private savers or, if necessary, directly from the Federal Reserve system itself. While the Federal Reserve usually buys only existing government securities from private owners, it can act as a lender of last resort and help finance the deficit by buying newly issued government debt securities; such "lending" by the Federal Reserve system is potentially highly inflationary, however, because it greatly expands the money supply (see Chapter 7).

The practical effect of adopting a capital budget in the early 1990s would be to diminish the incentive to reduce the deficit, resulting in continued substantial annual increases in federal borrowing and the accompanying high interest rates. Thus, while excluding certain government spending from investment hinders economic analyses of investment and saving, it seems unwise to develop a capital budget until the federal deficit is truly under control.

But even before developing a capital budget, it is desirable to have supplementary measures of investment that include education, research and development, transportation, and perhaps other items as investment. As noted by Carol Carson and Bruce Grimm, the U.S. government plans to develop such measures as "satellites" to the national economic accounts.[64] These satellites are included in the framework of the System of National Accounts developed by the United Nations; the SNA was discussed previously in this chapter.

Postscript on Definitions

In comparing investment in the United States to that in other nations, Robert Lipsey and Irving Kravis redefine investment to include spending for consumer durable goods, education, and research and development, as well as the conventional plant and equipment and housing.[65] Education and research and development improve productivity by improving the quality of the labor force and technology, while consumer durables increase productivity by facilitating automobile transportation to work and by reducing housework. Using this broadened definition, in 1980 U.S. investment as a percentage of gross domestic product was at 97 percent of the average for seven European nations and Japan, as compared to 90 percent under the conventional definition. This calculation suggests that lagging investment is not responsible for the decline in U.S. international competitiveness. However, there are several problems with this interpretation. First, the broader investment measure requires considerable statistical estimating which significantly reduces the reliability of the figures. Second, while some consumer durables do lead to productivity increases, it is not reasonable to treat them on a par with plant and equipment investment as an income-producing asset. Indeed, equating housing investment with plant and equipment is not reasonable either. Housing does not produce as much of an increase in productivity as plant and equipment, and excluding it from the international comparisons would probably further widen the gap in investment between the United States and other countries. Third, the returns on expenditures for education and research and development are much less certain than the returns on plant and equipment investment. While the United States spends more on education than other countries, the investment has not improved the low-quality education of high school graduates or the dearth of college students in the sciences and engineering. And despite the continued greater dollar level of spending on research and development by American companies than by foreign companies, U.S. industry is no longer the preeminent leader in technological breakthroughs.

As noted in this and previous sections, the decline in U.S. competitiveness that emerged in the early 1970s was seriously aggravated by the rise in the value of the dollar in the first half of the 1980s, the relatively high interest rates resulting from the large federal budget deficit in the 1980s, the mergers and takeovers of the 1980s, and the concomitant lack of commitment to long-term investments by American industry. All of these developments had negative effects on plant and equipment investment. *In short, using a more broadly defined measure of investment will not explain away the role of lessened plant and equipment investment and national saving in the decline in U.S. competitiveness in the 1980s.*

Summary

Analyses of GNP trends may take both an overall top-down perspective and a building-block approach focusing on the main components. Total GNP and alternative summary GNP measures provide the overall view; the household, business, government, and international components give insight into the factors driving the overall movements.

Total GNP and Alternative Summary GNP Measures

The summary measures of the national accounts besides the GNP are final sales, final sales to domestic purchasers, gross domestic product, command GNP, and GNP on the income side. The GNP and the alternative summary GNP measures differ in the way they treat inventories, foreign trade, and statistical errors. The main difference in these measures over the nine expansions and nine recessions of the postwar period lies in the effect additions and depletions of business inventories have on total GNP. While inventory buildups in expansions are not nearly as important as inventory declines in recessions, monitoring inventories in expansions is important in determining if the buildup appears to be in balance or excessive in relation to sales. For periods shorter than the entire expansion or recession, the alternative GNP measures sometimes give slightly different pictures of overall trends in economic activity.

GNP Components

The four main GNP components are consumer expenditures, private investment, government spending, and exports and imports. When observing these components, the analyst should remember the key linkage of income to spending. For example, consumer spending is affected by personal income; plant and equipment investment is affected by business profits; government spending is affected by tax receipts; and exports are affected by income abroad, and imports by income in the United States.

Consumer expenditures for durable goods, nondurable goods, and services account for the bulk of the GNP and have also tended to be a stabilizing factor in business cycles. Of the three kinds of consumer expenditures, spending for consumer durables (items that ordinarily last at least three years, such as cars, furniture, and household appliances) is by far the most cyclical. The cyclical stability of consumer spending could be affected by shifts in the relative importance of durables, nondurables, and services, which could make consumer expenditures either more or less stabilizing in expansions and recessions.

The main source of financing for consumer spending is disposable personal income. Consumer purchasing power over the business cycle tends to be stabilized through the net effect of: (a) the rise in unemployment insurance payments in recessions, and (b) the rise in tax collections in expansions and decline in tax collections in recessions, because the federal government's progressive income tax takes proportionately more money out of the income stream as individual incomes rise to higher tax brackets. The indexing of federal income taxes for inflation starting with 1985 income will probably enhance the cyclical stability of disposable income in recessions and lessen it in expansions. Other important factors affecting consumer spending are how consumers view the macroeconomic environment for employment and inflation, the relationship of consumer installment credit to personal income, and personal saving rates.

Private investment for business plant and equipment and residential construction, along with inventory accumulation and depletion discussed previously with the alternative summary GNP measures, has the most extreme cyclical movements of all GNP components. *Plant and equipment investment* for new buildings and machinery is often deferrable, as business can "make do" with the existing facilities. This, plus the fact that business profits—the main motivation for plant and equipment investment—have extreme cyclical movements in their own right, causes investment in capital facilities to increase much more in expansions and to decline much more in recessions from GNP. Trends in business capital appropriations, contracts and orders for plant and equipment, and projections of plant and equipment spending provide advance indicators of plant and equipment investment.

Another funding source for plant and equipment investment is the depreciation allowances for wear and tear and obsolescence of plant and equipment which are deducted as an expense on business income tax returns. Tax cuts related to the accelerated depreciation allowances in the Economic Recovery Tax Act of 1981 were intended to stimulate plant and equipment investment. However, taxes do not appear to have a major affect on investment in factories and machinery, yet they may have a greater impact on certain other investments such as office buildings and shopping centers. The decline in net investment as a percentage of the GNP during the 1980s is an indicator of the decline in U.S. international competitiveness.

Residential construction of single-family homes and townhouses, multifamily apartment buildings, and hotels, motels, and dormitories is relatively small compared with other GNP components, but it is important for two reasons. It has a secondary impact on economic activity by generating consumer spending for items like furniture and household appliances, and it tends to lead business cycles, turning down before a general recession begins and turning up before recovery.

The long-term demand for housing construction is mainly determined by population trends and household formation. Demographic projections indicate an annual average of 1.3 million new housing units in the 1990s, unless there are unexpected sharp changes in household formation, geographic migration within the United States, or government programs to replace substandard housing. The year-to-year short-term demand for new housing fluctuates considerably, mainly in response to variations in personal income, employment, interest rates, and housing prices.

Government spending by federal, state, and local governments for civilian and defense needs has grown considerably over the postwar period. Government spending and taxation have a greater stabilizing effect on the overall economy through the "automatic stabilizers" of income taxes and unemployment insurance, which take proportionately more money out of the income stream in expansions and put proportionately more money into the income stream in recessions. In terms of charges in budget surpluses and deficits, the federal budget has had a greater stabilizing role than state and local budgets in most of the postwar expansions and recessions.

The federal budget is also used as a fiscal policy tool through the concept of the "cyclically adjusted" or "high employment" budgets. These indicate whether the federal budget's posture at any given time, as well as whether its direction from year to year, is inherently stimulating (in a deficit) or restraining (in a surplus) on the income stream. The five-year plan to reduce the federal deficit adopted in 1990 is a start in the right direction, but much more is necessary to reduce the deficit substantially in the 1990s.

Exports and imports of goods, services, and income from foreign investments have accounted for a growing share of the American economy over the postwar period, which also makes the economy more subject to economic and political developments abroad. Three main factors determining the demand for exports and imports are economic activity at home (imports) and abroad (exports), relative prices of competing American and foreign goods and services, and the foreign exchange value of the dollar. Several studies indicate that economic activity is more important than prices in determining the volume of exports and imports. This is particularly evident for periods up to a year and is valid for longer periods as well, although prices are increasingly important with the passage of time. Because the foreign exchange value of the dollar affects relative prices in the United States and abroad, it has the same secondary importance to economic activity as was noted for prices.

The large balance of payments deficit that appeared in the 1980s reflected the deteriorating competitive position of American business in world markets. Factors that should be monitored in efforts to improve the U.S. competitive position include foreign holdings of federal debt obligations, passthroughs of changes in the value of the dollar to prices of exports and imports, and actions taken by U.S. businesses in competing for world markets.

Investment and saving affect living conditions at home as well as U.S. prestige in world affairs. As a percentage of the GNP, investment and saving declined in the 1980s after gradual increases in the previous decades. The decline in the 1980s occurred despite tax cuts, lower regulatory standards, and relaxed enforcement of antitrust laws, all of which were intended to spur investment and saving. Investment and saving will not increase unless presidential and congressional candidates convince the American people of the need to reduce the federal deficit, and unless U.S. businesses refocus their attention toward productive investments and away from company mergers and buyouts.

REVIEW QUESTIONS

GNP CONCEPTS

• The GNP on the "product side" and the "income side" is the same in total (except for statistical problems). However, the components of the two measures are different. What is the nature of the difference?

• What type of additional information would be needed to develop supplementary GNP measures that would reflect a concept of well-being in contrast to the conventional concept of production?

• GNP figures are provided in absolute current dollars, absolute constant dollars (real GNP), and rates of change of both.

   a. Why is the main interest in rates of change of real GNP?

   b. Give examples of analytic uses of the absolute GNP figures.

• Government purchases in the GNP exclude transfer payments for social security and unemployment benefits, even though they are part of government budgets and affect the economy.

   a. Why are transfer payments excluded?

   b. How is this limited measure of government dealt with
      in economic analysis?

• Why is it deceptive to look only at "net exports" (exports minus imports) without considering the export and import components separately?

• Why are valuation adjustments for inventories and depreciation allow-ances more important during highly inflationary periods than when prices rise slowly?

SUMMARY GNP MEASURES

• There are several alternative measures of the GNP, such as final sales, final sales to domestic purchasers, gross domestic product, command GNP, and GNP minus the statistical discrepancy. What overall purpose do they serve?

INVENTORIES

• What is the difference between planned and unplanned inventories? Are they identified separately in inventory data?
• Anecdotal reports in the press mention examples of American business relying on smaller inventories than in the past, including the Japanese concept of "just-in-time inventories." What figures would you look at to assess how widespread this is?

CONSUMER SPENDING

• Consumer spending has been a major factor in moderating the extremes of cyclical expansions and recessions.
>   a. What trends over the past forty years are responsible for this?
>   b. Give an example of what could change this in the future.

• Why is disposable personal income a better measure of consumer purchasing power than personal income?
• Both unemployment benefits and the progressive income tax give greater stability to disposable income over business cycles.
>   a. Explain.
>   b. How can this be affected in highly inflationary periods by the indexing of inflation in the tax laws?

• Why is the saving rate problematic in short-term forecasts of consumer spending?
• Because of the lack of information in consumer borrowing data on house-holds in different income groups, debt burden (installment credit as a percentage of personal income) is difficult to use as a signal that borrowing is excessive, which in turn presages a cutback in borrowing and spending. Thus, instead of being an advance indicator of a downturn in consumer borrowing and spending, debt burden is of concern because of its later potential snowball effect once a recession sets in. Explain.

PLANT AND EQUIPMENT INVESTMENT

• What makes plant and equipment investment have extreme cyclical movements? Discuss in terms of the nature of investment and business profits.

• Why do tax depreciation allowances for plant and equipment on business income tax returns moderate the cyclical volatility of funds available for investment?

• In surveys of business plans to invest in plant and equipment, the experience has been that projections of spending one year ahead have an average forecasting error of plus or minus 3 percent. How would you use data on business profits and on construction contracts and equipment orders to check the reasonableness of business investment plans?

RESIDENTIAL CONSTRUCTION

• Residential construction accounts for only 4 to 5 percent of the GNP, but it gets a lot of analytic attention. Why?

• Short-run forecasts of housing construction emphasize trends in personal income, employment, mortgage interest rates, and housing prices, while long-run forecasts focus on expected demographic trends in terms of the number of households.

a. Why is this distinction made?

b. Give an example of when the short-run forecast should include demographic trends.

GOVERNMENT SPENDING AND FINANCES

• The federal government budget moderates the extremes of cyclical expansions and recessions through its role as an automatic stabilizer.

a. Explain both the spending and revenue aspects of automatic stabilizers in terms of unemployment benefits and the progressive income tax.

b. How may the automatic stabilizing property be affected by the 1985 change in the income tax law, which provides for the indexing of income taxes for inflation?

• State and local government budgets also tend to be cyclically stabilizing, although they lack the innate automatic aspects of the federal budget. Yet experience since 1975 has been that it is important to include the effect of state and local government budgets in the consideration of the stabilizing impact of government on the economy. What is that experience?

• When the president submits the federal budget for the coming fiscal year to

Congress, the spending and revenue projections are based on assumed rates of economic growth, unemployment, and inflation. What is the difference between the spending and revenue projections and the subsequent actual spending and revenues if economic growth, unemployment, and inflation all turn out to be lower than anticipated in the projections?

	Spending		Revenues	
Economic growth	____higher	____lower	____higher	____lower
Unemployment	____higher	____lower	____higher	____lower
Inflation	____higher	____lower	____higher	____lower

• Why is the five-year deficit reduction plan of the Omnibus Budget Reconciliation Act of 1990 only a first step in reducing the federal budget deficit?

EXPORTS AND IMPORTS

• Why are exports more related to economic growth abroad while imports are more related to economic growth in the United States?
• What long-run factors could tend to moderate the improved competitive position of American exports and imports resulting from the decline in the dollar during 1985–87? Discuss in relation to economic growth trends at home and abroad, pricing policies of foreign producers, plant and equipment investment by American producers, and protectionist sentiment at home and abroad.
• Why is there particular interest in the balance of trade as distinct from the balance of payments in discussions of the American competitive position?
• How can indexes of the value of the dollar that combine foreign currencies into a single number sometimes be misleading for their effect on the competitive position of American exports and imports? Discuss in terms of individual countries' trade volumes.
• Why are the globalization of production, the Leontief Paradox, and the terms of trade long-term rather than short-term issues?
• How do price passthroughs of changes in the value of the dollar affect the competitive position of U.S. products in world markets?
• What problems are generally assumed to have caused the deterioration of the balance of payments and the United States becoming a debtor nation in the 1980s?
• Why will a reversal of these problems in favor of the United States not necessarily result in U.S.-made products becoming preeminent in world markets?
• What is the problem with continued large deficits in the balance of payments and the associated growing foreign debt?

INVESTMENT AND SAVING

• How does investment equal saving if planned investment does not equal planned saving?

• Why are analyses of investment and saving related to long-term productivity and living conditions rather than to short-term cyclical fluctuations?

• What makes the decline in investment and saving during the 1980s difficult for elected officials to come to grips with?

• How would increased purchases of U.S. goods at home and abroad and a reduction in the federal government budget deficit affect investment and saving?

• A capital budget includes government spending for education and job training, research and development, and transportation facilities as investment.

        a. How would a capital budget affect the measure of the federal deficit?

        b. What is the governance problem with a capital budget?

• How would the "satellite" accounts planned for the System of National Accounts affect the GNP measure of investment?

NOTES

1. Use of demand and supply terminology refers to the distinction between the components of the GNP on the product and income sides. In total, both sides measure "production." The difference between the two is in the demand and supply nature of the components.

2. Carol S. Carson and Jeanette Honsa, "The United Nations System of National Accounts: An Introduction," *Survey of Current Business,* June 1990.

3. "Nominal" and "real" are the terms commonly used to denote the distinction in GNP measures with and without inflation. Some may object to these words as misleading; there is nothing nominal about the GNP in current prices because this is the only actual GNP, and there is nothing real about the GNP in constant prices because in the everyday world items are bought and sold in today's price, not in the unchanged prices of a particular year.

4. Edward Steinberg, "What's in a Base Year? The Net Exports Paradox," *The Margin,* September/October 1990, p. 40.

5. Allan H. Young, "Alternative Measures of Real GNP," *Survey of Current Business,* April 1989.

6. Because the growth rates are calculated from similar stages of the business cycle in which the final years of the comparisons—1909, 1929, 1948, 1959, 1969, 1979, and 1989—are years of economic expansion, they provide a consistent representation of long-term trends; calculating the rates from terminal periods that include both expansion and recession years would have distorted the averages.

7. As a technical note to the treatment of housing in the GNP, housing rents are included in consumer spending because they are current services, but purchases of new or existing housing are treated as a business, and consequently are in the investment component of the GNP, which is discussed in a later section.

8. An alternative measure of personal saving, developed by the Federal Reserve Board as part of the flow of funds accounts, is based on the change in net assets of households—that is, assets less liabilities. The assets are ownership of bank deposits, securities, pension reserves, owner-occupied homes, consumer durables, and unincorporated business plant, equipment, and inventories. The liabilities are debt and borrowing by households and unincorporated businesses. During most of the 1980s, these saving measures were 25 to 50 percent higher than the saving estimates derived from disposable personal income less spending discussed in the text. The differential is mainly due to the different data bases used in preparing both measures and to a definitional difference. The flow of funds measure counts consumer durables as saving, while the personal income measure excludes consumer durables.

The two measures cannot be reconciled statistically because the various sources of the differences cannot be quantified. For the type of economic analysis discussed in this book, either measure is acceptable so long as the same one is used over time, although most references to personal saving are to the income less spending measure.

9. Because personal income includes nonhousehold investment income of life insurance companies and nonprofit organizations, which account for 3 percent of personal income in 1989, the saving rate is 0.2 to 0.3 percentage points lower than it would be if the nonhousehold items were not included, assuming saving rates of 5 to 7 percent. This is a relatively small absolute amount, and because these components as a share of personal income are relatively stable, they do not significantly affect the saving rate over time.

10. The two main uses of home equity loans are for home improvements and repayment of other debts. See Glenn B. Canner, Charles A. Luckett, and Thomas A. Durkin, "Mortgage Refinancing," *Federal Reserve Bulletin,* August 1990, p. 609.

11. Some studies use disposable personal income rather than personal income as used here in the denominator of the consumer debt burden measure. The use of disposable personal income raises the proportion by about 2.5 percentage points, but the movements over time in both figures are similar. Personal income is used here because it is regularly charted in the saving ratio in the *Survey of Current Business.*

12. Charles A. Luckett and James D. August, "The Growth of Consumer Debt," *Federal Reserve Bulletin,* June 1985, p. 391.

13. As a historical footnote, John Keynes recognized the analytical usefulness of statistical measures of depreciation. But because of the imprecision in defining depreciation, he relegated the application of statistical measures to description rather than to explanatory analysis. Writing of A. C. Pigou in 1936, Keynes says:

"Moreover, he is unable to devise any satisfactory formula to evaluate new equipment against old when, owing to changes in technique, the two are not identical. I believe that the concept at which Professor Pigou is aiming is the right and appropriate concept for economic analysis. But, until a satisfactory system of units has been adopted, its precise definition is an impossible task. The problem of comparing one real output with another and of then calculating net output by setting off new items of equipment against the wastage of old items presents conundrums which permit, one can confidently say, of no solution. . . . But the proper place for such things as net real output and the general level of prices lies within the field of historical and statistical description, and their purpose should be to satisfy historical or social curiosity, a purpose for which perfect precision—such as our causal analysis requires, whether or not our knowledge of the actual values of the relevant quantities is complete or exact—is neither usual nor necessary. To say that net output today is greater, but the price-level lower, than ten years ago or one year ago, is a proposition of a similar character to the statement that Queen Victoria was a better queen but not a happier woman than Queen Elizabeth—a proposition not without meaning and not without interest, but unsuitable as material for the differential calculus. Our precision will be a mock precision if we try to use such partly vague and non-quantitative concepts as the basis of quantitative analysis."

John Maynard Keynes, *The General Theory of Employment, Interest, and Money* (Harcourt Brace Jovanovich: [1936] 1964 reprint), pp. 39–40. However, later in the book, Keynes seems to acknowledge the usefulness of depreciation as reported on income tax returns, although he is not fully comfortable with it (pp. 56–60).

14. Benjamin M. Friedman, *Day of Reckoning: The Consequences of American Economic Policy under Reagan and After* (Random House: 1988), pp. 223–32.

15. Depreciation is almost all of the capital consumption allowance category in the GNP, the remainder being accidental damage to capital facilities.

16. Leonard Sahling and M. A. Akhtar, "What Is Behind the Capital Spending Boom?" *Quarterly Review,* Federal Reserve Bank of New York: Winter 1984–85, p. 27.

17. Robert S. McIntyre and Dean C. Tipps, *The Failure of Corporate Tax Incentives* (Citizens for Tax Justice: January 1985.)

18. Barry P. Bosworth, "Taxes and the Investment Recovery," *Brookings Papers on Economic Activity,* 1985:1.

19. Herman L. Liebling, Peter T. Bidwell, and Karen E. Hall, "The Recent Performance of Anticipation Surveys and Econometric Model Projections of Investment Spending in the United States," *Journal of Business,* October 1976; Karen Bradley and Avril Euba, "How Accurate Are Capital Spending Surveys?" *Quarterly Review,* Federal Reserve Bank of New York, Winter 1977–78; and J. Steven Landefeld and Eugene P. Seskin, "A Comparison of Anticipatory Surveys and Econometric Models in Forecasting U.S. Business Investment," paper presented at the 16th Centre for International Research on Economic Tendency Surveys (CIRET) Conference, Washington, D.C., September 21–24, 1983.

20. For more detail on these differences, see Eugene P. Seskin and David F. Sullivan, "Revised Estimates of New Plant and Equipment Expenditures in the United States, 1947–83," *Survey of Current Business,* February 1985, pp. 24–25.

21. Ibid.

22. Joint Center for Housing Studies of Harvard University, *The State of the Nation's Housing 1990,* pp. 2–3.

23. Ibid., pp. 4–5.

24. A correlation coefficient of 1 occurs when the variables have identical relative movements in the same direction in a direct relationship (both increase or decrease in tandem), and a coefficient of −1 occurs when the variables move in opposite directions in an inverse relationship (one increases and the other decreases). A correlation coefficient of zero indicates no relationship.

25. George A. Kahn, "The Changing Interest Sensitivity of the U.S. Economy," *Economic Review,* Federal Reserve Bank of Kansas City, November 1989; Randall J. Pozdena, "Do Interest Rates Still Affect Housing?" *Economic Review,* Federal Reserve Bank of San Francisco, Summer 1990; and John Ryding, "Housing Finance and the Transmission of Monetary Policy," *Quarterly Review,* Federal Reserve Bank of New York, Summer 1990.

26. Kenneth R. Stiltner and David R. Barton, "Econometric Models and Construction Forecasting," *Construction Review,* U.S. Department of Commerce, March/April 1990.

27. National income covers employee compensation, business profits, rental income, and net interest, and is basically the same as the GNP on the income side except that it excludes depreciation allowances and sales and property taxes. National income is used here because it centers on income flows to the labor and capital factors of production, which are directly affected by the stage of the business cycle, although the results of the analysis would not differ if current dollar GNP were used.

28. In the American federal system, it is impractical to use state and local budgets as a fiscal policy tool because (a) each state or local economy is heavily influenced by econo-

mies in the surrounding region as well as by national economy; (b) institutional aspects vary considerably—there are differing constitutional limitations on debt, legislatures meet at different times of the year, and fiscal years cover different twelve-month periods; and (c) it is not politically and economically feasible to have a coordinated fiscal policy for even the five or ten largest states (abstracting from the other states and the over three thousand localities)—the complexity is far greater than that of the federal budget, which itself becomes quite complicated merely in the dealings between Congress and the president.

29. The Full Employment and Balanced Growth Act of 1978 (Humphrey–Hawkins Act) set an unemployment goal of 4 percent and inflation goal of 3 percent by 1983, with a further inflation goal of zero percent by 1988, provided that achieving the inflation goal would not impede achieving the unemployment goal. These goals are reported on in the annual *Economic Report of the President*. (See Joint Economic Committee of Congress, *Employment Act of 1946, As Amended, with Related Laws*, October 1985, Section 4, pp. 5–7.)

30. Frank de Leeuw and Thomas M. Holloway, "Cyclical Adjustment of the Federal Budget and Federal Debt," *Survey of Current Business,* December 1983.

31. The alternative cyclically adjusted budget based on the GNP long-term growth trend abstracts from specific normative unemployment rates. It is calculated by connecting the midpoints of cyclical expansions, which are defined to include up to twelve quarters after the recovery from a recession surpasses the real GNP at the peak of the previous expansion. While it is useful for assessing budget surpluses and deficits in terms of the stage of the business cycle, this alternative cyclically adjusted budget is not applicable for setting fiscal policy guidelines because it does not specify an unemployment rate. It was published by the Bureau of Economic Analysis in the *Survey of Current Business* until 1989, when it was temporarily discontinued because more work is needed to refine the estimating procedures; for example, the method of estimating income tax revenues needs to be changed to reflect the recent tax legislation.

32. Vito Tanzi, "Federal Deficits and Interest Rates in the United States: An Empirical Analysis," *International Monetary Fund Staff Papers,* December 1985.

33. This idea focuses on the fact that the ratio of the capital stock of existing plant and equipment to the GNP is inversely related to the ratio of government debt to the GNP. It was introduced in "Cyclical Adjustment of the Federal Budget and Federal Debt," *Survey of Current Business*, December 1983, and is elaborated in Frank de Leeuw and Thomas M. Holloway, "The Measurement and Significance of the Cyclically Adjusted Federal Budget and Debt," *Journal of Money, Credit and Banking,* May 1985.

The "crowding out" of private investment due to large amounts of government borrowing is associated with two conditions: (a) periods of full employment when, because of low utilized plant and equipment capacity and low unemployment (Chapters 4 and 5), additional demand for credit raises prices and interest rates rather than economic growth (Chapters 6 and 7), and (b) periods of less than full employment when, even though unutilized capital and labor resources are available to increase production, the Federal Reserve does not accommodate the increasing demand for credit because of concern that it will ignite inflation. "Crowding in" occurs during periods of less than full employment when the government deficit stimulates economic growth and thus private investment.

A refinement of the effect of the cyclically adjusted budget surplus or deficit on the economy relates to the fact that in periods of less than full employment, accompanied by budget deficits and high inflation and interest rates—as in the late 1970s and early 1980s—adjusting the deficit for the high inflation and interest rates would greatly reduce it, or even put the budget in surplus. Thus, Robert Eisner considers the conventionally measured budget deficits in the late 1970s and early 1980s to have misled economic policymakers into slowing economic growth to contain inflation: they instituted restrictive fiscal and monetary policies, which resulted in the severe recession in 1981–82. See Robert Eisner, *How Real Is the Federal Deficit?* (The Free Press: 1986).

34. Christopher L. Bach, "U.S. International Transactions, Fourth Quarter and Year 1990," *Survey of Current Business*, March 1991.

35. The importance of the United States as a political haven for funds from other countries in driving up the value of the dollar is difficult to quantify and has also been questioned on pragmatic grounds. See Peter Isard and Lois Stekler, "U.S. International Capital Flows and the Dollar," and Richard N. Cooper's "Discussion Paper" in *Brookings Papers on Economic Activity*, 1985:1, pp. 226–27 and 246–47.

36. Jeffrey H. Lowe, "Gross Product of U.S. Affiliates of Foreign Companies, 1977–87," *Survey of Current Business,* June 1990. All-U.S.-business gross product excludes the following items from the GNP: rest-of-the-world, banks, government and government enterprises, private households, imputed product of owner-occupied housing, rental income of persons, business transfer payments, subsidies, and the statistical discrepancy. In 1987, foreign companies operating in the U.S. accounted for 3.3 percent of the GNP, compared to their share of 4.3 percent of the all-U.S.-business gross product cited in the text.

37. Ned G. Howenstine, "U.S. Affiliates of Foreign Companies: Operations in 1988," *Survey of Current Business,* July 1990.

38. James Orr, "The Trade Balance Effects of Foreign Direct Investment in U.S. Manufacturing," *Quarterly Review,* Federal Reserve Bank of New York, Summer 1991.

39. Norman S. Fieleke, "The Terms on Which Nations Trade," *New England Economic Review,* Federal Reserve Bank of Boston, November/December 1989.

40. Morris Goldstein and Mohsin S. Kahn, "Income and Price Effects in Foreign Trade," in R. W. Jones and P. B. Kenan, eds., *Handbook of International Economics*, Vol. 2 (Elsevier Science Publishing: 1985), particularly pp. 1076–86.

41. William Alterman, "Price Trends in U.S. Trade: New Data, New Insights," National Bureau of Economic Research, Conference on Research in Income and Wealth, International Economic Transactions: Issues in Measurement and Empirical Research, Washington, D.C., November 3–4, 1989.

42. David Bigman, "Exchange Rate Determination: Some Old Myths and New Paradigms," in David Bigman and Teizo Taya, eds., *Floating Exchange Rates and the State of World Trade Payments* (Ballinger Publishing: 1984).

43. Jane Marrinan, "Exchange Rate Determination: Sorting Out Theory and Evidence," *New England Economic Review,* Federal Reserve Bank of Boston, November/December 1989, p. 44; and Cletus C. Coughlin and Kees Koedijk, "What Do We Know About the Long-Run Real Exchange Rate?" *Review,* The Federal Reserve Bank of St. Louis, January/February 1990, p. 37.

44. J. Steven Landefeld and Ann M. Lawson, "Valuation of the U.S. Net International Investment Position," *Survey of Current Business*, May 1991; and Russell B. Scholl, "The International Investment Position of the United States in 1990," *Survey of Current Business,* June 1991.

45.   "World power and influence have historically accrued to creditor nations. It is not coincidental that America emerged as a world power simultaneously with our transition from a debtor nation dependent on foreign capital for our initial industrialization, to a creditor supplying investment capital to the rest of the world. But we are now a debtor again, and our future role in world affairs is in question. People simply do not regard their workers, their tenants, and their debtors in the same light as their employers, their landlords, and their creditors. Over time the respect, and even deference, that America had earned as world banker will gradually shift to the new creditor countries that are able to supply resources where we

cannot, and America's influence over nations and events will ebb.

Most Americans continue to think of themselves as creditors. We readily offer unsolicited advice to other debtor countries, as if they had fallen into a trap that we had successfully avoided. Meanwhile, the Japanese and Germans appear still to think of themselves as debtors. As a result, world leadership arrangements do not yet reflect our changed circumstances or theirs. But self-perceptions on both sides will soon catch up to the new reality, in which our financial problems circumscribe our scope for maneuver in world affairs while other countries' financial strength does the opposite. Just how large a departure from recent history that reality represents will depend in part on whether, and how, we change our economic policy." [Friedman, *Day of Reckoning*, p. 13.]

46. For example, Friedman, *Day of Reckoning*, Chapter 7; Laurence S. Seidman, *Saving for America's Economic Future: Parables and Policies* (M. E. Sharpe: 1989), Chapters 1 and 2; and U.S. Council of Economic Advisers, "The Annual Report of the Council of Economic Advisers," *Economic Report of the President*, February 1990, pp. 136–42.

47. Eisner, *How Real Is the Federal Deficit?* Chapter 3.

48. For an enlightening discussion of the equivalence of investment and saving, see ibid., Chapter 13. This also points up the limitation of relying on interest rates to balance investment and saving because interest rates are only one factor in investment decisions. For example, if business is pessimistic about the economic outlook, the lowest available interest rate may not encourage sufficient investment to equal saving.

49. William A. Niskanen, *Reaganomics: An Insider's Account of the Policies and the People* (Oxford University Press: 1988), pp. 130–33.

50. Ibid., p. 134.

51. Susan J. Tolchin and Martin Tolchin, *Dismantling America: The Rush to Deregulate* (Houghton Mifflin: 1983).

52. Larry Margasak, "Bird-Dogging Bureaucracy: Quayle-Led Council Watches over Impact on U.S. Competitiveness," Associated Press Wire Release, May 20, 1991.

53. David A. Stockman, *The Triumph of Politics: The Inside Story of the Reagan Revolution* (Harper & Row: 1986). The thrust of this book is President Reagan's unwillingness to fight for spending reductions commensurate with the tax cuts. His basic interest was in lower taxes, regardless of rhetoric about lower spending. In negotiations with Congress, when Republicans as well as Democrats opposed spending reductions, he did not support using lower spending as a requirement for lower taxes.

54. Walter Adams and James L. Brock, *Dangerous Pursuits: Mergers and Acquisitions in the Age of Wall Street* (McGraw-Hill: 1988), Chapters 7, 8, and 9.

55. David Ravenscraft and F. M. Scherer, *Mergers, Sell-Offs, and Economic Efficiency* (The Brookings Institution: 1987), pp. 202–3 and 218–21.

56. Richard Cantor, "Effects of Leverage on Corporate Investment and Hiring Decisions," *Quarterly Review*, Federal Reserve Bank of New York, Summer 1990.

57. Frank Lichtenberg, "Industrial Diversification and Its Consequences for Productivity," National Bureau of Economic Research Working Paper No. 3231, 1990; and Paul Healy, Krishna Palepu, and Richard Ruback, "Does Corporate Performance Improve after Mergers?" National Bureau of Economic Research Working Paper No. 3348, 1990.

58. Benjamin M. Friedman, "Views on the Likelihood of Financial Crisis," National Bureau of Economic Research Working Paper No. 3407, 1990; and James J. O'Leary, "The U.S. Economy on the Edge of a Recession—How Serious Could It Be?" (mimeo), United States Trust Company, October 15, 1990.

59. For the development of a progressive consumption tax, see Seidman, *Saving for America's Economic Future*, pp. 37–38.

60. On the culpability of conservatives as well as liberals in not cutting their favorite

programs, see Stockman, *The Triumph of Politics.*

61. Studies indicating that government spending for roads, mass transit, airports, dams, water and sewer systems, etc., significantly increases productivity include David Alan Aschauer, "Is Public Expenditure Productive?" *Journal of Monetary Economics,* March 1989; David A. Aschauer, "Public investment and productivity growth in the Group of Seven," *Economic Perspectives,* Federal Reserve Bank of Chicago, September/ October 1989; and Alicia H. Munnell, "Why Has Productivity Growth Declined? Productivity and Public Investment," *New England Economic Review,* Federal Reserve Bank of Boston, January/February 1990. Studies that downplay the effect of public investment on productivity include some participants in a conference reported in Alicia H. Munnell, "Is There a Shortfall in Public Capital Investment? An Overview," *New England Economic Review,* Federal Reserve Bank of Boston, May/June 1991; John A. Tatom, "Public Capital and Private Sector Performance," *Review,* The Federal Reserve Bank of St. Louis, May/June 1991; and Congressional Budget Office, *How Federal Spending for Infrastructure and Other Public Investments Affects the Economy,* July 1991.

62. The development of a capital budget is recommended in Eisner, *How Real Is the Federal Deficit?* Chapter 3.

63. Barry P. Bosworth, "Testimony before the Committee on Ways and Means, House of Representatives, United States Congress," April 19, 1989. In addition to cautioning that a capital budget should not be used as a loophole to define away the deficit, this statement recommends that a capital budget should include a depreciation fund with dedicated revenues to finance the various investments.

64. Carol S. Carson and Bruce T. Grimm, "Satellite Accounts in a Modernized and Extended System of Economic Accounts," *Business Economics,* January 1991.

65. Robert E. Lipsey and Irving B. Kravis, *Saving and Economic Growth: Is the United States Really Falling Behind?* (The Conference Board: 1987), Chapter 2.

4
INDUSTRIAL PRODUCTION AND
CAPACITY UTILIZATION

The industrial production index and industrial capacity utilization rates are monthly indicators provided by the Federal Reserve Board. They encompass manufacturing, mining, and electric and gas utilities, which account for about one-fourth of the gross national product (GNP). The production index measures the quantity of nonfarm goods and energy produced; the capacity utilization rate measures actual production as a percentage of the maximum output the industry can produce when its plant and equipment facilities and work force are fully utilized.

The industrial production and capacity utilization indicators have a large concentration of cyclically sensitive markets such as consumer durable goods, plant and equipment investment, residential construction, and business inventories. Demand in these markets increases faster in expansions, and declines more sharply in recessions, than other GNP components (see Chapter 3). Thus, both indicators are dominated by the most cyclical aspects of the economy. The production index is used in assessing the relationship between the components of the economy that dominate business cycles and total economic activity. Capacity utilization rates are used mainly as indicators of future plant and equipment investment and secondarily as indicators of future price movements.

This chapter is divided into two sections, which treat respectively the industrial production index and the capacity utilization rates. The production index section includes a brief discussion of the new service production index.

INDUSTRIAL PRODUCTION INDEX

The industrial production index (IPI) provides a seasonably adjusted, monthly measure of the *percent change in the quantity of output* in manufacturing, mining, and electric and gas utilities since the base period (currently 1987 = 100). Because it excludes the effect of price changes, the index does not measure the value of production but rather focuses on the relative movement of the quantity of production. Manufacturing dominates the index, accounting for 84 percent of the total output; mining accounts for 8 percent, and electric and gas utilities, 8 percent. These industries are among the most capital-intensive in the economy— in their production operations, they use much more plant and equipment relative to labor than other industries, and consequently are the source of most plant and equipment spending. In 1989, the industries covered in the IPI generated one-fourth of the GNP, but accounted for one-half of the nation's private nonfarm plant and equipment investment.

The IPI measure is provided from two perspectives, although the total is the same for both. One measures production by market groups, distinguishing types of product by end use; the other measures production according to the industry in which the product is made. The market groupings have three broad categories: (a) final products, encompassing consumer durable and nondurable goods, business equipment, prefabricated homes, drilling for oil and gas wells, and defense and space equipment (46 percent of the total); (b) intermediate products, encompassing construction materials that become part of residential and nonresidential structures, and business supplies such as commercial energy produced and animal feeds (15 percent); and (c) materials, encompassing raw materials, parts, containers, and fuels (39 percent). The IPI industry measure centers on the industries that produce these products—manufacturing, mining, and utilities.

As a measure of domestic production, the IPI excludes imports. However, imports as well as the excluded industries of agriculture, construction, transportation, trade, and all services are indirectly included to the extent that the manufacturing, mining, and utilities industries use their products as intermediate production items (inputs), in which case they are implicitly part of the product or power produced.

From an economic perspective, the market measure focuses on the *demand* for products in the consumer, business, and government markets (export markets are not separately identified, although some of the products are sold as exports). The industry measure focuses on the *supply* of the products provided by the producing industries. Demand for the different types of products accounted for in the market measure determines the growth rates of the particular industries supplying the goods.

PART A: ESTIMATING METHODOLOGY

The IPI is a composite of detailed components that are weighted by their relative importance.[1] (General issues regarding index numbers were discussed in Chapter 1.)

The base period of the index is 1987 = 100, which means that the index (minus 100) for any period represents the percent change from the 1988 average. For example, the index in December 1989 was 108.6, representing an 8.6 percent increase from the 1987 average; and the index in March 1990 was 108.9, representing an 8.9 percent increase since 1987. The change between two dates is therefore figured as the percent change between the two index levels. For example, between December 1989 and March 1990, the IPI increased by 0.3 percent $(108.9/108.6 - 1.0 \times 100)$.

The weights used for combining the components into the index since 1987 are based on the costs and profits that each industry added to the value of the products it sold in 1987. This "value-added" measure counts the wages, depreci-

Table 12

Estimating the Industrial Production Index for March 1990 (1987 = 100)

(1) Industry	(2) 1987 weights	(3) Ratio Change, 1987 to March 1990	(4) March 1990 proportions (2) x (3)
Manufacturing	84.44	1.098	92.72
Mining	7.93	1.011	8.02
Utilities	7.63	1.062	8.10
Total	100.00	—	108.84 (Total index)

Note: Because these calculations were done at the three broad levels of total manufacturing, total mining, and total utilities rather than for each of the 250 component industries of the IPI, the actual March 1990 index of 108.9 is slightly higher than the 108.8 calculated here.

ation, purchased services, and profits in each producing industry; in this way it avoids double-counting the value of goods each industry buys from other industries, although it does double-count purchased services.[2] The weights always sum to 100 and are updated based on the most recent five-year economic censuses of American industry, which are conducted by the Census Bureau for the years ending in 2 and 7. For example, the weights between 1982–86 are based on 1982 value added and between 1977–81 on 1977 value added. These "benchmark" revisions also include statistical improvements such as the inclusion of new industry categories and updated industry classification to reflect the most current technologies, and updated seasonal adjustment factors (the general process of revisions was discussed in Chapter 1).

Table 12 shows in summary form how the IPI is figured for the major industry categories in March 1990. Although much more component detail is used in developing the index (250 component industries are weighted), the basic procedure for deriving the index is simple. In this example, value-added weights for the broad industry categories are multiplied by the relative change in production in each of the industries since the base period. The sum of the products of the industry components is the index for the new period—in this case, approximately 108.9 for March 1990 (see note to Table 12).

Current Period Revisions

Ideally, current movements in the index are based on data for the actual items of output. However, because output data are not available monthly for all items, indirect data based on employee hours from Bureau of Labor Statistics data (Chapter 5) and on electricity consumption from Federal Reserve Board surveys of utilities sales to consuming industries are also used for some industries. The indirect data are converted to production estimates based on projections of technological trends and changes in labor productivity and electricity use per unit of output in the different industries. Direct product data account for 39 percent of the IPI estimates, and the indirect electricity and employment information for 32 percent and 29 percent, respectively. This results in revisions to the current index when more complete direct output data become available, replacing the indirect estimates.

The IPI for each month is first published in the third week of the following month and is subsequently revised in each of the next three months as underlying information on which the indexes are based becomes available. The average revision from the first to the fourth estimate is plus or minus 0.36 percent—from a first estimate of 110.0, for example, to a fourth estimate of between 109.6 and 110.4. The typical revision for monthly percent movements is plus or minus 0.27 percentage point. In about 85 percent of the cases, the first and fourth estimates for the month are in the same upward or downward direction from the previous month. The indexes are also revised to incorporate still more complete underlying data and also to update the seasonal adjustment factors.

Effect of Benchmark Revisions

Each benchmark revision to the IPI distinctly affects short-term and long-term movements. The 1990 revision, which incorporated new weights for 1982 and 1987, had more prominent short-term than long-term effects.[3] The main short-term effect was to reduce the measured severity of the 1982 recession. Thus, the decline in output in 1982 was revised to 4.4 percent, smaller than the previous estimate of 7.1 percent. Over the longer-term 1977–89 period, the 1990 revision lowered the average annual growth rate from 2.9 percent to 2.7 percent. The revised figures also lowered the growth rate during the 1983–89 expansion. The original estimate of an average annual growth rate of 4.6 percent during this period was revised to 4.0 percent.

In the 1985 revision, which incorporated new weights for 1972 and 1977, the main change to the IPI affecting cyclical expansions and recessions occurred in determining the start of the 1974–75 recession.[4] The pre-1985 index showed the third quarter of 1974 as the peak of the previous expansion, rather than the end of 1973 as is now shown in the revised index; however, both indexes moved in a narrow range for most of 1974, and then clearly declined in the last quarter of 1974 and first quarter of 1975. For longer periods, the annual growth rates of the two differed. Between 1967 and 1977, the old rate was 2.9 percent compared to the new rate of 3.1 percent; for the 1977–84 period, the old rate was 3.4 percent compared to the new rate of 2.9 percent. Thus, the revision from 1967 to 1977

Figure 28a. **Business Cycle Movements of the Industrial Production Index and Real GNP: Expansions**

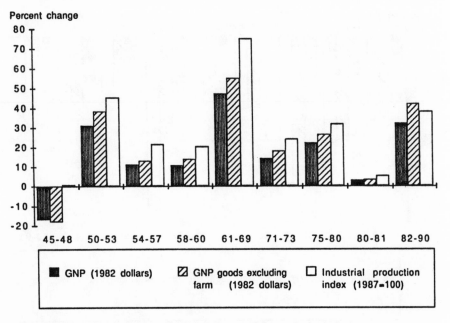

Note: Based on Federal Reserve Board and Bureau of Economic Analysis data.

was small, but the revised trend for 1977–84 showed a noticeably slower growth rate than previously depicted.

PART B: ANALYSIS OF TRENDS

As noted previously in this chapter, the IPI focuses on the most cyclically sensitive markets of the economy. This is apparent in the postwar business cycle patterns of the IPI and real GNP (Figures 28a and 28b). In the nine postwar expansions, the IPI typically increased 50 to 100 percent more than the GNP; in the nine postwar recessions, the IPI typically declined three to four times more than the GNP. The estimate of "GNP goods excluding farm," which is similar definitionally to the IPI, is more cyclical than total GNP. Nevertheless, the IPI has significantly greater cyclical movements than GNP goods (except for the 1982–90 expansion), although the differential is smaller than between the IPI and GNP.[5]

The relationship between the IPI and the GNP corresponds more closely, however, during periods of slow economic growth, typified by real GNP increasing at an annual rate of less than 3 percent. The designation of under 3 percent as

Figure 28b. **Business Cycle Movements of the Industrial Production Index and Real GNP: Recessions**

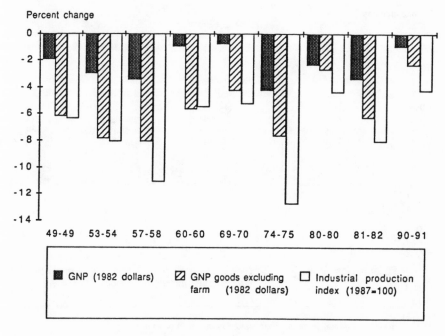

Note: Based on Federal Reserve Board and Bureau of Economic Analysis data.
Recession of 1990-91 in progress in Spring of 1991.

"slow growth" is based on the relationship between the GNP and unemployment (Chapter 5). This relationship indicates that the unemployment rate is relatively stable when GNP growth is in the 2–3 percent range; unemployment declines when GNP growth is above 3 percent; and unemployment rises when GNP growth is below 2 percent and of course when GNP declines.

Table 13 shows the growth in the IPI during 1948–89. Over the entire forty-one-year period, the IPI grew at an average annual rate of 3.8 percent. (Real GNP growth was somewhat slower at 3.3 percent over the same period, as noted in Chapter 3.) There was a marked slowdown in the 1970s and 1980s, however. Thus, from a peak of 5.5 percent in the 1960s, the IPI growth rate declined to 3 percent in the 1970s and to 2.4 percent in the 1980s. These patterns are similar for the manufacturing IPI, although in the 1980s the manufacturing IPI declined less than the total IPI.

Table 14 shows the average IPI–GNP relationship during the decades of 1950–89 for the three rates of GNP growth noted above. Specifically, it is the average ratio of annual growth in the IPI to annual growth in the GNP in each of years when GNP growth is 3 percent or higher, 2 to 2.9 percent, and under 2

Table 13

Average Annual Growth in the Industrial Production Index: 1948–89

	Total IPI (manufacturing, mining, utilities)	Manufacturing IPI
1948–59	4.3	4.2
1959–69	5.5	5.5
1969–79	3.0	3.2
1979–89	2.4	3.0
1948–89	3.8	4.0

percent. In years when the GNP increases less than 3 percent, the ratio is 1, indicating the IPI averages the same rate of growth; when GNP increases by 3 percent or more, the ratio is 1.5, indicating the IPI averages a 50 percent higher growth rate; and when the GNP declines, the ratio is 6.3, indicating the IPI declines at a rate over 6 times as fast. This suggests that annual increases in the IPI of at least 4.5 percent are typically necessary to lower the unemployment rate, because unemployment declines when GNP grows by at least 3 percent (at which point the IPI–GNP ratio averages 1.5). But this long-term relationship showed a noticeable change during the 1980s, particularly when GNP grew at 3 percent and higher: the IPI–GNP ratio dropped to average only 1.1 in these years. This change reflects the sharp increase in service industries employment in the 1980s. As in all long-term analyses, deviations from the trend suggest future movements should be monitored to determine if long-term rules-of-thumb remain relevant for particular periods.

While the manufacturing, mining, and utilities industries covered in the IPI account for a relatively small portion of the GNP—only one-fourth—they have wide secondary impacts. First, service industries are affected by movements in the IPI because the IPI industries generate a significant amount of business for services industries. When production is high, manufacturers use more transportation, communication, finance, insurance, repairs, and personnel services than when production is low. Second, because the IPI industries account for the major share of investment in plant and equipment, they heavily affect the demand for machinery, trucks, building materials, and construction workers. Third, because average incomes of workers in the IPI industries are higher than those in other industries, consumer spending is affected proportionately more by changing levels of IPI production in other industries.

The MIT Commission on Industrial Productivity has put the importance of manufacturing, which as noted above accounts for 84 percent of the IPI, in the context of American living standards and the world economy.[6] The commission points to manufacturing's role in high wages, technological progress, and the

Table 14

IPI and GNP for Different Rates of Economic Growth: 1950–89
(ratio of annual percent change in IPI to change in real GNP)

GNP growth (percent)	1950–59	1960–69	1970–79	1980–89	1950–89
3.0 and over	1.7	1.5	1.7	1.1	1.5
0 to 2.9	1.4	1.0	1.1	0.7	1.0
Less than zero	6.1	*	7.0	5.6	6.3

*There were no years of GNP decline in the 1960s.

foreign trade deficit. It anticipates that if manufacturing is treated as being obsolete to the U.S. economy, other countries will not only absorb the high-wage manufacturing industries, but that the supporting high-wage service industries such as design and engineering, repair and maintenance of equipment, testing services, market research, transportation, accounting, finance, and insurance are likely to follow abroad. Much technological progress based on manufacturing research and development spills over into other facets of the economy like health care and law enforcement, and thus a loss of the manufacturing base is likely to result in the loss of some of these benefits for other activities as well. The foreign trade deficit (Chapter 3) will not be solved without improved U.S. competitiveness in the sale of American-made products at home and abroad.

Because the IPI is dominated by manufacturing, it is highly pertinent to economic growth. *The analyst should assess the IPI for clues as to whether GNP growth will be modest or robust. On average, an annual growth in the IPI of at least 3.0 percent is necessary to generate sufficient GNP growth to lower the unemployment rate. This rate assumes a substantial increase in service industries employment relative to manufacturing industries employment in the 1990s, similar to that in the 1980s. If this pattern does not prevail, a greater increase in industrial production will be required to generate sufficient economic growth to lower the unemployment rate, because production in manufacturing industries is less labor intensive than production in service industries.*

Index of Service Production

In 1989 Zoltan Kenessey developed a new monthly service production index (SPI).[7] The SPI was published monthly by the Coalition of Services Industries until November 1991, when it was discontinued due to insufficient funding. The Bureau of Economic Analysis in the U.S. Department of Commerce is considering taking over the SPI and publishing an expanded index and/or the underlying data series; this decision will be made in 1992.

Historical measures begin with 1977. Four estimates for each month are prepared, similar to the IPI: an initial estimate in the following month and revisions in the three subsequent months. The SPI is seasonally adjusted and covers production in transportation, communications, utilities, wholesale and retail trade, finance, insurance and real estate, personal, business, and professional services, not-for-profit organizations, and public administration (federal, state, and local governments). Three subgroups are prepared: (1) the *tertiary sector,* composed of transportation, communications, utilities, and trade, relates to the movement and distribution of goods (transportation and trade) and to industries that use considerable amounts of equipment in their production similar to the goods-producing industries (communications and utilities); (2) the *quaternary sector,* composed of finance, insurance, real estate, public administration, and personal, business, and professional services; and (3) *private services,* composed of the tertiary and quaternary sectors except public administration.

The SPI accounts for three-fourths of the GNP, and thus provides a monthly output measure for the dominant portion of the economy. It is similar in concept to the IPI. The SPI measures the percent change in the quantity of output from the base period (currently 1977 = 100). Like the IPI, the SPI is composed of detailed component industries which are weighted by their relative importance to the GNP (see IPI Estimating Methodology). The source data for the monthly movements are based on employment figures mainly from the Bureau of Labor Statistics (55 percent); product indicators such as airline miles, hotel occupancy rates, patients admitted to hospitals, and shares traded on the New York Stock Exchange (16 percent); and the IPI and depreciation indicators (each 14.5 percent). The SPI is based on fifty data series for its component industries. There are no estimates of revision error.

During the 1980s, the SPI rose at an annual rate of 2.8 percent, which is modestly higher than the IPI increase of 2.4 percent. The SPI also showed less volatility than the IPI. For example, in the 1980 recession year, the SPI rose 0.7 percent while the IPI declined 1.9 percent; in the 1982 recession year, the SPI declined 0.4 percent and the IPI declined 4.4 percent; in the expansion years of 1983–89, the SPI rose 28 percent while the IPI rose 32 percent; and in the 1990–91 recession (as of the spring of 1991), the SPI was level while the IPI declined 4 percent.

The tertiary and quaternary groupings within the SPI had differential movements during the 1980s, with the tertiary industries (more goods-oriented) growing faster and also being more volatile than the quaternary industries. These patterns conform to the general perception that although service industries are not immune to recessions, they have steadier growth over the business cycle. Thus, the tertiary industries declined 1.4 percent in 1980 and 1.0 percent in 1982 (both were recession years), while increases in the quaternary industries slowed to 2.1 percent in 1980 and 0.1 percent in 1982. And the tertiary industries declined 1.6 percent while the quaternary industries increased 0.6 percent in the 1990–91 recession (as of the spring of 1991).

CAPACITY UTILIZATION RATES

Capacity utilization rates (CURs) are seasonally adjusted, monthly indicators of the relation of actual production to productive capacity. They cover the same industries as the IPI covers—manufacturing, mining, and electric and gas utilities.

CURs indicate the amount of unused capacity that industrial facilities could bring into production. For example, if a factory with the plant and equipment capacity to produce 1,000 cans of paint a month actually produces 800 cans a month, its utilization rate is 80 percent and its unutilized capacity is 20 percent. Unutilized plant and equipment is analogous to the unemployment of workers in the job market (see Chapter 5) as both measures indicate available resources that could be used to expand production. This does not imply that the two are equated, however, because on a social basis unemployment of workers is a more serious problem than unused industrial facilities.

Theoretically, the direction and level of CURs indicate the demand for plant and equipment investment and the degree of inflationary pressure in the economy. Rising CURs tend to *reduce* unit costs of production for a time, as the existing plant and equipment investment produces a larger volume of goods. The cost advantage of the larger volume (increasing returns to scale) continues until the utilization rate reaches a level at which further increases in production *raise* unit costs because of machinery breakdowns, increasing use of older and less efficient equipment, hiring of less productive workers as unemployment falls, and laxness by managements in holding down costs.[8]

The specific point at which the turnaround occurs on costs, and consequently on plant and equipment spending and on inflation, varies among industries and is hard to quantify precisely. The observed turnaround zone is based on movements of the figures—it does not mean that company decisions to invest or change prices are linked to a particular CUR zone. The rising production costs at the higher utilization rates spur companies to reduce costs by increasing capacity through new investment in plant and equipment. By contrast, relatively low and falling CURs reduce business incentives to expand capacity, and replacements of run-down and outmoded capacity account for greater shares of plant and equipment investment during such periods. Analogously, increasing production costs foster higher prices, and decreasing costs foster stable or declining prices.

PART A: ESTIMATING METHODOLOGY

CURs are provided for the total of all manufacturing, mining, and utility industries and for the component industries within each of these groups; the figures are available for manufacturing industries since 1948 and for mining and utilities since 1967.[9]

A CUR is the ratio of the IPI to industrial plant and equipment capacity. Consolidation of component industries to broader industry categories and the total CUR is based on the value-added weights used in the IPI. Because the IPI (in the numerator) was discussed earlier in this chapter, the following discussion concentrates on the capacity estimates as used in the denominator.

$$\text{Capacity utilization rate} = \frac{\text{Industrial production index}}{\text{Industrial capacity}} \times 100$$

Any discussion of capacity has a basic backdrop: Since actual capacity data in homogeneous units such as tons, barrels, feet, or number of units of the same item are available only for a limited number of industries, most capacity estimates are derived indirectly as a statistical artifact. The resultant capacity measures are close to the long-term rate of production growth (see Measurement Problems below).

An industry's capacity, while partly a result of its capital plant and equipment facilities, is also determined by the length of the typical working day and week. The capacity measures assume an eight-hour day and five-day working week for most industries, but these measures are higher for some industries such as steel, petroleum refining, and utilities, which maintain production around the clock. As in the case of the IPI, manufacturing dominates the movement of the CUR, accounting for 84 percent of the component industries. For manufacturing and gas utilities, capacity measures are developed through an indirect estimating procedure:

(a) For most manufacturing industries, year-end capacity levels are established by dividing the IPI by the Census Bureau's survey of plant capacity. A similar procedure for gas utilities is based on data from the U.S. Department of Energy, the American Gas Association, and industry sources. There are exceptions, however. More direct capacity estimates are derived from industry sources' data on hourly assembly line speeds for motor vehicles and for primary processing industries such as steel and nonferrous metals, paper, petroleum refining, and chemicals.

(b) The annual movements of the implied capacity measures in (a) are modified to be consistent with alternative figures on capacity data obtained from government agencies and private organizations, such as information on physical units (e.g., tons of steel), the dollar value of existing capital facilities (capital stocks), and direct surveys of capacity, and to allow for peak capacity to meet seasonal needs.[10]

(c) To estimate monthly capacity for previous years, the year-end capacity levels are connected and monthly trends for each year are calculated on the basis of the prorated rate of change between the two year-end monthly levels. Monthly estimates in the current year are based on continuing the rate of growth in the previous year.

Figure 29. **Industrial Production, Capacity, and Capacity Utilization: 1967–90**

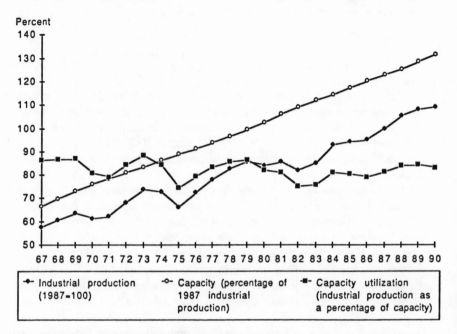

Note: Based on Federal Reserve Board data for manufacturing, mining, and utilities industries.

Different estimating procedures are used for electric utilities and mining. For electric utilities, data on kilowatt generating capacity from the Edison Electric Institute and the North American Electric Reliability Council are used. These are adjusted to take into account the need for reserve capacity for outages as well as power to meet peak summer and winter needs. For some mining industries, the capacity estimates are based on information from the U.S. Departments of the Energy and the Interior. For others, where such information is unavailable, capacity figures are inferred from long-term production trends based on connecting the production expansion peaks of business cycles.

Measurement Problems

The monthly CUR is published on the same schedule as the IPI, initially in the third week of the following month. It is revised in each of the next three months to reflect IPI revisions (the capacity figures are revised only once a year). Because of the capacity measure's synthetic nature, no estimates of average revision in the CUR are calculated. However, because CUR movements parallel those of the IPI so closely, one may assume the average revision of the CUR is probably close to that noted above for the IPI: plus or minus 0.36 percent for the monthly levels and plus or minus 0.27 percentage point for the monthly percent change (see previous examples for the IPI).

Figure 29 details the movements of the Federal Reserve Board figures for industrial production, capacity, and the CUR for all industries. While the CUR follows the cyclical pattern of the IPI, which is the numerator of the CUR ratio, capacity itself differs considerably from the highly cyclical IPI. Capacity rises at a relatively steady rate with no cyclical ups and downs because in any period, capacity is composed mainly of existing facilities, with only marginal net changes made for the addition of new investment and deduction of depreciated facilities. The overall CUR usually ranges from 75 to 85 percent, toward and above the upper end during expansions and toward and below the lower end during recessions. The range of CURs for individual industries varies from this overall average.

The overall CUR typically does not approach or exceed 100 percent. The major exception is high mobilization during wars, when industry undergoes a widespread conversion to two and three eight-hour shifts a day. Because such multiple shifts are not considered typical capacity levels that can be sustained over long periods in peacetime, they do not result in an upward adjustment in the estimated capacity levels; thus CURs theoretically may reach the 100 percent range. However, industry would probably operate at this level only during a full-scale war, and perhaps not even then. For example, the peak manufacturing CURs in the Korean and Vietnam wars were 92 percent and then only for a few months. There are no estimates for World War II because CURs were not developed until 1948. It remains unclear whether even a full-scale war would raise CURs to the 100 percent range.[11]

Production capacity is an elusive concept to define and measure. Theoretically, a business' ultimate capacity is the output it could produce if it operated seven days a week, twenty-four hours a day, with allowance for maintenance of existing equipment, shortage of materials, or other downtime. This level of operation is referred to as "engineering capacity." Other than in wartime, it is realistic only for industries with continuing process operations in which it is more efficient to operate around the clock. "Practical capacity" refers to the usual operations schedule that is realistically maintained on a continuing basis. These vary among industries from single and multiple eight-hour shifts over a five-day week to continuous operations seven days a week.

Practical capacity is the implied measure in the Federal Reserve Board figures. However, the measure is not always explicitly defined in the source data used for the estimates. For example, the McGraw-Hill CUR company level surveys, which were discontinued after 1988, do not define the capacity measure for the respondents.[12] This probably leads to inconsistent reporting by companies—for example, some may assume engineering capacity as practical capacity. This is less of a problem for the capacity figures that are based on Census Bureau

Table 15

Capacity Utilization Rates

	Total (manufacturing, mining, and utilities)	Manufacturing
1985	80.3	79.5
1986	79.2	79.0
1987	81.4	81.4
1988	84.0	83.9
1989	84.2	83.9
1990	83.0	82.3

plant level (establishment) survey data, because the Census provides respondents with qualitative definitions of capacity in terms of typical operational schedules; however, as noted below, the lack of quantitative definitions is still felt to cause some inconsistency.[13]

Another continuing problem with any statistical measure of capacity is whether plants that are closed down in recessions are considered permanently removed from production, or if this capacity is considered "found" and available again in expansions.[14] While the Federal Reserve uses consistency checks with alternative data and statistical procedures to modify aberrant movements in the capacity figures, a considerable amount of indirect estimating is associated with the preparation of the capacity figures. Finally, the capacity figures do not include imports, which are an important source of added supply in some industries and which in effect increase capacity. *For these reasons, the capacity figures, and therefore the CURs, should be considered orders of magnitude rather than precise numbers.*

PART B: ANALYSIS OF TRENDS

This section profiles the CUR trends since the late 1940s and compares them to trends in plant and equipment spending. It also considers the relationship between the CURs and price movements. Because manufacturing accounts for 84 percent of the industries covered in the CUR total, there is little difference in the *movements* of the CUR combined total for manufacturing, mining, and utilities and the manufacturing component (Table 15). There also is only a slight difference in the *levels* of the combined total and the manufacturing component—the combined total tends to be 0.5 to 1.0 percentage point higher. Thus, because manufacturing is dominant, and because of manufacturing's key role in the economy which was discussed in the previous section on the IPI, the following discussion centers on manufacturing industries.

Figure 30 shows the CUR trends for all manufacturing industries during the

Figure 30. **Capacity Utilization in Manufacturing Industries: 1948–90**

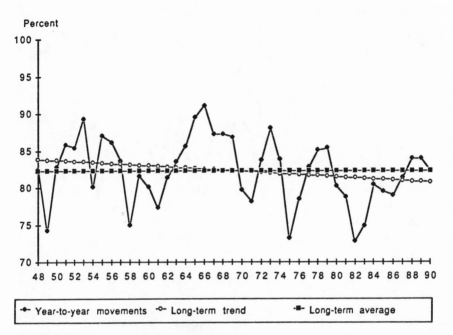

Note: Based on Federal Reserve Board data.

years 1948–90. The CUR averaged 82 percent, peaking at annual averages of 89.5 and 91 percent in 1965 and 1966 (the early part of the Vietnam War buildup), and at 89 percent in 1953 (the last year of the Korean War); the CUR fell to its lowest level of 73 percent twice—in 1975 (the last year of the 1973–75 recession) and in the 1982 recession year. The CUR has been in a long-term downward trend during 1948–90, as indicated by the diamond line in Figure 30. The long-term decline of 0.1 percent annually occurred despite periods of high CURs during 1963–69, 1972–74, 1978–79, and 1988–89. Viewed in terms of decades (see Table 17 below), the average CURs of 82 percent during the 1970s and of 79.5 percent during the 1980s were progressively lower than the average of 85 percent during the 1960s (or of 83 percent during 1948–59); the relatively high average CUR of 85 percent during the 1960s is an interruption of the general downward trend.

CURs and Plant and Equipment Investment

Manufacturing is capital intensive, accounting for 19 percent of the GNP but 36 percent of plant and equipment investment in 1988. CURs give important clues

Figure 31. **Capacity Utilization and Real Plant and Equipment Investment in Manufacturing Industries: 1948–89**

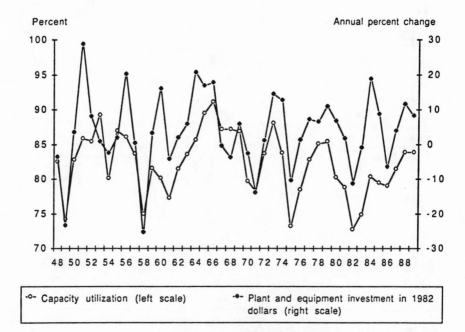

Percent   Annual percent change

-○- Capacity utilization (left scale)   -●- Plant and equipment investment in 1982 dollars (right scale)

Note: Based on Federal Reserve Board and Bureau of the Census data.

to future plant and equipment investment in manufacturing. There is generally a direct relationship from one year to the next, with higher CURs associated with increased investment and lower CURs associated with either a decline in the rate of increase or an actual drop in investment. This relationship is detailed in Figure 31, which shows percentage levels of the CUR in each year and the percentage change in real plant and equipment spending (in 1982 dollars) from the previous year for all manufacturing industries over the 1948–89 period. However, the rates of change associated with the CUR and investment vary considerably from one year to the next, so that a one percentage point change in the CUR may result in a wide range of percentage changes in investment depending on other economic factors in different periods.

Figure 32a depicts the differential rates of change between the CUR and investment more directly. Each year is plotted as the point where the CUR level on the horizontal axis intersects investment annual percent change on the vertical axis as a black diamond. The long-term average relationship for all years is represented by the line of white diamonds. This line slopes upward to the right, which indicates a general direct relationship. The slope of the line indicates that,

Figure 32a. **Capacity Utilization vs. Real Plant and Equipment Investment in Manufacturing Industries: 1948–89**

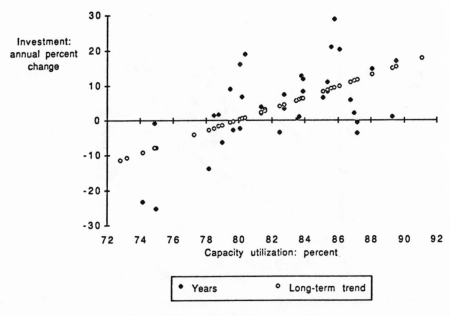

Note: Based on Federal Reserve Board and Bureau of the Census data.

on average, a 1 percentage point change in the CUR is associated with a 1.6 percent change in plant and equipment investment. The correlation coefficient is .65. A correlation coefficient of 1 indicates identical movements while a coefficient of zero indicates no similarity in the movements. (A perfect relationship with a correlation coefficient of 1 would be one in which the points for all years coincide with the average line.[15]) Thus, the wide dispersion of individual years above and below the average line shows that the long-term average relationship between the CUR and investment is highly unpredictable for year-to-year movements. (This analysis is based on the aggregate for all manufacturing industries; there would certainly be differences if similar assessments were made for particular industries in paper, rubber, chemicals, steel, machinery, transportation equipment, etc.)

Figure 32b shows the same CUR and investment data as Figure 32a except that it displays the year-to-year movements by connecting the yearly points from one year to the next (Figure 32b excludes the average long-term line to avoid cluttering). The varying slopes of the lines connecting each two years highlight the disparities in the rates of change between the CUR and investment, even when they move upward to the right like the average long-term relationship. The

Figure 32b. **Capacity Utilization vs. Real Plant and Equipment Investment in Manufac-turing Industries: 1948–89**

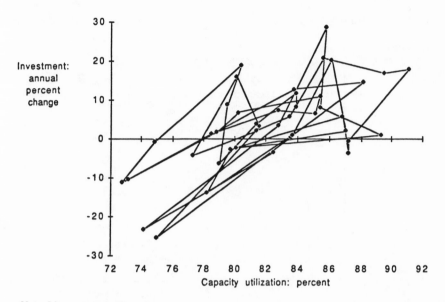

Note: Lines connect adjacent years.

disparity is most extreme when the line connecting two years slopes downward to the right, which indicates that the rate of change in investment is in the opposite direction of the percentage point change in the CUR (i.e., investment increases when the CUR declines, or investment falls when the CUR increases). Examples of such extremes are 1951–52, 1955–56, 1964–65, and 1977–78.

The year-to-year variability between changes in the CUR and investment highlights the complexity of the factors determining investment. The CUR is only one factor among many. Past and anticipated future profits also play a key role in determining plant and equipment investment, as does the volatility of profits (see Chapter 3). In addition, however, the relationship between the CUR and investment is complicated by four factors discussed in detail below. These are: (1) the time lag from when the decision to invest is made and when actual investment spending occurs; (2) the tendency of the CUR to function as a thresh-old, where investment is usually robust above a certain level of the CUR and weak below the threshold; (3) the fact that investment is determined by both the level and the annual change of the CUR; and (4) the effect of changes over time in the propensity to invest at given CUR levels.

The statistical relationship between the CUR and investment is problematic in part because of the time lag between the investment decision and the actual ·

investment. The length of this lag depends on the type of investment. Some equipment items such as trucks may be purchased within a few months of the initial decision, while the construction of new plant facilities or the installation of large equipment may require several years. In the case of investments with long time lags, economic conditions may change radically from buoyant sales when the investment decision is made, to slack demand when the investment comes on line for production. The complexity of the relationship is illustrated when we examine how CURs in one year are related to investment in the following year. Such an analysis results in a correlation coefficient of .22, compared to the coefficient of .65 in Figures 32a and 32b, which results when the same year is used for the CUR and investment. One reason for this weaker relationship may be the opportunity to postpone or cancel investment decisions with long time lags between the time a construction contract is made or an equipment order is placed and the time when the capital facility is used in production.

Another factor complicating the relationship between the CUR and investment is the CUR's tendency to function as a threshold in this relationship: or, what is sometimes referred to as a "flashpoint." That is, above a particular CUR level, businesses are assumed to increase plant and equipment expenditures substantially to expand capacity in order to meet the increased demand for their products, while below the threshold businesses are assumed to retrench capital spending and concentrate on modernizing by replacing inefficient and outmoded facilities rather than on expanding capacity. The CUR threshold is often cited at about 83 percent, which is slightly above the 1948–89 average of 82.3 percent. (Over the forty-one-year period, the CUR ranged from 73 percent in 1982 to 91 percent in 1966.) My own statistical analysis suggests that the threshold is probably higher.

I first performed separate analyses of the type in Figures 32a and 32b for CURs above and below the following assumed thresholds: 72–79 vs. 80–91 percent; 72–82 vs. 83–91 percent; and 72–83 vs. 85–91 percent. (There were no years when the CUR averaged 84 percent, that is, was between 84.0–84.9 percent, although there were months when the CUR was within that range.) With this approach, a threshold is indicated when the slopes of the two lines representing the long-term average relationship in each of the paired CUR ranges changes, with the line in the higher range of each pair tilting up more sharply. Specifically, the average line for 80–91 percent would tilt upward more than the line for 72–79 percent, and the same would be true for 83–91 compared to 72–82 percent and for 85–91 compared to 72–83 percent. However, this did not occur in these cases. In fact, the opposite pattern occurred: investment rose more sharply for each percentage point increase in the lower range of the CUR than in the higher range.[16] This reflects the fact that although investment typically declines when the CUR is at 72–79 percent, the *fall in the rate of decline* for each percentage point increase in the CUR in this range is greater than the rate of increase in investment for each percentage point increase in the CUR above 80 percent. Thus, this analysis for determining whether there is a threshold neither

Table 16

Capacity Utilization and Plant and Equipment Investment: 1948–89

Capacity utilization rate (percent)	Plant and equipment investment in 1982 dollars (percent change from previous year)	Number of years at each CUR
72	−11.3	1
73	−10.5	1
74	−12.1	2
75	−25.4	1
77	−4.2	1
78	−3.7	3
79	−0.1	3
80	9.8	4
81	3.0	3
82	2.4	3
83	6.7	6
85	15.0	5
86	13.0	2
87	−0.8	3
88	14.5	1
89	8.9	2
91	17.8	1

Average	82	Average	3.7	Total	42

confirmed nor disproved the hypothesis. However, comparing the slopes of the average line for the 83–91 and 85–91 percent CUR ranges (as noted above, there are no years when the CUR averaged 84 percent) suggests a modest threshold when the CUR reaches 85 percent. At this level and above, the rate of investment increases for each percentage point increase in the CUR, rising from a 0.54 percent increase in the 83–91 range to a 0.74 percent increase in the 85–91 percent range.[17] The caveat in this analysis, however, is that the statistical tests of significance are weak, and the findings are therefore only suggestive.

A simpler way to search for a CUR threshold is represented in Table 16. The average change in investment for each two-digit CUR level—that is, 72, 73, . . . , 91 percent—is compared with the long-term average annual increase in plant and equipment investment. The long-term average CUR of 82.3 percent is rounded to 82 percent in the table. Investment rose at an average annual rate of 3.7 percent over the 1948–89 period. Thus, a threshold would be suggested if investment substantially exceeded this average for a sustained period when the CUR was

Table 17

Capacity Utilization and the Propensity to Invest

	(1) Capacity utilization rate (percent)	(2) Plant and equipment investment in 1982 dollars (average annual percent change during period)	(3) Propensity to invest (2)/(1)	(4) Decade propensity as a proportion of the long-term average (3)/0.045 x 100 (percent)
1948–59	82.8	1.0	0.012	27
1960–69	85.0	7.6	0.089	198
1970–79	81.9	2.7	0.033	73
1980–89	79.5	4.1	0.052	116
1948–89	82.3	3.7	0.045	100

above a certain level. The table shows the following: When the CUR was in the 72–79 percent range, investment declined (although at the 79 percent CUR, investment declined only 0.1 percent); at an 80 percent CUR, investment rose 10 percent, much faster than the long-term rate; at an 81–82 percent CUR, the investment increase fell to 2 to 3 percent, which was slower than the long-term rate; at an 83 percent CUR, investment accelerated to 7 percent, which was significantly faster than the long-term rate but slower than at the 80 percent CUR; and at an 85–91 percent CUR, investment increased from 9 to 18 percent, much faster than the long-term rate, with the single exception that when the CUR was at 87 percent, investment declined 1 percent.

These patterns indicate an incipient threshold at the 83 percent CUR, but it becomes robust at an 85 percent CUR. The rapid rise in investment at the 80 percent CUR seems to be an anomaly. There is also a caveat in this analysis: averaging investment at the two-digit CUR masks large differences in investment within the same CUR in different years. For example, in the three years that averaged a 79 percent CUR, investment declined by 2.8 and 6.4 percent in two years and increased 8.8 in the other year; similarly, for the six years that averaged an 83 percent CUR, investment increases ranged from 0.4 to 12.7 percent.

The CUR–investment relationship is further complicated by the fact that investment typically responds both to the level and the annual change of the CUR. That is, while a higher CUR tends to generate more investment than a low CUR, it is also true that a rising CUR will generate more investment than a declining CUR quite apart from the absolute value of the CUR. However, including both the level and percentage point change in the CUR in assessing trends in investment resulted in only a slight improvement in the correlation coefficient to .68, up from the .65 in Figures 32a and 32b.

Figure 33. **Real Plant and Equipment Investment Propensity in Manufacturing Industries: 1948–89**

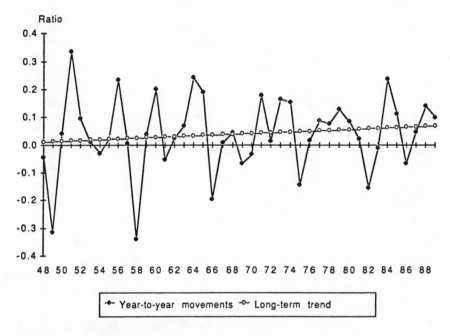

Note: Investment propensity is the annual percent change in investment divided by the capacity utilization rate.

Lastly, the variability between changes in the CUR and plant and equipment investment may also reflect changes in the propensity to invest at given CUR levels. The propensity to invest is calculated by taking the ratio of the percent change in investment to the CUR level in the same period. Table 17 shows the average propensity to invest during 1948–89. The long-term propensity over the 1948–89 period is 0.045. During 1948–59, the propensity was only 27 percent of the long-term average, but it jumped to 98 percent above the average in the 1960s, dropped to 73 percent of the average in the 1970s, and rose to 16 percent above the average in the 1980s. This considerable fluctuation in the propensity to invest over the forty-two-year period reflects the importance of factors other than the CUR, such as profits, in driving investment.

Figure 33 shows the yearly investment propensity and the long-term average trend during the 1948–89 period. It indicates continuous yearly volatility, although the gyrations since the late 1960s, while still significant, are less extreme. One reason the movements have dampened since the 1960s is that businesses appear to have become more cautious in responding to short-term increases in the CUR. Rather than risk overexpanding with quick increases in plant and equipment investment, they seem to wait longer until larger markets for their products become more certain.

Over the 1948–89 period, the investment propensity rose at an average annual rate of 4.8 percent (the straight line in Figure 33). Thus, the rate of investment has been increasing at a given CUR level. The long-term upward movement is also evident in Table 17 which shows that investment during the 1980s rose 4.1 percent when the CUR averaged only 79.5 percent, making the 1980s the decade with the highest investment propensity over the forty-two-year period, except for the 1960s. The rising propensity in the 1980s may be due to the increasing use of computers and their frequent upgrading, including that by small businesses.

In conclusion, CURs represent a partial but important segment of the economy. However, the statistical relationship between the CUR and investment in manufacturing over time is only a broad order of magnitude. *In assessing the effect of the CUR movements on future investment, the analyst should include the effect of the other indicators of future investment discussed in Chapter 3: the underlying role of profits, as well as interest rates and actual investment decisions reflected in business plans to invest, contracts and orders for capital facilities, and capital appropriations by companies.*

CURs and Prices

The relationship between the CUR in manufacturing industries and price movements may be assessed in comparing changes in the CURs to three different measures of price change: the producer price index for industrial commodities (composed of manufactured and mineral products) prepared by the Bureau of Labor Statistics; the consumer price index (CPI) prepared by the Bureau of Labor Statistics (Chapter 6); and the GNP implicit price deflator prepared by the Bureau of Economic Analysis (Chapter 3). Figures 34, 35, and 36 show these relationships, in which the percentage levels of the CUR are compared to the annual percent changes of the three price measures during 1948–89. The correlation coefficients are .05 for industrial commodities prices, –.08 for the CPI, and –.08 for the GNP price deflator. Thus, the analysis shows almost no relationship between the CUR and the three price measures, since a coefficient of 1 indicates identical movements and a coefficient of zero indicates no similarity in the movements, as discussed in the previous section on investment.[18]

Moreover, the CUR relationships with the CPI and the GNP price deflator indicated by the negative correlation coefficients and the negative long-term average relationships (depicted by the lines of white diamonds in Figures 35 and 36 which slope downward to the right) are suspect. These inverse relationships suggest prices rise more slowly as the CUR reaches higher levels—that is, prices decline when the CUR increases. As noted in the introduction to the CUR section, such movements are to be expected when the economy is recovering from the low CURs of a recession because unit costs of production decline with the

Figure 34. **Capacity Utilization in Manufacturing Industries vs. the Industrial Commodities Price Index: 1948–89**

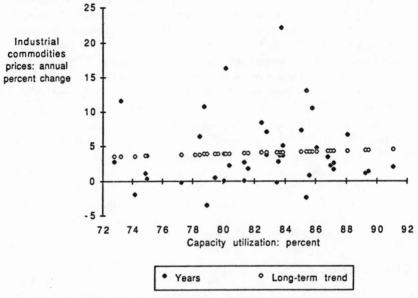

Note: Based on Federal Reserve Board and Bureau of Labor Statistics data.

greater volume of production. But inverse movements are not expected when the economy is operating above the economic activity levels of the previous business cycle expansion, which occurs most of the time (Chapter 2). In these periods, unit costs of production tend to rise because of machinery breakdowns, use of less efficient equipment, the hiring of less productive workers when unemployment is low, and a certain laxness among management noted above, which is referred to as X-efficiency.[19] While the long-term relationship between the CUR and industrial commodities prices is direct (positive), with prices rising faster as the CUR reaches higher levels, this relationship is not consistent. At the higher CUR levels of 83–91 percent and 85–91 percent, the relationship is inverse, at a time when one would expect it to be most robustly direct.

However, for some industries these inverse relationships between the CUR and price changes may not be as contradictory as the theory suggests. It is conceivable that in some cases equipment does not break down any more often at high operating rates than at low rates and indeed may even perform better when continually in use. Similarly, hiring less productive workers when unemployment is low may not be very much of a problem in the basic processing industries, such as textiles, paper, chemicals, and petroleum refining, where output is typically expanded by using more raw materials and running the equipment longer rather than by hiring more labor. Thus, at least in the basic processing industries, an

Figure 35. **Capacity Utilization in Manufacturing Industries vs. the Consumer Price Index: 1948–89**

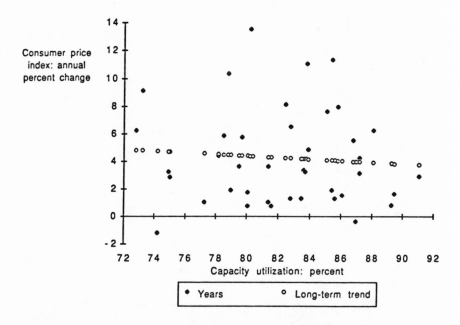

Note: Based on Federal Reserve Board and Bureau of Labor Statistics data.

inverse CUR–price relationship may be realistic. Still, for all manufacturing industries in the aggregate, the correlation coefficient is very low, suggesting that on the whole the relationship between CURs and prices is not significant.

At the same time, a close relationship between the CUR and industrial prices and between the CUR and the CPI occurred during 1983–89. The correlation coefficient over the seven-year period was 0.6 in both cases, indicating a direct relationship, but the year-to-year movements varied widely. Although the correlation for the GNP price deflator during 1983–89 also showed a direct relationship, it was still almost nonexistent at 0.06. The improved relationship for industrial prices and the CPI probably reflects two significant features of the 1980s: a sharp decline followed by relative stability in oil prices, and a marked slowdown in the rate of wage increases (see Chapter 5). These changes in oil prices and wages affected prices much less than they had previously, however, and the CUR therefore appears to have a correspondingly greater impact.

This closer relationship during 1983–89, while substantial, has been too short to consider the CUR as a weighty factor affecting price movements. For the new relationship to continue, the economy will have to remain relatively free of sharp changes in oil prices, wages, or other price factors that override the significance of the CUR. Also, even though the average relationship is more closely corre-

Figure 36. **Capacity Utilization in Manufacturing Industries vs. the GNP Implicit Price Deflator: 1948–89**

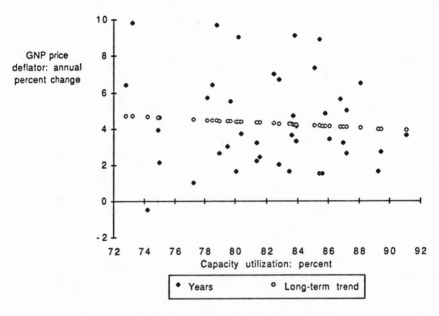

Note: Based on Federal Reserve Board and Bureau of Economic Analysis data.

lated, the yearly movements' wide variation from the average relationship severely hampers using CURs to predict price movements in particular periods.

Relationships developed from analyses done at the economy wide level typically do not hold for all components within the aggregate, such as for all industries. For example, in an econometric analysis, William Kan, Reva Krieger, and P. A. Tinsley conclude that CURs noticeably affect prices for primary processing and materials industries.[20]

To sum up, there is little observed long-term relationship between the CUR and overall price movements. *The analyst should monitor the closer relationship that appeared in the 1980s to determine if CURs will be a significant factor to consider in future price movements.*

SUMMARY

The IPI covers the economy's most cyclically volatile segments. While the manufacturing, mining, and utilities industries covered in the IPI represent only one-fourth of the GNP, they generate a significant business for service industries and account for the bulk of plant and equipment investment. They therefore have a large secondary impact on the entire economy. On average, an annual growth rate in the IPI of at least 3 percent is needed to generate sufficient GNP growth to reduce the unemployment rate.

The CUR provides a theoretical basis for assessing future demand for plant and equipment and inflationary pressures. Experience over the post–World War II period indicates that the CUR is related to capital investment in manufacturing. No simple empirical relationship is apparent between the CUR and economywide price movements over the postwar period, although a relationship between the CUR and industrial and consumer prices did occur in the 1980s.

REVIEW QUESTIONS

• Why is the industrial production index more cyclically volatile than real GNP?

• The industrial production index accounts for only one-fourth of the GNP, but it has important secondary impacts that affect a much greater share of the GNP. What are the secondary impacts?

• In the 1980s, less of an increase in the industrial production index was required to lower the unemployment rate than in previous decades.

What caused this change?

How may this relationship change again in the 1990s?

• Why are movements of the capacity utilization rate determined more by industrial production (numerator) than by capacity (denominator)?

• Capacity utilization affects plant and equipment investment differently when capacity utilization is above or below a threshold level.

What is the difference?

Is the threshold concept viable for economic analysis?

• Why is the capacity utilization rate of limited usefulness for analyzing inflation?

NOTES

1. For a description of the methodology, see Kenneth Armitage and Dixon A. Tranum, "Industrial Production: 1989 Developments and Historical Revision," *Federal Reserve Bulletin,* April 1990. A more detailed description of the methodology is available in Board of Governors of the Federal Reserve System, *Industrial Production 1986 Edition: With a Description of the Methodology,* December 1986.

2. These weights are based on Census Bureau value-added data. They differ from GNP value-added measures which do not double-count purchased services or purchased goods, but include sales and property taxes.

3. Armitage and Tranum, "Industrial Production."

4. Joan D. Hosley and James E. Kennedy, "A Revision of the Index of Industrial Production," *Federal Reserve Bulletin,* July 1985, p. 488.

5. Because of several technical differences in the measurement of the IPI and the GNP, attempts to "reconcile" differences in the cyclical movements of GNP goods and the IPI by modifying the definitions to make the two indicators conform more closely have only been partially successful.

6. Michael L. Dertouzos, Richard K. Lester, Robert M. Solow, and The MIT Commission on Industrial Productivity, *Made in America: Regaining the Productive Edge* (The MIT Press: 1989), pp. 39–42.

7. Zoltan E. Kenessey, "The Development of a Monthly Service Output Index," *The Service Economy,* Coalition of Services Industries, April 1989, pp. 1–5.

8. In prosperous times, managers probably have less pressure to seek more efficient operations and eliminate marginal activities than in periods of slow growth or recessions, when businesses tend to be more aggressive in cutting costs. These practices over the business cycle are difficult to quantify, but they are intuitively plausible and also appear anecdotally in the press. They are related in the economic literature to the idea of "X-efficiency," which typically associates differences in competitive pressures in monopolistic and more competitive industries. See Harvey Leibenstein, "Allocative Efficiency vs. 'X-Efficiency,' " *American Economic Review*, June 1966, and F. M. Scherer, *Industrial Market Structure and Economic Performance*, 2d ed. (Rand McNally College Publishing: 1980), pp. 464–66.

9. For a description of the methodology, see Richard D. Raddock, "Recent Developments in Industrial Capacity and Utilization," *Federal Reserve Bulletin*, June 1990.

10. Using capital stock data to estimate capacity poses several problems: (1) capital stock data are developed indirectly by cumulating annual capital expenditures and deducting annual depreciation, rather than from direct measures of capital stocks based on industry survey data; (2) how to account for plant and equipment investment intended primarily to reduce pollution and improve worker health and safety; and (3) how to account for the differing importance of long-lasting equipment items compared to those that are replaced frequently. For a general discussion of the use of capital stock data in economic analysis, see Stephen D. Oliner, "Private Business Capital: Trends, Recent Developments, and Measurement Issues," *Federal Reserve Bulletin*, December 1989.

11. One analyst suggests that even in a major mobilization it is unrealistic to expect CURs in the 100 percent range. See Zoltan E. Kenessey, "Capacity Utilization Statistics: Further Plans," *Measures of Capacity Utilization: Problems and Tasks*, Board of Governors of the Federal Reserve System (Staff Studies 105), July 1979, pp. 245–48.

12. Richard D. Raddock, "Revised Federal Reserve Rates of Capacity Utilization," *Federal Reserve Bulletin*, October 1985.

13. Bureau of the Census, U.S. Department of Commerce, "Survey of Plant Capacity, 1987," *Current Industrial Reports*, January 1989, Appendix B, p. B-1.

14. Raddock, "Revised Federal Reserve Rates," pp. 761–62.

15. A correlation coefficient of 1 occurs when the variables move in the same patterns in a direct relationship (both rise or fall in tandem), and a coefficient of −1 occurs when the variables move in opposite patterns in an inverse relationship (one rises and the other falls).

16. The statistical relationships are:

Capacity utilization rate	Percentage increase in plant and equipment for a one percentage point increase in the CUR
72–91%	1.59%
72–79	2.39
80–91	0.57
72–82	2.35
83–91	0.54
72–83	2.10
85–91	0.74

17. See note 16.

18. See note 15.

19. See note 8.

20. William Kan, Reva Krieger, and P. A. Tinsley, "The Long and Short of Industrial Strength Pricing," Finance and Economic Discussion Series, Federal Reserve Board, November 1989.

5
UNEMPLOYMENT, EMPLOYMENT, AND PRODUCTIVITY

Labor is the dominant source of household income. It is also the dominant cost item to business and governments in producing the nation's goods and services: employee compensation (wages and fringe benefits) accounts for about 60 percent of the GNP (see Chapter 3). Hence, trends in employment and unemployment have tremendous economic significance.

This chapter focuses on the main labor indicators of unemployment, employment, and productivity. The basic data for these indicators are provided monthly and quarterly by the Bureau of Labor Statistics in the U.S. Department of Labor. The unemployment rate, probably the most familiar indicator, is discussed first, followed by employment (which includes hours worked and wage rates) and productivity (which includes the relationship of unit labor costs to inflation).

The discussion of trends in employment and unemployment is limited to what they indicate about economic growth and material living conditions. However, the analyst should note that these trends may also affect the economy in more intangible ways, such as the effect they may have on personal satisfaction and social stability. While, strictly speaking, these factors are not "economic," they can affect economic developments. For example, voters experiencing high unemployment are more likely to vote for politicians who offer new economic theories and the promise of job creation. While such cause-and-effect relationships are difficult to quantify, the analyst should bear them in mind when considering the economic policy implications of employment data.

UNEMPLOYMENT

The unemployment rate (UR) is the proportion of the nation's working population sixteen years of age and older that is out of work and looking for a job. It functions as a relative measure of the degree of slack in job markets. A relatively high UR indicates that production may be expanded without generating inflation, because the available labor supply will tend to moderate wage rate increases and in some cases reduce wage rates. Conversely, in periods of low unemployment, rapid economic growth will frequently raise wages—the tighter labor supply pushes up wages as more jobs are filled with less experienced and less productive workers. It should be noted, however, that the overall UR may mask significant differences among local markets, occupations and industries, and demo-graphic groups.

PART A: ESTIMATING METHODOLOGY

There are several measures of unemployment. All are calculated by figuring the number of unemployed persons as a proportion of the labor force, which is defined as the sum of employed plus unemployed persons. The basic difference among the various measures is the definition of the unemployed.[1]

$$\text{Unemployment rate} = \frac{\text{Unemployed persons}}{\substack{\text{Employed plus unemployed persons} \\ \text{(Labor force)}}} \times 100$$

The most widely accepted UR measure defines the labor force as consisting of persons at least sixteen years old who have a job or are actively seeking work. This conventional definition has two variants, one covering both civilian and armed-forces employment and the other including only civilian employment. The employment component includes full-time and part-time jobs as paid em-ployees, self-employment, and persons working at nonpaid jobs in a family business for at least fifteen hours a week. Thus, the employed population con-sists of wage earners and of those who work for profit, the latter being the self-employed and unpaid workers in family businesses who are assumed to share in the profits. All persons are counted equally if they are paid for an hour or more of work per week. If a person has two or more jobs, the job with the most hours worked in the week is the only one counted in the figures. (The effect of this treatment is compared with a different employment measure in the next section on employment). Unemployed persons are those who looked for a job at least once in the previous four weeks and specify an acceptable job search (for example, answered a newspaper advertisement or checked with an employment agency, employer, friends, or relatives).

Persons under sixteen years of age (regardless of their employment status) and those with no job who are not actively seeking work are "not in the labor force" and therefore are not included in the UR figures. For example, "discour-aged workers"—persons sixteen and older who are not looking for a job because they believe jobs are unavailable in their area or in their line of work, or because they believe that they would not qualify for existing job openings—are not included in the labor force or UR measures because they are neither working nor looking for work. Typically, discouraged workers represent from 0.6 to 1.2 per-cent of the labor force, tending toward the lower figure in expansions and the higher in recessions.

The information used in deriving the UR is obtained from a monthly survey of a sample of about 60,000 households, called the Current Population Survey

(CPS), which the Census Bureau conducts for the Bureau of Labor Statistics. The survey refers to the individual's employment status during the calendar week that includes the twelve day of the month, while the survey is conducted during the following week. Because the sample may not be fully representative of the demographic and economic characteristics of America's 93 million households (as of 1989), the chances are that in two of three cases, the error in the level and monthly movement of the UR is plus or minus 0.1 percentage point.[2] For example, if the UR is 7 percent, it most likely is in the range of 6.9 to 7.1 percent. Because of this sampling error, a single month-to-month change of 0.1 percentage point is not statistically significant, but a change of 0.2 percentage point or more is statistically significant. By the same token, cumulated changes in the UR in the same upward and downward direction of 0.1 percentage point a month for two or more months in a row are statistically significant. If the reliability range is raised to nineteen of twenty cases—thus raising the accuracy of the figures from the above example of two out of three cases—the sampling error for the level and change rises to 0.2 percentage point, and the above examples are increased accordingly. Thus, a UR of 7 percent would have an error range of 6.8 to 7.2 percent, and a monthly change would have to be at least 0.3 percentage point to be statistically significant.

Some economists believe that the measured UR is too high because the labor force figures do not include persons working in the underground economy (see Chapter 1 for a general discussion of the underground economy). In a 1984 review of the literature on the problem, the Bureau of Labor Statistics questioned the validity of other analysts' estimates, such as that in 1978 the official UR was overstated by 1.5 percentage points.[3] They concluded that there are no sound estimates of the underground economy's effect on the UR, and that their analysis of the household survey data did not substantiate the claims of a significant effect on the UR. However, this issue is still unresolved, and the analyst should follow new findings on the topic. If such estimates are developed, they also would affect the employment figures discussed in the next section.

The CPS is a voluntary personal interview survey of the employment status of one adult member of each household selected in the sampling frame. If the survey participant is unavailable at the time of the interview, another adult member of the household (such as a spouse) who is familiar with the individual's employment status may answer the questions by proxy. In order to reduce reporting burden, a fraction of the survey sample is continually replaced with new households. Each survey participant is interviewed for four months, dropped from the survey for the next eight months, and finally included in the survey for the subsequent four months; participation in the survey ends after this sixteen-month period. As indicated by the sample of questions summarized below, people are not asked if they are unemployed. Rather, unemployment is determined from the consistency of their answers to the questions to ensure that the same unemployment definitions are used for all survey participants.

• Did you do any work at all last week, not counting work around the house?

• Several questions on your employment status (including cross-checks) on hours worked per week, pay rate, and time off from the job.

• Have you been looking for work during the past four weeks?

• What have you been doing in the last four weeks to find work?

• At the time you started looking for work, was it because you lost or quit a job or was there some other reason?

• How many weeks have you been looking for work?

• Could you have taken a job last week if one had been offered?

• When did you last work for pay at a regular job or business either full-time or part-time?

• Why did you leave that job?

• Do you want a regular job now, either full- or part-time?

• What are the reasons you are not looking for work?

• Do you intend to look for work of any kind in the next twelve months?

• Several questions on your job search (including cross-checks) on when last worked, when laid off, and how long looking for work.

Discouraged Workers

The Bureau of Labor Statistics is reviewing the CPS during the early 1990s to determine if survey questions accurately measure the labor force, given the existing labor force definitions. Changes to the questionnaire based on this research are planned for 1994. An important purpose of the review is to find better means of identifying discouraged workers who, as noted above, are currently excluded from labor force counts.

The current method counts persons as discouraged workers if they say they want a job but are not seeking work because they think they cannot get a job. However, such persons are not asked when they last looked for work; the answer to this question would provide some indication of how committed the discouraged worker is to finding a job. Previous research by Harvey Hamel, and Kennon Copeland and Jennifer Rothgeb suggests that counting workers as discouraged only if they looked for work at least once during the past six months would lower the number of discouraged workers by about 50 percent.[4] The National Commission on Employment and Unemployment Statistics (Levitan Commission) recommended that the BLS adopt this method.[5] The BLS is currently developing methods to count persons as discouraged workers only if they actively looked for a job at least once during the past year. The BLS plans to use the one-year criterion because of the small difference in the number of persons who say they conducted at least one job search in the past twelve months compared to the number who say they looked during the past six months. In part this reflects a tendency of survey respondents known as "telescoping": when asked to recall events of the past six months, people find it easier to recollect in a time span of one year and thus often include events of the past twelve months as occurring in the past six months.

The Levitan Commission also recommended that the BLS should continue excluding discouraged workers from the labor force, although a minority of the commission's members felt that the BLS should include discouraged workers in the labor force. Including discouraged workers in the unemployment figures would raise the unemployment rate by approximately 0.6 to 1.2 percentage points, based on the current count of discouraged workers. However, under the new method of identifying discouraged workers, which is planned to be instituted in 1994, including discouraged workers in calculating the unemployment rate would only raise the UR by approximately 0.3 to 0.6 percentage point since the number of discouraged workers will be about 50 percent lower.

Alternative Unemployment Rates

The BLS provides eight alternative URs based on the household survey (Table 18). The lowest UR is associated with persons unemployed for fifteen weeks or longer. The highest includes persons working part-time who would work full-time if jobs were available, plus "discouraged" workers who do not look for work because they think there are no jobs for them. The range between these extremes is considerable—1.3 to 9 percent in the fourth quarter of 1990, with the conventional definitions at 6 percent. URs are also calculated from the household survey for demographic groups by age, race, ethnic origin, gender, and family responsibility to highlight variations that different population segments have in obtaining work. In addition, there is a measure of unemployment based on unemployment insurance data, although as discussed below, it is not comparable to the eight URs.

The two conventional URs that are the most widely accepted (U–5a and U–5b in Table 18) are the "official" measures. These two are the most neutral in terms of value judgments related to the widely accepted labor force definitions. They include all unemployed workers and give equal weight to each unemployed person. The only difference between them is the inclusion of the resident armed forces (those stationed in the United States) as a portion of the labor force in the 5a measure. Typically, their measures differ by only 0.1 percentage point—the UR (5a) including the armed forces being lower than the civilian UR (5b).

Although their movements over time are similar, the different UR definitions indicate a varying absolute range of slackness in the economy. They therefore tend to be cited selectively by persons characterizing the extent of unemployment, depending on social or political perspectives. For example, those who wish to emphasize the economy's success in generating employment highlight the U–1 end of the spectrum giving the lower URs (political conservatives), and those who wish to emphasize the economy's failure to provide jobs highlight the U–7 end giving the higher URs (political liberals). This does not necessarily reflect

Table 18

**Alternative Unemployment Rates Using Varying Definitions
of Unemployment and the Labor Force** (in percent)

		1990:4[a]
U–1	Persons unemployed 15 weeks or longer as a percentage of the civilian labor force	1.3
U–2	Job losers as a percentage of the civilian labor force[b]	3.0
U–3	Unemployed persons 25 years and over as a percentage of the civilian labor force	4.7
U–4	Unemployed full-time jobseekers as a percentage of the full-time civilian labor force	5.7
U–5a	**Total unemployed (16 years and older) as a percentage of the labor force, including the resident armed forces**	**5.8**
U–5b	**Total unemployed (16 years and older) as a percentage of the civilian labor force**	**5.9**
U–6	Unemployed persons seeking full-time jobs plus ½ of unemployed persons seeking part-time jobs plus ½ of employed persons who are working part-time for economic reasons as a percentage of the civilian labor force less ½ of the part-time labor force[c]	8.1
U–7	U–6 plus discouraged workers as a percentage of the civilian labor force plus discouraged workers less ½ of the part-time labor force	8.9

Source: Bureau of Labor Statistics, U.S. Department of Labor, "The Employment Situation: April 1991" (News Release), May 3, 1991, Table A–8.

[a]Fourth quarter of 1990.

[b]Job losers are unemployed because they were laid off or fired.

[c]"Part-time for economic reasons" refers to persons who wish to work full-time but who are working less than 35 hours a week because of slack work, materials shortages, or other factors beyond their control.

the tendency of the political party in power, which whether liberal or conservative, would seek to show they are providing more jobs.

Unemployment and Unemployment Insurance

A different measure of unemployment based on persons collecting unemployment insurance benefit payments is provided weekly and monthly by the Employment and Training Administration in the U.S. Department of Labor. Its main use for macroeconomic analysis is that the figures on persons filing initial claims for benefit payments when they become unemployed are a component of the composite index of leading indicators (see Chapter 8). In addition, because the insured UR data are available weekly and because their monthly movements (the average of the four weeks) tend to be similar although not identical to those for the household UR, they are sometimes used as a clue to the forthcoming monthly household UR.

The unemployment insurance data coverage is limited to persons filing claims for unemployment insurance benefits and consequently is a much less comprehensive unemployment measure than those based on the household survey discussed above. In 1989, for example, on average 2.3 million unemployed workers filed for benefits in state and federal unemployment insurance programs, compared with 6.5 million workers counted as unemployed in the household survey. Thus, insured unemployment represented only 36 percent of all unemployment. Overall, in 1989 the insured UR was 1.9 percent compared to the household UR of 5.2 percent.

Many unemployed persons cannot receive unemployment insurance because benefits are payable only to those who (a) lost their job, with exceptions in some states for those who quit their jobs with good cause, (b) previously worked long enough to be eligible for benefit payments (e.g., six months), (c) applied for benefit payments, and (d) have not exhausted the period (e.g., twenty-six weeks) during which they may collect the payments. Thus, insured unemployment excludes such groups as young persons looking for their first job after graduation, former workers who are re-entering the labor force, and those who are otherwise ineligible or have exhausted their unemployment benefits.

The basic purpose of unemployment insurance is to cushion workers who have lost their jobs against personal and economic hardship. In addition, by bolstering household incomes, unemployment insurance helps stabilize the economy and lessen the overall economic decline during recessions (see Chapter 3 under Consumer Expenditures). However, there has been a long-term decline in the proportion of laid-off workers who collect unemployment insurance benefit payments, which accelerated sharply in the 1980s. (In most states, workers who are fired for a work-related cause do not collect unemployment benefits; in a few states, fired workers are paid unemployment benefits after a fixed period of time.) Based on the number of workers receiving unemployment benefits and the number of workers laid off from their jobs who are covered by unemployment insurance, unemployment benefits were paid to practically all workers who lost their jobs in 1979 (98 percent) and 1980 (97 percent); however, this proportion then dropped sharply, reaching a low of 58 percent in 1984, and subsequently partially rebounded to 78 percent by 1989. Thus, by 1989, over 20 percent of workers who lost their jobs failed to receive unemployment benefits. In addition to the greater personal hardship, economists are concerned that this trend will diminish the stabilizing effect of unemployment insurance during recessions that may occur in the 1990s.

The *national* patterns of unemployment insurance vary widely among the states. State governments run the unemployment insurance program under general federal standards that give the states complete discretion to determine who is eligible for unemployment benefits, how much in benefits they are paid, and how long they are paid. Legally, the states are not required to pay any unemployment benefits, but all states do pay them since it would be politically impractical not to do so. However, the generosity of the benefits varies considerably among the states: as of mid-1990, unemployed persons collecting unemployment benefits as a proportion of total unemployment (as defined by the UR measure of unemployment) ranged from 13 percent in South Dakota to 52 percent in Rhode Island; and average weekly benefit payments ranged from $102 in Louisiana to $218 in Massachusetts. Employers in all states must pay a federally-mandated tax for each employee into the unemployment insurance state trust fund regardless of the state's benefit program. The employer's tax varies according to the level of unemployment insurance benefits paid to former employees who were laid off— that is, an employer with a high layoff rate pays a higher tax than an employer with a low layoff (the layoff rate is referred to as the "experience rating").

Walter Corson and Walter Nicholson found that the 1980s' sharp decline in the proportion of laid-off workers who collect unemployment insurance is attributable to several changes in economic factors and in federal and state government policies:[6]

• The continued decline in manufacturing reduced the unemployment insurance coverage because workers in manufacturing industries have higher rates of applying for and receiving unemployment benefits than workers in the faster-growing service industries.

• The distribution of unemployed workers shifted geographically from the high unemployment insurance coverage states in the northeast to the low coverage states in the southern and central states.

• The federal government made many cutbacks in unemployment insurance programs. In the 1970s, these made unemployment benefits taxable and required that Social Security benefits be offset when unemployment benefits are collected at the same time. In the 1980s, the extended unemployment benefits available when the twenty-six-week regular benefit period expires were made less generous, unemployment insurance trust fund and loan provisions to state governments were made more stringent, a cut in federal funds to the states for administering the program led to a tightening of state budgets for unemployment insurance, and the taxation of unemployment benefits was extended to include the benefits of lower income persons.

• The state governments tightened eligibility rules in part because of the cutback in federal funds described above.

• Employers increasingly challenged their workers' initial claims for unemployment benefits. As noted above, the experience rating feature of the employer unemployment insurance tax penalizes the employer for greater numbers of former employees collecting unemployment benefits. Most of the challenges are brought by the nonunionized companies, which dominate the faster-growing service industries.[7]

In a survey of unemployed workers who did not apply for unemployment insurance benefits during 1989–90, Wayne Vroman found that 45 percent of those who had lost their jobs believed they were ineligible for the benefits.[8] He concludes that research is needed on the effects of the above-noted tightening of eligibility requirements in the 1980s on declining applications (the study lacked funds to examine this topic) and on the question of how well workers understand eligibility criteria for receipt of benefits.

Economists have also studied the effect of unemployment insurance benefits on the UR and concluded that unemployment insurance probably raises the UR above what it would be in the absence of unemployment insurance, but the extent is not known. On the one hand, unemployment insurance increases the UR because by providing some income it lessens an unemployed worker's immediate need to take a job. The availability of unemployment insurance also may encourage some people to enter the labor market to build up unemployment insurance benefits to be covered in the event of future unemployment; the immediate effect of this increase in the labor force is to raise the UR, although if the new entrants become employed it then lowers the UR. On the other hand, unemployment insurance helps lower the UR because it increases consumer spending, and thereby production and employment, above what they would be without the income supplements. Unemployment insurance also tends to lower the UR because the employer's tax varies directly with the benefits paid to former employees who are laid off (experience rating), and thus the employer has an incentive to minimize layoffs.

Estimates of the effect of unemployment insurance on unemployment typically focus on the impact of *changes in the generosity* of the benefits as measured by which unemployed persons are eligible for unemployment insurance benefits, the dollar payments of the benefits, and the length of time that benefits are paid. In general, the research indicates that increasing the generosity of unemployment benefits lengthens the time unemployed persons take to find a new job (known as a "disincentive" effect), and lessening the generosity shortens the job search time ("incentive" effect), although estimates of these impacts on the UR are not available. Disincentive effects tend to be most apparent during periods of tight labor markets when the UR is low and workers believe it will be easy to become re-employed; in contrast, when labor markets are slack unemployed workers are prone to accept job offers sooner due to their fear that they will not get a subsequent job offer. In a study comparing the U.S. and Canadian unemployment insurance systems, Vivek Moorthy concludes that Canada's more generous unemployment insurance system caused the UR in Canada to be over 2 percentage points higher than the UR in the United States during the 1980s.[9] The Canadian system is more generous than the U.S. system in three ways: it includes people who have left the labor force and then re-entered the job market, not just those who were laid off; it provides broader coverage to those who have quit their jobs; and it pays higher and longer benefits. While these differences may not account for the entire differential in the URs of the two countries, it seems plausible that the more generous Canadian system has some disincentive effect compared to the U.S. system. Analogously, the tightening of unemployment insurance in the United States during the 1980s had an incentive effect on work effort and thus lowered the UR during the decade, although there are no estimates of how much.

To assess the cyclical stabilizing properties of consumer spending, the analyst should monitor the flow of unemployment benefits during recessions to determine the extent to which these benefits are maintaining household incomes (Chapter 3). The assessment should include the effect of changes in the unemployment insurance system on the proportion of laid-off workers who collect unemployment insurance benefit payments. The analyst should also keep in mind that changes in the generosity of unemployment benefits may affect UR movements. However, the weekly unemployment insurance data cumulated for four weeks should be treated only as suggestive of the official monthly UR because the unemployment insurance information does not always reflect the official UR movements.

Dynamic Factors in Labor Force and Unemployment Analysis

Long-term and short-term movements in and out of the labor force complicate UR analysis. As previously stated, the labor force is the sum of employed and unemployed persons. The "labor force participation rate" represents the number of persons in the labor force as a proportion of the population sixteen years of age and older.

Long-term demographic cycles are important in assessing UR trends over several years. Population changes resulting from long-term birthrate cycles have the most pronounced impact on the labor force over long-run five- and ten-year periods, mainly because of the lag in the effect of birthrates in previous decades on the working-age population. (Changing immigration, emigration, and death rates are less important factors affecting the working-age population.) For example, the low birthrates of the depression in the 1930s led to a low compounded annual increase of the working-age population in the 1950s of 1.0 percent; the baby boom of the latter 1940s and the 1950s resulted in faster average annual increases in the working-age population of 1.5 percent in the 1960s and 2.1 percent in the 1970s. The subsequent drop in birth rates during the 1960s and 1970s lowered the annual working-age population increases in the 1980s to 1.2 percent. Similar patterns appear when the working-age population is defined to exclude persons sixty-five years and older, despite the increasing proportion of the elderly in the population.[10]

Changes in the labor-force participation rate over the long run mainly reflect changes in life-style. These are typified by the tendency for increasing proportions of women to pursue a career while greater proportions of men have shortened their working careers by going to school longer and retiring earlier. The overall effect of these tendencies on the combined civilian participation rate for men and women has changed since 1950; while this total rate increased from only 59 percent to 60 percent from 1950 to 1970, the relatively large growth of women in the labor force during the 1970s raised the total rate in 1980 to 64 percent. In the 1980s, the influx of women slowed as the total rate in 1989 reached 66 percent. On balance, the long-run rising rates for women and declining rates for men have led to an upward trend in the total rate.

Over shorter cyclical periods, changes in the participation rates of persons entering and leaving the labor market are more likely to respond to short-term economic conditions. Typically, more people enter the labor force in expansions than in recessions, as the prospects of finding a job are higher in expansions than in recessions. Yet even in recessions there tends to be a general upward thrust in participation because of the underlying upward trend.

Monthly and quarterly movements of the participation rate are key items affecting the short-run UR because they indicate how individuals perceive their immediate chances of finding work. Intuitively, one would expect that more persons would enter the labor force during expansions than during recessions because they would be more hopeful of getting a job when the economy is growing. However, short-term movements in and out of the labor force do not always follow such expected patterns. For example, Carol Leon notes that in recessions it is not clear what the typical behavior is if one member of a family loses a job—whether this causes another family member to seek work to supplement the family's income (the added-worker effect), or if the declining job market discourages the second family member from seeking work (the discouraged-worker effect).[11] These alternative responses introduce an uncertain short-term factor into the labor force and the UR. At the extremes, a greater optimism about job prospects could cause a rise in the UR at the same time that employment is rising if more people enter the labor force than can be hired; conversely, if declining employment causes large numbers to withdraw from the labor market because of the pessimistic outlook for jobs, the UR could decline along with the falling employment (although this is more hypothetical than experiential, since unemployment has always increased in recessions).

In some months these movements in and out of the labor force lead to UR changes that outweigh changes in employment. In these cases, large numbers of persons leaving the labor force lower the UR while large numbers of persons entering the labor force raise the UR. Thus, UR trends may give a different picture of the economy than employment trends. In September 1990, for example, the UR increased although employment also increased. *Therefore, in evaluating UR movements, the analyst should consider the monthly effects of flows in and out of the labor force.*

PART B: ANALYSIS OF TRENDS

Over the post-World War II business cycles, the UR moved as expected—declining in expansions and rising in recessions. The only exception was the expansion from 1945 to 1948; the exceptionally low UR of 1.9 percent in 1945 was not sustained in the subsequent demobilization of war production and the reduction of the resident armed forces (from 11.4 million in 1945 to 1.5 million in 1948). Thus, the UR averaged 3.9 percent in 1946 and 1947 and 3.8 percent in 1948. In retrospect, these were the lowest "peacetime" URs in the postwar period, as discussed below. The relatively low URs in 1946–48 resulted from the strong civilian economy noted in Chapter 3, and from the return of many veterans to full-time schooling, which removed them from the labor force. In terms of timing at cyclical turning points, the UR is a leading indicator at the peak of expansions and a lagging indicator at the trough of recessions (see Chapter 8).

Several long-term features of the UR movements are noteworthy. First, unemployment levels worsened during the 1970s and early 1980s, drifting upward so that typically the low point at the peak of each expansion was higher than it was at the peak of the previous expansion. But during the 1983–90 expansion this pattern was reversed as the UR fell below that in the two previous expansions. Second, the UR has not been below 3 percent other than in the 1952–53 Korean War period, and since then it was below 4 percent for a sustained period only in the 1966–69 Vietnam War period. Third, the goal of achieving through fiscal and monetary policies, a minimum level of unemployment, corresponding to a notion of "full employment," without causing inflation has changed. In the 1960s it was believed the lowest feasible UR was 3 to 4 percent. In the 1970s this figure was raised to 5 to 7 percent, and there was little discussion of minimum unemployment goals in the 1980s, although as noted below, the Full Employment and Balanced Growth Act of 1978 specified unemployment goals of 4 percent for the 1980s.

Figure 37 shows the UR at the peaks of expansions and troughs of recessions from 1948 to 1990. The UR's shifting patterns over this postwar period are primarily the net effect of changes in the rate of economic growth, the demographic composition of the labor force, and labor productivity. The two consecutive decades of slowdown in the real GNP growth rate during the 1970s and 1980s damaged the economy's capacity to absorb the increasing numbers of persons seeking jobs (see Chapter 3). Although economic growth in the 1980s quickened after back-to-back recessions from 1980 to 1982, for the entire decade the growth rate was below that of the 1970s. The changing composition of the labor force, primarily the increased number of teenage workers and, secondly, the increasing participation of women in the labor force, raised the unemployment rate in the 1970s and lowered it in the 1980s. These effects are treated in detail in the following two sections. Finally, labor productivity improvement slowed in the 1970s and 1980s. Since the rate of labor productivity increase measures changes in workers' efficiency in producing goods and services, one might expect that the lower productivity improvement would have lowered the UR in the 1970s and 1980s. However, as discussed later in this chapter, the effect of productivity movements on the UR is indeterminate. The relationship

189

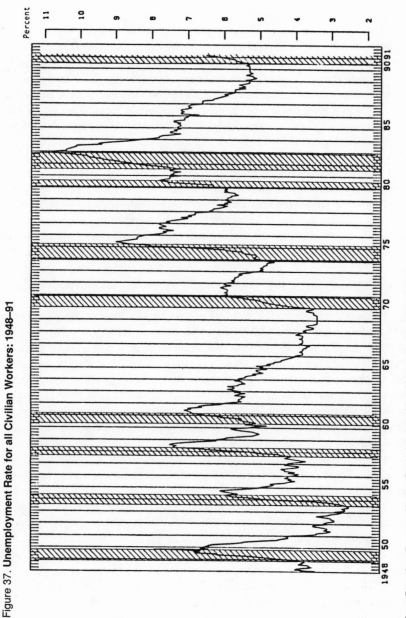

Figure 37. Unemployment Rate for all Civilian Workers: 1948–91

Note: Based on Bureau of Labor Statistics data. Lined bars are recession periods.

between productivity and employment is simply too complex to assume that they always move in either the opposite or the same directions.

Unemployment and Inflation Goals

Economic analysis has a major policy interest in determining the lowest UR level that can be sustained over long periods without causing inflation. Over the years this concept has been referred to variously as "full," "maximum," or "high" employment, "natural" unemployment, and the "nonaccelerating inflation rate of unemployment." Regardless of the terminology, the intent is to establish an employment level toward which the national should strive. Two major issues are relevant to developing a minimum UR: determining an "acceptable" inflation rate and adjusting the UR for the changing composition of the labor force.

With respect to inflation, a minimum UR raises the question of what rate of price increase accompanying minimum unemployment goals is acceptable. The 1956 UR of 4 percent and the 1.5 percent rise in the consumer price index were sometimes referred to as a desirable goal because that was the lowest peacetime UR since the Korean War. However, one year later, when the UR rose only slightly, to 4.2 percent, inflation rose much more (contrary to economic theory), to 3.6 percent, which emphasizes the poor rationale of using one year as an ideal. The 1962 *Economic Report of the President* cited a 4 percent minimum UR as an interim goal, implying that it could be driven below 4 percent, but did not specify the accompanying inflation rate.[12] Nor did commentaries in the 1970s that mentioned minimum URs of 5 to 7 percent specify the inflation rate. Then in 1978 the Full Employment and Balanced Growth Act (Humphrey–Hawkins Act) established a UR goal of 4 percent and an inflation goal based on the consumer price index (CPI) of 3 percent by 1983, with a further reduction of inflation to zero by 1988; however, the act permits the inflation goals to be relaxed if pursuing them would hinder achieving the unemployment goal. In 1989 (the year before the recession began), the UR was 5.2 percent while the CPI increased by 4.6 percent. Thus, progress toward the goals appears modest when compared to the actual levels of 6.0 percent unemployment and 7.6 percent inflation that existed in 1978 when the goals were established. However, progress seems more impressive considering the deterioration of the economy after the goals were established in 1978: the UR peaked at annual averages of 9.5 percent in 1982 and 1983 (the monthly UR peaked at 10.8 percent in December 1982) and the rise in the CPI peaked at 13.5 percent in 1980. By the end of the 1980s, the UR was 1.6 percentage points and the CPI was 1.2 percentage points above the 1983 goals. However, the original act's goals for 1988 appeared much more distant, particularly that for zero inflation.

The Humphrey-Hawkins Act goals continue in effect, even though the time-tables have passed, unless and until the legislation is modified or repealed. However, no one goes to jail and neither the president nor any members of Congress are voted out of office because the goals are not reached. Rather, the effects of such goal-setting are more intangible. On the one hand, the goals represent a clearly defined end for the nation, one that will bring significant improvements and that encourages everyone to continue to try to do better. On the other hand, if the goals are unrealistic, they will not only be disregarded but also may lead to cynicism that can discourage efforts for improvement and thereby ultimately have a negative effect. Thus, developing meaningful goals requires balancing the tension between ideal aspirations and feasible achievements. As noted above, interpretation of the historical record is a matter of perspective. Viewed from the perspective of 1978 when the Humphrey–Hawkins goals were established, progress has been modest; viewed from the perspective of the subsequent deterioration of the economy, progress has been striking. In the author's judgment, these goals are useful because they are a constant reminder of an ultimate end of economic policymaking even when disappointing trends in unemployment and inflation make it "practical" to lower hopes for improvement in the immediate future.

In estimating a minimum UR, it is recognized that there will always be some unemployment, for two reasons. First, there is never a perfect match between persons in the labor force and the skills required by employers, because of residual outmoded skills from declining industries, lack of training, geographic immobility of workers, or age, race, gender, and other discrimination in hiring (structural unemployment). Second, there is an inherent time lag in finding jobs whether persons are newly entering the labor force or whether they have lost their jobs (frictional unemployment).[13] In practice, determining a minimum UR that would accommodate this structural and frictional unemployment has been based on past relationships between unemployment and inflation rather than on an analysis of what the structure of the economy would generate (this approach is referred to as the "Phillips curve" and is discussed in Chapter 6). Although a structural analysis is theoretically more appealing, it would require an assessment of the micro transactions of buyers and sellers in product, labor, and financial markets that could be translated into the overall macro economy. This is a monumental task, and the methodology of economics is not yet capable of it (see the Macro vs. Micro Analysis section in the Introduction).

Moreover, a certain level of long-term price inflation seems to be built into the economy (Chapter 6). One reason is that some prices and wages are set by multiyear contracts that call for scheduled increases over the life of the contract regardless of changing economic conditions. Another is that while some prices and wages actually decline during recessions or during periods of slow economic growth (as seen in the wage givebacks of the 1980s), more typically during such periods the rate of increase merely slows, or wages and prices hold steady. Businesses and workers apparently believe that while price and wage declines would increase the quantity of goods and services sold and the number of workers employed, such increases would be insufficient to offset the resultant decline in company profits or of worker incomes. This long-term inflation bias in the economy makes the Humphrey-Hawkins goal of zero inflation ultimately unrealistic. There is also a view held by Milton Friedman and other "monetarist" economists (who are discussed in Chapter 7) that the trade-off between unemployment and inflation occurs only in the short run; in the long run, according to this view, there is no trade-off, as all attempts to stimulate economic growth will only increase inflation without lowering unemployment.[14]

In the political arena, this trade-off debate is played out with liberals emphasizing the unemployment problem and conservatives emphasizing the inflation problem. It is also reflected in the differing views that political liberals and conservatives take of the eight alternative URs noted above (Table 18). But Philip Klein questions the premise of this view that there is something "natural" about certain unemployment levels while there is nothing natural about inflation.[15] The traditional trade-off approach assumes that counteracting an accelerating rate of inflation is more important than lowering unemployment. Klein's critique points out, however, that historically inflation has been as persistent as unemployment and is therefore just as natural. In fact, zero inflation is quite unnatural since it hardly ever occurs. Because of the persistence of inflation, Klein argues that trying to cure inflation by slowing economic growth and raising unemployment is futile.

In theory, the Humphrey–Hawkins Act does not rely on the concept of a natural unemployment rate as a policy guide since it provides for the inflation goal to be suspended if pursuing it will impede reaching the unemployment goal. In carrying out the intent of the act through fiscal and monetary policies, the president, Congress, and the Federal Reserve are authorized to decide if and when to waive the inflation goal. In practice, however, inflation remains a central concern of policymakers, and the inflation goal has never been waived (either explicitly or implicitly) up to the time of this writing in 1991. Indeed, despite the fact that, as noted above, the Humphrey–Hawkins goal of zero inflation is quite unrealistic, in 1990 the Federal Reserve adopted the long-run goal of "price stability," which is another phrase for zero inflation.[16]

Yet in 1990, the economy had not even reached the 3 percent inflation goal set for 1983. In the long run, a zero-inflation goal is probably a disservice, since it leads to lessening or even destroying the national will to reduce inflation other than through higher unemployment. Modifying the Humphrey–Hawkins Act and the Federal Reserve policies to establish a more meaningful and feasible inflation goal above zero, such as in the 1 or 2 percent range, would probably encourage efforts to reach the inflation goal by raising productivity and lowering production costs rather than by slowing economic growth and raising unemployment.

Demographic and Growth Factors
Affecting Unemployment

As noted previously, unemployment goals drifted upward from 3 to 4 percent in the 1960s to 5 to 7 percent in the 1970s, and then dropped to 4 percent in the

1980s with the Humphrey-Hawkins Act. The upward drift reflected the perception that because teenagers and adult women, who had higher URs than men, were accounting for an increasing proportion of the labor force, this demographic change alone would increase a minimum UR over time. In a study of the effect of these demographic changes, Paul Flaim estimated that if the labor force composition had remained the same between 1959 and 1979, the civilian UR would have been 1.4 percentage points lower than it was in 1979 (4.4 percent compared with the actual 5.8 percent).[17] The study also found that most of the rise in unemployment due to the demographic factors over the period resulted from the increased number of teenagers in the population rather than from the increasing labor force participation rates of women: adult male URs greatly differ from teenage URs, while adult male and female URs are much closer. In fact, since the 1980s there has been no consistent difference in URs between adult men and women; in some years men have higher URs and in some years women have higher URs. Examples of these URs from 1959 to 1989 during expansion years at the end of four decades are shown below.

	1959	1969	1979	1989
Adult men (20 years +)	4.7	2.1	4.2	4.5
Adult women (20 years +)	5.2	3.7	5.7	4.7
Teenagers (16 to 19 years)	14.6	12.2	16.1	15.0

However, the upward creep in the UR due to the demographic shifts was reversed in the 1980s. Because of the birthrate cycle discussed in Part A, the teenage proportion of the labor force, which had increased from 6.4 percent in 1959 to 9.2 percent in 1979, fell to 6.4 percent in 1989. The above-noted study estimates that this decline in the teenage share of the work force accounted for approximately 0.5 percentage point of the 0.6 percentage point decline in the UR from 1979 to 1989—that is, approximately 80 percent of the decade decline in the UR.[18] The study also projects that the lower birthrates of baby-boom parents will contribute to a further UR decline in the 1990s by 0.3 percentage point because of the resulting lower proportion of teenage workers. As noted earlier in the section on unemployment insurance, the tightening of unemployment insurance benefits during the 1980s also probably contributed to the lower UR during the decade. However, quantitative estimates of the unemployment insurance impact on the decline are not available.

In addition, the above tabulation of unemployment for selected age and gender categories of workers indicates that independent of the demographic compositional shifts, the expansion of the 1980s left URs for adult men, adult women, and teenagers in 1989 significantly above those in 1969, and closer to those in 1959 and 1979. This reflects the faster rate of economic growth during the

1960s than during the 1950s, 1970s, and 1980s (see Chapter 3). In sum, although the UR declined during the 1980s, most of the decline appears to be the result of factors other than economic growth.

The *employment–population ratio* provides another measure of job markets, although from a different perspective than the UR. The employment–population ratio is calculated by dividing the total civilian employment by the civilian noninstitutional population age sixteen years and older. Because the ratio excludes the effect of changes in the labor force, it is not affected by people moving in and out of the job market whether due to job market perceptions or to personal factors. Since the population age sixteen and over (the denominator of the ratio) increases steadily over time, changes in the ratio are dominated by changes in employment (the numerator). Thus, the ratio is a ready indicator of changes in the employment rate, and is useful for that reason. However, the employment–population ratio should not be viewed as a normative indicator. The share of the working-age population that should be employed does not represent an established societal goal, unlike the UR which policymakers agree should be kept as low as possible without igniting inflation. Similarly, although the employment–population ratio has the attributes of a labor capacity utilization measure, it should not be treated as having a threshold that triggers different economic responses when the ratio rises above or falls below a certain level (see discussion of the threshold level of the capacity utilization rate for plant and equipment investment in Chapter 4).

Economic Growth and Unemployment: Okun's Law

Economic growth is a key factor affecting unemployment: rapid economic growth lowers the UR, and slow or declining growth raises the UR. These relationships have been studied by comparing economic growth, as represented by movements in the real GNP, to changes in the UR. Such relationships develop a break-even point indicating (a) the level of growth required for maintaining a steady UR, and (b) the unemployment effects of growth rates above and below the break-even point. This is referred to as "Okun's Law" after Arthur Okun, who developed such relationships in the 1960s.

The basic break-even rate of GNP growth can be understood with the following example. Assume the UR is 5 percent, the labor force grows by 1 percent per year, and productivity increases 1.5 percent annually. Then the real GNP must grow 2.5 percent annually to absorb 95 percent of the labor force growth.

Figure 38 shows the UR/GNP relationship from 1948 to 1989. The black diamonds represent the intersection of the GNP and UR points for each year, and the line of white diamonds is the long-term average relationship. The long-term average indicates the basic inverse relationship: as the GNP increases, the UR falls, and vice versa. Graphically, this relationship appears in the direction of the

Figure 38. **Okun's Law: 1948–89**

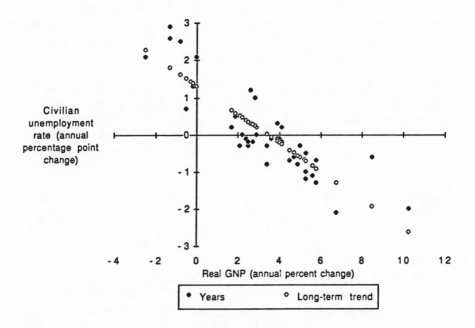

Note: Based on Bureau of Economic Analysis and Bureau of Labor Statistics data.

line of white diamonds, which slopes downward to the right. This general relationship is expected from economic theory. The correlation coefficient of -.88
indicates a substantial inverse relationship over the forty-two-year period (a perfect inverse relationship is represented by −1.)[19] For periods approximating decades, the correlation coefficient varied from the highest during the 1950s and
1980s (1948–59: -.90, and 1979–89: -.97), to the lowest during the 1960s and
1970s (1959–69: -.77 and 1969–79: -.74). These variations reflect continuing
changes in the many factors determining the UR/GNP relationship that make it
more consistent in some periods than in others, as discussed below.

A central task of analysts studying the Okun's Law relationship is to estimate
the break-even point. In a 1984 study, Douglas Woodham suggested that the
break-even point is reached at an annual real GNP growth rate of 3 percent.[20] At
the 3 percent rate, the UR tends to be stable; and for every percentage point of
annual GNP growth above or below 3 percent, the UR tends to decrease (increase) by 0.4 of a percentage point over the year. These relationships are averages and, consistent with the above discussion, do not hold for every period.
Thus, it subsequently became evident that during the 1980s the GNP break-even
point was lower than 3 percent due to the previously noted demographic trends

which have led to a declining proportion of teenagers (who have very high unemployment rates) in the labor force. The effect is particularly evident in the years 1986 and 1989 when real GNP grew by less than 3 percent while the UR also declined. The decline in teenage workers that began in the mid-1970s has apparently reduced the break-even point in the 1980s to a GNP growth rate of 2 to 2.5 percent. Since the teenage proportion will continue to decline in the 1990s, the break-even point by the end of the decade will likely be about 2 percent. Successive estimates of Okun's Law are also affected by GNP data revisions, including the effect of changing the base year of the price deflator used in preparing the constant-dollar GNP measures on real GNP growth rates, as discussed in Chapter 3.

It is also apparent from the many divergences of the forty-two years above and below the long-term average line in Figure 38 that the relative UR and GNP movements are not the same in all years. For example, in 1984 the GNP rose by 6.8 percent and the UR declined by 2.1 percentage points, a UR percentage point change of approximately one-third the GNP percent change; but in 1988, the GNP increased by 4.5 percent and the UR declined by 0.7 percentage point, a UR percentage point change of only one-sixth the GNP percent change. Such variations reflect the fact that the UR is unchanged at the break-even GNP growth rate of 2 to 2.5 percent; consequently, the closer the growth rates are to the break-even point, the smaller is their proportionate impact on the UR. The variations also indicate other complexities underlying the UR/GNP relationship.

For example, GNP is driven directly by employment, weekly hours worked, and productivity, and these factors do not always move in tandem with the UR trends. As noted previously in Part A, short-term monthly unemployment movements are not always consistent with the movements of employment. Both weekly hours and productivity are discussed below, but their impacts on Okun's Law are noted briefly here. The response of weekly hours worked to changes in economic activity, while tending to lead overall economic activity at the business cycle turning points, fluctuates considerably during the expansion and recession phases, and thus does not always increase in expansions and decrease in recessions as expected. Productivity shows noticeable changes in longer-term growth rates that affect GNP movements, but which do not necessarily parallel UR movements.

With these caveats, Okun's Law provides an overall perspective for linking economic growth with unemployment. In assessing these trends, the analyst should observe special conditions that may cause large divergences from the long-run trend for particular periods. In addition, the long-run relationship should be reviewed every few years to determine if there are significant changes that should be brought into the analysis.

Digression on Job Vacancies

One approach for assessing the magnitude of unemployment is to compare it with available job vacancies. To make such a comparison meaningfully, the distribution of job skills among the unemployed would have to be matched with those required in the available jobs. Only with appropriate data on both of these factors would it be plausible to make unemployment-vacancy comparisons at the overall macro level. If there were a reasonable match, it could be assumed that part of the unemployment could be absorbed. Such an analysis could provide a clearer perspective on the extent of unemployment requiring fiscal and monetary policies or special job programs.

However, no such information on job vacancies is available that would allow absolute comparisons with unemployment levels. The Bureau of Labor Statistics' previous attempts to collect such data from employers were discontinued in the 1970s. From the late 1960s to 1973, the BLS collected job vacancy data by industry, but discontinued the effort because sufficient funds were not available to expand the program to cover the entire economy, as initially intended. In the late 1970s, the BLS undertook a pilot study of the feasibility of collecting job vacancy data by occupation at the state level, which indicated that collecting representative and reliable data was possible but difficult. The BLS did not extend the pilot study into a regular collection program because it was too costly. Thus, both prior efforts were terminated because of a lack of funding. A decade later in 1990, however, the fiscal year 1990 budget appropriation for the Department of Labor directed the Department to develop a methodology to identify annual national labor shortages. In response the BLS conducted a series of experimental surveys to assess the feasibility of collecting job vacancy data from employers by occupation. This experimental work was completed in 1991, and the BLS project team concluded that it is feasible to collect job vacancy data on an annual basis for $11–12 million per year. Assuming a full-scale program is funded in the early 1990s, the initial data would be available in the mid-1990s.

As an alternative to collecting job vacancy data from employers, there are The Conference Board figures on employer hiring plans from help-wanted newspaper advertisements. They are collected from one newspaper in each of fifty-one cities (including their suburbs) which comprise local labor markets. This sample is raised to an estimated national total by the national employment proportions accounted for by the sample cities. The data are provided monthly as an index of the percent change in the number of jobs advertised. The index is a leading indicator at business expansion peaks and a lagging indicator at business recession troughs (see Chapter 8).

The help-wanted data broadly estimate the relative change in job vacancies. However, they are not comprehensive or representative enough to be converted to absolute levels for comparisons with the actual number of unemployed persons because many jobs are not advertised in newspapers. The help-wanted figures also do not distinguish job vacancies by occupational skills, which as noted above is necessary for matching with unemployment skills. Thus, while some job vacancy figures are available from help-wanted advertising, data problems prevent their use at this time for assessing the overall magnitude of unemployment.

EMPLOYMENT: PERSONS, HOURS, AND WAGES

This section covers three aspects of employment: the number of employed persons, the hours per week they work, and the wages they earn.

Employed Persons

There are two monthly estimates of the number of persons with jobs: (a) the household survey discussed in the previous section on unemployment, and (b) the survey of workers on employer payrolls. They are based on different definitions and data collection methods and as a result sometimes show noticeably different monthly and cyclical trends. Therefore, it is important to know which figures are used in analyses of trends.

The definitional differences in the two employment surveys also result in each providing different types of detailed data. A basic distinction is that the employer survey provides a count of *jobs* with considerable industry and geographic detail, while the household survey counts employed *persons*, with a focus on demographic characteristics.

PART A: ESTIMATING METHODOLOGY

The employer survey counts all paying jobs of nonagricultural civilian employees. It includes *all* jobs held by each worker (not just the primary one as in the household survey), workers under sixteen years old, residents of Canada and Mexico who commute to the United States for work, and institutionalized persons on payroll jobs—all of whom are excluded form the household survey. However, it excludes the self-employed; private household, agricultural, and unpaid family workers; and workers on the job rolls but temporarily not receiving pay such as those on strike or on unpaid vacations or sick leave. All of these are in the household survey. Neither survey makes any distinction between a full-time and a part-time worker—both are counted as one person—and unpaid work around the house by homeowners and renters is excluded in both surveys. In addition, there are substantial differences in the sampling and data collection aspects of both surveys.

The net effect of these differences in coverage is that the household survey shows more employment than the employer survey—in 1990 the household survey's civilian employment figure was 118 million, while the employer survey showed 110 million. Most of this 8 million difference is accounted for when both measures are put on a similar definitional basis, although this reconciliation cannot be done fully because of the lack of information on all groups of workers that differ between the surveys.[21] In 1990, the reconciliation resulted in the initial difference of 8 million more workers in the household survey being shifted to 7 million more workers in the employer survey, mainly because of dual job holding in the employer survey.

Employment based on the household survey was covered in the section on unemployment; the new information noted here concerns the sampling error of the household employment information. In two cases out of three, the monthly level of employment is within a range of plus or minus 293,000 persons, and the monthly change in employment is within a range of plus or minus 224,000 persons;[22] if the reliability is raised to 19 cases out of 20, these ranges are increased to 586,000 and 448,000, respectively. By way of perspective, civilian employment in the household survey in November 1990 totaled 117.4 million and the monthly change from October was 347,000. The sensitivity of the monthly change to sampling error is apparent from the comparison of the October–November 347,000 change to the sampling error in two of three cases of 224,000. The proportionate sampling error for the monthly change is much greater than that for the monthly level. *Thus, no single month's employment should be considered as establishing a trend, but rather should be considered in light of the movements for several months to indicate if something different is occurring.*

The employment figures based on the employer survey are derived from the records of companies, nonprofit organizations, and governments.[23] A sample of these employers is surveyed for the pay period that includes the twelfth day of the month. The surveys are conducted for the Bureau of Labor Statistics by state employment agencies. The survey covers the number of workers employed as well as their paid weekly hours and earnings (discussed in the next section). The monthly sample of over 360,000 employer establishments (places of work including individual establishments of large companies) covered about 37 percent of all nonagricultural employment in 1989.

The monthly figures go through two sets of revisions. They are initially published as "preliminary" in each of the first two months after the survey is taken, and in the third month are "final" based on the most complete returns from the employer sample. These are subsequently revised annually to conform to benchmark figures for the month of March, which are based on data from the *universe* of all employers reporting their unemployment insurance tax payments to the state employment offices. The new March levels are then used to revise the previous eleven months, which were based on data obtained from the *sample* of employers, and extrapolations are carried forward to the most current month as well. The unemployment insurance reports covered 98 percent of all nonagricultural employment in 1989; these are supplemented by other reports for industries exempt from unemployment laws, such as those available from Social Security records. Table 19 shows that over 1985–89, the benchmark revisions for all employees ranged from –0.5 percent to less than 0.05 percent. They reflect differing revision patterns for individual industries—for example, in 1989 transportation was lowered by 3 percent and state governments were increased by 1 percent.

Despite the relatively small revisions in annual benchmarks, there remain

Table 19

**Percentage Difference between Monthly Survey and
Benchmark Nonagricultural Employment**

(+ : benchmark exceeds monthly survey
− : benchmark less than monthly survey)

1985	less than 0.05
1986	−0.5
1987	less than 0.05
1988	−0.3
1989	less than 0.05

Source: Patricia M. Getz, "Establishment Estimates Revised to March 1989 Benchmarks and 1987 SIC Codes," *Employment and Earnings,* September 1990, p. 19.

some longstanding concerns regarding the sampling procedures for the employer survey. One issue is how up-to-date the sample of participating firms is. Because new firms are added to the universe frame only once each quarter, the monthly survey data first reflect these firms' employment several months after the firms have been in operation. The understatement of employment due to the delayed inclusion of new firms in the sample is compensated by an indirect adjustment of the new firms' additional employment based on benchmark revisions of the past several years and differential growth rates between the most recent quarter and the past several years. A second issue is the sample itself. Because the current sample is not a probability sample, no range of sampling error is associated with it. While formal sampling error estimates do not exist for the employer survey, the annual benchmark provides a comprehensive annual measure of overall survey error, containing both sampling and nonsampling components. Thus the existing range of past benchmark revisions are analogous to a range of sampling error (i.e., a confidence interval) and suggest that a true probability sample would not result in significantly different annual levels, although it could result in noticeably different monthly movements during the year.

Use of Alternative Employment Surveys

Statistically, both surveys have strengths and weaknesses. The household survey is stronger in terms of general sample survey methodology as it has a probability sample. This advantage is lessened by the typical undercounting in household surveys of minority-group males, who also have relatively high cyclical employment experience. The information source for the employer survey is better because the data are obtained from employer payroll records, which are used for tax returns, rather than from answers by household members, which are not documented.

Over the years, the employer survey has been considered to better measure the

Table 20

Nonagricultural Employment: 1948–89 (annual percent change)

	Employer survey	Household survey
1948–59	1.6	1.4
1959–69	2.8	2.3
1969–79	2.5	2.5
1979–89	1.9	1.8
1948–89	2.2	2.0

monthly change in total employment.[24] This is discussed in Part B, which includes guidance for assessing the monthly and cyclical trends. The employer survey is also a component of the composite index of coincident indicators (see Chapter 8).

PART B: ANALYSIS OF TRENDS

The two surveys' long-term movements are similar, although not identical. Table 20 shows both surveys' movements in nonagricultural employment at compound annual rates for the 1950s, 1960s, 1970s, and 1980s.[25] Over the forty-one years from 1948 to 1989, employment based on the employer survey increased at an annual rate of 2.2 percent, slightly faster than the growth of 2.0 percent indicated by the household survey. The decade increases in both surveys were highest in the 1960s and 1970s, and lowest in the 1950s and 1980s. The most prominent decade-to-decade changes were the acceleration of employment increases in the 1960s and the deceleration in the 1980s. The two surveys represent divergent movements in the 1970s when the employer survey shows employment rising at a slower rate than in the 1960s, while the household survey shows it increasing at a faster rate. Because of their general long-run similarities, however, the main interest in the differential movements of the two surveys is in the short-term monthly and quarterly patterns.

There are noticeable differences in the monthly and cyclical movements of employment as measured by the employer and household surveys. The employer survey has both steadier growth rates over three to six months, and more extreme cyclical movements in the longer expansion and recession periods, than the household survey.

Monthly Movements

Figure 39 shows monthly employment trends of both surveys in 1989 and 1990. The employer survey data show steadier movements in the same direction

Figure 39. **Monthly Civilian Employment from Employer and Household Surveys: 1989–90**

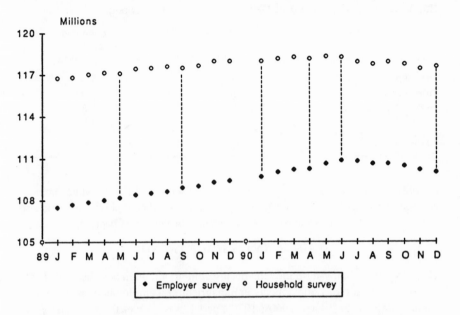

Note: Vertical lines indicate months when the two surveys moved in different directions.

over several months, in contrast to the household survey, which has more frequent monthly changes in direction.

These monthly differences are perplexing because it is not known whether the labor market, after the data are seasonally adjusted, actually has the employer survey's relatively smooth monthly movements or the household survey's more frequent interruptions of directional movement. The varying short-term movements of the two surveys reflect the difference in coverage and methodology noted in Part A. But it is difficult to say which survey better depicts the actual economy. *Over any period of months, the analyst should compare the employment movements from both surveys. If they are similar, they may be considered to confirm the trend. If they differ significantly, definitional and statistical differences between the surveys should be examined to see if there is a reasonable explanation. If there is no plausible explanation, the trend for that short period may be treated as within the lower and upper range of both survey figures.*

Cyclical Movements

Figures 40a and 40b show the changes in both employment surveys and in the real GNP during the postwar expansions and recessions (the cyclical turning points are the same as those used in Chapter 3 for the GNP). In almost all cases, the employer survey showed more extreme cyclical movements, increasing more in expansions and decreasing more in recessions than the household survey. The typical cyclical difference between the two surveys was 1 to 2 percentage points; the exceptional cases of much larger differences occurred in the expansions of 1950–53 (10 percentage points) and 1961–69 (13 percentage points). While the differentials have been relatively stable since the 1970s, the differences in definition and methodology suggest that large variations may again occur, although probably not as great as in 1950–53 and 1961–69.

Employment as measured in both surveys is typically less cyclical than the GNP, rising less in expansions and falling less in recessions. The GNP is more cyclical because in addition to employment, it takes into account weekly hours and productivity, both of which are more cyclical than employment. (They are discussed later in this chapter.)

John Stinson suggests reasons for the varying cyclical patterns based on qualitative assessments of the likely effect of the differences between the two surveys.[26] In recessions, there are two situations that lead to employment decreases in the employer survey and no decrease in the household survey. These are cases in which a dual jobholder loses one job, and cases in which a person loses a job with a large employer who is a respondent in the employer survey and switches to a marginal employer who is not in the employer survey (perhaps even switching to the underground economy). In expansions, the reverse situation occurs for persons who had been with marginal employers not in the employer survey and switch as demand increases to larger employers that are in the employer survey; this appears as an employment increase in the employer survey but as no change in the household survey. Another supposition on the greater cyclical volatility of the employer survey is considered more speculative: it is possible that because the persons typically undercounted in household surveys, such as minority males, are those with the greatest cyclical changes in employment, the undercount may reduce that survey's employment fluctuations.

There also are cyclical fluctuations in self-employment, which is included in the household and excluded from the employer survey. Eugene Becker notes that self-employment increases in expansions along with other employment, but in recessions it tends to decline less sharply and to start increasing sooner than wage and salary employment.[27] These countercyclical movements in recessions may result from two factors: (a) persons who are self-employed as a second job, and thus are counted only in their primary job in the household survey, are counted as self-employed when they lose their employee job, and (b) some workers who have lost their jobs and are not able to find another one try self-employment and thus are still counted in the household survey.

As an overall assessment of which survey is most appropriate for cyclical analysis, the employer survey's conceptual emphasis on jobs, including dual jobholders, gives a better picture of employment in expansions and recessions

Figure 40a. **Business Cycle Movements of Civilian Employment and Real GNP: Expansions**

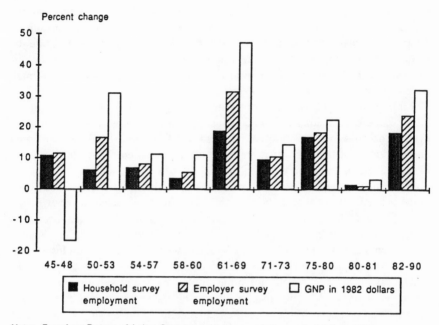

Note: Based on Bureau of Labor Statistics and Bureau of Economic Analysis data.

than the household's survey emphasis on demographic groups. Main coverage drawbacks of the employer survey are the exclusion of nonagricultural self-employed and most agricultural workers (these account for about 10 percent of the household survey's civilian employment), and that the survey does not specify the number of persons (as distinct from jobs), and which demographic groups are gaining and losing. Statistically, the weaknesses in both surveys seem to produce a standoff. *But, on balance, the concept of jobs seems most relevant for assessing cyclical employment trends, which suggests that the analyst should focus on the employer survey.*

Labor Hours, Earnings, and Costs

Compensation payments (money wages and salaries plus fringe benefits) represent income to workers and costs to employers. They affect consumer purchasing power, job security, business profits, and inflation. They also have an impact on collective bargaining.

The total amount of wage payments in the economy reflects three factors: the number of jobs (discussed in the previous section), average hours on the job, and

Figure 40b. **Business Cycle Movements of Civilian Employment and Real GNP: Recessions**

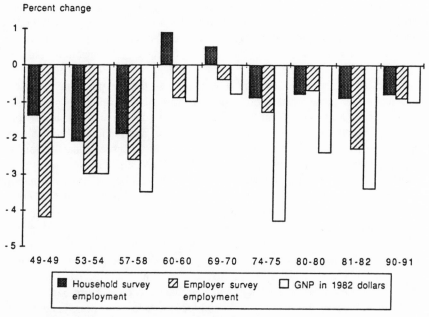

Percent change

| 49-49 | 53-54 | 57-58 | 60-60 | 69-70 | 74-75 | 80-80 | 81-82 | 90-91 |

| ■ Household survey employment | ▨ Employer survey employment | ☐ GNP in 1982 dollars |

Note: Based on Bureau of Labor Statistics and Bureau of Economic Analysis data.
Recession of 1990-91 in progress in spring of 1991.

average wage rates of pay. *Weekly hours* represent the average length of the workweek. *Weekly earnings* are the average weekly paycheck, from the combined result of the hourly pay rate and the weekly hours. Both hours and earnings are averages for all private nonfarm industries and occupations, and thus can change if jobs shift between industries or occupations that have longer and shorter workweeks or higher and lower pay rates, such as manufacturing and services or clerks and pharmacists. *Wage costs* represent changes in the average paycheck for all private nonfarm industries, assuming that the distribution of jobs between industries and occupations remains constant. Thus, wage costs measure labor expenses for doing the same kind of work. Weekly hours and weekly earnings are provided monthly and wage costs are provided quarterly by the Bureau of Labor Statistics.

The data are based on survey information obtained from employers for the pay period that includes the twelfth day of the month for the total of full-time and part-time workers in all private nonagricultural industries. Similar information is available for particular industries. The hours and earnings data are obtained mainly from the employer survey on the number of jobs which was covered in the previous section. The indicator of wage costs—the employment–cost index—is based on a different survey, which is discussed below.

The hours, earnings, and costs are averages for the total of full-time and part-time workers and of overtime hours that are paid a premium over the straight-time rate in private nonagricultural industries. Technically, they are based on "hours paid for," which includes employees on paid vacations and sick leave, as distinct from the actual working time on the job (hours worked) as discussed below under Productivity. This is done so that the payments represent the actual earnings and costs, rather than simply the hours worked.

The data on hours and earnings are limited to "production and nonsupervisory workers," which in all industries exclude executives and managers; in manufacturing, construction, and mining, workers engaged in professional, technical, office, and sales activities are excluded as well.[28] Thus, the data represent "line" workers as distinct from administrative and support employees. The information on wage costs is more comprehensive on two counts. It includes all workers—production and nonsupervisory workers as well as executives, managers, administrative, and support personnel. The cost figures also include money wages and fringe benefits in a combined total as "compensation." In contrast to the earnings figures, which only cover money wages, the cost data include the employers' payments for Social Security, unemployment insurance, and private health and life group insurance. The earnings and cost data are on a gross basis before employee deductions for income and social security taxes and fringe benefits.

Weekly Hours

The figure for weekly hours is an early indicator of changes in labor utilization. Typically, employers change existing employees' hours before hiring new employees when sales turn up in the initial stage of an expansion and before laying off workers when sales first turn down in a recession. Because recent sales trends may be reversed in a short period, it is simpler for employers to adjust work schedules first. Hiring new employees involves administrative costs and training time, which may not be justified by future business activity. Laying off workers in temporary downturns may result in losing efficient labor to other employers just as demand picks up. Retaining workers during slack periods that are expected to be of short duration—sometimes referred to as "hoarding"—is one way to avoid this possibility. Other factors encourage employers not to lay off workers immediately before there is a more definitive indication of sales trends. They recognize the importance of the job to the worker and, on a personal level, some may be reluctant to lay anyone off. Employers also seek to avoid higher unemployment insurance premiums, which can result from increasing layoffs because the premiums are based on the employer's unemployment experience (see earlier section on unemployment insurance).

The figure for average weekly hours in manufacturing industries is so sensitive to changes in demand that it is a component of the composite index of leading indicators (see Chapter 8). It includes overtime and typically ranges from 39 to 41 hours; for short periods, typically of one to three months, it has fallen below 39 hours in some recessions, and less frequently has risen above 41 hours in expansions.

On average, it takes at least three months for the weekly hours figures for manufacturing to establish a cyclical upward or downward trend. A one- or two-month upward or downward movement is affected by too many factors to be considered a statistically reliable trend. However, even within the longer expansion and recession periods, the weekly hours series is quite erratic. *Consequently, the analyst should consider current trends in weekly hours only as a broad clue to developments in labor markets.*

Weekly Earnings

The data on workers' average weekly earnings in constant dollars provide trends on the material well-being of all workers from their job earnings after correcting for effects of price inflation. This estimate of the purchasing power of wage income is obtained by modifying the actual income for price changes as measured by the consumer price index (see Chapter 6).

A simplified version of the relationship between income, prices, and spending (assuming no change in saving rates) may be summarized as follows: If both income and prices change at the same rate, income keeps pace with inflation and will have a neutral effect on consumer spending; if income rises faster than prices, the increased purchasing power will be a stimulus for consumers to buy more goods and services, and thus production and employment will increase; and if prices rise faster than income, the decline in consumer spending will result in lower production and employment. Analogous relationships between income and spending occur if prices are declining, although price declines in nondepression periods occur only in occasional months; for example, if income remains constant and prices decline, purchasing power increases. In this schema, income is used synonymously with earnings of each jobholder, although as discussed below, income for the broader household spending unit includes income for all workers in the family plus income from investments and income maintenance programs, as measured in personal income (see Chapter 3 under Consumer Expenditures).

In Figure 41 the trend from 1950 to 1990 of average weekly earnings per worker corrected for price change is represented through an index using 1982 = 100. Real weekly earnings generally rose during the 1950s and 1960s, reaching a peak in 1972–73, and then generally declined from 1974 to 1990. While there were short-term interruptions in these trends, the long-term decline in earnings from 1974 to 1990 is striking. By 1990, real earnings per worker had declined to the 1959 level.

Figure 41. **Real Average Weekly Earnings Per Worker and Real Disposable Personal Income Per Capita: 1950–90**

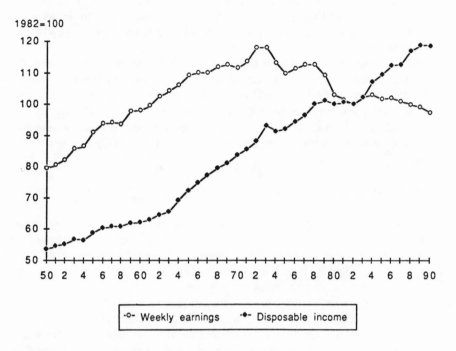

1982=100

Note: **Bureau of Labor Statistics and Bureau of Economic Analysis data in 1982 dollars converted to 1982=100.**

These data on job earnings per worker differ significantly from those on disposable personal income per capita (which are derived from the personal income measures discussed in Chapter 3). Disposable income per capita (i.e., income per person including all adults and children) is a far more comprehensive measure than job earnings per worker. Personal income includes the combined job earnings of *all* workers in the household (e.g., the combined earnings of both spouses), plus income received by all household members from self-employment, interest, dividends, rent, unemployment insurance, Social Security, and other income maintenance programs. As indicated in Figure 41, the trend of real disposable income per capita has with a few exceptions risen continuously over the 1950–90 period. The growth continued even during 1974–90 because the increasing proportion of families in which both spouses have paying jobs, the rising receipt of income maintenance payments stemming from the Social Security program and the Great Society programs of the 1960s, and the greater interest income received from higher interest rates more than offset the decline in job earnings per worker. Based on this measure the real income of each person *on average* has continually risen, although not all families and individuals have shared in this average increase, and many adults of this generation have not reached the income levels and living conditions of their parents.

The measures of job earnings per worker and of disposable income per person are pertinent for assessing changes in the economic well-being of Americans, although each provides a different perspective. For example, in terms of the next section on labor–management collective bargaining, job earnings per worker is the relevant indicator because compensation for work is based on such factors as the job's value to the employer, the union's bargaining power, and the number of workers with the occupational skills relative to the number of available jobs in the occupation (referred to as a labor shortage or surplus), rather than on a consideration of the worker's earnings when combined with the spouse's earnings and other income the worker derives from self-employment, investments, or income maintenance transfer payments. In contrast, the income per capita data are useful for assessing changes in the average rate of improvement in Americans' living conditions as well as for comparisons of living conditions in the United States with those in other nations. (Living conditions are also discussed below under Productivity and in Chapter 6 in the section on The CPI and Measuring Poverty.)

Labor–Management Collective Bargaining

Compensation settlements in collective bargaining can indicate future changes in compensation rates, which will affect household and business incomes, employment, and inflation. ("Compensation" is the sum of cash wages and salaries plus fringe benefits.) Unions strive to ensure that compensation increases keep pace with inflation and productivity improvements so that workers' material well-being continually improves. When compensation increases less than prices, living conditions decline, and unions will press for greater pay increases. However, rapidly rising compensation may perpetuate inflation or lead to a loss of jobs due to plant shutdowns or to American industry becoming less competitive with imports. Rapidly rising compensation may also contribute to a shift of jobs from unions to nonunion companies, either in the same region or through plant relocation and the startup of new firms in areas where wages are lower. In assessing the effect of compensation on plant shutdowns and shifts to lower-paid nonunion workers, it should be kept in mind that labor costs are only one factor affecting competitiveness, and not always the dominant one. Examples of others are the market for the firm's products, management and labor skills, and the utilization of modern equipment.

Unions accounted for only 16 percent of all workers in 1990. Although union membership increased continually over the postwar period until the 1980s, the share declined as union membership increased more slowly than the total employment.[29] Actual union membership fell from 21.0 million in 1979 to 16.7 million in 1990. The weakened bargaining position resulting from the declining membership affects the union movement as a whole, with the exception of a few individual unions that have grown in membership such as those representing teachers. More specifically, because the decline in union membership was confined to private industry, the weakened bargaining position centered on workers in private industry as distinct from those in government employment. For example, from 1983 to 1990, union members as a share of all workers in their respective groups showed the following patterns: in private nonfarm industries, union membership declined from 17 to 12 percent; in farm industries, union membership declined from 3 to 2 percent; while in federal, state, and local governments, union membership remained steady at 36.5 percent. Linda Bell concludes that the decline in union bargaining strength was partially responsible for the wage cuts, slower wage increases, and greater use of other types of compensation that dampened wage growth in the 1980s.[30] Examples of the other types of compensation are two-tier contracts in which newly hired workers are paid less than previously hired workers, lump-sum payments that are not a permanent part of the wage base, and profit-sharing plans whose benefits are related to the economic fortunes of the company.

Even though unions represent a relatively small percentage of American workers, union wage rates and fringe benefits influence compensation rates in general. Because unions are the dominant bargaining agent in several industries, their compensation patterns often are a guideline for compensation of nonunion workers in the same industry or company. For example, some nonunion companies make it a policy to increase compensation in accordance with their union counterparts in order to reduce incentives for their workers to join a union, and some union agreements for wage freezes or cuts in the early 1980s had similar provisions requiring "equality of sacrifice" for nonunion counterparts in the same firm. There is not a one-to-one relationship between union and nonunion compensation; in fact, the trends discussed below indicate they have not always moved in tandem. However, as the pacesetter for improving workers' incomes, union compensation often is used as a standard by which to measure nonunion compensation increases in efforts to unionize nonunion companies.

Figure 42 compares annual changes in union and nonunion compensation with the consumer price index over 1970–90. This index of job costs is based on maintaining the same distributions of industry and occupational employment, and thus differs from the weekly earnings figures, which incorporate changes over time in the employment distributions of industries and occupations.[31] Maintenance of the same industry and occupational distributions more accurately measures compensation changes because shifts in the distributions of employees among low- and high-paying industries and occupations do not affect the measures. From 1970 to 1983, union wage increases typically exceeded nonunion wage increases by 1 to 2 percentage points. But this pattern was reversed during

Figure 42. **Annual Changes in Union Compensation, Nonunion Compensation, and Consumer Prices: 1970–90**

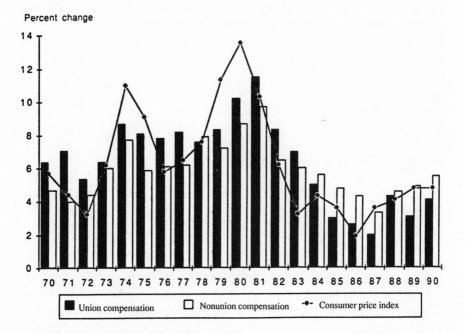

Percent change

Note: Based on Bureau of Labor Statistics data.
See Chapter 5, footnote 31 for breaks in compensation series.

1984–90, when nonunion compensation increases exceeded union increases by 1 to 2 percentage points.

The net effect of these trends is that the spread between union and nonunion wages remained substantial at the end of the 1980s. The Bureau of Labor Statistics prepares three different measures of the spread, one from the household current population survey, one from the employer industry wage survey, and one from the employment cost index. As noted in a study by Kay Anderson, Philip Doyle, and Albert Schwenk, the union advantage is apparent in all three measures, although as expected the magnitude of the advantage varies due to differences in the surveys' coverage and methodology.[32] Table 21 shows the differential in 1989 of compensation in private nonfarm industries of union workers relative to nonunion workers. (The data are drawn from the employment cost index because it gives the most comprehensive picture for similar categories of industries and workers.) For all industries, compensation per worker in 1989 was 35 percent higher for union workers than for nonunion workers. The union advantage was much greater in nonmanufacturing industries than in manufacturing

Table 21

**Earnings of Union Workers Relative to Nonunion Workers
in Private Nonfarm Industries: 1989** (nonunion = 100)

	Compensation	Wages and salaries	Fringe benefits
Manufacturing and			
nonmanufacturing	135	121	178
Blue-collar	166	148	214
Manufacturing	112	101	139
Blue-collar	149	136	180
Nonmanufacturing	141	128	182
Blue-collar	183	163	243

Source: Kay E. Anderson, Philip M. Doyle, and Albert E. Schwenk, "Measuring Union-Nonunion Earnings Differences," *Monthly Labor Review*, June 1990. The author obtained unpublished data for the nonmanufacturing blue-collar category.

industries, for blue-collar workers than for other workers in both manufacturing and nonmanufacturing, and for fringe benefits than for wages and salaries in both manufacturing and nonmanufacturing. The only category with similar pay for union and nonunion workers was wages and salaries in manufacturing industries for all workers.

Inflation slowed considerably in the 1980s, and became much less significant in raising worker pay rates than it had been in the 1970s (Figure 42). But job earnings did not keep pace with inflation during the 1980s, as apparent from Figure 41. However, the data suggest that a delayed response to this lag occurred in union–management collective bargaining settlements during the late 1980s and in 1990. Figure 43 shows that annual wage rate increases in settlements involving 1,000 workers or more over the multiyear life of the contracts declined from 1981 to 1986, reaching a low of slightly under 2 percent in 1986, and subsequently rose to slightly over 3 percent in 1989 and 1990. This upturn reflected unions' stronger stance, but the increases were still below the inflation rate (although actual earnings were higher for workers in unions having cost-of-living provisions in their contracts, the settlements data exclude prospective pay increases linked to future rates of inflation). Figure 43 indicates that the increases during 1987–90 were modest in another respect: 1989 was the first time since 1981 that the negotiated wage settlements were greater than those when the same parties had last bargained. (Data for compensation rate increases show similar movements as the wage rate settlements during 1981–90, but compensation data for the last time the same parties bargained have not been compiled.)

These collective bargaining data on wage and compensation "rate" adjustments exclude the effect of lump-sum payments by employers. Lump-sum remu-

Figure 43. **Annual Wage Rate Adjustments by Collective Bargaining Settlements in Private Industry: 1981–90**

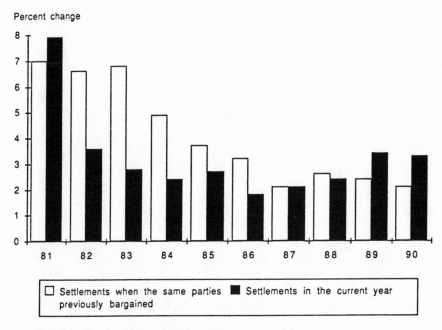

Note: Based on Bureau of Labor Statistics data over term of the contract for settlements of 1,000 workers or more.

neration is a one-time payment to the worker that is not part of the permanent earnings base; because the permanent earnings base is the starting point for the next round of bargaining, lump-sum payments tend to lower future pay increases. The pay rate data also measure the average annual increase for the total of all years in the contract, regardless of which year each increase went into effect. The Bureau of Labor Statistics introduced a supplementary data series in 1990 on collective bargaining compensation "cost" adjustments that includes lump-sum payments.[33] Only lump-sum payments that are guaranteed in the contract are included; contingent lump-sum payments such as those that are linked to the company's future profits are excluded. This cost adjustment series also allocates the multiyear pay increases to the year (or period within the year) they go into effect. Thus, the cost adjustment data differ from the rate adjustment data in the treatment of lump-sum payments and the timing of the pay increases.

The rate adjustment and cost adjustment data are different ways of measuring the effect of collective bargaining settlements. For settlements in 1988, 1989, and 1990, both series had similar year-to-year movements, although the cost adjustment measure increased less than the rate adjustment measure, as indicated in the tabulation below. The cost adjustment measure shows smaller increases because the pay increases are first counted in the period when they go into effect (e.g., which may be in the second or third year of the contract), in contrast to the rate adjustment measure, which counts all pay increases as covering the entire term of the contract regardless of the period when they go into effect. All told, however, both series indicate modest pay increases in collective bargaining settlements during 1988–90.

Collective Bargaining Settlements over the Life of the Contract for Settlements of 5,000 Workers or More: Average Annual Increase

	"Cost" adjustment	"Rate" adjustment
1988	1.7%	2.5%
1989	2.8	3.4
1990	2.4	3.2

Management plays a key role in determining wages. Trends in sales, profits, and unemployment affect employers' willingness to give wage increases. Following the back-to-back recessions in 1980 and 1981–82, the bargaining power shifted from unions to management, leading to the sharp decline in collective bargaining compensation increases during the 1980s.

Employers were aggressive and successful in bargaining to hold down the amount of wage increases. This has led to two-tier wage scales, which pay new workers lower wages than existing workers in the same job, albeit occasionally the arrangement has a planned phase-out. In some cases, wages have been reduced as "givebacks" to save jobs. Wage costs have also been lowered by changes in work rules, such as using less experienced workers and contracting out to lower-wage nonunion companies. And employers increasingly utilized strikes to replace union workers with permanent lower-paid nonunion workers, thus eliminating unions in their companies.

The reduced bargaining power of most unions stems from the high unemployment and low economic growth of the early 1980s, the loss of high paying jobs to foreign competition and the threat of a further loss to competition from abroad, the growth of nonunion companies due to industrial shifts to the Sunbelt states that have less forceful laws requiring union representation, interpretations of federal labor laws less favorable to unions, and a more aggressive posture by employers in hiring nonunion workers to continue operations during strikes as well as using nonunion workers as permanent replacements after strikes.

The magnitude of this shift in bargaining power is difficult to quantify. As noted previously, part of the smaller negotiated wage settlements occurred because inflation dropped substantially in the 1980s. The shift is based on a qualitative judgment. *The analyst should monitor trends affecting both sides of the bargaining table: efforts by unions to make up for losses in the purchasing power of workers' income, and employers' resistance to large compensation increases. These will be affected by how each side perceives the relationship between compensation and jobs. If a strong linkage between compensation and jobs is assumed, compensation would tend to increase less than if job security were not an overriding issue. The bargaining power relationship will include the unions' ability to organize workers, since negotiating strength is affected by the number of union workers. In addition, the composition of settlements between cash wages and fringe benefits could be affected by rising health insurance costs; thus, unions may trade part of a cash wage increase to maintain health insurance benefits.*

PRODUCTIVITY

Productivity is the general term referring to the efficiency of production operations; rising productivity is fundamental to improvements in living conditions. Increasing total output is a key factor in improving the material well-being of the population and maintaining a secure defense. There are two ways to increase the volume of goods and services available for private and public use: increase the amount of labor and capital equipment used in production, or increase the efficiency of these factors in producing the output. The latter defines the economy's productivity and is a primary factor determining the nation's total output.

Sustained productivity increases over time are the basic means by which the economy generates overall improved living conditions for each generation. Thus, higher productivity is required for children to have a higher level of material well-being than their parents. Productivity is increased through improvements in technology and equipment, education and skills of the work force, and managerial know-how. In some situations, however, new technology can temporarily lower productivity. Productivity may be reduced in the initial transition period when lack of familiarity with new equipment causes workers to take longer to do a job than they took with the older technology, or when breakdowns and bugs occur in the new equipment and have to be ironed out. (The problems associated with the introduction of computers and advanced telephone systems provide recent examples of this phenomenon.) Moreover, because new technology causes some workers to be unemployed or to work at lower-paying jobs, not everyone shares equally in productivity improvements. This section assesses productivity's effect on unemployment and inflation.

Productivity is defined as the output produced in relation to the inputs of labor, machinery, materials, and services required for production.[34] It is economic output per unit of input. Traditionally, the inputs are limited to labor, and so for the economy as a whole productivity is measured as the real gross domestic product per labor hour (real GDP is covered in Chapter 3, and labor hours are the product of employment and hours, as covered earlier in this chapter). The figures on labor hours include paid employees, the self-employed, and unpaid family workers. In the case of paid employees, who account for about 85 percent of labor hours in the GDP business sector, the definition of hours represents hours at work, which excludes paid leave for vacations, sickness, or other reasons. The data on hours for the self-employed and family workers are less clear. Given the nature of the compensation for these groups, measures of their labor input can be described as "hours worked" or "hours paid." As noted by Mary Jablonski, Kent Kunze, and Phyllis Otto, the introduction of the hours-worked in place of the hours-paid data in 1989 changed growth rates on overall productivity measures during the 1948–88 period by only 0.1 percentage point.[35] The rate changed by as much as 0.2 percentage point only for manufacturing during 1973–79. The productivity measures are provided quarterly due to their link to the GDP measures.

Because of statistical problems in measuring the productivity of government, nonprofit organization, and household workers, in the GDP their output is equivalent to their labor input of wages and salaries adjusted for inflation; consequently, there is no statistical change in their productivity. Therefore, the measure of output used in estimating productivity excludes government, nonprofit organization, and household output, because to include them would bias the productivity measures downward. The rental value of owner-occupied housing and the "rest-of-the-world" sector (which is part of the gross national product) are also excluded because there are no corresponding labor hours for these components. Thus, the output measure is gross domestic product for the business sector.

$$\text{Productivity} = \frac{\text{Output}}{\text{Input}} = \frac{\text{Real GDP*}}{\text{Labor hours**}} = \text{Real GDP per labor hour}$$

*Gross domestic product in the business sector.
**Paid employees, the self-employed, and unpaid family workers.

Many underlying factors affect productivity: the skills and effort of workers; use of capital equipment in production; scientific technology in the production process; managerial know-how; level of output; utilization of capacity, energy, and materials; organization of production that integrates output, transportation, and distribution; and the interaction of these and all other factors. The measure of productivity above reflects the total effect of all of these labor, capital, and other elements. Because productivity is calculated as output per labor hour, the effect of changes in the quantity of labor (number of workers and weekly hours) is eliminated. However, changes in the quality of labor such as workers' expertise and work effort are included. As noted above, this is the traditional measure of productivity and is called labor productivity.

Table 22

Alternative Measures of Productivity: 1948–89 (annual percent change)

	Labor Productivity		Multifactor Productivity	
	Business sector	Manufacturing	Business sector	Manufacturing
1948–59	3.3	2.6	2.1	1.8
1959–69	3.0	2.9	2.0	2.1
1969–79	1.5	2.4	0.7	1.5
1979–89	1.3	3.2	0.8	2.5
1948–89	2.3	2.8	1.4	2.0

Note: Based on Bureau of Labor Statistics data.

An alternative productivity measure eliminates the effect of the quantity of plant and equipment investment as well as the quantity of labor, but includes some changes in the quality of capital investment. (The plant and equipment quality improvements stem from two factors: (a) more weight is given to shorter-lived equipment items, and (b) quality improvements are included in the producer price indexes used to convert the value of capital facilities to constant dollars.) This formula includes the services of capital facilities along with labor hours in the denominator of the above equation and is called multifactor productivity. Thus, it captures the underlying elements driving productivity as defined in the previous paragraph by excluding changes in the quantity of labor and capital facilities. Since labor productivity only excludes the quantity of labor, it shows greater productivity increases than multifactor productivity.

Table 22 shows the average annual movements of labor productivity and multifactor productivity separately for the GDP business sector and manufacturing industries for the period from 1948 to 1989 as well as for the decades of the 1950s, 1960s, 1970s, and 1980s.[36] Over the long-term 1948–89 period, labor productivity rose one percentage point faster than multifactor productivity for the business sector and manufacturing. Manufacturing productivity grew one-half percentgage point faster than business sector productivity. The productivity slowdown in the 1970s appears in all four measures. The productivity stagnation in the business sector and the productivity improvement in manufacturing in the 1980s appears in the labor and multifactor measures.

The greater productivity increase in manufacturing industries probably reflects the relatively greater use of equipment in manufacturing, even though many nonmanufacturing industries are also capital intensive. Some of the differential is also probably due to the problems of measuring the output of service industries included in nonmanufacturing because the output of educational, medical, legal, and other labor-intensive industries is not readily quantifiable. The

Figure 44a. **Productivity in the Business Sector: 1950–90**

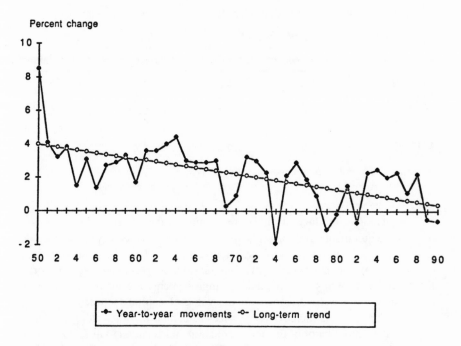

Percent change

Note: Based on Bureau of Labor Statistics data.

methodology used in measuring the output of service industries probably understates their productivity. However, it is puzzling that the faster productivity growth in manufacturing occurs only in the 1970s and 1980s; in the 1950s, productivity growth was actually faster in the business sector, and in the 1960s productivity grew at the same rate in both categories.

In addition, part of the slower productivity improvement in the business sector compared to manufacturing appears to reflect a problem with the data series on the GNP by industry. Lawrence Mishel found that the distribution of the GNP among the various industries allocates too much output to manufacturing industries and not enough to nonmanufacturing, and thus overstates the productivity increase in manufacturing and understates it in nonmanufacturing.[37] In response to this critique, the Bureau of Economic Analysis is refining the statistical procedures for this allocation. Initial effects of these refinements on the differential productivity movements show a relatively small reduction in the annual rate of increase of manufacturing output from the previous estimate of 2.7 percent to the revised figure of 2.5 percent for the 1977–87 period.[38] Revised estimates for years before 1977 will be prepared later in the 1990s. The manufacturing mea-

Figure 44b. Productivity in Manufacturing: 1950–90

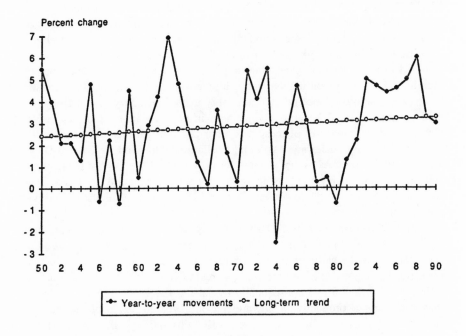

Percent change

Year-to-year movements   Long-term trend

Note: Based on Bureau of Labor Statistics data.

sure is of particular interest because of concern about the competitive position of U.S. manufactured products in world markets and the role of manufacturing in the overall economy as discussed in Chapters 3 and 4.

Figures 44a and 44b show the yearly labor productivity change for the business sector and for all manufacturing industries, and the long-run trends in productivity change during 1950–90. As indicated by the steeper upward and downward movements for manufacturing industries, productivity is more volatile in manufacturing than in the business sector. This reflects the greater year-to-year volatility of manufacturing output. The long-run trend in productivity improvement during the forty years has been slowing in the business sector (downward sloping line) and accelerating slightly in manufacturing industries (upward sloping line), consistent with the decade movements noted in Table 22. Multifactor productivity is not shown in Figures 44a and 44b but it has similar business sector and maufacturing patterns as those for labor productivity.

Cyclical productivity changes generally arise from the previously discussed tendency of employers not to make immediate changes to their work force when business turns down in a recession from the previous expansion peak or when it first turns up in an expansion from the previous recession trough (see the section Weekly Hours, above). Lawrence Fulco points out that because of this practice, productivity rises more in expansions than in recessions irrespective of changes in labor skills, capital equipment, and other basic factors affecting productivity.[39]

Various explanations have been offered for the productivity slowdown in the 1970s: decreasing technological advance due to lower research and development spending, less investment in plant and equipment as higher energy prices caused business to use more labor relative to energy-using machinery, and more hours paid for than worked because of increases in paid vacations and sick leave. However, actual measures of these and other possible reasons related to multi-factor productivity by Jerome Mark and William Waldorf and by Edward Denison have yielded estimates that account for only about 20 percent of the decline, and the factors causing the slowdown are not well understood.[40] It is also of interest that productivity slowdowns occurred in virtually all industrialized nations in the 1970s.

(Charles Morris and Michael Darby have suggested that the measured productivity growth slowdown in the 1970s is a statistical illusion associated with the price controls in the early 1970s.[41] Their analysis is based on the assumption that the official price measures used to estimate real GNP in 1973 did not adequately reflect price inflation and consequently overstated the 1973 productivity level, thus indicating a productivity slowdown from 1968 to 1973, but no further slowdown after 1973. However, empirically substantiating the extent of the price-measurement problem is difficult. It requires accounting for changes in the quality of goods in determining price changes, a technical aspect discussed in Chapter 3, Part A, under Real GNP and Inflation, and in Chapter 6 on the consumer price index. Because this assessment hinges on the assumed price-measurement problem that has not been demonstrated empirically, it has not replaced the generally accepted view that productivity slowed down during most of the 1970s.)

Figures 44a and 44b show that the year-to-year measures of productivity growth fluctuate substantially. This is due to the sharper cyclical changes in the GNP (numerator) than changes in labor hours (denominator). Again, employers tend to delay laying off and hiring workers at the turning points of business cycles. Although not shown in the figure, the same phenomenon occurs in the quarterly trends. However, despite substantial fluctuations in the measure, the underlying factors driving productivity cumulate slowly over time as they become more widely diffused throughout the economy, and thus they do not have significant quarterly and annual changes. *Therefore, in assessing the prospect for productivity trends, the analyst should be aware of the differing cyclical and longer-term factors affecting productivity.*

Additionally, as the average for all industries, the overall productivity measure conceals wide variations among individual industries. For 1973–86, Figure 45 shows little relationship between productivity and output change for several

Figure 45. **Output Per Employee Hour and Employment in Selected Industries: 1973–86**

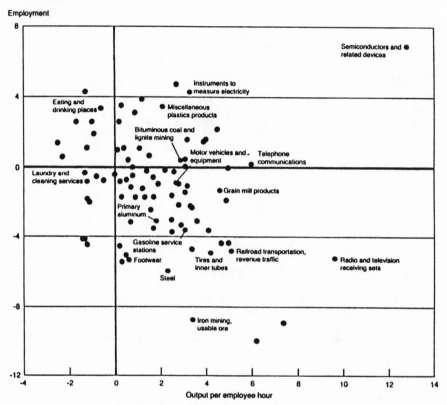

Source: Bureau of Labor Statistics, *Productivity and the Economy: A Chartbook*, March 1988.

individual manufacturing industries. Industries with high productivity show both high and low increases in employment, as do industries with low productivity increases or actual productivity declines. Thus, these data do not support the concern that advanced technology, by displacing workers with outmoded skills, leads to lower employment. Rather, the net effect on employment seems more closely related to demand for each industry's product. It should be noted, however, that these relationships refer to total employment. Persons with particular or limited skills who lose their jobs because of the introduction of labor-saving machinery, such as factory workers and laborers, are not always able to find new work, and many work at new jobs at lower income levels.[42]

Table 23

International Productivity Levels: 1950–89 (United States = 100)

	Gross domestic product per employed person[a]					Manufacturing output per hour[b]
	1950	1960	1970	1980	1989	1987
United States	100	100	100	100	100	100
Canada	76	79	83	92	94	85
Italy	29	42	63	82	87	94
France	38	48	64	80	86	75
Belgium	47	51	63	80	84	99
Norway	43	50	58	74	80	NA
Germany	35	49	62	76	78	75
Netherlands	52	58	70	81	77	91
Japan	15	23	46	63	73	71
Austria	31	39	54	68	72	NA
United Kingdom	54	55	58	67	72	51
Sweden	NA	52	63	67	68	NA
Denmark	NA	53	60	66	65	NA
Korea	NA	13 (1963)	17	26	40	27

[a]Office of Productivity and Technology, Bureau of Labor Statistics, U.S. Department of Labor.

[b]Peter Hooper and Kathryn A. Larin, "International Comparisons of Labor Costs in Manufacturing," *Review of Income and Wealth,* December 1989.

NA: Not available

Comparison with Other Countries

Table 23 shows productivity as measured by gross domestic product per employed person for the United States and twelve other industrialized nations and industrializing Korea for 1950, 1960, 1970, 1980, and 1989, with the United States indexed as 100 in all years, based on Bureau of Labor Statistics data. Productivity in the United States in 1989 is higher than in other industrialized countries, although the gap has been narrowing over the past forty years. As of 1989, productivity in Canada is 6 percent below the United States; Italy, France, Belgium, and Norway are 13 to 20 percent below; Germany, the Netherlands, Japan, Austria, and the United Kingdom are 22 to 28 percent below; Sweden and Denmark are 32 to 35 percent below; and Korea is 60 percent below the United States.

The BLS does not prepare international productivity measures for manufacturing industries because it believes the lack of comparable price data for many industrial products among the nations prevents the development of meaningful estimates. Because the loss in United States competitiveness is most apparent in manufacturing, economists are interested in international comparisons of productivity in manufacturing. Peter Hooper and Kathryn Larin have prepared international productivity measures for manufacturing by applying economywide price data to manufacturing industries (also shown in Table 23).[43] As of 1987, these broad and tentative estimates show an overall U.S. superiority similar to that in the BLS measures of gross domestic product, although there are noticeable differences in the standing of some countries. Part of the similarity in the overall superiority may reflect the use of economywide price measures in preparing the manufacturing estimates.

In an assessment of international productivity movements since the 1860s, William Baumol, Sue Anne Blackman, and Edward Wolff develop the idea that international productivity levels in the long run tend to converge.[44] This occurs because new technology is transferred relatively rapidly from the country in which it was developed to other nations. An imitating country often narrows the productivity gap created by the new technology in a process of "catch-up," and sometimes, because of a wider and more advanced exploitation of the new technology, even surpasses the originating country. But according to this study, although the U.S. productivity advantage has narrowed over the post–World War II period, productivity improvement in the United States remains sufficiently rapid that the United States is not in danger of losing its overall advantage. Naturally, studies of this type are based on considerable inferences and should be considered as suggestive only.

Despite substantial technical limitations, these measures imply that the loss of U.S. competitiveness in export and import markets discussed in Chapter 3 is attributable to factors other than international differences in productivity. For example, even Japan and Germany, two major competitors of the United States, show surprisingly lower productivity levels than the United States.

Productivity and Inflation

Prices are determined by both the markets for goods and services (demand) and production costs (supply). Prices tend to rise faster when economic growth is strong than when it is slow or declining because households and businesses are more willing to buy items at higher prices when employment and incomes are rising rapidly (higher demand). This section, however, focuses on the supply effect of production costs on prices. Price movements are discussed more fully in Chapter 6 on the consumer price index.

Productivity affects inflation through its effect on the costs of producing goods and services. If costs rise, business will be motivated to increase prices in order to maintain profits rates (profits as a percentage of sales). If costs remain the same or decline, they do not exert a pressure for higher prices to maintain profit rates; in fact, if costs decline, prices can decline and profits can still be maintained.

Of key interest in considering production costs is the relation between com-

Figure 46. **Unit Labor Costs and Prices, Business Sector: 1975–90**

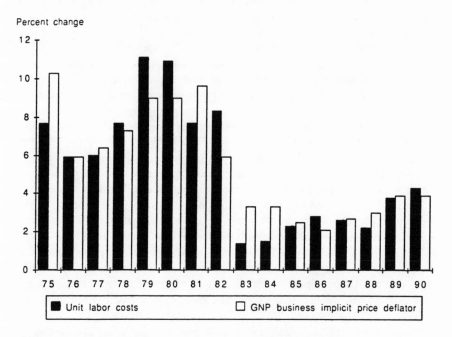

Note: Based on Bureau of Labor Statistics and Bureau of Economic Analysis data.

pensation (money wages and salaries plus fringe benefits) and productivity, which is referred to as unit labor costs (ULC).[45] ULC also may be expressed as compensation per unit of output because, in the identity below, labor hours is the common term in both compensation and productivity, and thus cancels out in the numerator and denominator. As in the case of productivity, the term ULC refers to the business sector—that is, it excludes output of governments, nonprofit organizations, and households.

$$\text{Unit labor costs} = \frac{\text{Compensation per hour}}{\text{Productivity}} = \frac{\dfrac{\text{Compensation*}}{\text{Labor hours}}}{\dfrac{\text{Output}}{\text{Labor hours}}} = \frac{\text{Compensation}}{\text{Output}}$$

*Money wages and salaries plus fringe benefits.

If compensation rises faster than productivity, ULC increase and there is an upward pressure on prices; if compensation increases slower than productivity, ULC decline and there is a downward pressure on prices. Figure 46 shows the annual changes of ULC and the GNP business sector implicit price deflator from 1975–90. The figure indicates parallel movements in both indicators. On an annual basis, the relative movements tend to be within 1 to 2 percentage points of each other.

ULC are an important but not determining factor affecting prices. *In using ULC to assess trends in price pressures, the analyst should supplement ULC with economic growth rates and market conditions that have important spillover impacts on other prices, such as the secondary effects of energy and food prices.*

SUMMARY

Unemployment Rate

The unemployment rate (UR) moves in accordance with business cycles, declining in expansions and rising in recessions. The UR is a leading indicator at expansion peaks and a lagging indicator at recession troughs. However, its monthly movements sometimes are contrary to trends in economic growth because of persons newly seeking jobs or unemployed persons giving up in their job search, which makes short-term UR movements difficult to interpret. It is thus useful to supplement UR analyses with a consideration of flows in and out of the labor force. The changing proportion of teenagers in the labor force has been the main factor affecting long-term movements in the UR in relation to concepts of "full" or "high" employment.

The relationship between economic growth and unemployment is quantified in Okun's Law. Broad measures of this relationship establish break-even points indicating the required growth in real GNP necessary to maintain a steady unemployment rate as well as indicating the economic growth rates above or below the break-even point that lower or raise the unemployment rate by particular amounts. However, these are long-term averages that can diverge substantially from the theory in particular points.

Employment

Employment measures are provided by two surveys that have differing definitions and data-collection methodologies. One is a survey of employers, and the other is a survey of households (the household survey is also the source of the unemployment rate figures). The employer survey typically has more extreme cyclical movements than the household survey—increasing more in expansions and decreasing more in recessions—and is considered more relevant for assessing cyclical changes in employment.

Weekly Hours

Changes in weekly hours worked in manufacturing are an early indicator of turning points at cyclical expansion peaks and recession troughs, and are included as a leading indicator of economic activity. However, the erratic monthly movements in the weekly hours figures make it difficult in some periods to establish a trend; they are best treated as a clue to future economic activity that should be compared with indicators on employment and unemployment.

Earnings and Collective Bargaining

Wages and fringe benefits represent income to workers and costs to employers. Average weekly earnings in constant dollars declined from the early 1970s through 1990. Such measures of the material well-being of workers, plus assessments of the competitive position of U.S. business and the strength of unions, are the main factors determining collective bargaining settlements.

Productivity

Productivity refers to the efficiency of production operations. Basic factors affecting productivity are the skills of workers, use of capital equipment, level of technology, and managerial know-how. These factors change gradually and are reflected in productivity movements over several years. By contrast, shorter-term quarterly and annual movements in productivity mainly reflect cyclical changes in economic growth. Productivity in the United States was noticeably above that in other countries at the end of the 1980s, although the U.S. advantage has been narrowing.

Productivity also affects inflation through its relationship to unit labor costs. Unit labor costs are an important but not determining factor affecting prices; in assessing price trends, data on unit labor costs should be supplemented with measures of economic growth and market developments that impact heavily on prices, such as food and energy.

REVIEW QUESTIONS

UNEMPLOYMENT

• Characterize how the official unemployment measures (total and civilian unemployment) differ from the alternative unemployment figures that focus on special characteristics of the unemployed.

• Why are the official unemployment figures higher than those based on unemployment insurance data?

• What is the macroeconomic concern about the decline during the 1980s in the proportion of laid-off workers receiving unemployment insurance benefit payments?

• The increasing proportion of teenagers and women in the labor force raised the unemployment rate during most of the 1970s. What changes occurred in these demographic components that lower the unemployment rate in the 1980s and 1990s?

• The goals for lowering unemployment and inflation established in the Full Employment and Balanced Growth Act of 1978 (Humphrey–Hawkins Act) have not been reached as of 1991. Discuss the arguments for maintaining, repealing, and modifying the unemployment and inflation goals in the act.

• How does the employment–population ratio differ from the unemployment rate as a measure of job markets?

• Using a formulation of Okun's Law that puts the break-even point for unemployment at an annual growth in real GNP of 2.5 percent, what is the effect on the unemployment rate of:

	No change	Higher	Lower
GNP growth of 2.5%	___	___	___
GNP growth of 4.0%	___	___	___
GNP growth of 1.0%	___	___	___

EMPLOYMENT

• The survey of employment based on employer payroll records counts jobs, while the household survey of employment counts people. Why would the employer survey be a better measure of production?

• Are differences in employment trends of the household and employer surveys more significant for periods within one year or over several years?

• Employers tend to change the weekly hours of workers in response to changes in company sales before hiring or laying off workers. What cyclical property does this give weekly hours data?

• How has the trend in real earnings per worker changed since the early 1970s?

• Why has the trend in real earnings per worker differed from the trend in real disposable income per capita since the early 1970s?

COLLECTIVE BARGAINING

• Although union workers account for less than 20 percent of the labor force and the share has been declining, the terms of collective bargaining agreements are closely followed for their impact on future income, employment, and inflation. Why?

• What are the main factors that will affect the bargaining power of labor and management in the 1990s?

PRODUCTIVITY

• Using the traditional productivity measure of output per worker hour, short-run productivity changes of one or two years reflect cyclical changes in economic growth more than basic changes in efficiency associated with worker skills, technology, and managerial know-how. Explain.

• Why is multifactor productivity a better measure of efficiency than the traditional measure of labor productivity?

• Japan and Germany are major competitors of the United States in world markets, but U.S. productivity appears to be significantly above that in both countries. What other factors account for the decline in U.S. competitiveness?

• Inflation is influenced by trends in unit labor costs. On average, what would inflation be if the components of unit labor costs are:

Productivity	Compensation per hour	Inflation				
		2%	6%	9%	−1%	−6%
5%	4%	___	___	___	___	___
2	4	___	___	___	___	___
0	6	___	___	___	___	___

NOTES

1. For a detailed description of the methodology, see Bureau of Labor Statistics, U.S. Department of Labor, *BLS Handbook of Methods*, April 1988, Chapter 1. For the evolution of unemployment measurements, see John E. Bregger, "The Current Population Survey: A historical perspective and BLS' role," *Monthly Labor Review*, June 1984.

2. Bureau of Labor Statistics, U.S. Department of Labor, *Employment and Earnings*, September 1990, Table C, p. 160.

3. Richard J. McDonald, "The 'underground economy' and BLS statistical data," *Monthly Labor Review*, January 1984, pp. 11–13.

4. Harvey R. Hamel, "Two-fifths of discouraged workers sought work during prior six-month period," *Monthly Labor Review*, March 1979; and Kennon R. Copeland and Jennifer M. Rothgeb, "Testing Alternative Questionnaires for the Current Population Survey," Proceedings of the Section on Survey Research Methods, American Statistical Association, 1990.

5. National Commission on Employment and Unemployment Statistics, *Counting the Labor Force* (U.S. Government Printing Office: 1979), pp. 44–49.

6. Walter Corson and Walter Nicholson, *An Examination of Declining UI Claims during the 1980s* (prepared by Mathematica Policy Research for the U.S. Department of Labor), Unemployment Insurance Occasional Paper 88–3, Employment and Training Administration, U.S. Department of Labor, 1988. A condensed version of this report is in Employment and Training Administration, U.S. Department of Labor, *The Secretary's Seminars on Unemployment Insurance,* Unemployment Insurance Occasional Paper 89–1, 1989.

7. David E. Rosenbaum, "Unemployment Insurance Aiding Fewer Workers," *New York Times*, December 1, 1990, pp. 1, 38.

8. Wayne Vroman, "The Decline in Unemployment Insurance Claims Activity in the 1980s," The Urban Institute, Washington, D.C., December 1990.

9. Vivek Moorthy, "Unemployment in Canada and the United States: The Role of Unemployment Insurance Benefits," *Quarterly Review*, Federal Reserve Bank of New York, Winter 1989–90.

10. Annual percentage growth rates for the noninstitutional population age 16 to 64 years are: 1950s: 0.7; 1960s: 1.5; 1970s: 2.0; 1980s: 1.1

11. Carol Boyd Leon, "The employment-population ratio: its value in labor force analysis," *Monthly Labor Review*, February 1981, pp. 37–38.

12. *Economic Report of the President*, January 1962, pp. 46–48.

13. Sherman J. Maisel, *Macroeconomics: Theories and Policies* (W. W. Norton & Company: 1982), pp. 555–57.

14. Milton Friedman, "The Role of Monetary Policy," *American Economic Review*, March 1968, pp. 7–11.

15. Philip A. Klein, "What's Natural about Unemployment?" in Philip A. Klein, ed., *Analyzing Modern Business Cycles: Essays Honoring Geoffrey H. Moore* (M. E. Sharpe: 1990).

16. "The Federal Open Market Committee is committed to the achievement, over time, of price stability. The importance of this objective derives from the fact that the prospects for long-run growth in the economy are brightest when inflation need no longer be a material consideration in the decisions of households and firms." Board of Governors of the Federal Reserve System, "Monetary Policy Report to Congress Pursuant to the Full Employment and Balanced Growth Act of 1978," February 20, 1990, p. 1.

17. Paul O. Flaim, "Population changes, the baby boom, and the unemployment rate," *Monthly Labor Review*, August 1990.

18. Ibid. The unemployment rate declined from 5.85 percent in 1979 to 5.27 percent in 1989. Of this 0.58 percentage point decline, 0.46 percentage point (79 percent) is attributable to the decline of teenagers in the labor force.

19. A correlation coefficient of 1 means the variables have identical percentage movements in the same direction in a direct relationship (both increase or decrease in tandem), and a coefficient of −1 means the variables move in opposite directions in an inverse relationship (one increases and the other decreases). A correlation coefficient of zero indicates no relationship.

20. Douglas M. Woodham, "Potential Output Growth and the Long-Term Inflation Outlook," *Quarterly Review*, Federal Reserve Bank of New York, Summer 1984.

21. John F. Stinson, Jr., "Comparison of Nonagricultural Employment Estimates from Two Surveys," *Employment and Earnings*, March 1984. For more detail on the factors contributing to these differences, see Gloria P. Green, "Comparing employment estimates from household and payroll surveys," *Monthly Labor Review*, December 1969. These annual reconciliations have not been published since 1984, but they are available for later years from the Bureau of Labor Statistics.

22. *Employment and Earnings*, September 1990, pp. 159–60 (particularly Table B).

23. For a detailed description of the methodology, see Bureau of Labor Statistics, *BLS Handbook of Methods*, Chapter 2.

24. Green, "Comparing employment estimates," p. 19. This 1969 assessment tends to be repeated in current newspaper reports on monthly employment trends.

25. The 1950s are calculated from 1948–59 instead of 1949–59 because 1949 was a recession year and 1959 was an expansion year, which would distort the calculation. Both terminal years for the other decades are expansion periods (i.e., 1959 and 1969, 1969 and

1979, and 1979 and 1989). To maintain this consistency of using all terminal years as expansion periods, the entire four decades are calculated as 1948–89.

26. John F. Stinson, Jr., "Comparison of Nonagricultural Employment Estimates from Two Surveys," *Employment and Earnings*, March 1983, pp. 8–9.

27. Eugene H. Becker, "Self-employed workers: an update to 1983," *Monthly Labor Review*, July 1984, pp. 15–16.

28. In manufacturing, mining, and construction, for employees up through the level of working supervisors, "production" designates workers who engage directly in the work. The analogous designation in other industries—transportation, utilities, trade, finance, and other services—is "nonsupervisory" workers.

29. The union share of all wage and salary workers declined over the postwar period from 35.5 percent in 1945 to 23 percent in 1980 to 16 percent in 1990. Actual membership increased until 1979, although at a slower rate than employment; however, from 1979 to 1990 the number of union members also declined, which accelerated the falling share in the later period. The above percentages refer to farm and nonfarm labor organizations involved in collective bargaining. For 1945, they are limited to organizations designated officially as unions, while by the 1970s they include employee associations of professional groups that subsequently began to act as unions although not called unions, such as the National Education Association and the Fraternal Orders of Police. See Larry T. Adams, "Changing employment patterns of organized workers," *Monthly Labor Review*, February 1985, p. 26, and subsequent January issues of *Employment and Earnings*.

30. Linda A. Bell, "Union Concessions in the 1980s," *Quarterly Review*, Federal Reserve Bank of New York, Summer 1989.

31. Because of changes in data availability on wage rates in the 1970s and 1980s, there are breaks in the continuity of the figures between 1976 and 1977 and between 1980 and 1981. Data from 1970 to 1976 are for scheduled wage adjustments (excluding fringe benefits) in manufacturing; from 1977 to 1980 they cover wages (excluding fringe benefits) in all private nonagricultural industries; and from 1981 to 1990 they cover wages and fringe benefits in all private nonagricultural industries. However, the union/nonunion differentials are consistent in each year, as the same definition for union and nonunion wages is used in each year. This Bureau of Labor Statistics information is based on the survey of wage developments in manufacturing for 1970–76 and the employment cost index for 1977–90.

32. Kay E. Anderson, Philip M. Doyle, and Albert E. Schwenk, "Measuring union-nonunion earnings differences," *Monthly Labor Review*, June 1990.

33. Alvin Bauman, "A new measure of compensation cost adjustments," *Monthly Labor Review*, August 1990.

34. For a detailed description of the methodology, see Bureau of Labor Statistics, *BLS Handbook of Methods*, Chapter 10.

35. Mary Jablonski, Kent Kunze, and Phyllis Flohr Otto, "Hours at work: a new base for BLS productivity statistics," *Monthly Labor Review*, February 1990.

36. See note 25.

37. Lawrence R. Mishel, "The Late Great Debate on Deindustrialization," *Challenge*, January/February 1989.

38. Frank de Leeuw, Michael Mohr, and Robert P. Parker, "Gross Product by Industry, 1977–88: A Progress Report on Improving the Estimates," *Survey of Current Business*, January 1991.

39. Lawrence J. Fulco, "Strong post-recession gain in productivity contributes to slow growth in labor costs," *Monthly Labor Review*, December 1984.

40. Jerome A. Mark, William H. Waldorf, et al., *Trends in Multifactor Productivity*, Bureau of Labor Statistics, Bulletin 2178, September 1983, Chapters III and IV; and

Edward F. Denison, *Trends in Economic Growth, 1929–1982* (The Brookings Institution: 1985).

41. Charles S. Morris, "The Productivity 'Slowdown': A Sectoral Analysis," *Economic Review*, Federal Reserve Bank of Kansas City, April 1984; and Michael R. Darby, "The U.S. Productivity Slowdown: A Case of Statistical Myopia," *American Economic Review*, June 1984.

42. Jerome A. Mark, "Technological change and employment: some results from BLS research," *Monthly Labor Review*, April 1987; and Ronald E. Kutscher and Richard W. Riche, "Impact of Technology on Employment and the Workforce—The U.S. Experience," World Bank Seminar on Employment and Social Dimension of Economic Adjustment, Washington, D.C., February 27–28, 1990.

43. Peter Hooper and Kathryn A. Larin, "International Comparisons of Labor Costs in Manufacturing," *Review of Income and Wealth*, December 1989.

44. William J. Baumol, Sue Anne Batey Blackman, and Edward N. Wolff, *Productivity and American Leadership: The Long View* (The MIT Press: 1989), Chapter 5.

45. For a detailed description of the methodology, see Bureau of Labor Statistics, *BLS Handbook of Methods*, Chapter 13.

6
CONSUMER PRICE INDEX

The consumer price index (CPI) measures changes in the prices of goods and services bought by households. It is the most widely recognized gauge of inflation, a key measure of consumer purchasing power and economic well-being. There are three broad uses of the CPI: (a) it is central to macroeconomic analysis and policy decisions about balancing unemployment and inflation; (b) it is the basis of cost-escalation estimates used to compensate for inflation in wage contracts, pensions, income-maintenance programs, business contracts, and indexing of federal individual income taxes; and (c) it is used to deflate economic measures of the gross national product (for detailed goods and service items in the GNP based on item detail in the CPI), wage earnings, and interest rates. Additionally, CPI futures contracts are traded on the Coffee, Sugar, and Cocoa Exchange as a hedge against future price increases or declines. In cost escalation, the CPI directly affected the income of close to 150 million persons through its impact on collective bargaining agreements and statutory payments associated with Social Security, military and federal civilian retirement programs, and the food stamp and school lunch programs in 1980.[1]

The CPI is provided monthly by the Bureau of Labor Statics. It covers household spending for everyday living expenses such as food and beverages, housing, apparel, transportation, medical care, education, entertainment, tobacco products, and other personal goods and services. In addition to the national CPI, there are CPIs for certain metropolitan areas and regions of the country.

Two CPI indexes are provided at both the national and local levels. One is based on the spending patterns for goods and services of all urban *consumers* (CPI-U); the other is based on the spending patterns of urban *wage and clerical workers* (CPI-W). The CPI-U includes all urban employed, unemployed, and retired persons (80 percent of the noninstitutional population in 1981).[2] It is assumed that price changes for the remaining 20 percent of the population (18 percent rural and 2 percent military) differ from those for urban consumers.

The CPI-W represents urban household units in which one of the members worked at least thirty-seven weeks during the year in jobs usually paid on an hourly or commission basis in the craft, operative, clerical, sales, service, and laborer occupations. These workers and their households accounted for 30 percent of the noninstitutionalized population in 1980.

Both indexes are provided monthly. Although the CPI-W coverage of the population is less than half the coverage of CPI-U, many cost escalations under labor and business contracts are based on the CPI-W. The CPI-W has been in existence longer and is thus more familiar (it was first published in 1919 and regular, periodic publication began in 1921, while the CPI-U was begun in 1978). The CPI-W was initially started for use in wage negotiations, and because its uses broadened, the CPI-U was introduced to provide a more representative measure of price changes.[3] Different spending patterns for particular goods and services in the two indexes have resulted in the CPI-U increasing slightly faster than the CPI-W—for example, from 1980 to 1990, the CPI-U increased at an annual compound rate of 4.7 percent compared to the CPI-W increase of 4.5 percent. The pattern was similar for the intervening periods of 1980–85 and 1985–90. The slight differential between the CPI-U and the CPI-W figures results from the different spending patterns associated with the two measures. Compared to the CPI-W, the CPI-U assumes that a greater proportion of the consumer's budget is spent for housing and medical care and less for food and transportation. (These assumptions are discussed below in Part A under Index Number Weights). The general properties of index numbers were discussed in Chapter 1.

The CPI measures the relative change in prices as the percent movement between two periods rather than the dollar amounts of the costs. For example, the CPIs for the New York and Cleveland metropolitan areas may show prices rising faster in Cleveland than in New York, but in dollars it still may cost more to live in New York.

Specifying the appropriate distribution of goods and services for measuring price change is elusive, and the CPI concept of using buying patterns that are constant for periods of about ten years is only one way of doing it. Measures of consumer price movements based on alternative methodologies are available from the gross national product measures (see Chapter 3) and are compared to the CPI in this chapter.

The CPI is sometimes referred to as the cost of living, although it does not conform to a theoretical cost of living. As Patrick Jackman notes, a cost-of-living index allows for the substitution of perfect substitute products when the substitute product has a lower price, while the CPI does not permit this substitution.[4] Thus, a cost-of-living index measures price movements associated with the *minimum* expenditures necessary to maintain a constant standard of living. In contrast, the CPI measures price movements for purchasing only the same items between two periods, regardless of the availability of lower-priced substitutes. The CPI also does not include other attributes of a cost-of-living index, such as accounting for household preferences between work and leisure and how changes in income tax rates affect the household's after-tax income and thus the household's financial ability to buy the same goods and services as in the base period.

Underlying Rate of Inflation

Fluctuations in the CPI are partly due to the highly volatile food and energy prices. Crop harvests are subject to changing weather conditions and oil production is subject to the effectiveness of the Organization of Petroleum Exporting Countries as a cartel in controling oil output of the member nations. Daniel Yergin has explicated the political aspects of maintaining discipline among the OPEC nations in adhering to agreed-on country output quotas.[5] Since climate and OPEC are "extra market" conditions which typically temporarily affect the supply and therefore the price of food and oil products, they are likely to be reversed more quickly than the factors affecting the production of other items in the CPI. Therefore, the CPI is also published excluding food and energy prices. This measure is referred to as the *underlying rate of inflation* or sometimes as *core inflation,* since it focuses on the more permanent factors affecting price movements.

The CPI and Measuring Poverty

It is worth noting here that the CPI represents price change only as it affects *living conditions* based on actual purchases, but it does not measure the impact of price change on *living standards.* That is, the CPI measures the relative increase or decrease in the purchasing power of consumers' dollars but does not indicate the amount of dollars necessary under current prices to purchase adequate nutrition, housing, health care, etc. Some measure of the impact of price increases on living standards can be found in the official poverty line measure, which the government uses to count the number of poor persons. Each year the government establishes a cash-income line that represents the threshold income necessary for a family of four to purchase a minimum standard of living in that year (suitably adjusted threshold incomes are provided for larger and smaller families) and counts the number of persons whose cash income falls below that threshold as poor.

The poverty measure is prepared annually by the Census Bureau based on data from a survey of households in the Current Population Survey. The measure was originally developed in the early 1960s using Department of Agriculture data on the cost of a nutritious diet and the average proportion of income spent on food. However, the poverty measure's methodology has been widely criticized, particularly because it has never been updated in any way except to adjust it for the effect of rising prices according to movements in the CPI. Research indicates that if the poverty measure were updated to reflect the CPI's more recent spending-pattern weights for food, the poverty line would have been progressively raised and more people would be counted in poverty than presently are included in the official figures. On the other hand, if the many noncash in-kind income maintenance benefits established since the 1960s were included as income, the official count of people whose income falls below the poverty line would fall.

From a policy standpoint a good case can be made that the poverty measure should be updated to reflect the more current spending patterns used by the CPI as well as the receipt of noncash income. A more accurate measure of the numbers of persons living in poverty could result in more equitable and efficient government spending on income maintenance programs. From an economic standpoint, the poverty measure has some effect on government spending on entitlement programs, since eligibility for many income maintenance programs is based on establishing poverty-level income. Patricia Ruggles recommends that a new poverty standard for the 1990s should include more fundamental changes: these are detailed minimum need budgets for several consumption categories (not just food), refinement of the method of adjusting the poverty income line depending on the number of persons in the family, an after-tax definition of income and inclusion of in-kind benefit payments that are most fungible into cash such as food stamps and rent supplements, reconsideration of the current use of a lower poverty income line for the elderly, and consideration of ways to account for assets in gauging income.[6] She also recommends that statistics be provided on the number of people whose income falls below the poverty line for spells of several months during the year, although since their calendar-year annual income would be above the poverty income line they would not be included in the official annual counts of the poverty population.

The measurement of poverty is a subjective concept based on the nation's perception of minimum living requirements. The measure also rises over time in line with the population's rising expectations of minimum standards of subsistence. For example, Eugene Smolensky estimates that when President Lyndon Johnson declared war on poverty in 1964 " ... To help that one-fifth of all American families with income too small to even meet their basic needs," he used a poverty standard that was 90 percent higher than the one President Franklin Roosevelt used in 1937 when he said, "I see one-third of the nation ill-housed, ill-clad, ill-nourished."[7] Similarly, the poverty standard of the 1930s was undoubtedly higher than that used around 1900. Establishing a new poverty standard for the 1990s would probably raise the number of people counted as living in poverty, even with noncash benefits included in the measure. Because this would increase federal spending for income maintenance programs, and thus increase the federal budget deficit, there has been only limited political support for reassessing the poverty standard.

PART A: ESTIMATING METHODOLOGY

By definition, the CPI measures the actual price charged for items. This includes sales taxes, premiums and discounts from list prices, and import duties. In practice, there probably are a minority of cases in which actual prices net of premiums and discounts from list prices are not obtained.

Quality

As a measure of price change, the CPI includes the effect of quality change in the goods and services prices. The CPI's measure of quality change includes improvements or reductions in the performance of an item, but not changes in its aesthetic qualities. For example, if a loaf of bread is increased (decreased) in size or nutrients, the changes are quality improvements (declines), which will be included in the CPI. Similarly, if a car's design is changed to increase (decrease) its braking power, maneuverability, pollution controls, or comfort, the changes are quality improvements (declines), which the CPI will take into account as cost changes. By contrast, a change in styling such as sculptured lines or chrome is not a quality change.

The idea behind the CPI is that the measured price movements from one period to the next should reflect only those price changes that occur independent of quality changes. Thus, in the monthly pricing of the CPI items, prices are compared to the item's specifications to determine if changes in specifications have occurred, as well as to obtain an estimate of the value of the specification changes. Changes in quality and selling price affect the price used in the CPI, as shown below. The implementation of quality changes in CPI is governed by the availability of data on the extent of the change—the CPI reflects the changes only if the dollar value of the quality change can be quantified.

Quality change	Selling price	CPI price
Improvement	Increase by amount of improvement	No change
Improvement	Increase less than improvement	Decrease
Improvement	No change	Decrease
Improvement	Increase more than improvement	Increase
Decline	Decrease by amount of decline	No change
Decline	Decrease less than decline	Increase
Decline	No change	Increase
Decline	Decrease more than decline	Decrease

Index Number Weights

The CPI is an index number that combines the prices for a wide range of goods and services into a single figure.[8] The goods and service items are combined by using the percentage shares of households' total dollar spending for each item in the base period as weights. Data on the spending patterns are obtained from surveys of representative samples of households in geographic areas around the country conducted for the Bureau of Labor Statistics by the Census Bureau. These spending patterns are updated about every ten years—the weights from 1978 to 1986 are based on spending patterns in 1972–73, except that in 1983 a new method of pricing owner-occupied housing was introduced that further modified the weights. Starting in 1987, the weights reflect spending patterns in 1982–84; these will be used until more current spending patterns are introduced in the late 1990s.[9]

As a fixed-weight index for the approximate ten-year periods between the updating of the spending patterns, the CPI measures the effect of price changes assuming a constant quantity and quality of the same goods and services over the period. Because of the fixed weights, the effect of changing consumer preferences for spending among different goods and services (say, between food, housing, and recreation) or for substituting products due to changes in taste or relative prices (for example, beef vs. chicken) is not fully included in the estimation of the CPI.

Changing consumer preferences are, however, partially reflected to the extent that changing demand for particular items affects their prices. Surveyors obtain current monthly price data by visiting the same retail stores and service businesses and pricing the same items (or close substitutes) every collection period, monthly or bimonthly depending on the city and item in the survey samples. The businesses included in the sample from which the price data are obtained are selected proportional to their sales volume as reported in a household survey of where consumers buy, thus giving greater importance to price changes in the larger outlets. Only prices obtained for identical items in two successive months are used in the CPI measures.

Price data on electricity are obtained from utilities by personal interview. Data on rents are obtained from a sampling procedure in which six groups of single-family homes and apartment buildings are each visited every six months to obtain rental charges for the current and previous months; this technique, which is used to hold down the rental survey's size and cost, provides the monthly rent change by weighting the one-month and six-month changes for comparable housing units.

Although highly simplified, Table 24 shows the basic procedure for calculating the monthly CPI-U seasonally unadjusted level using December 1990 as the example. The table is calculated for the unadjusted CPI level because the seasonally adjusted level is not published; the unadjusted level and the month-to-month changes for both the seasonally adjusted and unadjusted measures are published.[10] The weights of the major components are from the spending patterns introduced in 1987 using December 1986 as the based period. These are multiplied by the relative price change between December 1986 and December 1990 to obtain the proportions of each component in December 1990, and the proportions are summed to obtain the total CPI on a base of December 1986 = 100. To convert this level to the base of 1982–84 = 100, which is the actual base period used in the published CPI, the summed total is multiplied by the ratio of the CPI price change between 1982–84 and December 1986. The resultant index of 133.8 means that the CPI increased by 33.8 percent between 1982–84 and De-

Table 24

Estimating the CPI-U for December 1990* (1982–84 = 100)

(1) Item	(2) Base-period weights, Dec. 1986	(3) Ratio change, Dec. 1986 to Dec. 1990	(4) December 1990 Proportions (2) x (3) (Dec. 1986 = 100)
Food and beverages	17.758	1.207	21.4
Housing	42.791	1.170	50.1
Apparel and upkeep	6.309	1.166	7.4
Transportation	17.172	1.254	21.5
Medical care	5.749	1.345	7.7
Entertainment	4.385	1.192	5.2
Other	5.836	1.321	7.7
Total	100.000	—	121.1

Adjustment to 1982–84 = 100:
CPI for Dec. 1986 (1982–84 = 100): 110.5
CPI for Dec. 1990 (1982–84 = 100): 133.8
    (121.1 x 1.105)
*Not seasonally adjusted.
Note: Detail does not equal totals due to rounding.

cember 1990. In practice, the computations are made at a much greater level of detailed items within each major component—food prices, for example, are calculated for a wide range of bakery, meat, dairy, produce items, beverages, and the like—and distinctions are made between food consumed in homes and restaurants. The percent change in the CPI between any two periods is calculated as the relative movement in the CPI levels between the periods. For example, from June to December 1990, the CPI, seasonally unadjusted, increased by 3 percent as follows:

December CPI	133.8
less: June CPI	129.9
equals: Index point change	3.9
Ratio of index point change (3.9/129.9)	0.030
Percent change (0.030 x 100)	3.0%

Price Effect of Updating Weights

The effect of updating the CPI weights to reflect more recent spending patterns can be analyzed by comparing the official CPI based on new weights to hypothetical figures based on continued use of old weights. For example, from 1983 to 1990 the official CPI, calculated according to 1982–84 spending patterns, increased 31.8 percent. However, the CPI increase is 31.4 percent for the same period when calculated using the old 1972–73 spending patterns (as modified in 1983 for the new method of measuring housing costs). This differential is approximate since the CPIs are calculated at summary levels for the major components of food and beverages, housing, apparel, transportation, medical care, entertainment, and all other items, rather than for the hundreds of detailed items. Previous changes in weights based on new spending patterns also had a relatively small impact on the overall CPI. Thus, the ten-year periods in which the weights remain constant do not appear to cause exceptional discontinuities in the measure of price change. Despite these relatively small effects on measured price change due to changing weights, the BLS continues to publish the CPI using the old weights for a period of six months after the new weights are introduced, which allows users of the CPI to assess the impact of the new weights during a transition period.

Reliability of the CPI

Because the monthly price data are collected from a sample of retail and other businesses selling to households, the CPI is subject to errors associated with sampling rather than surveying an entire group. On average, for every monthly percent change in the CPI, the sampling error is 0.05.[11] For example, if the CPI increases by 0.4 percent from one month to the next, in two of three cases the increase ranges from 0.35 to 0.45 percent due to sampling error.

PART B: ANALYSIS OF TRENDS

Many terms are used to characterize various rates of price change. *Inflation* is the rate at which the overall level of prices increases; *deflation* is the rate of price decline; *disinflation* is a substantial slowdown in the rate of inflation such as occurred in the first half of the 1980s; *creeping inflation* is a low increase in inflation as from 1950–65; and *accelerating inflation* is a speedup in the rate of price increase as from 1973–81. These characterizations are of price movements during the periods as a whole, although prices in particular years diverge from the general pattern. A steady price level may be referred to as *zero inflation*. Because the CPI represents the weighted average price level for all household goods and services, of which some components are increasing and others are decreasing in price, zero inflation occurs when the CPI remains unchanged—that is, when increases and decreases in prices of the components are offsetting in the aggregate.

Long-term Shifts in the Rate of Inflation

Figure 47 shows inflation rates in the CPI for 1950–90, highlighting periods during which the inflation rate changed noticeably. The CPI increased at an

Figure 47. **Inflation Patterns Based on the Consumer Price Index: 1950–90**

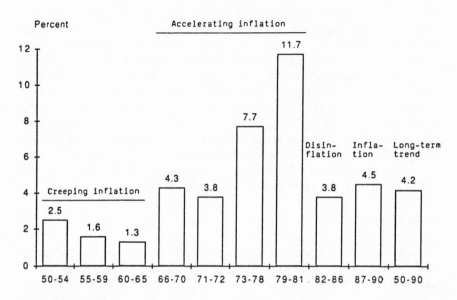

Note: Based on Bureau of Labor Statistics data. Annual percent change for multiyear periods at compound rates.

average annual rate of 4.2 percent over the entire period. Because prices as a whole almost always rise—they increased in all but one year (in 1955 prices decreased by 0.4 percent)—the rate of increase is what concerns the analyst. Even during periods of general inflation, however, certain components of the CPI show declines—gasoline and oil in several years of the 1980s, for example.

From 1950–90, the periods that are of interest for the changing rate of inflation are the low and declining creeping inflation of 1950–65; the acceleration during 1966–81 (this period included an inflation slowdown in 1971–72 while mandatory price controls were in effect); the disinflation in 1982–86; and the upturn in inflation in 1987–90. Despite the sharp drop in inflation in the first half of the 1980s, inflation during 1982–90 was twice the rate of the 1950–65 period.

The inflation acceleration in the late 1960s resulted from the Vietnam War buildup. In the 1970s, several factors converged to cause the sharp acceleration in inflation: energy prices increased substantially when the Organization of Petroleum Export Countries (OPEC) became an effective cartel in 1973; the value of the dollar declined following the shift to floating exchange rates; unit labor costs rose because of a productivity slowdown and higher wage increases; and the wage–price spiral fed an inflationary psychology of expected continued higher inflation.

These factors generally turned around in the first half of the 1980s, which together with the slowdown in economic growth weakened the inflationary pressures. The result was the disinflation of 1982–86. The subsequent upturn in inflation during 1987–90 in part reflected the productivity declines in 1989 and 1990, which in turn were accompanied by a rise in unit labor costs (see Chapter 5 for productivity and unit labor costs). Albert Hirsch notes that various analyses differ regarding the importance of each of the factors in the disinflation, although the slowdown in economic growth is generally given the largest single weight.[12]

Expectations of price changes are an important intangible to monitor since they affect the behavior of lenders, businesses, and labor in the setting of interest rates, prices, and wages. An expectation of high inflation tends to be a self-fulfilling forecast: the various groups insulate themselves by raising interest rates, prices, and wage demands in order to maintain the purchasing power of their future incomes. Similarly, an expectation of low inflation tends to lead to smaller price increases. Inflationary expectations fueled the large price increases in the 1970s; while they lessened substantially in the 1980s, uncertainties regarding oil prices, the value of the dollar, unit labor costs, or other developments could again generate inflationary behavior.

A structural tendency toward inflation is resulting from the continuing shift in the American economy from the consumption of commodities to the consumption of services. From 1950 to 1990, prices of services increased at an annual rate of 5.4 percent, compared with 3.7 percent for commodities; this pattern of higher price increases for services occurred in all four decades of the period. The higher prices for services are partially due to the higher labor content in the production of services in contrast to commodities, which use proportionately more machinery in their production; services do not benefit as much as commodities from cost-saving productivity improvements in machinery. Another part of the difference may be statistical inadequacies resulting from the difficulty of quantifying quality changes in services such as housing, transportation, medical care, education, and entertainment. If quality improvements are understated in services, the price increases would be overstated (see Part A of this chapter).

Cyclical Inflation Movements

Table 25 shows the pattern of CPI movements at the peak of expansions and trough of recessions in the post–World War II business cycles. As would be expected, prices tend to rise faster in expansions and slower in subsequent recessions. There were, however, two exceptions: in the 1949 recession overall prices declined faster at the expansion peak than at the recession trough, and in the 1957–58 recession, prices increased faster at the recession trough than at the expansion peak. In both of these cases, food prices played a partial role. Because food prices are often driven by supply shortages or surpluses caused by weather

Table 25

CPI Movements at Cyclical Turning Points
(three-month annual rates at expansion peak and recession trough)

Expansion peak		Recession trough	
Nov 48	−4.3	Oct 49	−0.6
Jul 53	1.5	May 54	−0.8
Aug 57	4.1	Apr 58	4.3
Apr 60	2.3	Feb 61	0.8
Dec 69	6.3	Nov 70	5.9
Nov 73	8.2	Mar 75	6.6
Jan 80	15.8	Jul 80	8.3
Jul 81	11.7	Nov 82	1.7

Source: John F. Early, Mary Lynn Schmidt, and Thomas J. Mosimann, "Inflation and the business cycle during the postwar period," *Monthly Labor Review*, November 1984, Table 1, p. 4.

conditions and harvests, they are not directly related to cyclical price fluctuations. Two additional factors in 1949 were the still-unsatisfied demand after World War II for automobiles and the rapidly growing market for television sets that propped up prices in 1949. While overall prices typically do not decline in recessions (slight declines occurred only in the first two of the eight postwar recessions), the slower rate of increase in recessions indicates they are responsive to declining sales volume. Prices for the broad groups of both commodities and services (not shown in the table) have the same pattern of faster increases in expansions.

The tendency in recessions for the rate of price increase to slow down rather than for prices to decline reflects the business perception that price declines would not generate enough additional sales to raise profits. This reluctance to lower prices is referred to as the "stickiness" of prices.

CPI and GNP Price Measures

In addition to the CPI, three alternative measures of changes in consumer prices are available from the GNP figures: the implicit price deflator, the fixed-weighted price index, and the chain price index for personal consumption expenditures. They differ from each other in their treatment of expenditure weights: the implicit price deflator has continually changing weights to reflect current spending patterns; the fixed-weighted index maintains the same weights in all years; and the chain price index utilizes both current and constant weights by maintaining constant spending patterns only between two consecutive quarters (annually for two consecutive years), and then updating the weights to the cur-

Table 26

Alternative Measures of Price Change: 1984–90 (annual percent change)

	Consumer price index	Fixed-weighted price index*	Chain price index*	Implicit price deflator*
1984	4.3	4.0	3.9	3.8
1985	3.6	3.5	3.5	3.2
1986	1.9	2.7	2.7	2.4
1987	3.6	4.6	4.6	4.6
1988	4.1	4.1	4.0	3.8
1989	4.8	4.8	4.7	4.6
1990	5.4	5.2	4.9	5.0
Average	4.0	4.1	4.0	3.9

*Based on the gross national product price measures for personal consumption expenditures.

rent spending patterns (see Chapter 3, Part A, under Real GNP and Inflation).

The implicit price deflator reflects households' spending substitutions among different goods and services due to price changes or consumer preferences, and thus reflects these changes immediately. In contrast, the fixed-weighted price index does not reflect these product shifts, while the chain price index does reflect them, but with a time lag.

Since the CPI retains fixed weights for about ten years, conceptually it is closest to the fixed-weighted price index. There are differences, however. The CPI has used 1982–84 weights since 1987; in the previous years 1972–73 weights were used as noted in Part A. By contrast, the fixed-weighted price index in this analysis uses 1982 weights for all years (1987 weights are used for all years after the GNP benchmark revision in December 1991). The CPI and GNP price measures also differ in the coverage and measurement of several items. For example, life insurance is excluded from the CPI and included in the GNP price measures.

Table 26 compares the CPI with the GNP consumer price measures for 1984 to 1990. A change in the CPI method of pricing owner-occupied housing in 1983 made the CPI and GNP price measures of price change conceptually much more comparable beginning in 1984. The CPI and the fixed-weighted price index moved in similar directions in five of the seven years during 1984–90; the exceptions were 1984 and 1988, when the CPI inflation rate increased while the fixed-weighted price index rate decreased. In 1986 and 1987, the CPI increased by one percentage point less than the fixed-weighted price index. Thus, the movements of the two indexes have noticeable year-to-year differences. Over several years these differences tend to be offsetting; for example, the average annual price increase over the seven years was only marginally different, 4.0 percent for the CPI and 4.1 percent for the fixed-weighted price index. Among the three GNP price measures, the implicit price deflator tends to show the least amount of inflation and the fixed-weighted price index shows the most; the chain price index's inflation rate lies between them. The average annual price increase over the seven-year period for the various price measures differed by only 0.2 percentage point: the fixed-weighted index rising by 4.1 percent and the implicit price deflator rising by 3.9 percent. (Before the GNP base period year [in this analysis 1982], the pattern of annual increases among the three GNP price measures is reversed: the implicit price deflator shows the largest annual increases and the fixed-weighted price index shows the smallest ones. I have not found an explanation for this phenomenon.)

No single concept of constructing index numbers is necessarily best for capturing actual economic trends (see Chapter 1). For example, if the analyst wants to assess the effect of price movements on purchases of the same basket of goods and services over time, the CPI and the fixed-weighted price index are the most appropriate; if the interest is in price trends of items actually bought, the implicit price deflator and the chain price index are the most appropriate; and if the focus is on the "true" rate of inflation, the range between the lowest and highest rates of the various measures may be considered as bracketing the actual amount. In general, the advantage of alternative measures is that they emphasize the inherent ambiguity in measuring price movements by providing a range rather than a single figure of price movements.

Because the types and quality of goods and services change considerably over long periods of time, measures of average price change become less meaningful the further back in time one goes. This applies to all price indexes regardless of their weighting structure. However, to reduce the effect of these discontinuities, it is preferable to use the CPI or the implicit price deflator rather than the fixed-weighted price index over long time periods. This reflects the fact that new expenditure patterns are incorporated in the CPI every ten years and in the price deflator continuously, while the fixed-weighted price index maintains the same expenditure patterns for all years. Over the 1959–90 period (the fixed-weighted price index was first published for 1959), prices rose at an average annual rate of 5.0 percent in the CPI, 4.8 percent in the implicit price deflator, and 4.5 percent in the fixed-weighted price index. These differences are relatively small over the thirty-one-year period, although the CPI and the implicit price deflator show a greater rate of inflation than the fixed-weighted price index.

Relation of Inflation to Unemployment

Inflation and unemployment are the most obvious indicators of the economy's performance. Clearly, the economic well-being of individuals is enhanced by low inflation and low unemployment. However, much of the debate on economic policies focuses on the compatibility of the two for the economy as a whole. To the extent that low inflation and low unemployment are incompatible, debate centers on whether emphasis should be placed on reducing unemployment or reducing inflation. Much of the public policy discussion is influenced by the Phillips curve, which depicts a direct trade-off between unemployment (see Chapter 5) and inflation. As discussed below, the trade-off is apparent primarily in period when both unemployment and inflation are relatively low. This limits the application of the Phillips curve considerably. It is discussed here in some detail because of its perceived importance in the economic debate.

While the trade-off between unemployment and inflation concerns policy analysts and government officials, the population is concerned with the effects of both factors in daily life. Everyone experiences inflation continuously in the cost of household items. Fewer persons are directly affected by unemployment, but for those out of work the impact can be severe. Since the 1960s, the combined effect of unemployment and inflation, termed the misery index, has reflected the pocketbook issue in voter behavior. Its impact on presidential elections over the postwar period is discussed below.

Phillips Curve

The most direct measure of the relationship between inflation and unemployment is the Phillips curve. It is named for A. W. Phillips, who in the late 1950s assessed the relationship between wage rates and unemployment in England over a 100-year period.[13] In recent analyses, the wage-rate component is replaced by prices; it is this adaptation, termed the augmented Phillips curve, that is used here.[14]

The Phillips curve depicts graphically the idea of an inverse relationship between unemployment and inflation: as unemployment decreases, inflation increases, and vice versa (i.e., the Phillips curve is a downward-sloping line to the right). The underlying principle is that declining unemployment leads to higher production costs as more outmoded and inefficient machinery is used and less-productive workers are employed; in addition, when unemployment is low or declining, unions tend to get higher wage increases because they are in a stronger bargaining position. Conversely, when unemployment is high or rising, production and wage increases are lower. In addition, changes in the position of the Phillips curve indicate if the unemployment–inflation trade-off has improved or worsened between two periods. The trade-off improves when unemployment in both the past and current periods is unchanged and inflation lessens in the current period. The trade-off worsens when unemployment is unchanged in both periods and inflation increases in the current period. Graphically, when the trade-off improves, the Phillips curve shifts to the left; and when the trade-off worsens, it shifts to the right.

Figures 48a, b, c, and d show annual Phillips curve trends for approximately

Figure 48a. **Phillips Curve: 1948–59**

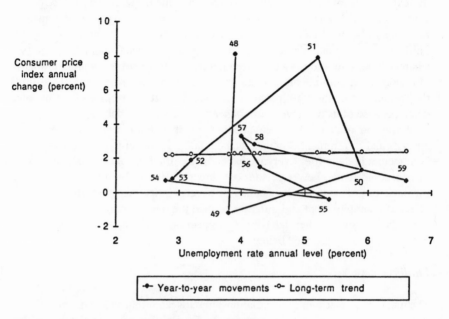

Note: Unemployment rate of previous year corresponds to
CPI change of current year (e.g. UR 1958 and CPI 1959).

four decades from 1948 to 1990. The unemployment rate is shown one year
before the change in the CPI, on the premise that changes in the unemployment
level do not immediately affect prices—for example, unemployment in 1989
affects prices in 1990.[15]

The figures loosely conform to the concept of a trade-off between unemployment and inflation when the plotted line connecting one year to the next slopes
downward to the right. The average relationship for all years is represented by
the straight line with white diamonds. The theoretical inverse relationship was
most evident in the 1960s when both unemployment and inflation were relatively
low. Experience was contrary to the theory in the 1950s, when there was a slight
direct relationship (upward-sloping line). The relationship was tenuous in the
1970s (slightly downward-sloping line). More strikingly, as the 1970s pro-
gressed, the unemployment–inflation trade-off worsened, as the Phillips curve
continually moved to the right from the early 1970s to the late 1970s. For
example, in 1973 unemployment was 5.5 percent and inflation was 6.2 percent,
while in 1979 not only was unemployment higher at 6 percent, but inflation had
increased to 11.3 percent (80 percent higher than the 1973 rate). In the 1980s and
1990, the average experience was consistent with the theory, but the average

Figure 48b. **Phillips Curve: 1960–69**

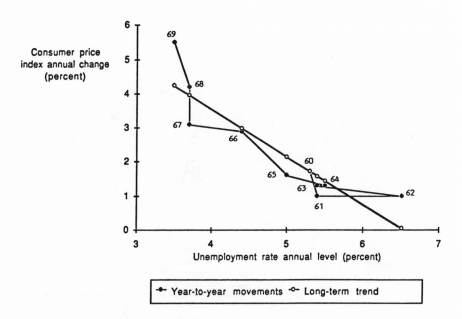

Note: Unemployment rate of previous year corresponds to
CPI change of current year (e.g. UR 1968 and CPI 1969).

masks major differences between the early and later years. Thus, a downward-sloping line was evident during 1980–83, but from 1984–90 a horizontal line was more apparent. The experience of the 1987–90 period also indicates that the trade-off had improved considerably since the early 1980s. In general (other than the 1960s), there were wide variations in the year-to-year movements, making them highly unpredictable, as evidenced by the wide dispersion of the individual years from the average long-term relationship (straight white diamond line).

This divergence between the theory and experience indicates that, for the most part, the economy is too complex for simple Phillips curve relationships. The relationship breaks down in two very different economic environments. In the 1970s both inflation and unemployment were relatively high, and in some years both were rising; in part this reflected the substantial increase in inflationary expectations, which became self-fulfilling when they led to rapid price and wage increases as business and labor tried to make up for declines in real income and to insulate their incomes against further price increases. In the expansion from 1982 to 1990, which followed periods of high unemployment during the recessions of 1980 and 1981–82, both inflation and unemployment declined from the previous high levels, although inflation turned up again during 1987–

Figure 48c. **Phillips Curve: 1970–79**

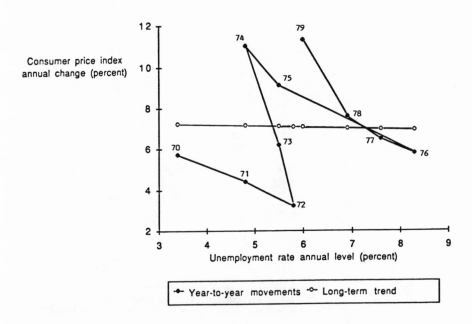

Note: Unemployment rate of previous year corresponds to CPI
change of current year (e.g. UR 1978 and CPI 1979).

90. Fuller utilization of resources during this period raised productivity by lowering fixed overhead costs, which was also an incentive to business to hold down the rate of price increases even though the economy was expanding. (As noted previously, inflation also slowed in this period because oil prices fell following the weakening of the OPEC cartel, the value of the dollar increased in the first half of the 1980s, and inflationary expectations slowed.)

Another problem of Phillips curve analysis is that the threshold level of unemployment below which inflation tends to accelerate and above which inflation tends to slow down is hard to pinpoint. This threshold is referred to as the nonaccelerating inflation rate of unemployment. As noted in Chapter 5, it is perceived by some to have risen from about 4 percent in the 1960s to as high as 7 percent in the 1970s. The higher rate is ascribed mainly to the influx of teenagers (who have high unemployment rates) into the labor force and to a small extent to the increase in working women (whose unemployment rates before the 1980s had been slightly higher than those for men). In the early 1990s the threshold is considered to have declined to the 5 percent range because of the fall-off in the teenage population and the similarity of unemployment rates for men and women workers. Other long-term factors affecting the nonaccelerating inflation

Figure 48d. **Phillips Curve: 1980–90**

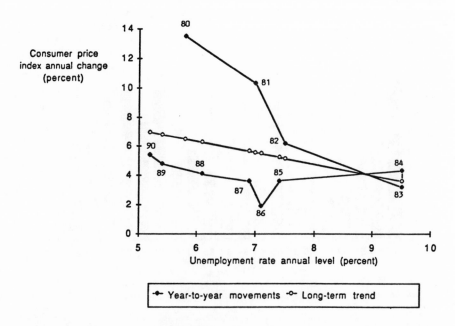

Note: Unemployment rate of previous year corresponds to CPI change of current year (e.g. UR 1989 and CPI 1990).

rate of unemployment are productivity increases, tariffs and other import restrictions, farm subsidy price supports, minimum wages, monopolistic pricing, deregulation or industry pricing, and social compacts between business and labor to hold down price and wage increases. The threshold unemployment rate falls when these factors change in the direction of causing lower prices, and it rises when changes in these factors tend to increase prices. These changes in the threshold unemployment rate are referred to as improving or worsening the Phillips curve trade-off noted above.

The Phillips curve trade-off between inflation and unemployment is most apparent when inflation and unemployment are in relatively low ranges. During other periods, experience reveals considerable divergence from the theory. For example, high inflation and low unemployment may not be compatible over sustained periods as spending by households and businesses is moderated or lowered because the higher prices reduce the purchasing power of their incomes, leading to lower economic growth and higher unemployment. By contrast, Robert Kuttner notes that low unemployment and low inflation may be compatible if business and labor pursue a concerted anti-inflation policy by deliberately holding down the rate of wage and price increases and thus maintain the purchasing

Figure 49. **Misery Index in Presidential Election and Immediately Preceding Years**

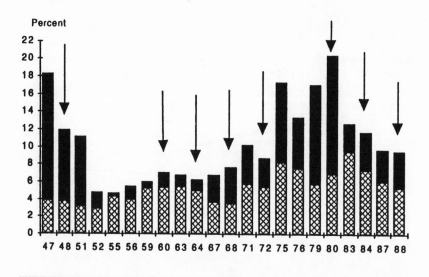

Note: Arrow indicates that the winning presidential candidate had advantage of the misery index movement.

power of incomes, leading to faster economic growth and lower unemployment.[16] *The analyst should consider Phillips curve projections of inflation rates at various unemployment levels most relevant during periods when both unemployment and inflation are relatively low.*

Misery Index

In recent national elections, the CPI has become part of the debate between candidates because of its inclusion in a figure called the misery index. The misery index is the sum of the CPI inflation rate and the unemployment rate, and it has been used in election campaigns since 1976 as a summary measure of the pocketbook issue. Because high rates of inflation and unemployment are undesirable, economic well-being and the misery index are inversely related. Thus, the nation is better off when the misery index is low than when it is high, and the incumbent party will gain from a low index and be at a disadvantage from a high one.

The misery index is only a rough guide to how voters perceive their economic well-being. Its limitations are that it gives equal weight to unemployment and inflation, which may be an accurate reflection of the public's perceptions only when the two components are at certain levels; it excludes employment, which may be rising while unemployment also is rising, as discussed in Chapter 5; and it does not distinguish whether the index level is particularly high or low except in relation to past periods. However, because of its use in recent campaigns, it is interesting to review the experience of the index with the outcome of presidential elections.

Figure 49 shows the misery index in the eleven postwar presidential election years from 1948 to 1988 and in each of the years preceding the election year. The adjacent years are included as an indication of the recent economic record of the incumbent party, which may be best remembered by the voters. In eight of eleven elections, the party won when the recent movement in the misery index favored it—for example, the incumbent party benefited if the index declined between the pre-election year and the election year. This pattern did not occur in the first three postwar elections, when in two cases (1952 and 1956) the misery index did not favor the winner; however, in seven of eight elections from 1960 to 1988 (1976 was the exception), the party that won was favored by the recent movement of the misery index.

Since 1960, then, the change in the misery index in the election year has generally corresponded to the outcome of the presidential election. However, it should be remembered that the change in the misery index is a highly simplified view of pocketbook issues. It also does not reflect the level of the index, other important domestic and international election issues, or the personalities of the candidates. Elections are won on a combination of factors, of which the pocketbook issue is important but not necessarily decisive. *Thus, while the misery index may suggest which candidate has an advantage because of the economic environment, it does not necessarily presage the outcome of the election.*

SUMMARY

The CPI has moved consistently upward over the postwar period but at varying rates. Even in recessions, the CPI tends to show a slower rate of increase rather than an absolute decline. Thus, although prices for particular items sometimes decline, assessments of overall price movements focus on changes in the rate of increase.

The relationship between inflation and unemployment is most directly expressed in Phillips curve analysis. Experience with the Phillips curve indicates that the assumed inverse relationship, in which a change in the unemployment rate leads to a change in the inflation rate in the opposite direction, holds up best during periods of low unemployment and low inflation; by contrast, the relationship has been quite limited during periods of high unemployment, high inflation, or both.

The combined effect of inflation and unemployment, referred to as the misery index, has been used as an indication of the pocketbook issue in presidential elections since 1976. The index is a broad measure of how the economic environment affects voters' perceptions of their economic well-being. Movements in the misery index in the year preceding the election and in the election year tend to be consistent with the result of the election. However, they are more useful as a guide to which candidate has the advantage because of economic conditions, and not as a prediction of the winner.

REVIEW QUESTIONS

• How do price movements differ during periods of inflation, disinflation, and deflation?

• What does the change in the CPI weights about every ten years mean for the measure of price change between each ten-year period?

• Why would the CPI be expected to increase more (or decrease less) than the personal consumption expenditure implicit price deflator in the GNP?

• How does the CPI differ from a cost-of-living index?

• The CPI and the poverty income line are both based on a standard of living concept.

_____true _____false

• The CPI measures prices of items having comparable functional characteristics over time, including the effects of quality and quantity changes. What is the effect of the following market price changes on the CPI?

Market Price	CPI Price		
	No change	Increase	Decrease
A loaf of bread is made smaller and the price is unchanged.	—	—	—
Air bags are made standard equipment on a new car and the price of the car is increased by the cost of the airbags.	—	—	—
An apartment building is renovated by dividing each four-room apartment renting for $800 a month into two two-room apartments each renting for $600 a month. The renovation cost is $100 a month for each two-room apartment.	—	—	—

• What does an improved trade-off in the Phillips curve mean?

• The Phillips curve trade-off between inflation and unemployment breaks down in two economic environments: (1) when both inflation and unemployment are high, and (2) when both inflation and unemployment are declining. What causes the breakdown during these periods?

• Although the misery index gives equal weight to inflation and unemployment, inflation directly affects many more people than unemployment. What is a rationale for giving equal weight to each?

NOTES

1. Bureau of Labor Statistics, U.S. Department of Labor, *BLS Handbook of Methods*, April 1988, p. 157.
2. The noninstitutional population excludes persons in prisons, long-term care hospitals, and old-age and other protected homes, a group that makes up 1 percent of the population.
3. Bureau of Labor Statistics, *BLS Handbook of Methods*, p. 154.
4. Patrick C. Jackman, "The CPI as a Cost of Living Index," paper presented at the 65th annual conference of the Western Economic Association, San Diego, California, June 29–July 3, 1990.
5. Daniel Yergin, *The Prize: The Epic Quest for Oil, Money, and Power* (Simon & Schuster: 1991), pp. 522–25, 636–38, 718–21, 746–51, and 758–64.
6. Patricia Ruggles, *Drawing the Line: Alternative Poverty Measures and Their Implications for Public Policy* (The Urban Institute Press: 1990), pp. 170–72.
7. Eugene Smolensky, "The Past and Present Poor," in *The Concept of Poverty* (Chamber of Commerce of the United States: 1965), pp. 45, 54–55.
8. For the detailed methodology of constructing the CPI, see Bureau of Labor Statistics, *BLS Handbook of Methods*, Chapter 19.
9. Because the Consumer Expenditures Survey data refer to 1982–84 but were introduced in the CPI in 1987, they were modified to be more representative of 1987. This was done by allowing for the effect of price changes between 1982–84 and December 1986 on the dollar expenditures on each item. This adjustment assumed that the relative price changes did not affect the quantities of each item bought—in other words, that no substitution occurred because of price changes.
10. Seasonally adjusted total CPI levels are not published because cost-escalation contracts are typically calculated using unadjusted levels, and the publication of two levels could confuse the parties to the contracts regarding the appropriate index to use. However, unpublished seasonally adjusted total CPI levels are provided on request, and seasonally adjusted levels for the major components are published.
11. Thomas J. Mosimann, "Measures of Error for Changes in the Consumer Price Index January 1978–December 1986," *CPI Detailed Report,* Bureau of Labor Statistics, U.S. Department of Labor, February 1991.
12. Albert A. Hirsch, "An Analysis of Disinflation: 1980–83," *Business Economics*, January 1985.
13. A. W. Phillips, "The Relation between Unemployment and the Rate of Change of Money Wage Rates in the United Kingdom, 1861–1957," *Economica*, November 1958.
14. For a good discussion of the conceptual aspects of the Phillips curve, see Sherman J. Maisel, *Macroeconomics: Theories and Policies* (W. W. Norton & Company: 1982), pp. 443–60.
15. Detailed studies using monthly or quarterly data have shorter lags of about six months between unemployment and prices. Lagging the effect of unemployment on inflation one year improves the observed relationship in terms in the Phillips curve theory in the 1970s and 1980s, has no appreciable effect in the 1960s, and worsens the relationship in the 1950s.
16. Robert Kuttner, *The Economic Illusion: False Choices between Prosperity and Social Justice* (Houghton Mifflin: 1984), p. 22 and Chapter 4.

7
MONEY SUPPLY AND INTEREST RATES

Money is a lubricant for the economy. It allows a greater specialization of production and division of labor and thus higher productivity and better living conditions than is possible in a barter economy. Money also has a life of its own in financial markets, which affects the economy. These financial aspects of money are the subject of this chapter.

The money supply measures certain financial assets held by households, businesses, nonprofit organizations, and state and local governments that are available for consumer, business, and government spending. It is used, along with other economic indicators, by the Federal Reserve (FR) to determine monetary policies. Monetary policy refers to Federal Reserve actions that affect bank reserves, the money supply, and interest rates. The FR influences the money supply by affecting the levels of bank reserves available for loans, and thus affecting interest rates on loans to households and business. Monetary policies aim at moderating extreme cyclical fluctuations of high inflation during expansions and high unemployment during recessions, with the goal of achieving steadier economic growth, high employment, and low inflation over the long run.

The money supply is an intermediate economic indicator, in contrast to ultimate indicators such as the real gross national product, unemployment, or the consumer price index. The money supply is of policy interest because it influences interest rates. Interest rates are the price of money, and thus the level of interest rates more closely affects the quantity of loans and the ultimate indicators.

In preparing the money supply measures, the FR provides three alternative definitions—M–1, M–2, and M–3—which range in coverage of financial assets from M–1 as the most limited to M–3 as the broadest. For example, M–1 includes only currency, demand (checking) deposits, interest-bearing negotiable order of withdrawal (NOW) accounts (which are also used by households for writing checks), and nonbank traveler's checks, while M–3 includes all of these plus savings and time deposits, money market deposits and money market mutual funds, Eurodollars, and more. The money supply excludes such financial assets as corporate stocks, commercial and government bonds, and life insurance. The FR publishes all of the money supply measures weekly.

The various assets included in the three measures also differ in terms of liquidity (the ease with which they can be used immediately as money without the risk of losing value) and in the amount of control the FR has over their rate of expansion (through regulation of reserve requirements for commercial banks and other depository institutions). M–1 is the most liquid and theoretically subject to the most FR influence; M–2, and M–3 are increasingly less liquid and subject to less FR influence.

The money supply differs from other economic indicators in this book in a basic way: it is the only indicator on which a governmental authority acts solely and directly to affect its performance. The federal budget deficit is acted on directly, but as noted below, the federal budget is not solely associated with managing the economy. The other indicators reflect economic activity but are not active instruments in economic policy. Even when incomes policies of voluntary price and wage guidelines or mandatory controls are in effect, the consumer price index and wage rate indicators, while they record the impact of those policies, are not used as instruments to achieve the price and wage goals.

Monetary policy and fiscal policy are the federal government's main tools for influencing the overall economy. As noted in Chapter 2 under Economic Policies, monetary policy is more focused than fiscal policy because it is geared solely to influencing the economy, while fiscal policy is derived secondarily as the outcome of spending programs and tax laws to meet the nation's civilian and defense needs in the most efficient and equitable manner. Monetary policy is also more flexible because it can be modified quickly and often; fiscal policy responds more slowly to changing economic conditions because of the lengthy legislative process involved in changing spending programs and tax laws. (Fiscal policy is discussed in Chapter 3 under Government Spending and Finances.)

MONEY SUPPLY, INTEREST RATES, AND ECONOMIC ACTIVITY

The money supply in part reflects the decisions of households, businesses, non-profit organizations, and state and local governments to hold their assets in certain financial forms—currency, checking accounts, savings accounts, money market mutual funds, money market deposit accounts, large time deposits, Euro-dollars, etc. The money supply is also influenced by FR monetary policies.

In economic theory, the amount of money is related to spending and the resultant economic growth, employment, and inflation. A larger money supply means more spending, and a smaller money supply means less spending. The FR affects the supply of money by expanding or restraining the amount of commercial bank reserves available for loans, and in turn the amount of bank reserves affects interest rates (the techniques for managing the money supply are discussed in the next section).

There is an assumed short-run inverse relationship between bank reserves and interest rates—more bank reserves lead to lower interest rates, and fewer bank reserves result in higher interest rates. As more reserves become available, banks, finance companies, and other lending institutions increasingly compete to extend credit, tending to lead to lower interest rates. In turn, lower interest rates induce households to borrow money for consumer items and housing mortgages and prompt businesses to borrow money for inventories and plant and equipment investment. Because these loans become checking accounts for borrowers, the money supply increases. The opposite occurs when fewer reserves are available, which tends to raise interest rates and lower borrowing, and consequently lowers the money supply.

Schematically, these relationships appear as:

Reserves → Interest rates → Spending →Money Supply
→ Growth, employment, inflation.

There tends to be a direct relationship between money supply growth rates on the one hand and economic growth, employment, and inflation on the other, although as discussed below under Part B, the relationship is statistically weak. There are also time lags from when changes in the money supply occur to when they affect economic activity. The time lags are difficult to quantify with precision; estimates range from less than one year to about two years because other factors affecting the economy (unemployment levels and economic growth, the federal deficit, the value of the dollar, oil prices, inflationary expectations, etc.) vary over time.

These nonmonetary conditions also sometimes override the effects of money supply movements assumed in the theoretical schematic. During periods of high inflation or expected increases in inflation, rapid growth in the money supply may be perceived by lenders as overstimulating the economy and causing further price increases; therefore, interest rates may continue to increase (contrary to the expected theoretical decrease), as lenders act to keep the purchasing power of their incomes from deteriorating due to inflation when the loan is repaid. When lenders and borrowers raise interest rates above what they would be in periods of less inflation, the increment in the rate is referred to as an "inflation premium." This occurred from the late 1970s through 1990. A similar pattern of nonmonetary factors weighing heavily may occur during recessions and periods of high unemployment when, despite lower interest rates, households and businesses do not increase their borrowing and spending because of declining incomes.

The limited power of FR policies in the face of these nonmonetary factors is suggested by the use of the colloquial expressions "pulling the string" and "pushing the string" to describe FR policies. Generally, the FR is considered to be more effective at slowing economic activity by raising interest rates (pulling the string) than at quickening economic activity by lowering interest rates (pushing the string).

FR MONEY SUPPLY TARGETS
AND THEIR IMPLEMENTATION

As discussed previously, the Full Employment and Balanced Growth Act of 1978 (the Humphrey–Hawkins Act) established goals for reducing unemployment and inflation (see Chapter 5 under Unemployment). The act also requires the FR to report to Congress twice a year, in February and July, on its objectives and plans for growth rates of the money supply during the calendar year.[1] In these reports to Congress, the FR provides target ranges for the growth of M–1, M–2, and M–3. However, the FR does not always provide targets for all of the money supply measures. For example, during 1987-91 no target was given for M–1 in reports to Congress because of its higher sensitivity to interest rates and problems in understanding its behavior relative to income and interest rates (see Part B below under Money Supply Targets and Velocity).

These target ranges are set to provide the amount of money estimated to be necessary to accommodate what the FR considers to be a desirable and realistic path for economic growth, employment, and inflation. However, as Paul Volcker notes, they do not represent preconceptions of how fast the economy should grow over particular periods.[2] Such goals are appropriately set by elected officials, such as the president or Congress, as in the Humphrey–Hawkins Act. By contrast, the Federal Reserve is a central bank, and the FR Board is composed of appointed officials (see Note on FR Organization and Independence below). While the FR could work with the president and Congress in reaching a consensus on these goals, Spence Hilton and Vivek Moorthy note that this could compromise the independence of the FR.[3]

Through its effect on bank reserves, the FR seeks to influence a panoply of economic functions, starting with short-term credit costs, in a continental, post-industrial economy that is enormous, complex, increasingly open to international influences, and highly variable by region. But monetary policy, although capable of being finely tuned from day to day, is a crude device for achieving all the good things the American public wants and tends to expect the government to bring about: jobs, high wages, profits, price stability, predictability. Over the years, FR polices have centered on combating inflation. For example, in 1990 the FR adopted the long-run goal of "price stability," which is zero inflation in the overall price level (see Chapter 5 for a discussion of zero inflation under Unemployment and Inflation Goals).[4] The FR view is that with price stability undergirding the economy, the natural generative forces of American life bring about jobs, high wages, profits, and so forth.

The target ranges typically allow the FR considerable discretion in modifying growth rates in the money supply as economic trends and the demand for money evolve through the year. For example, in the February 1991 report, the ranges for 1991 are 2½ to 6½ percent for M–2 and 1 to 5 percent for M–3. The Humphrey–Hawkins Act treats these targets as guides rather than requiring that they be met, so long as reasons for not achieving them are reported to Congress.

The FR uses three tools to influence the money supply: open market operations, the discount rate, and reserve requirements.[5] All three tools can be used to affect commercial bank reserves, the volume of bank loans, the money supply, and interest rates. *Open market operations* are the purchase and sale of federal government debt securities by the FR. Since commercial banks invest in federal securities as a source of income and nonbank investors in federal securities maintain bank checking accounts, bank reserves are increased when the FR buys and decreased when it sells. These operations can be carried out daily, if needed, and are the FR's primary means of controlling bank reserves on a current basis. Open market operations are reflected in the movement of federal funds interest rates, which in turn indicate whether the thrust of current monetary policies is aimed at stimulating or restraining economic activity (federal funds are discussed below under Interest Rate Differentials).

The *discount rate* is the interest rate that the FR Banks charge commercial banks for loans. Banks typically obtain such loans (a) when smaller agricultural banks need longer-term liquidity during crop-growing seasons to meet seasonal demands for loans, or (b) to meet short-term liquidity needs when other sources of funds are unavailable. Banks may also need longer-term loans (referred to as extended credit) when they have more serious liquidity or management difficulties that can be resolved only over protracted periods. When necessary, the FR changes the discount rate to bring it in line with other short-term interest rates, or to signal a change in FR policy on the growth rate of the money supply. The discount rate is changed more frequently when market interest rates are rising or falling, and less frequently when market rates are relatively stable. The FR restricts borrowing from the "discount window" for the emergency-type purposes noted above in order to prevent banks from using it as a general source of low-interest funds—for example, the discount rate is lower than the federal funds rate—which the banks would then lend at higher rates (the federal funds rate is discussed below under Interest Rate Differentials). The symbolic importance of the discount rate exceeds its importance as a price of money actually borrowed.

Reserve requirements are the legally required reserves that banks must maintain with the FR Banks (these twelve regional banks are discussed below) in proportion to their demand deposits and NOW accounts. Since the Depository Institutions Deregulation and Monetary Control Act of 1980, banks that are members of the FR system, as well as nonmember banks, are subject to the reserve requirements. The direct purpose of reserve requirements is to ensure that banks maintain sufficient liquidity to conduct daily operations such as clearing checks and meeting the ongoing needs of customers. These reserves also make it possible to implement monetary policies in conjunction with open market operations. If there were no reserve requirements, the FR would have no fulcrum for inducing banks to expand or contract loans. Thus, open market operations would be less effective because there would be no regulatory limit on the volume of money and loans that the banking system could create. The FR Board (the Board of Governors is discussed below) may change reserve requirements within certain legally prescribed limits, but because such changes can drastically affect banks' liquidity, the requirements are changed infrequently and then typically open market operations are undertaken to ensure no net change in bank reserves. Reserve requirements have been used to counteract developments in particular financial markets—such as varying international interest rates that cause money to flow between the United States and other nations in a way that hinders the implementation of domestic monetary policies—or as a signal that the FR is changing its policies toward expansion or restraint.

Under the Monetary Control Act of 1980, the FR has had less flexibility to change reserve requirements.[6] In fact, the first change in reserve requirements since 1980 occurred in December 1990 when reserve requirements were eliminated for nonpersonal time deposits and net Eurocurrency liabilities.[7] This was done to encourage banks to relax their standards of creditworthiness of potential borrowers and the terms and conditions of loans as a means of stimulating an increased volume of loans to stem the recession that began in July 1990. Lower reserve requirements lead to lower bank costs since banks do not earn interest on reserves and thus raise the profitability of loans to banks, which encourages banks to increase their loans. While the FR acknowledged that the tightened standards had been desirable for improving the financial soundness of banks in light of the concern about bank failures, the FR felt the standards had become too stringent and were counterproductive.

However, reserve requirements are not used to maintain the financial solvency of banks. This is done by the banking regulatory agencies—the FR for state-chartered FR member banks, Comptroller of the Currency (Department of the Treasury) for nationally-chartered banks, and Federal Deposit Insurance Corporation for state-chartered nonmember banks that have FDIC insurance—in their supervision of bank operations. The supervision includes ensuring that banks meet capital requirements, which specify the levels of bank owners' equity investment as a percentage of total bank assets. It also should be noted that proposals have been made to reorganize the banking regulatory system which, if enacted in legislation, would change the supervisory responsibilities of the existing three agencies and/or create a new agency.

Reserve requirements also put an upper limit on the ultimate increase in the money supply resulting from bank loans. When a bank gives a customer a loan, it increases the customer's checking deposits by the amount of the loan. Because checking deposits are part of the money supply, the loan increases the money supply. The expansion of the money supply from when the customer first uses the loan to buy a car, pay school tuition, or purchase other goods and services multiplies several times as the car dealer and school deposit their receipts in their respective banks, and those banks in turn extend loans with the new deposits, and so on.[8] Since the re-lending and re-spending occur in successive time periods, it may be several years before the cumulative ultimate expansion of the money supply from a single loan is reached.

Over the long run, independent of changes in the demand for money during cyclical expansions and recessions, an increase in the money supply is needed to accommodate the increasing population. This continuing increment is put into the economy by the FR's purchase of Treasury securities in open market operations.

MONETARY POLICIES

Economists differ over the appropriateness of monetary policies adopted by the FR. The differences center on two points: (a) whether monetary policies should emphasize the level of interest rates or growth in the money supply, and (b) whether money supply targets should continue to be developed as a range, giving the FR discretion in adjusting to changing economic conditions, or if a single figure should be adhered to as the target. Those who emphasize the use of the money supply rather than interest rates and who opt for a single figure for the money supply targets are referred to as monetarists; Milton Friedman and the Federal Reserve Bank of St. Louis are among those who are identified with the monetarist approach.[9] By contrast, the FR approach is eclectic in that it modifies the emphasis placed on money supply or interest rate targets based on its assessment of current and future economic conditions.

Monetarists believe economic history shows that, in the long run, the money supply is the ultimate determinant of economic activity as measured in current dollars. While some monetarists may reassess this view in light of the weak relationship of changes in the money supply and current dollar GNP in the 1980s, their basic argument has been as follows: because little is known about forecasting economic activity, frequent changes in monetary policies cause undue uncertainty in the business community and volatile interest rates and economic activity, while a steady and predictable growth in the money supply would be conducive to a more certain economic environment encouraging more business investment and a higher rate of long-run economic growth. Monetarists recommend a steady annual growth in the money supply (typically M–1) that would reflect what they consider to be the potential growth in the real gross national product based on long-run employment and productivity trends. The money supply growth rate tends to be about 4 percent, but the precise number is less important than that it be steady. This approach emphasizes holding down inflation—for example, a 4 percent annual increase in the money supply would be consistent with a zero rate of inflation, in which the overall price level is steady. Supporters of a discretionary monetary policy, on the other hand, believe that emphasizing the money supply over all other factors would cause excessively high unemployment by not allowing for some price inflation. To them, monetarism is based on a simplistic view of the economy and would hamstring the FR in its job of promoting economic growth and moderating inflation in the short run. They take an eclectic view by assessing trends in a variety of economic indicators and then modifying monetary policies in light of changing economic conditions. This discretionary (or eclectic) approach dominates FR actions.

There are fundamental differences between eclectics and monetarists. However, as Alan Greenspan notes, they generally agree on the differential short-run and long-run impacts of monetary policy: in the short run, monetary policy has more impact on economic growth and employment and less on inflation, while in the long-run monetary policy has more impact on inflation.[10] Also the debate has continued about the effects of a monetarist policy stance vs. a discretionary (i.e., eclectic) monetary policy stance on short-run trade-off between economic growth and inflation. Steven Englander reviews this literature on the effectiveness of monetary policies in the United States and other member nations of the Organization of Economic Cooperation and Development. He assesses the claims by proponents of monetarist and rational expectation theories that verifiable rules for money supply growth have greater credibility with the public of the government's intention to lower inflation, and are not only more effective in reducing inflation than the discretionary monetary policies advocated by eclectics but also are relatively costless in terms of higher unemployment.[11] He finds that these claims cannot be substantiated empirically. (Rational expectations theory, which states that the market adjusts to and therefore frustrates government intervention in the economy, results in the same prescription for monetary policies as monetarism.)

Opinions also differ within the eclectic approach on the desirable degree of expansion or restraint and on whether the focus should be on raising rates of economic growth (as measured by the real gross national product) or lowering inflation. This divergence of opinion is apparent in the public record of the meetings of the Federal Open Market Committee. The committee—which is composed of the seven Federal Reserve governors, the president of the Federal Reserve Bank of New York, and a rotating panel of the presidents of four of the eleven other regional Federal Reserve Banks—often has near-unanimous rather than unanimous opinions on open market operations. *In assessing the future course of FR monetary targets, the analyst should consider the underlying assumptions of those policies and their consistency with trends in economic growth, employment, and inflation.*

NOTE ON FR ORGANIZATION
AND INDEPENDENCE

The Federal Reserve System is headed by a seven-member Board of Governors in Washington, D.C., which establishes overall monetary policies, and twelve regional Federal Reserve Banks located around the country. The seven governors are appointed by the president, subject to confirmation of the Senate, and are permanent members of the Federal Open Market Committee (FOMC). Each FR Bank has a board of nine directors—six are elected by the commercial banks in the district (three represent the member banks and three represent the public) and three public members are appointed by the FR Board; the FR Board designates the chairman and deputy chairman from the three public members it appoints. The FR Bank's board of directors appoints the Bank's president subject to FR Board approval. The presidents of the FR Banks are members of the FOMC (on a rotating basis as noted above).

As members of the FOMC, the presidents of the FR Banks bring to the FOMC deliberations a special knowledge of the patterns of economic growth in different sections of the country as well as of the economic concerns of each geographic region. Because these regional concerns vary (for example, local areas have different levels of unemployment), they could lead the presidents of the FR Banks to vote on the FOMC from a regional rather than from a national vantage point. In addition, because the presidents are representatives of commercial banks, they may concentrate on fighting inflation and thus vote for higher interest rates more often than persons who do not represent commercial banks. In analyses of the voting records of all FOMC members, Geoffrey Tootell concludes there is no significant difference between the voting records of the FR Bank presidents and the FR Board governors.[12] However, others believe the voting records show that the FR Bank presidents favor higher interest rates more frequently than the FR Board governors.

Because of concern about the role of the FR Bank presidents in determining monetary policy, Representatives Lee Hamilton and Byron Dorgan and Senators Paul Sarbanes and Jim Sasser introduced identical congressional bills in both houses of Congress called the "Monetary Policy Reform Act of 1991." The proposed legislation has two main components: (1) it dissolves the FOMC and gives the FR Board Governors sole voting power on open market operations; and (2) it creates a Federal Open Market Advisory Council through which the twelve FR Bank presidents advise the FR Board governors on economic conditions. The rationale for ending the voting on open market operations by the Bank presidents is that since the presidents are private individuals who are neither appointed by the president nor confirmed by the Senate, they should not actively participate in policy decisions that have major impacts on the economic well-being of the nation. By contrast, as an advisory body, the Bank presidents would fulfill a useful role in a democratic society. (Proposed legislation to make the operations of the FR System less secretive are discussed below under the Federal Reserve Reform Act of 1991.)

The FR Board, the FR Banks, and the FOMC have different monetary policy powers: the FR Board determines reserve requirements, each FR Bank proposes changes in its discount rate subject to FR Board approval, and the FOMC establishes the money supply targets and directs open market operations. In general, there is considerable interplay between the Board and the Banks (particularly through the FOMC), but the FR Board has greater authority. Thus, the Board alone changes reserve requirements (although after consulting with the Banks), the Board approves proposed changes on the discount rate, and the Board's governors represent seven of the twelve members of the FOMC.

Institutionally, the FR Board reports to Congress; it is legally independent of the president. Since the executive branch does not participate in formulating monetary policies and the FR does not participate in formulating fiscal policies, coordination can be a problem. The FR and the president are in fact sometimes at odds, a situation that has been criticized for leading to unbalanced fiscal and monetary policies. Such disagreement usually occurs when unemployment is rising (or when unemployment is high and is not declining or is declining only slowly) and the president wants to stimulate employment growth while the FR emphasizes its traditional inclination to hold inflation down.

This leaves Congress as the only branch with direct links to all parties engaged in developing fiscal and monetary policies. While congressional review of the FR's annual and semiannual reports could provide a vehicle for coordination, in practice this does not occur. Congress has the authority to redirect FR policies if it is dissatisfied with them, but because it feels uneasy, and perhaps even inadequate, in assessing the economic and financial relationships, it does not take an active role in devising monetary policies. Indeed, while individual members of Congress occasionally express their opinions, Congress as a legislative body does not articulate its own view of FR policies. More members express disagreement with FR policies when unemployment is rising, similar to when the president disagrees, as noted above. Obviously, Congress and the president are more responsive to election prospects than are appointed FR officials.

Over the years, proposals such as that by Lester Thurow have been made to bring the FR under the direction of the president so that responsibility for monetary policies will be lodged *directly* with elected officials.[13] Any such change would require new legislation. This would have to balance the benefits of greater coordination between fiscal and monetary policies (as in the United Kingdom where the Bank of England is directed by the Prime Minister's party) against concern that the change would unduly politicize the FR's guidance of the economy, gearing it to help the party in power win elections. One theory (conspiratorial in nature) of why Congress and the president have not placed the FR under the president is that it would remove the FR as a visible entity to blame when the economy does not perform well.

Representatives Lee Hamilton and Byron Dorgan have proposed a more limited change that they say would increase the accountability of the FR but not diminish its independence. The thrust of their proposal is to give the public and Congress more detailed and prompt information about FR policymaking, and improve the coordination of monetary and fiscal policy between the FR and the president. Their 1991 congressional bill, "The Federal Reserve Reform Act of 1991," has the following provisions:

264 TRACKING AMERICA'S ECONOMY

• The secretary of the Treasury, chairman of the Council of Economic Advisers, and director of the Office of Management and Budget will hold three formal meetings a year on a nonvoting basis with the Federal Open Market Committee.

• The four-year term of the chairman of the FR Board will correspond more closely with the term of the president—specifically, the president will appoint a new Chairman (with the consent of the Senate as now) one year after taking office.

• Changes in the targets of monetary policy will be disclosed immediately after they are made, in contrast to the current procedure of disclosure six weeks later.

• The General Accounting Office (GAO) will audit complex aspects of FR operations that are currently inadequately dealt with in congressional hearings, such as the usefulness of information available at the Federal Open Market Committee meetings, the costs of purchases and sales of Treasury securities and the efficiency of these open market operations, and the terms and collateral of discount loans used to aid failing banks. This provision would give the GAO and Congress access to FR files that are now confidential and which successive FR chairmen have said should remain so.

• Complete accounting of the receipts and expenditures of the Federal Reserve System in the president's budget will be required for the current year with projections for the two succeeding years, in contrast to the current procedure of providing budget figures only for FR Board operations in Washington, D.C., but not for the regional banks, and only for the current and past years but not for future years. Although this comprehensive inclusion of FR finances in the president's budget would not require congressional approval, the FR fears that such a requirement would be a step toward less independence.

Despite the general principle of FR independence, the FR has been subject to political pressures from presidents. William Greider discusses such pressures involving Harry Truman and Richard Nixon, and William Safire gives a White House insider's view of Nixon's actions.[14] In both cases, the presidents advocated low interest rates to stimulate economic growth, and in the case of President Truman also to hold down interest costs on the federal debt. The episode with President Truman led to the "Treasury–Federal Reserve Accord" of 1951, which freed the FR to act independently, and thus enacted a major change in the relationship between the FR and the president. Twenty years later, President Nixon tried to undo the 1951 accord by pressuring Arthur Burns, chairman of the FR at that time, to influence the Federal Open Market Committee to lower interest rates in 1971 in order to boost the economy and thus help Nixon win re-election in 1972. The effect of presidential pressure on FR actions is disputed, but that it occurs is indisputable. One view of the effect of such pressure is that when the pressure is public, the FR resists in a show of independence—integrity, the FR family would call it—and that the White House effort may be counterproductive.

Table 27

Money Supply Measures (billions of dollars, December 1990)

M–1	**$825.4**
Currency (excludes bank-owned cash in bank vaults)	246.4
Demand (checking) deposits	276.9
NOW accounts (used for checking and saving)	293.7
Travelers checks, nonbank (e.g., American Express)	8.4
M–2	**3,330.0**
M–1	825.4
Small time deposits (less than $100,000) including open accounts and certificates of deposit	1,164.2
Savings deposits	410.8
Money market deposit accounts	505.9
Money market mutual funds (households, business, broker-dealers)	347.7
Overnight repurchase agreements (used in open market operations)	54.7
Overnight Eurodollars held by U.S. residents at overseas branches of U.S. banks	19.4
M–3	**4,114.1**
M–2	3,330.0
Large time deposits ($100,000 and more)	507.1
Term Eurodollars (maturities longer than 1 day)	71.4
Money market mutual funds (institutions only)	125.7
Term repurchase agreements (longer than 1 day)	90.2

Note: The M–1, M–2, and M–3 totals and certain components are seasonally adjusted. Other components are not seasonally adjusted. The sum of the components do not equal the totals because certain adjustments are made at the total level to avoid double-counting. For example, deposits of one bank held by another are excluded, as are assets held by money market mutual funds in other components of M–2 and M–3.

PART A: ESTIMATING METHODOLOGY

Table 27 shows the components of the M–1, M–2, and M–3 measures of the money supply. The measures encompass increasingly broader definitions of money and "near money" (assets that can readily be converted to cash) in progressing from M–1 toward M–3; each successive measure takes the previous one as a base and adds new elements. The differences in the dollar levels of the alternative measures are substantial, most notably between M–1 and M–2; as of December 1990, M–2 was four times as large as M–1, and M–3 exceeded M–2 by 25 percent.

More significant for economic analysis are the differential growth rates in the money supply measures from year-to-year. The relationships of these differential rates to economic growth and inflation are discussed in Part B.

From an analytic perspective, the various money supply measures are distinguished by two factors: FR control and financial liquidity. Theoretically, M–1 is subject to the greatest FR control because it has the highest proportion of assets subject to FR reserve requirements. Analogously, M–3 is subject to the least FR control because it has the lowest proportion of assets with reserve require-ments—reserve requirements are imposed only on demand (checking) deposits and NOW accounts and these components are included in all three money supply measures. However, the effect of FR control over money supply growth dimin-ished considerably during the 1980s as holders of checking accounts, savings deposits, and other financial assets—in seeking the best place for their funds—transferred them from one type of asset to another with much greater frequency than previously. This greater movement of funds resulted from the lifting of interest rate ceilings on bank deposits under the Depository Institutions Deregu-lation and Monetary Control Act of 1980, the creation of a variety of new income-earning financial instruments, and the increased internationalization of the U.S. economy. It also led the FR to discontinue inclusion of M–1 targets in its reports to Congress since 1987 (noted previously under FR Money Supply Targets and Their Implementation).

Distinctions in terms of liquidity are based on assessments of the risks of particular assets losing value if converted to cash. For example, nonbank traveler's checks function as currency; demand deposits often require minimum balances below which penalty fees are paid; saving deposits may forfeit some interest payments if withdrawn before certain dates; and money market securities are subject to current market interest rates, which impose a greater risk regarding the future value of these assets. M–1 is the most liquid of the money supply measures, while M–2 and M–3 are increasingly less liquid because they include progressively greater proportions of assets that are based on current market rates.

Monthly data for the money supply measures are based on reports from sam-ples of large and small commercial banks, savings and loan associations, mutual savings banks, credit unions, and brokers and dealers. Because the weekly data are based on fewer reports, they should be used with caution: they fluctuate considerably from week to week and are sometimes substantially revised based on the more complete information underlying the monthly measures.

PART B: ANALYSIS OF TRENDS

A previous section of this chapter discussed the theoretical relationships between movements in the money supply, GNP, and interest rates (see Money Supply, Interest Rates, and Economic Activity). Because comparable data for the three money supply measures are available only since the fourth quarter of 1959, comparisons of money supply trends with economic growth, inflation, and inter-est rates are made here for the 1960–90 period only.

Money Supply, GNP, and Inflation

Relationships between growth in the money supply and the gross national prod-uct are theoretically most consistent for the GNP in current dollars because

Figure 50. **Money Supply (M–1) vs. GNP, 1959–90: Money Supply Impact for Two Years**

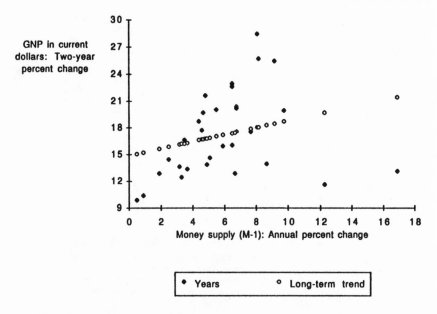

Note: Money supply annual change and GNP same year and next year change
(e.g. MS 1988-89 = GNP 1988-90).

money supply measures are in current dollars and thus relate to actual price levels. As for which of the three money supply measures is most closely related to GNP movements, theoretical arguments could probably be made in support of any one of them.

In the comparisons shown here, the change in the money supply in one year is assumed to affect the GNP growth rates in the same year and the year following, showing in effect a two-year impact on the GNP. The money supply's impact on the GNP for (a) only the same year as the money supply change, and (b) the same year and the two years following the money supply change, did not result in as close a correspondence; therefore, these other relationships are not shown here.

Figure 50 shows M–1 in relation to the GNP in current dollars, and Figures 51 and 52 compare M–1 movements to real GNP and inflation (measured by the GNP implicit price deflator). The points representing each year show the money supply growth rate in the initial year and the GNP measure used in the particular figure for that year and the following year. For example, 1961, which is the first year shown in the figures, represents the change in the money supply in 1960 and the change in the GNP in 1960 and 1961. The change in each year is calculated

Figure 51. **Money Supply (M–1) vs. Real GNP, 1959–90: Money Supply Impact for Two Years**

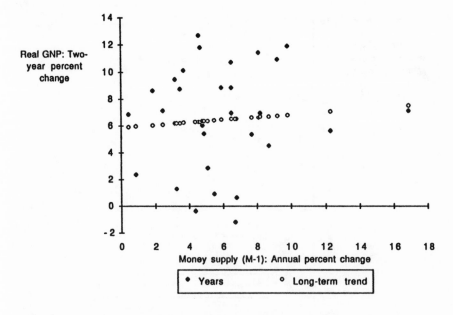

Note: Money supply annual change and real GNP same year and next year change (e.g. MS 1988-89 = GNP 1988-90).

from the fourth quarter to the fourth quarter—1959:4 to 1960:4, 1960:4 to 1961:4, and so on. Over the long run, the closest relationship appears as an upward-sloping line to the right—thus, an increase or slowdown in the rate of money supply growth would be associated with similar movements in GNP and inflation. The closest comparison is with GNP in current dollars (Figure 50); but it is not stable or predictable from year to year. The upward-sloping line to the right (of white diamonds) represents an average relationship over the years; because of the wide dispersion of the years around the line, there would be a large margin of error in using it to predict GNP in any particular year.

The M–1 relationships with real GNP and inflation (Figures 51 and 52) are both less consistent than that with GNP in current dollars (Figure 50), although M–1 corresponds more to inflation than to real GNP. In fact, the money supply has little linkage to current-dollar GNP, real GNP, and inflation. Benjamin Friedman and Kenneth Kuttner note that these relationships declined considerably in the 1980s.[15] The correlation coefficients are: GNP in current dollars (.27); inflation (.17); and real GNP (.08)—the closer the correlation coefficient is to 1 or –1, the more similar are the movements of the variables, while the closer they are to

Figure 52. **Money Supply (M–1) vs. GNP Implicit Price Deflator, 1959–90: Money Supply Impact for Two Years**

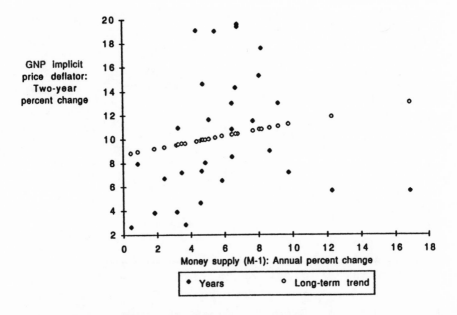

Note: Money supply annual change and GNP implicit price deflator same year and next year change (e.g., MS 1988-89 = IPD 1988-90).

zero, the less similar are the movements.[16]

These measures show that using the money supply to determine current-dollar GNP, real GNP, or inflation is difficult. Similar comparisons between current-dollar GNP and M–2 and M–3 also showed weak relationships.

In assessing movements of the money supply measures as a gauge of future economic activity, the analyst should consider the money supply as a clue only for GNP in current dollars. The money supply is irrelevant as a guide for future short-term movements of real GNP or inflation. M–1 typically shows similar relationships to GNP as do M–2 and M–3. This suggests that unless special circumstances such as the development of new financial instruments indicate the use of a particular money supply measure, in most cases it is appropriate to use M–1, which also is the most widely cited figure.

Money Supply Targets and Velocity

The money supply targets used by the FR in conducting monetary policy are based on an expectation of the demand for money in relation to economic activ-

Figure 53a. **M–1 Velocity: 1959–90**

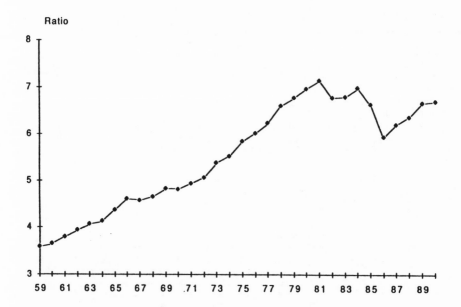

Note: Velocity is current dollar GNP divided by M-1 money supply.
Each year is represented by the fourth quarter.

ity. One simple measure of this relationship is the ratio of the GNP to the money supply. This ratio is called velocity of money and indicates the relative extent to which households, businesses, nonprofit organizations, and state and local governments hold financial assets in the most liquid form (it also may be thought of as the turnover of money). If the GNP grows faster than the money supply, velocity increases; if the money supply increases faster than the GNP, velocity decreases. Velocity is a behavorial relationship of the public's tendency to hold money in the most liquid forms, such as low-interest or non-interest bearing assets, because the public perceives a need for the money in the near future and wants it readily available, or because it does not want to risk a loss in capital value. The future need may be for consumer and business spending, investments in anticipation of higher interest rates, and so forth.

Figures 53a, 53b, and 53c show trends from 1959 to 1990 of velocity for M–1, M–2, and M–3, respectively. Each year is represented by the fourth quarter of the year—1959:4, 1960:4, and so on. Movements of the three measures are quite different. M–1 velocity rose continually from 3.6 in 1959 to 7.1 in 1981, and then fluctuated noticeably from 1982 to 1990, reaching 6.7 in 1990. M–2

Figure 53b. **M–2 Velocity: 1959–90**

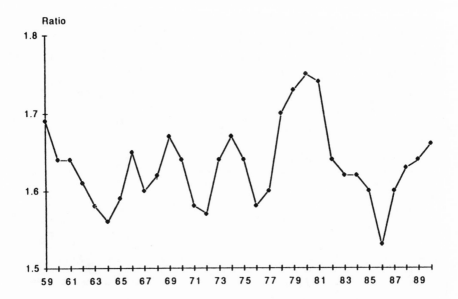

Note: Velocity is current dollar GNP divided by M-2 money supply.
Each year is represented by the fourth quarter.

fluctuated within a range of 1.55 to 1.75, with no discernible long-term trend. M–3 showed a long-term decline, although with some interruption, from around 1.7 in 1959 to 1.2 in 1986, and then turned upward, reaching 1.35 in 1990. This general volatility reflects the fluid reactions of households and businesses to changing patterns of economic growth, inflation, and interest rates, as well as the development of new financial instruments such as interest-bearing NOW accounts and money market funds and the solvency problems of financial institutions including failures of savings and loan associations and commercial banks.

Movements in velocity are difficult to predict. Consequently, money supply targets are subject to the uncertainty of the movement of velocity. For example, when the GNP growth rate turns out to be close to the rate assumed when the money supply targets were projected, the money supply will exceed the target if velocity is much lower than anticipated; the money supply will be lower than the target if velocity is much higher than expected. This occurs even with the wide upper and lower limits set by the FR for its money supply targets.

An instance of the money supply exceeding the upper range of the target occurred in 1985. Apparently because of the declining interest rates in that year,

Figure 53c. **M–3 Velocity: 1959–90**

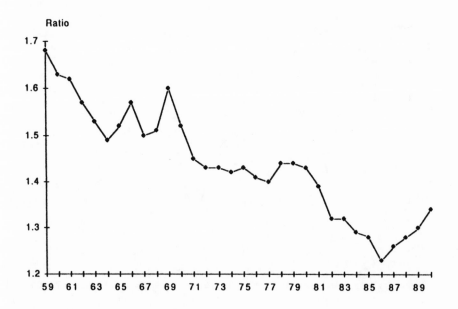

Note: Velocity is current dollar GNP divided by M-3 money supply.
Each year is represented by the fourth quarter.

households, businesses, nonprofit organizations, and governments tended to keep more of their financial assets in interest-bearing M–1 NOW accounts. Another possible reason noted by the FR for the 1985 decline in velocity was that companies and banks adopted more cautious cash-management policies in light of financial problems in certain markets (such as risky bank loans, bank failures, and investment companies' abuses in handling securities funds).[17] The further decline in velocity in 1986 caused M–1 to grow much faster than the target for the year. As a result, the FR did not provide a M–1 target for 1987 in its February 1987 report to Congress because of the increasing uncertainties regarding the M–1 relationships to GNP and interest rates.[18] As noted previously, the FR continued this practice of not including M–1 targets in its reports to Congress in later years.

The uncertainty of velocity movements points up the difficulty of projecting money supply targets in relation to the GNP. *In assessing the likely outcome of money supply targets, the analyst should keep in mind that while the Federal Reserve can influence the quantity of money, underlying economic factors such as economic growth, unemployment, capacity utilization, the federal deficit, the*

Figure 54. **Money Supply (M–1) vs. Interest Rates, 1959–90: Money Supply Impact for One Year**

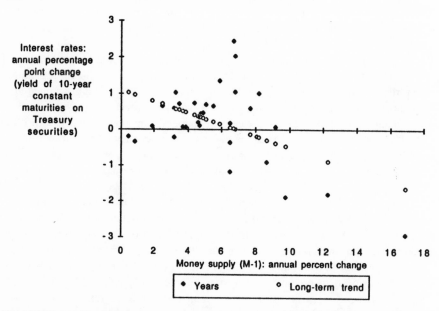

Note: Money supply annual change and interest rate annual change for the same year (e.g. MS 89 to 90 = IR 89 to 90).

value of the dollar, oil prices, and inflationary expectations dominate movements in the money supply.

Money Supply, Interest Rates, and Economic Activity

Interest is the price of money. Major elements determining the interest rate on a loan include: (a) competing outlets for lenders' funds in other loans or invest-ments (referred to as "opportunity cost"); (b) risk of default on the loan; (c) expectation of inflation in discounting the future value of interest payments and repayment of the principal of the loan; and (d) availability of alternative sources of funds for loans (i.e., the supply of loanable funds). There is a direct relation-ship between the first three elements and the level of interest rates—the greater the opportunity cost, the risk of default, or the expectation of inflation, the higher the interest rate. In contrast, a greater supply of loanable funds tends to lower interest rates, which is an inverse relationship.

While influencing the money supply is an important intermediate tool for conducting monetary policy, decisions to borrow and spend are directly affected by interest rates. Households, businesses, and other borrowers think in terms of interest rates because they represent the cost of credit, while money supply movements as such are removed from borrowing decisions. Theoretically, in the short run a speedup in the money supply's growth rate would lower interest rates, and a slowdown in the money supply's growth would raise interest rates, as indicated at the beginning of the chapter.

Figure 54 shows the relationships for 1960–90 of changes in M–1 and interest rates. The interest rates are yields on Treasury securities with a ten-year remaining maturity.[19] The ten-year rate is used to reflect long-term borrowing for plant and equipment investments. The comparison is based on money supply and interest rate changes in the same year—the percent change in the money supply from 1989 to 1990, for example, is related to the percent change in interest rates from 1989 to 1990. Comparisons using a two-year impact of the money supply on interest rates as well as using M–2 and M–3 did not have as close a correspondence and are not shown here.

The figure shows an inverse relationship between the money supply and interest rates; however, although consistent with economic theory, the relationship is rough. The inverse relationship is represented by the downward-sloping line to the right, which is the average for all years. The individual yearly points are widely dispersed around the average line, and thus there is a wide margin of error for using it to predict interest rates in a particular year. Statistically, the correlation coefficient is –0.49, which indicates a limited relationship, as –1 would show identical inverse movements and zero would show no similarity in their movements.

One of the factors affecting the general inverse relationship between the money supply and interest rates is the risk of inflation. When inflationary expectations rise, lenders and borrowers raise interest rates above what they would be when lower inflation is expected; as noted at the beginning of the chapter, this "inflation premium" is intended to protect the purchasing power of the loan when it is repaid. Inflationary psychology thus reverses the expected relationship between money supply growth and interest rates. In this situation, an acceleration of money supply growth is associated with fueling inflation by making money more readily available for borrowing and spending; the resulting rate of economic growth, higher than the economy can sustain without causing further inflation, leads to higher interest rates as lenders act to compensate for expected higher inflation. In short, an easing of monetary policy, which the credit markets perceived as inflationary, may be counterproductive and produce higher interest rates.

There have been several studies of the sensitivity of growth in real GNP to changes in interest rates over the post–World War II period, but the findings have varied. As noted by Beverly Hirtle and Jeanette Kelleher, some studies show a decline in interest sensitivity, while others indicate no change or even an increase.[20] Their own research indicates a decline in interest sensitivity from the 1950s to the 1970s, followed by an increase in the 1980s.

The issue is complicated by recent developments in financial deregulation,

Figure 55. **Real Interest Rate vs. Real Gross National Product: 1955–90**

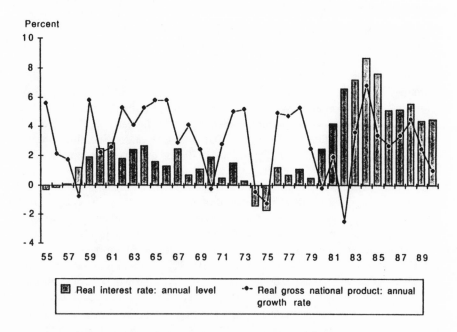

Note: Real interest is Treasury securities 10-year yield minus the
GNP implicit price deflator annual change.

increased corporate leverage resulting from buyouts and mergers, and greater internationalization of the economy. More research is needed to understand fully the nature and impact of interest rate sensitivity. The findings of such research could have important implications for FR monetary policies. For example, George Kahn (whose studies indicate a decline in interest sensitivity) argues that because of the longer time now required for changes in interest rates to affect the economy, the FR should institute monetary policy changes more quickly in response to economic shocks, such as changes in tax laws and oil prices (supply shocks) or changes in fiscal policies and inflationary expectations (demand shocks).[21]

Real interest rates, defined as the market rate minus expected inflation, represent the cost of borrowing adjusted for lenders' expectations of future inflation. Real interest rates rise when lenders are concerned that inflation will accelerate and they decline when inflation is expected to recede. Higher real interest tends to retard borrowing and economic growth, while lower real interest tends to stimulate borrowing and growth. For this reason, inflation is not likely to lead to higher, sustained growth.

Figure 55 shows trends in real interest rates and real GNP over 1955–

90. Real interest rates are calculated as the yield on Treasury securities with ten-year remaining maturities less the current inflation rate represented by the GNP implicit price deflator (this assumes that the current inflation rate is expected to continue in the future). Real interest rates over the thirty-five-year period averaged 2.4 percent. However, it was much higher in the 1980s than in the earlier years, averaging 1.1 percent during 1955–80 and 5.9 percent during 1981–90. The sharp increase during 1981–90 occurred when both market (i.e., nominal) interest rates and inflation were declining, but real interest rates rose more because experience had raised expectations of inflation (the lower real interest rates during 1986–90 compared to those in the early 1980s were still substantially above those during 1955–80). For that reason, nominal interest rates fell less than did inflation. During the 1970s, on the other hand, real interest rates were low, even though inflation and nominal interest rates were high and accelerating. One explanation is that lenders assumed that the high inflation was only temporary and therefore that nominal interest rates were sufficiently high to compensate for any loss in purchasing power due to inflation when in later periods the interest payments are made and the principal of the loan is paid back.

Figure 55 also shows that economic growth (real GNP) during 1955–90 was faster through the 1970s than during 1980–90. This is consistent with the theoretical expectation that low real interest rates stimulate growth. Although there is no existing hypothesis of a threshold level of real interest in relation to economic growth—what real interest rate is the break-even level above which economic growth slows and below which economic growth accelerates—the high real interest rates of the 1980s appear to have retarded economic growth.

In assessing the impact of changes in the money supply on interest rates, the analyst should review both the changing demand for money and inflationary expectations. The changing demand for money arises from the desires of borrowers—consumers, businesses, and governments—to spend. Inflationary expectations reflect lenders' and borrowers' perceptions of future price movements. Thus, while the money supply affects interest rates, it is not sufficient to explain interest rate movements. Moreover, unless inflationary expectations as expressed in real interest rates, and the demand for money as expressed in real GNP are considered, a mechanical interpretation of money supply movements can often lead to an incorrect assessment of future changes in interest rates.

Interest Rate Differentials

Interest rate differentials on different debt instruments are intensely scrutinized every day in the trading of debt securities on financial exchanges and in other financial markets. Although the general economic effects of interest rate differentials are not readily apparent, the variations are briefly discussed here to introduce the reader to the complexities of financial markets.

Figure 56. **Illustrative Yield Curves**

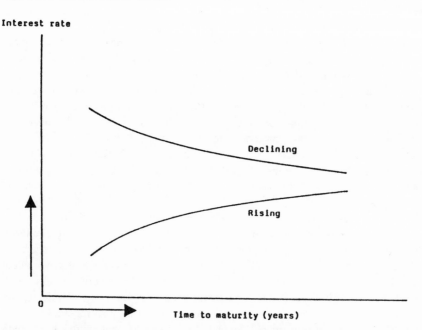

The different interest rates that are charged on the various kinds of debt instruments are influenced by several factors, including the maturity period of the debt (i.e., the length of time before repayment is due), the relative risk of default by borrowers, and the differing tax rates assessed on interest from commercial and government securities. The interest rate on federal funds is also heavily influenced by FR monetary policies.

The differential interest rates on short-term and long-term debt instruments reflect distinctions in liquidity as well as expectations regarding the future course of interest rates. Generally, short-term rates are lower than long-term rates because short-term debt instruments can be sold for cash more quickly and with less risk of a significant capital loss on the initial amount of the loan than is the case for long-term debt. These interest rate differentials are often depicted with a *yield curve* which shows that interest rates typically increase as the maturity of the debt lengthens.[22] Figure 56 shows illustrative rising and falling yield curves.

Expectations about future interest rates drive the yield curve. For example, when short-term rates are expected to rise in the future, the yield curve will rise more steeply than usual. Such a steeply rising curve typically occurs when a recession is perceived to be bottoming out and the anticipated recovery and subsequent expansion are expected to provoke greater demand for loans and concomitantly higher interest rates. By contrast, the yield curve will decline when short-term interest rates are expected to fall in the future. A declining yield curve typically occurs during an inflationary period when the FR tightens credit to curb the inflation: the resulting expectation of slower economic growth or recession reduces demand for loans, leading to lower interest rates.

This model of rising and falling yield curves is not unanimously accepted, however.[23] Some analysts say that the focus on the importance of short-term interest rates is misguided and more attention should be paid to the long-term rates. Others claim that because lenders tend to specialize in either short-term or long-term loans, the interest rates charged on the two kinds of debt in fact have little relation to each other. At any rate, yield curves are statistically related to macroeconomic indicators of economic growth and inflation. Thus, Arturo Estrella and Gikas Hardouvelis note that yield curves add useful information in forecasting economic activity, although it is difficult to deduce from these statistical relationships that the yield curve is a causal factor in future economic growth and inflation.[24]

Yield spread refers to the range of differential interest rates paid on securities representing household, commercial, and government debt of the same maturity (i.e., repayment of the principal due in three months, one year, five years, etc.).[25] There are many reasons for this spread in interest rates. Federal government securities invariably pay lower interest than household and commercial debt of the same maturity because the risk that the federal government will default on repayment of the interest and principal is lower. The U.S. government has never defaulted on interest or principal. State and local governments with a high credit rating typically pay lower interest rates on their debt than households, businesses, and the federal government because interest received from state and local debt securities is exempt from federal income taxes. (Interest from U.S. Treasury securities is similarly exempt from state and local government income taxes.) Like the yield curve, the yield spread undoubtedly has macroeconomic effects, but they are more difficult to reduce to direct relationships.

The *federal funds* interest rate is the rate charged for loans between banks.[26] These typically are for overnight loans that allow banks to meet reserve requirements, although there are "term" federal funds with maturities from a few days to over one year (the average is less than six months). Because banks do not receive interest on their reserve accounts with the FR, the federal funds market has dual incentives: banks typically keep their reserves at the minimum required, but they sometimes fall below the minimum which causes the need to borrow, while banks holding reserves above the minimum requirement gain interest by lending the surplus. The name "federal funds" reflects the transfer of these funds at FR Banks.

The federal funds interest rate on interbank loans is the clearest indicator of current FR monetary policy. The FR's open market operations (typically conducted a few days a week), which raise or lower bank reserves and thus the availability of bank credit for loans, virtually determine movements in the federal funds rate as well as the need for banks to borrow to meet their reserve requirements. In addition, interest rates on commercial short-term securities such as certificates of deposit and commercial paper reflect movements in the federal funds rate. The federal funds rate should not be confused with the FR discount rate (the interest charge to banks when they borrow directly from the FR) discussed earlier under "FR Money Supply Targets and Their Implementation."

SUMMARY

The money supply is the main measure used by the Federal Reserve to formulate monetary policies. It is the only indicator discussed in this book that is acted on directly to affect its performance. The FR influences the money supply in its use of targets by the role it takes in affecting the level of commercial bank reserves through open market operations, the discount rate, and reserve requirements.

Money supply movements are mainly of interest because of their effect on interest rates. Of the three money supply measures (M-1, M-2, and M-3), M-1 is the appropriate one to use in most cases.

A key problem in using money supply targets in relation to projections of the GNP is the uncertainty of velocity movements. Because of substantial fluctuations in velocity, it is evident that while FR monetary policies influence movements in the money supply, other factors significantly affect the growth rate in the money supply.

The immediate impact of changes in the money supply is on the level of interest rates. In the short run, a rapid growth in the money supply tends to lower interest rates, and a slower growth tends to raise interest rates. But the relationship is limited because inflationary expectations and the demand for money by household, business, and government borrowers strongly affect interest rates. In addition, real interest rates—the market rate minus inflation—appear to have an important impact on economic growth. Thus, while the money supply influences interest rates, a mechanical use of money supply movements to assess future trends in interest rates can often be misleading.

REVIEW QUESTIONS

• The money supply differs from other economic indicators in the nature of actions taken to affect it. What is the difference?
• The Federal Reserve is required to report its money supply targets to Congress twice a year. How does this affect Federal Reserve independence in conducting monetary policy?
• How does the independence of the Federal Reserve differ from the independence of the Supreme Court?
• What is the concern about including Federal Reserve Bank presidents on the Federal Reserve Open Market Committee?
• What would happen to the effectiveness of open market operations if reserve requirements were abolished?

• Reserve requirements are used to oversee the financial solvency of banks.

_____True_____False?

• How does monetarism differ from discretionary monetary policy?

• How was the effectiveness of the Federal Reserve's influence over M–1 affected during the 1980s?

• Characterize the relationship between movements in the money supply and those for GNP in current dollars, real GNP, and prices.

• Why doesn't the generally inverse relationship between the money supply and interest rates hold during periods of inflationary expectations?

• Although inflation and nominal interest rates in the 1970s were significantly higher than they were in the 1980s, real interest rates were significantly lower during the 1970s. What could have caused these different patterns?

• How have inflationary expectations made real interest rates a deterrent to economic growth since the 1980s?

• Contrast the monetary policy roles of the discount rate and the federal funds rate.

• How do yield curves suggest expected changes in borrowing and economic activity?

NOTES

1. Full Employment and Balanced Growth Act of 1978, Section 108. The act is discussed in Board of Governors of the Federal Reserve System, *Federal Reserve System: Purposes and Functions*, 1984, p. 20.

2. Paul A. Volcker, chairman of the Board of Governors of the Federal Reserve System, Statement to the Committee on Banking, Housing, and Urban Affairs, U.S. Senate, February 20, 1985, Attachment III ("Targeting Real Growth").

3. Spence Hilton and Vivek Moorthy, "Targeting Nominal GNP," in *Intermediate Targets and Indicators for Monetary Policy: A Critical Survey*, Federal Reserve Bank of New York,: July 1990, pp. 247–48.

4. Board of Governors of the Federal Reserve System, *Monetary Policy Report to Congress Pursuant to the Full Employment and Balance Growth Act of 1978*, February 20, 1990, p. 1.

5. For a detailed discussion of these methods, see Board of Governors of the Federal Reserve System, *Federal Reserve System*, Chapters 3 and 4.

6. For example, reserve requirements may be changed solely to conduct monetary policy; changes within the prescribed range of 8 to 14 percent of deposits for large bank transactions accounts (i.e., interest and noninterest bearing checking accounts) must be reported to Congress; supplementary reserve requirements up to 4 percentage points above 14 percent must be approved by five Board members, would earn interest in contrast to no interest earned on the 8–14 percent regular schedule, and must be reported to Congress; and reserve requirements may be changed outside the 8–14 percent schedule and applied to nontransaction accounts for periods up to six months if approved by five Board members, would not earn interest, and must be reported to Congress.

7. "Announcements," *Federal Reserve Bulletin*, February 1991, p. 95.

8. Reserve requirements in 1991 are 3 percent for banks holding deposits up to $41.1 million and 12 percent for banks holding deposits over $41.1 million. In this example of

how loans create new bank deposits, we will use the 12 percent reserve requirement for large banks. Suppose customer A deposits $10,000 in the Atlantic bank. The Atlantic bank then lends $8,800 of the new deposits (allowing a 12 percent reserve) to customer B, and adds the $8,800 to customer B's checking account. Customer B buys a car for the $8,800 and the car dealer deposits the payment in the Pacific bank, which increases that bank's deposits by $8,800. At this point, deposits in the Atlantic bank are reduced by $8,800, resulting in a net increment of $1,200 from customer A's initial $10,000 deposit. The Pacific bank then lends $7,744 of the new deposits of $8,800 it obtained from the car dealer (again allowing a 12 percent reserve) to customer C. Customer C spends the $7,744 for college tuition and the college deposits the $7,744 in the Continental bank, which reduces the Pacific bank's net increment in deposits to $1,056 (8,800 − 7,744). The chain continues with the Continental bank lending $6,815 (12 percent less than 7,744) to customer D and so on. The total amount of new deposit creation through this mechanism is the sum of the net increment of deposits that each bank has after its loan is spent by the borrower. Thus, the increments to the deposits of the Atlantic and Pacific banks of $1,200 and $1,056 add $2,256 to the money supply.

This fractional reserve system adds decreasing increments to the money supply in the successive rounds of lending and spending from the initial $10,000 deposit by customer A until the process diminishes to zero. Mathematically, the limit to the increase in the money supply is obtained by dividing the initial deposit by the reserve ratio, in this case $10,000/0.12, which amounts to $83,333. That is, the initial deposit of $10,000 can result in an ultimate increase of $83,333 in the money supply. This is also referred to as the deposit multiplier, which in this case is 8.3 (83,333/10,000), and in a simple form is obtained by 1/0.12 (i.e., 1/reserve ratio). For a good explanation of how bank deposits are created through the fractional reserve system, see Edwin Mansfield, *Principles of Macroeconomics*, 4th ed. (W. W. Norton & Company: 1983), pp. 362–69.

9. For example, Milton Friedman, "The Role of Monetary Policy," *American Economic Review*, March 1968; Dallas S. Batten and Courtenay C. Stone, "Are Monetarists an Endangered Species?" *Review*, The Federal Reserve Bank of St. Louis, May 1983; and David Laidler, "The Legacy of the Monetarist Controversy," *Review*, The Federal Reserve Bank of St. Louis, March/April 1990.

10. Alan Greenspan, "Economic Forecasting in the Private and Public Sectors," *Business Economics*, January 1991, p. 55.

11. A. Steven Englander, "Optimal Monetary Design: Rules versus Discretion Again," *Quarterly Review*, Federal Reserve Bank of New York, Winter 1991.

12. Geoffrey M. B. Tootell, "Regional Economic Conditions and the FOMC Votes of District Presidents," *New England Economic Review*, Federal Reserve Bank of Boston, March/April 1991; and Geoffrey M. B. Tootell, "Are District Presidents More Conservative than Board Governors?" *New England Economic Review*, Federal Reserve Bank of Boston, September/October 1991..

13. For a proposal in the mid-1980s to bring the Federal Reserve under the president, see Lester C. Thurow, *The Zero-Sum Solution: Building a World-Class American Economy* (Simon and Schuster: 1985), pp. 325–27.

14. William Greider, *Secrets of the Temple: How the Federal Reserve Runs the Country* (Simon and Schuster: 1987), Chapter 10; and William Safire, *Before the Fall: An Inside View of the Pre-Watergate White House* (Doubleday & Company: 1975), pp. 491–96.

15. Benjamin M. Friedman and Kenneth N. Kuttner, "Money, Income and Prices after the 1980s," Working Paper No. 2852, National Bureau of Economic Research, February 1989.

16. A correlation coefficient of 1 occurs when the variables move in identical patterns

in a direct relationship (both increase or decrease in tandem), and a coefficient of −1 occurs when the variables move in identical patterns in an inverse relationship (one increases and the other decreases). A coefficient of zero indicates no statistical relationship.

17. Board of Governors of the Federal Reserve System, *Monetary Policy Report to Congress Pursuant to the Full Employment and Balanced Growth Act of 1978.* February 19, 1986, p. 26. The Federal Reserve statement on this topic is worded generally, with no specific examples of the financial problems leading to the more cautious cash-management policies. Examples of the problems cited here are based on discussions with the Federal Reserve staff.

18. Board of Governors of the Federal Reserve System, *Monetary Policy Report to Congress Pursuant to the Full Employment and Balanced Growth Act of 1978*, February 19, 1987, pp. 6–8.

19. These estimates are based on constructing yield curves (interest rates and years to maturity) for the most actively traded Treasury securities, and reading the ten-year interest rate from the curve. See Joint Economic Committee of Congress, *1980 Supplement to Economic Indicators*, p. 108.

20. Beverly Hirtle and Jeanette Kelleher, "Financial Market Evolution and the Interest Sensitivity of Output," *Quarterly Review,* Federal Reserve Bank of New York, Summer 1990.

21. George A. Kahn, "The Changing Interest Sensitivity of the U.S. Economy," *Economic Review,* Federal Reserve Bank of Kansas City, November 1989.

22. For discussions of yield curves, see Ann-Marie Meulendyke, *U.S. Monetary Policy and Financial Markets,* Federal Reserve Bank of New York, 1989, pp. 185–88; and Henry Kaufman, *Interest Rates, the Markets, and the New Financial World* (Times Books: 1986), Chapter 12.

23. Ibid.

24. Arturo Estrella and Gikas Hardouvelis, "Possible Roles of the Yield Curve in Monetary Policy," in *Intermediate Targets and Indicators for Monetary Policy: A Critical Survey*(Federal Reserve Bank of New York: July 1990).

25. For a discussion of yield spreads, see Timothy Q. Cook, in "Treasury Bills," *Instruments of the Money Market* (Federal Reserve Bank of Richmond: 1986), pp. 88–90.

26. For a discussion of federal funds, see Marvin Goodfriend and William Whelpley, "Federal Funds," in *Instruments of the Money Market,* Federal Reserve Bank of Richmond, 1986, Chapter 2; and Meulendyke, *U.S. Monetary Policy and Financial Markets,* 1989, pp. 72–75.

8
LEADING, COINCIDENT, AND
LAGGING INDEXES

The leading, coincident, and lagging (LCLg) indexes of economic activity are based on the concept that each phase of the business cycle contains the seeds of the following phase. By focusing on the factors operating in each phase, the LCLg system provides a basis for monitoring the tendency to move from one phase to the next. The LCLg system assesses the strengths and weaknesses in the economy as clues to a quickening or slowing of future rates of economic growth as well as to cyclical turning points in moving from the upward expansion to the downward recession and vice versa, but it does not provide specific forecasts.

Development of the LCLg system evolved over a quarter of a century. In 1937, Secretary of the Treasury Henry Morgenthau, Jr., requested Wesley Mitchell to compile a list of statistical series to observe for clues as to when the recession that began in 1937 would turn up into a recovery, which Mitchell did in collaboration with Arthur Burns. In 1950, Geoffrey Moore revised this list and added a new set of indicators to observe when an expansion is likely to turn down into a recession. Finally, in 1961 Julius Shiskin developed the composite indexes that group several component indicators in the summary form of the LCLg system.[1] The U.S. Department of Commerce began regular monthly publication of the composite indexes in 1968. Currently, the experimental recession indexes developed by James Stock and Mark Watson are a promising innovation in the leading indicator system, as discussed in this chapter.

The system has been criticized for being excessively empirical and lacking a theoretical framework. Critics often refer to a 1947 article by Tjalling Koopmans that criticized the work by Mitchell and Burns in general and particularly attacked their 1946 book, *Measuring Business Cycles*.[2] However, the author disagrees with these criticisms and argues below that the system is grounded in economic theory.

The Bureau of Economic Analysis of the U.S. Department of Commerce provides the LCLg indexes monthly in the *Survey of Current Business*. The indexes are the most systematic quantification of how various aspects of the economy behave in cyclical expansions and recessions.

The three classifications of leading, coincident, and lagging refer to the timing in the turning points of the business cycle: the leading index turns down before a general recession begins and turns up before the recovery from the recession begins; the coincident index moves in tandem with the cyclical movements of the overall economy, tending to coincide with the designations of expansions and recessions (discussed in Chapter 2); and the lagging index turns down after the beginning of a recession and turns up after the beginning of a recovery.

The LCLg system is based on Wesley Mitchell's theory that expectations of future profits are the motivating force in the economy.[3] When business executives believe their sales and profits will rise, companies expand production of goods and services and of investment in new plant and equipment, but when they believe profits will decline, they reduce production and investment. These actions generate the expansion and recession phases of the business cycle. As discussed below, the LCLg indexes suggest the future course of profits by indicating businesses, expectations of future rising sales (leading index), and by the differential movements in current business activity (coincident index) and production costs (lagging index).

THE PROCESS OF CYCLICAL CHANGE

As background for the role of the three indexes, it is useful to summarize the cyclical phenomena considered to be the major elements underlying the LCLg system. To illustrate, assume as the cyclical starting point the beginning of the expansion from the previous recession (sometimes referred to as the recovery). In this initial stage, an impetus for increasing production starts an upward movement. Sales increase as consumers begin purchasing durable goods they had deferred during the recession; unit costs of production decline because the increasing volume of sales is spread over the fixed depreciation and maintenance costs of existing plant and equipment, as well as over the lowered work force and other services resulting from the cutbacks of nonessential costs in the preceding recession. Thus, profits (sales minus costs) increase. As this momentum spreads and employment and consumer spending increase, business executives become more optimistic about future sales and order more goods for inventories and invest in new plant and equipment to increase and modernize productive capacity; this is heightened by the accelerated increase in the numbers of new businesses that come into existence in anticipation of continued growing markets and higher profits, which in turn stimulates more production, hiring, and spending.

However, at some point the upward momentum slows. Sales of some items are no longer as brisk because consumers' needs have changed, and higher prices cause consumers to defer purchases. Unsold inventories of goods accumulate, leading to reduced prices to sell them, and to reduced orders for new goods to replace them, and thus lower future production. When capacity utilization rates rise to high levels, production costs rise because of increasing use of outmoded and less efficient equipment, hiring of less efficient workers when unemployment rates fall to low levels, and obtaining loans at high interest rates when the overall demand for money is strong. The higher production costs lead businesses to maintain prices in order to limit reductions in profit margins, but the higher prices in turn lead to lower sales; the combination of lower sales and higher production costs reduces profits enough to dampen the incentive for investing in new plant and equipment capacity. This slowdown in demand leads to lower production, and thus less employment and income for consumers, resulting in lower spending. The slowdown has a snowballing effect (analogous to the upward spiral in the earlier stages of the expansion) as consumers and business retrench in their spending. There is less incentive to take out additional loans (which would bolster spending), because, thanks to lower incomes, existing loans have become a greater burden to repay. Thus, production and employment are further reduced, bringing on a recession.

Increasing numbers of businesses close down during the recession, and existing businesses cut costs by maintaining lower inventories and reducing employment. This depressed level of economic activity ultimately runs its course as consumers who have deferred spending because of the economic uncertainty begin to replace their older goods and buy new housing at the lower recession-induced interest rates. This turnaround in sales encourages businesses to order more goods for inventories, thus stimulating production, and the stage is set for the recovery phase, which completes the cycle.

While this is a highly simplified version of cyclical economic movements, it depicts the basic rationale of the LCLg system. Each business cycle will have its unique characteristics because of other factors that vary over time, such as the intensity of inflation, unemployment level, population growth, development of new products, soundness of the banking system, and competition from abroad.

CONCEPTS OF THE LCLg SYSTEM

The LCLg system is based on the idea that profits are the driving force in the private enterprise economy. Business decisions on production, prices, employment, and investment are understood in relation to profits—both past trends in profits and the perception of future profits. Thus, changing expectations for profits affect the direction and pace of economic activity.

The LCLg system combines several data series into a composite leading index, a composite coincident index, and a composite lagging index. The following discussion capsulizes the three composite indexes and the rationale for each of the components; the rationale was articulated by Feliks Tamm.[4] The component data series that have been discussed in previous chapters are noted in parenthesis.

The *leading* index indicates business perceptions of future profits. It represents businesses' anticipation of future economic developments, and the response in actions and plans to those expectations. The eleven components of the leading index are:

1. *Average weekly hours of manufacturing production workers* (see Chapter

5). Because of uncertainty in the economic outlook, employers are more likely to adjust the hours of previously-hired workers before hiring new workers during recovery or laying off workers during recession.

2. *Average weekly initial claims for unemployment insurance, state programs.* Increases or decreases in unemployment indicate business expectations of the demand for labor.

3. *Manufacturers' new orders for consumer goods and materials, in constant dollars.* Business commitments to buy items indicate future levels of production.

4. *Vendor performance (percentage of companies receiving slower deliveries).* Delivery time reflects the strength of demand—brisk when the time from the placement of the order to delivery is long (because of the large backlog of orders), and weak when the delivery time is short.

5. *Contracts and orders for plant and equipment, in constant dollars* (see Chapter 3). These business commitments indicate future production and employment.

6. *New private-housing building permits, index* (see Chapter 3). Permits provide advance indication of housing construction, which is cyclically sensitive to changes in employment and interest rates. Home construction generally leads the economy.

7. *Manufacturers' unfilled orders in durable goods industries, monthly change.* The backlog of orders influences future production, and production is typically more volatile in these cyclical industries.

8. *Prices of crude and intermediate materials, monthly change.* Prices of certain farm, mineral, and scrap products in which supplies cannot be changed quickly (because of production lead times and delays in obtaining used goods for scrap) are sensitive to sharp changes in demand.

9. *Prices of 500 common stocks, index.* Stock prices reflect investor expectations of economic growth and profits, and thus future investment and consumer spending. High stock prices make it easier for businesses to raise funds for plant and equipment investment and other ventures by selling new stock to the public (equity financing), which entails no required payback to the buyer of the value of the stock or the payment of dividends. By contrast, low stock prices make it more likely that businesses will obtain funds from the public by selling bonds (debt financing, in which the principal is repaid and there are specified interest payments). Stock prices also affect household wealth and in turn, future consumer spending. Stockholders perceive they have more money to spend when stock prices (and thus their wealth) are rising than when they are falling. However, stock market prices also reflect speculation, insider trading, and program trading, which are not associated with underlying economic factors.

10. *Money supply (M–2), in constant dollars* (see Chapter 7). The amount of financial liquid assets reflects the purchasing power available for business and household transactions such as buying materials, hiring labor, investing in plant

and equipment, and buying consumer goods. M–2 is used rather than M–1 because M–2 includes money market instruments that are quite liquid; it thus provides a broader measure of funds available for economic transactions.

11. *Consumer expectations, index* (see Chapter 3). Consumer attitudes on the outlook for the economy and their own financial well-being give clues to future household spending. In a sense, expectations are self-fulfilling.

In assessing monthly changes in the composite indexes, the analyst should consider whether the movements represent a broad-based pattern of most of the indicators, or if they result from relatively large movements of a small number of the component indicators.

The *coincident* index measures various aspects of production that reflect the current level of economic activity. It indicates whether the economy is growing or declining, and thus is the primary quantitative gauge of expansion and recession periods. The four components of the coincident index are:

1. *Employees on nonagricultural payrolls* (see Chapter 5). This measures the labor component in the current production of goods and services.

2. *Personal income less transfer payments, in constant dollars* (see Chapter 3). Real income earned by labor and investors reflects the resources used in producing the nation's output.

3. *Industrial production index* (see Chapter 4). Because manufacturing, mining, and gas and electric utilities tend to be the more cyclically volatile industries, current production levels in these industries are a good indicator of the cyclical elements in the economy.

4. *Manufacturing and trade sales, in constant dollars.* Movement of goods within the economy between manufacturing plants, from manufacturers to wholesalers, from wholesalers to retailers, and from retailers to consumers indicates the flows of goods in production and from production to distribution.

The *lagging* index reflects production costs and inventory and debt burdens that may encourage or retard economic growth. A slow increase or a decline in the lagging index is conducive to economic growth, while a rapid increase in the lagging index is conducive to a recession. The seven components of the lagging index are:

1. *Average duration of unemployment, weeks.* Persons unemployed for long periods, such as displaced workers who lost their jobs because of plant closings or young people with limited education and training, are assumed to have less marketable skills than those unemployed for short periods. Recruiting and training costs are therefore higher if there are large numbers of long-term unemployed persons.

2. *Inventory-to-sales ratio for manufacturing and trade, in constant dollars* (see Chapter 3). Inventories are a major cost factor for businesses, and the higher they are relative to sales, the more expensive they are to hold—either because

they represent borrowed money which results in interest costs, or because they tie up company funds.

3. *Labor cost per unit of output in manufacturing, monthly change* (see Chapter 5). Labor costs in relation to production affect profits, which in turn affect decisions to expand or contract production and employment.

4. *Commercial and industrial loans outstanding, in constant dollars.* Interest burden on existing loans is higher and the availability of money for new loans is lessened the greater the level of outstanding loans.

5. *Ratio of consumer installment credit outstanding to personal income* (see Chapter 3). The debt burden of consumers suggests they are likely to take on more loans for further spending when the ratio is low, and pay off existing loans when the ratio is high, thus contracting spending.

6. *Average prime rate charged by banks.* Interest rates charged for business loans indicate the cost of borrowing, which affects profits and the willingness to borrow.

7. *Consumer price index for services, monthly change* (see Chapter 6). Prices of services reflect price pressures stemming from production costs in labor-intensive industries.

LIMITATION FOR FORECASTING

The LCLg system provides a striking example of how revisions to preliminary data affect analyses of the state of the economy (see Chapter 1 for a general discussion of data revisions). The analyses in Part B of this chapter are based on revised data. They indicate that the LCLg system provides early signals of a cyclical downturn well before the onset of most recessions and of a cyclical upturn that is observable in about half of all recoveries. However, as noted by Evan Koenig and Kenneth Emery, the contemporaneous preliminary data which are available to analysts during the critical months preceding recessions and recoveries do not always provide such early indications of cyclical turning points.[5]

Table 28 compares the contemporaneous preliminary data of the leading index to the revised data (as currently published) of the leading index for the months preceding recessions and recoveries from 1969 to 1991. (The U.S. Department of Commerce first published data on the LCLg system in 1968, initially by the Bureau of the Census and since 1972 by the Bureau of Economic Analysis.) The preliminary data measures in the table were derived by the author from previously published data. Specifically, the preliminary measures are based on taking the data series as they existed on the eve of the peak of each expansion and the eve of the trough of each recession (the leading index data are first available one month after the reference month). For example, data for July 1990, which is the peak of the expansion preceding the recession that began in August 1990, first became available at the end of August. In reviewing these data, which where available at the end of August, the author determined that the leading

Table 28

Leading Index: Advance Indication of Cyclical Turning Points (months)

	Contemporaneous preliminary data[a]	Revised data[b]
Peak expansion month on the eve of recession		
December 1969	3	8
November 1973	0	8
January 1980	10	15
July 1981	3	2
July 1990	0	0[c]
Trough recession month on the eve of recovery		
November 1970	1	1
March 1975	0	1
July 1980	2	2
November 1982	8	10
1991?[d]	NA	NA

Source: Bureau of Economic Analysis.
[a]Measures derived by the author. See text.
[b]Published in the *Survey of Current Business*.
[c]Subject to further revision.
[d]The recession of 1990–91 was in progress when this manuscript was completed.
NA. Not available as of the spring of 1991.

index was level for the preceding eighteen months with no discernible rising or declining trend. Of the five recessions, the preliminary data gave no advance indication of a downturn in two cases, only three months' notice in two cases, and eight months notice in one case. In contrast, the revised data, which became available in subsequent years, showed strong early indications of a downturn in three of the five cases. BEA has adopted July 1990 as the peak of the expansion preceding the recession of 1990–91, but following its long-standing policy, it will first add recession shading to its charts for this recession only after the National Bureau of Economic Research determines that the recession is over (as of spring 1991, no such determination has been made); the NBER is the arbiter for designating cyclical turning points, as noted in Chapter 2. There was little difference between the preliminary and revised data in regard to advance indication of recovery.

The revised data are superior because the structure of the three composite indexes in general and the leading index in particular is revamped at ten- to fifteen-year intervals to take into account changes in the economy and to incorporate better-performing component series. Two types of changes are usually made: (a) the composition of the indexes is changed to replace some data components with new or modified ones, and (b) new formulations of the statistical factors such as weights and trend factors are used. In addition to these infrequent structural changes, monthly data are continually revised on a current basis as part of the routine preparation of revised economic data series. Revised LCLg data are important for developing historical analytic relationships, but they obviously do not ensure that the subsequent contemporaneous preliminary data will give observable advance signals of cyclical turning points. Thus, because the economy is continually changing and every business cycle is different, indicators selected on the basis of their performance in past cycles do not always provide the same level of performance in future cycles. For example, in 1989 BEA changed the composition of the leading index to one that would have provided an earlier warning of the 1980 recession than did the leading index that was in fact in use on the eve of the 1980 recession; and the revised composition of the leading index instituted in 1976 showed an early warning of the recession starting at the end of 1973 that was not at all apparent in the leading index which was in use on the eve of that recession.

The lack of advance indications of cyclical turning points in the preliminary data significantly limits use of the LCLg system for economic forecasting, although as noted by Koenig and Emery, it may be the best available early warning system. *Consequently, the analyst should include assessments of rates of change in the composite indexes in addition to their changes in direction for clues of future cyclical turning points.*

PART A: ESTIMATING METHODOLOGY

The LCLg composite indexes are developed by combining the component data series into three overall indexes. The three indexes for each new month are calculated based on the monthly movements of the components. The general concept is similar to that used for the index numbers on industrial production (Chapter 4) and consumer prices (Chapter 6), although the procedures have some differences. In the current version of the indexes, equal weights are assigned to all components because research indicated that differential weights used in previous versions did not materially affect movements of the composite indexes.[6] Thus, in calculating the composite indexes, all components within each composite have the same importance. Comprehensive evaluations and revisions of the LCLg system are conducted every ten to fifteen years.

Table 29 shows the components of the composite indexes. Many economic indicators are evaluated to determine their appropriateness for inclusion in the composite indexes.[7] The overall considerations in selecting them are: (a) their theoretical role in the leading, coincident, and lagging process, and (b) how they perform empirically in terms of leading and lagging general business cycles over

Table 29

Components of the Composite Indexes

Leading Index:
1. Average weekly hours of manufacturing production workers
2. Average weekly initial claims for unemployment insurance, state programs
3. Manufacturers' new orders for consumer goods and materials, in constant dollars
4. Vendor performance (percentage of companies receiving slower deliveries)
5. Contracts and orders for plant and equipment, in constant dollars
6. New private-housing building permits, index
7. Manufacturers' unfilled orders in durable goods industries, monthly change
8. Prices of crude and intermediate materials, monthly change
9. Prices of 500 common stocks, index
10. Money supply (M–2), in constant dollars
11. Consumer expectations, index

Coincident Index:
1. Employees on nonagricultural payrolls
2. Personal income less transfer payments, in constant dollars
3. Industrial production index
4. Manufacturing and trade sales, in constant dollars

Lagging Index:
1. Average duration of unemployment, weeks
2. Inventory-to-sales ratio for manufacturing and trade, in constant dollars
3. Labor cost per unit of output in manufacturing
4. Commercial and industrial loans outstanding, in constant dollars
5. Ratio of consumer installment credit outstanding to personal income
6. Average prime rate charged by banks
7. Consumer price index for services, monthly change

Note: Each component is weighted equally.

the post–World War II period. The specific criteria used are economic significance (theoretical importance); statistical adequacy (quality of the underlying survey and other statistical data from which they are calculated); timing (consistency in leading, coinciding, or lagging general business cycles); conformity to business cycle directional movements (upward in expansions and downward in recessions); smoothness (extent of erratic increases and decreases that obscure cyclical movements); and currency (promptness of the availability of current data; they must be monthly, not quarterly, series—in time for preparing the monthly indexes). Numerical scores for each of these categories determine whether they qualify for inclusion in the composite indexes.

The component data series selected for use are then combined into the three composite indexes. Statistical adjustments are made so that the long-run trends of the indexes (over several cycles abstracting from the cyclical movements) will be similar; this ensures that the monthly percent changes in the three indexes are comparable for cyclical comparisons because they are not affected by differential long-run trends. The trend in the real gross national product is used for this purpose since it reflects overall economic activity. Additional modifications are made to ensure that components with relatively large upward and downward movements do not dominate the index. This result is achieved by dividing each component's monthly change by the long-term average monthly change without regard to sign.

Inversion of Unemployment Indicators

Statistical data that are plotted on charts typically are depicted as rising when the line moves upward and as declining when the line moves downward. These upward and downward movements conform to the directional movements of the upward (expansion) and downward (recession) phases of the business cycle. However, in two indicators of the LCLg system—initial claims for unemployment insurance (leading index) and average duration of unemployment (lagging index)—this movement is reversed. For these two, for example, a decline indicates a rise in or stimulus to economic activity. They thus conform to the business cycle phases in the reverse direction. For these two indicators, the scales on the charts' vertical axes are inverted so that, graphically, an increase is shown as declining and a decrease is shown as rising. This makes their directional movements visually consistent with general business cycle movements. These two unemployment components are also inverted when used to calculate the monthly movements of the leading and lagging composite indexes, so that the unemployment figures do not distort the indexes' movements; if they were not inverted, they would offset part of the cyclical movement of the other components.

PART B: ANALYSIS OF TRENDS

The behavior of the three composite indexes over the general business cycle in the expansions and recessions since World War II is summarized below. Their behavior is consistent with their theoretical role discussed earlier—the leading index turns down in a recession and up in a recovery before these movements occur in the general business cycle; the direction and timing of the coincident index are close to those of the general economy (Figure 57 shows that since the 1970s, the turning points of the coincident index were identical to those in the overall economy with only minor exceptions); and cyclical turns in the lagging index occur after those in the general economy.

The tabulation below excludes the recession beginning in July 1990, which was in progress as of April 1991. It is excluded because the Bureau of Economic Analysis will first provide estimates of when the leading index turned down before the onset of the recession after the recession ends. However, based on the data available in 1990, the leading index had been level for six quarters before the recession began and first showed a downward trend beginning in August

Figure 57. **Leading, Coincident, and Lagging Composite Indexes: 1948–90**

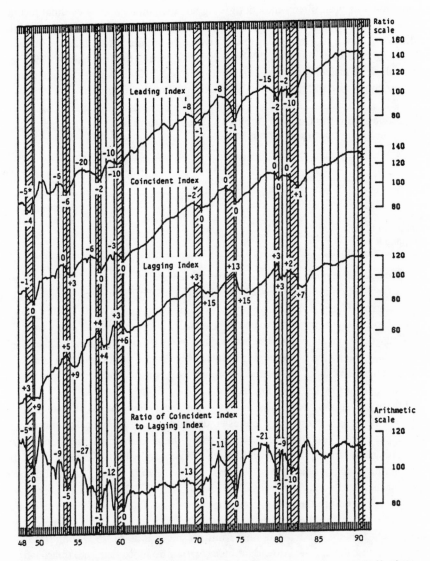

Note: Based on Bureau of Economic Analysis data. Lined bars are recession periods. Numbers are monthly leads (–) and lags (+) from cyclical turning points.

*Not necessarily the peak but is the high for the available data.

1990. The contemporary data did not give advance notice of the coming of the recession, although they showed a clear slowdown in the growth rate over the previous 1½ years. This is a continuation of the general problem with the contemporaneous preliminary data not giving advance indication of cyclical turning points (see above section Limitation for Forecasting). In addition, the ratio of the coincident index to the lagging index (which is an alternative leading index as discussed below) declined in 1989 but then rose during the first half of 1990, and only showed a declining trend beginning in July 1990. Thus, this alternative leading index also did not give an advance signal of the recession.

Difference from the General Business Cycle in Months
(average for the postwar business cycles)

	(– lead; + lag)	
	Peaks	Troughs
Leading Index	–9	–5
Coincident Index	–2	+1
Lagging Index	+5	+9

Because the lagging index is last in the sequence of cyclical movements, it plays a role (in addition to its conceptual one of costs) in confirming that a cyclical turn has occurred. Generally, the lagging index turns down about two quarters after a general recession begins and turns up three quarters after a general recovery from the previous recession, although these time lags have not been systematically quantified. The actual designation of the turning points of the general business cycle is made by the National Bureau of Economic Research, and is based on the movements of several indicators as discussed in Chapter 2.

Figure 57 shows that leads and lags for individual cycles do not always parallel the long-term average patterns above. Using differences of more than one quarter (i.e., four months or more) from these averages as a guideline for determining relatively high variations, the most noticeable deviations from the long-term averages occurred as follows: in the leading index, at the business cycle peaks before the recessions of 1953–54, 1957–58, 1980, and 1981–82, and at the troughs before the upturn from the recessions of 1960, 1969–70, 1974–75, and 1981–82; and in the lagging index at the peak before the 1974–75 recession, and at the troughs after the upturn from the recessions of 1957–58, 1969–70, 1974–75, and 1980. The coincident index varied by more than one quarter from the long-term average only at the peak before the 1957–58 recession.

Variations of more than one quarter do not dominate the LCLg system. However, they occur often enough to make it difficult to portray the current phase of any cycle as having average lead and lag characteristics. *The analyst should keep this limitation in mind when using the system as a clue to future economic trends.*

Coincident/Lagging Ratio

The coincident index divided by the lagging index is considered by some as an additional leading indicator.[8] Theoretically, this ratio is significant because it relates production to costs, providing in effect a view of profits—the underlying concept of the LCLg system. For example, if the coincident index (production) increases or decreases at the same rate as the lagging index (costs), there is no change in the profit picture, thus signifying continued economic growth at the current rate. However, differential movements in the two indexes suggest other tendencies in the economy. If the coincident index increases at a faster rate or decreases at a slower rate than the lagging index, this indicates an increase in profits (since revenues are rising faster than costs) and higher economic growth in the future; but if the coincident index increases at a slower rate or decreases at a faster rate, a decline in profits and lower future economic growth are indicated. Algebraically, it appears as follows:

$$\frac{\text{Coincident}}{\text{Lagging}} = \frac{\text{Production}}{\text{Costs}} = \text{Profit rate}$$

Over the postwar business cycles, on average the coincident/lagging ratio led the general recessions at the expansion peaks by thirteen months and led the general recoveries at the recession troughs by two months. As indicated below, these leads exceed those of the leading index by four months at peaks, but they are shorter than the leading index by three months at the troughs. Thus, during expansions the coincident/lagging ratio tends to give an earlier signal than the leading index of an impending recession, while the leading index gives an earlier signal during recessions of the subsequent recovery. In the latter stages of expansions, the lagging index typically increases rapidly while the increase in the coincident index slows down, causing the coincident/lagging ratio to decline. This indicates a squeeze on profits (costs rising faster than revenues) and signals lower economic growth in the future. By contrast, during recessions the lagging index declines proportionately more than the coincident index, indicating that costs have been reduced relative to revenues and thus suggesting a future upturn in profits.

Difference from the General Business Cycle in Months
(average for the postwar business cycles)

	(− lead; + lag)	
	Peaks	Troughs
Coincident/Lagging Ratio	−13	−2
Leading Index	−9	−5
Difference	−4	+3

Figure 57 shows that the coincident/lagging ratio differs from the leading index in the long-run trend as well as from cycle to cycle. While the leading index over the long run has a rising trend, the coincident/lagging ratio is generally level because the upward trend in both components cancels out in dividing through to obtain the ratio:

$$\frac{\text{Coincident (upward trend)}}{\text{Lagging (upward trend)}} = \text{Coincident/Lagging ratio}$$

This partially accounts for the longer lead before expansion peaks of the coincident/lagging ratio compared with the leading index. Experimental data have indicated that if a long-term upward trend were added to the coincident/lagging ratio, its lead time would be closer to that of the leading index. However, this technique needs more work before it can be used in the official methodology. The coincident/lagging ratio shows significantly different patterns from decade to decade—it declined in the 1950s, was steady in the 1960s, and rose in the 1970s and 1980s back to the 1950s level. These differential movements in the coincident/lagging ratio over the long run may reflect structural changes in the economy, but they are difficult to explain.

As in the case of the leading index, the coincident/lagging ratio shows noticeable variations in the pattern of lead times for individual cycles compared with the average lead time for all cycles; this limits applying average relationships to the current phase in any cycle. Using the criterion of variations of more than one quarter from the long-term average noted above, relatively large variations occurred at the peaks before the 1948–49, 1953–54, 1957–58, 1980, and 1981–82 recessions and at the trough before the recovery from the 1981–82 recession.

An advantage of using the coincident/lagging ratio to predict economic movements is that it is based on different data and a different concept from those in the leading index. The independent data base provides a consistency check on the leading index. In addition, the coincident/lagging ratio suggests a concept of equilibrium between sales and costs in which the economy is considered to be relatively well balanced with no significant excesses or deficiencies in production, incomes, costs and prices. Yet, this state may never be reached in practice, as adjustments are made continually to production, prices, wages, and interest— all aimed at increasing profits.[9] Despite these continually changing relationships, one tendency that may be observed from historical behavior of the coincident/lagging ratio is that the economy is more balanced when the ratio is unchanged at a relatively high level during the expansion period, suggesting that further expansion is likely.[10]

Cyclical patterns of the coincident/lagging ratio vary sharply from the long-term average and from the timing of the leading index. *In periods when such divergences are marked, the analyst should consider other economic tendencies as being dominant—for example, a downturn in the coincident/lagging ratio that is accompanied by a rising leading index suggests a slowdown in economic growth rather than an impending recession, as during 1985–86.*

False Signals

The economy moves unevenly in both expansions and recessions, slowing down and speeding up as well as declining for short spells in expansions and rising for short spells in recessions. Because of these variations, it is often difficult in the current period to determine if a changing rate of growth or a reversal of direction signifies a fundamental change or a temporary counter-movement from which the previous trend will reappear. Temporary reversals of direction in the LCLg system—reversals, that is, suggesting a cyclical change that didn't follow—are known as "false signals." For example, the leading index declined temporarily in 1951, 1966, and 1984. Those downturns could have suggested pending recessions, but the movements were subsequently reversed. Slowdown in economic growth as measured by the coincident index did follow these downturns, but the changes were limited and did not turn into a recession. Therefore, these downturns were false signals.

False signals bring into focus the limitations of the LCLg system as a forecasting tool. The system suggests changes in the direction and pace of economic activity that will occur. As noted by Julius Shiskin, it also gives additional information for analyzing the economy's strengths and weaknesses.[11] But it does not specifically forecast cyclical turning points or growth rates. *In using the LCLg system, the analyst should recognize that it can only give clues as to future economic movements both for cyclical turning points and for economic growth rates. Because lead times for turning points vary from cycle to cycle, a mechanical application of the average lead times for all cycles is likely to be misleading.*

Probability of Future Recessions: Experimental Indexes

The LCLg system does not forecast when turning points in the business cycle will occur, as noted above. Rather, a committee of economists under the auspices of the National Bureau of Economic Research designates when a recession has begun or ended (see Chapter 2). In 1989, however, James Stock and Mark Watson developed on an experimental basis a recession index that predicts the likelihood of a recession in the future.[12] Their measures are published monthly in a press release by the NBER, although their forecasts do not necessarily represent the views of other researchers or of the officers of the NBER.

Stock and Watson's recession index is based on establishing a leading index and a coincident index that are rigorously linked to each other in terms of their historical relationship. The rationale behind their system is that a coincident index that represents actual economic activity should be a reasonable predictor of the state of the economy at a future date. Using the historical experience of the indicators, they constructed a leading and a coincident index so that the leading index typically leads the coincident index by six months. Using these indexes, Stock and Watson are able to make statements such as, "The probability that the economy will be in a recession six months from now is X percent."

The coincident index in the experimental indexes has the same four components as the coincident index in the LCLg system except that the experimental index uses "employee-hours" in place of "employees" in nonagricultural industries.

The component indicators of the experimental leading index differ substantially from the LCLg system. The LCLg system leading index has eleven components of which two are financial, while the experimental leading index has seven components of which three are financial. The experimental index excludes several nonfinancial components that are in the LCLg leading index. In contrast, the experimental index has one more financial component and thus a much greater proportionate representation of financial variables. The experimental index also includes an international item and employment related to slack work, neither of which are in the LCLg system. The component items of the experimental leading index are:

1. Building permits for new private housing;
2. Manufacturers' unfilled orders for durable goods industries, in constant dollars;
3. Trade-weighted index of nominal exchange rates between the United States and the United Kingdom, West Germany, France, Italy, and Japan;
4. Part-time workers in nonagricultural industries because of slack work;
5. Ten-year Treasury bond interest rate (constant maturity);
6. Interest rate spread between six-month commercial paper and six-month Treasury bills;
7. Yield curve difference between ten-year Treasury bonds and one-year Treasury bonds (constant maturity).

The experimental recession index is constructed by using the seven indicators of the leading index to develop a range of forecasts of overall economic conditions over the next twelve months based on statistical regression techniques. Each forecast is assessed for whether it will likely be classified in a recessionary or expansionary period, technically using the tools of statistical pattern recognition (this is a way of estimating the probability that a given data set matches or is in a class of prespecified patterns based on earlier recession and expansion periods).

An alternative recession index (which is derived from an unpublished alternative leading index) is based on forecasts of seven *nonfinancial* leading indicators. Three of these are the same as those in the published experimental leading index: housing building permits, manufacturers' unfilled orders, and foreign exchange rates. The other four indicators are a help-wanted index (which is a substitute for the slack-work indicator), average weekly hours in manufacturing, vendor performance (percentage of companies receiving slow deliveries), and capacity utilization in manufacturing.

The recession indexes did not well predict the recession that began in 1990. For example, as late as September 1990 (based on August data), the recession index for all components indicated a 3 percent probability that the economy would be in a recession in February 1991, while the probability for the index excluding financial variables was still only 24 percent. And in December 1990 (based on November data), the probability of a recession in May 1991 for all components was 14 percent and excluding financial variables was 53 percent.

The low probability of both recession indexes mirrors the previously noted failure of the LCLg system to provide advance indication of the onset of the 1990 recession in the LCLg system. This experience with the recession indexes may also be related to the general problem with contemporaneous preliminary data for the LCLg system (see above section, Limitation for Forecasting). The higher probability of a recession in the recession index excluding financial variables reflects the fact that monetary policy preceding the recession generally was neutral rather than restrictive. For example, the federal funds rate on interbank loans, which is a good indicator of Federal Reserve monetary policies, declined during the last half of 1989 and was level during the first half of 1990 (the federal funds rate is discussed in Chapter 7). Mark Watson notes that financial variables in the recession index were modestly optimistic.[13] This differs from the tight monetary policies that typically occurred before previous recessions, and which in statistical analyses of previous time periods retrospectively led to the recession index that includes financial variables performing better than the nonfinancial recession index. However, despite this reversal in the performance of the two recession indexes, even the nonfinancial index did not perform well in predicting the 1990–91 recession or in identifying the recession after it began.

Overall, the experimental indexes are a promising development in the field of leading indicators, but they need more research to improve their forecasting capability. This research should particularly focus on the forecasting power of the experimental indexes using contemporaneous preliminary data.

SUMMARY

The leading, coincident, and lagging indexes provide clues to business cycle turning points and the future course of economic growth. The indexes are based on the theories that profits are the primary force driving the economy and that each phase of the business cycle contains the seeds of the next phase.

The leading index reflects businesses' expectations, plans, and actions for economic developments. During the expansion phase of the business cycle, the leading index turns down before the general economy declines into a recession, and during the recession phase it turns up before the general economy moves into a recovery. The coincident index measures current economic activity and moves in tandem with the cyclical turning points of the general economy. The lagging index represents business costs; it turns down after the general economy moves from expansion into recession, and it turns up after a general recovery from a recession begins.

A fourth measure, the ratio of the coincident index to the lagging index, relates trends in production (coincident index) to costs (lagging index). As a general indicator of profits, which determines business decisions to expand or contract production, employment, and investment, the movements of this ratio also lead the general business cycle at cyclical turning points.

The LCLg system suggests future changes in economic activity. It provides information for assessing the strengths and weaknesses of the economy. But it does not specifically forecast economic growth rates and cyclical turning points. Current analyses also must allow for the possibility that some changes in direction of the leading index are reversed before an actual cyclical turn occurs and thus give a false signal. Statistically, the preliminary contemporaneous data that are available during the current period when the system is used for forecasting do not indicate advance signals of cyclical turning points nearly as well as revised data that become available in later years. When applying the long-term average relationships of the system to the analysis of a particular time period, it is important to recognize that each business cycle has unique characteristics. The special factors in the period under analysis that may cause its movements to diverge from the long-term averages must be taken into account.

The new experimental recession indexes, which indicate the probability that a recession will occur six months in the future, are a promising area for further research.

REVIEW QUESTIONS

• The LCLg system is based on two main ideas: (1) the current phase of the business cycle contains the seeds of the next phase, and (2) profits are the prime mover of the economy. Describe the role of profits as the economy moves from expansion to recession to recovery to expansion.

• How do data revisions affect the usefulness of the LCLg system?

• What is the conceptual difference between the leading index and the ratio of the coincident index to the lagging index ?

• In reporting on the leading index, newspaper articles sometimes state that a decline in the index for three consecutive months signals a coming recession. What is wrong with this interpretation?

• During an expansion, assume that for several months the leading index turns down but the coincident/lagging ratio continues to rise. What does this suggest for future economic activity?

• The lead time of the leading index before a recession differs from the lead time before a recovery. Which of the following best represents the average lead periods?

Before recession:	Before recovery:
_____ 5 months	_____ 2 months
_____ 10 months	_____ 5 months
_____ 15 months	_____ 10 months

• What causes false signals in the LCLg system?
• What do the experimental recession indexes contribute to the LCLg system?

NOTES

1. This history is recounted in Geoffrey H. Moore, *Business Cycles, Inflation, and Forecasting*, 2d ed. (Ballinger: 1983), Chapter 24. There are three milestone publications: Wesley C. Mitchell and Arthur F. Burns, *Statistical Indicators of Cyclical Revivals*, Bulletin 69 (National Bureau of Economic Research: 1938), which was reprinted in Geoffrey H. Moore, ed., *Business Cycle Indicators* (National Bureau of Economic Research: 1961); Geoffrey H. Moore, *Statistical Indicators of Cyclical Revivals and Recessions*, Occasional Paper 31 (National Bureau of Economic Research: 1950); and Julius Shiskin, *Signals of Recession and Recovery*, Occasional Paper 77 (National Bureau of Economic Research: 1961).

2. Tjalling C. Koopmans, "Measurement without Theory," *Review of Economics and Statistics,* August 1947.

3. Wesley C. Mitchell, *Business Cycles: The Problem and Its Setting* (National Bureau of Economic Research: 1927), pp. 105–7.

4. The itemization draws heavily on Feliks Tamm, "An Introduction to the System of Coincident, Leading and Lagging Indexes," Bureau of Economic Analysis, U.S. Department of Commerce, October 1984 (unpublished), pp. 2–11.

5. Evan F. Koenig and Kenneth M. Emery, "Misleading Indicators? Using the Composite Leading Indicators to Predict Cyclical Turning Points," *Economic Review*, Federal Reserve Bank of Dallas, July 1991.

6. Marie P. Hertzberg and Barry A. Beckman, "Business Cycle Indicators: Revised Composite Indexes," *Survey of Current Business,* January 1989.

7. These are detailed in two articles by Victor Zarnowitz and Charlotte Boschan: "Cyclical Indicators: An Evaluation and New Leading Indexes," *Business Conditions Digest*, May 1975, and "New Composite Indexes of Coincident and Lagging Indicators," *Business Conditions Digest*, November 1975. An elaboration of how the monthly indexes are calculated is in Bureau of Economic Analysis, *Handbook of Cyclical Indicators: A Supplement to the Business Conditions Digest*, 1984, pp. 65–70.

8. See Geoffrey H. Moore, "Generating Leading Indicators from Lagging Indicators," *Western Economic Journal*, June 1969, for the initial formulation of the coincident/ lagging ratio. It also is discussed in Zarnowitz and Boschan, "New Composite Indexes," and Tamm, "An Introduction to the System of Coincident, Leading and Lagging Indexes."

9. Mitchell, *Business Cycles*, pp. 186–88.

10. Tamm, "An Introduction to the System of Coincident, Leading and Lagging Indexes," p. 12.

11. Discussion by Julius Shiskin on the paper by Saul H. Hymans, "On the Use of Leading Indicators to Predict Cyclical Turning Points," *Brookings Papers on Economic Activity*, 2:1973, pp. 378–79.

12. James H. Stock and Mark W. Watson, "New Indexes of Coincident and Leading Economic Indicators," *NBER Macroeconomics Annual*, vol. 4 (The MIT Press: 1989).

13. Mark W. Watson, "Using Econometric Models to Predict Recessions," *Economic Perspectives,* Federal Reserve Bank of Chicago, November/December 1991.

9
GENERAL PROPERTIES OF
ECONOMIC FORECASTING

The economic indicators discussed in this book are statistical measures of the past. As extrapolations from these historical indicators, macroeconomic forecasts may be viewed as another kind of economic indicator. Forecasts of economic growth, unemployment, inflation, interest rates, and other economic indicators are developed by government and private organizations and disseminated in summary form through the news media. Organizations that prepare such forecasts for public dissemination include Data Resources, Inc. (DRI), Wharton Econometric Forecasting Associates (WEFA), Blue Chip Economic Indicators, the Federal Reserve Bank of Philadelphia, university-affiliated research groups (such as those at Georgia State, Michigan, and UCLA), the Congressional Budget Office, and the U.S. Council of Economic Advisers.

Because perceptions of the future have an important effect on spending, investment, and saving decisions, forecasts about the future of the economy provoke widespread interest. Households, businesses, and governments rely on these forecasts in making a variety of economic decisions. Thus, forecasts not only predict the economic future, they also may influence that future. For example, forecasts of future interest rates may affect a prospective home owner's decision to buy, or a business owner's decision about whether to invest in new equipment or change the level of inventories. Economic forecasts also affect how the president and Congress budget and appropriate funds for federal programs and establish federal tax laws for stabilizing economic fluctuations; how the Federal Reserve conducts monetary policy; and how state and local governments determine whether and when to sell bonds for building schools, sewer treatment plants, or other capital facilities.

In controversies over public policies, economic forecasts spotlight the uncertainty of the future. Various forecasts provide divergent views of trends in the pace of economic growth and inflation, and these differences sharpen public debate on the likely outcome of private and public actions. Effective forecasts take into account the effect of current actions, such as current fiscal and monetary policies, on the future economy. Forecasts should help lead us to a better selection of goals and methods to improve economic well-being.

There are two kinds of economic forecasts: informal predictions based on personal experience and formal analyses derived from statistical research. Perceptions of householders and business owners about the overall economy and their own economic prospects constitute the informal type of economic forecast. Informal forecasts are likely to reflect knowledge gained from the news media as well as personal experience. Frequently, therefore, these forecasts implicitly incorporate elements of the formal macroeconomic forecasting which is the subject of this chapter.

In economic as in political or weather forecasting, many scenarios are possible. The challenge in making any forecast is to recognize the range of these possibilities and determine which is most probable. Alternatively a forecast may seek to assess the likely effects of a given set of forecasting assumptions (often referred to as "What if" forecasting). For example, what would be the effect on the gross national product growth rate if the labor force remains stable over the forecast period? This chapter focuses on how such formal economic forecasts are developed and used in order to help the analyst make such forecasting judgments as well as to evaluate others' forecasts.

FORECASTING METHODOLOGY:
HISTORICAL ANALYSIS AND FUTURE ASSUMPTIONS

Quite simply, a macroeconomic forecast uses past and current economic data to determine economic relationships and in turn uses these relationships to predict the future state of the economy. In interpreting the current data, a forecaster may utilize econometric models, analyses of past trends, or mechanical extrapolations of past trends. A forecast based on an econometric model uses sophisticated mathematical and statistical techniques in a system of equations to integrate the theoretical and empirical interrelationships among such economic variables as employment, inflation, interest rates, and the value of the dollar. The model builder exercises judgment in specifying which variables are included in the model and the mathematical form of the equations. The forecaster also exercises judgment in modifying the forecasts generated by the model. These adjustments reflect assessments of current economic trends and anticipated future developments that are too subtle to be incorporated in the structural equations of the model.

A forecast based on analyses of past trends extrapolates from the statistical experience of selected components of the economy to predict the likely future direction and pace of observed trends. Like economic modeling, these extrapolations incorporate the forecaster's judgment, the statistical relationships observed in past behavior of the components, and current data like surveys of anticipated spending by households and businesses or prognostications of government budgets.

Mechanical forecasts extrapolate from the past trends of given variables to predict future developments. This forecasting technique is referred to as "autoregressive" because future rates of growth are projected only by patterns of the variable's past growth rates. For example, the future growth rate of real GNP is determined solely by past growth rates of real GNP. Mathematical equations used in developing these autoregressive forecasts include the Box–Jenkins and autoregressive integrated moving average (ARIMA) methodologies. Autoregressive forecasts predict cyclical turning points as well as rates of growth. However, as in all forecasts, the identification of cyclical turning points is limited to short-term predictions. (This limit is discussed in more detail below.) Autoregressive forecasts incorporate the forecaster's judgment primarily in specifying the mathematical structure of time lags in the forecasting equation, although the use of autoregressive methodology itself reflects the forecaster's judgment that an indicator's past behavior is the best predictor of its future movements. Contrary to the practice with econometric modeling, however, forecasters using autoregressive methodology typically accept the forecast yielded by the equation rather than modifying the forecast based on subjective judgments about more likely outcomes. There is no intrinsic reason for this tendency of autoregressive forecasters not to modify their forecasts, however.

Assumptions about fiscal and monetary policies, technology, and institutions are key to making a forecast. All forecasts—econometric models, analyses of trends, and mechanical extrapolations—explicitly or implicitly include such assumptions and try to capture the interactions among them. These economic, scientific, and political elements form the regime under which the economy operates. A sharp departure from past patterns can significantly affect historical relationships of income, spending, productivity, unemployment, inflation, business cycles, and economic growth. Forecasts that make different assumptions about the economic regime can vary substantially. For example, a significant change in the federal deficit or Federal Reserve monetary policies can alter the outlook for unemployment and inflation. Further examples abound: technological breakthroughs such as electric cars or superconductors, or more widespread adoption of existing technology, such as solar energy or robots, can create major new product markets; a shift in labor–management relations from wage givebacks to wage takebacks may affect the morale and consequently the productivity of workers; the large corporate debt resulting from junk bond financing of company takeovers may inhibit additional plant and equipment investment and make more companies vulnerable to bankruptcy during a recession; the tendency for transnational companies to conduct more research and development abroad may lower U.S. international competitiveness; an accelerated trend toward global warming may limit the production of certain items or change the method of producing them; and the demise of the Soviet Union may shift federal spending from defense to social programs to address homelessness, schooling, and the environment, with consequent effects on productivity, health, and crime.

SHORT-TERM AND LONG-TERM FORECASTS

The distinctions among short-term, medium-term, and long-term forecasts are not precise. Moreover, terminology varies with the user. One extreme is seen in the preoccupation of some participants in financial markets with how the stock and bond markets are likely to respond to late-breaking news within the next few days; such a focus implicitly defines any period longer than a few days as long-term.

Generally, however, short-term forecasts refer to economic projections for periods of up to two years which typically chart movements on a quarterly or semiannual basis (less frequently, movements are charted monthly). Some short-term forecasts are prepared for as long as four years ahead, but they emphasize the first two years. Short-term forecasts center on the cyclical dimensions of the economy and highlight changes in the rates of economic growth, employment, and inflation as well as identify the cyclical turning points from expansion to recession to recovery. These forecasts typically assume a continuation of the economic, scientific, and political regime of the recent past, except for expected changes in fiscal and monetary policies. The short time frame under consideration limits the extent to which basic changes in economic arrangements, technology, and political factors may be expected to affect the mainstream of economic life.

Medium-term forecasts are associated with a three- to five-year horizon and chart changes on an annual basis. There is some overlap between medium-term forecasts and the latter part of short-term forecasts that extend four years into the future, although, as noted above, quarterly or semi-annual movements of short-term forecasts usually are not developed beyond the first two years. Medium-term forecasts incorporate more change in the economic, technical, and political regime than do short-term forecasts. The five-year federal budget deficit reduction plan of 1990 is an example of a medium-term forecast (see Chapter 3 under Government Spending and Finances).

Long-term forecasts refer to projections extending more than five years. They typically predict the state of the economy year-by-year, although very long forecasts of twenty or more years may use averages of five- or ten-year periods. Over such long periods, fundamental changes can occur in the underlying regime of economic arrangements, technology, and political factors. Thus, long-term forecasts provide a framework for evaluating and planning for developments that require long lead times such as the impact of demographic and industrial changes on education, job training, housing, transportation, and other public infrastructure. Like medium-term forecasts, long-term forecasts do not include cyclical turning points from expansion to recession to recovery because relationships of such short-term volatility are too complex to trace far into the future. Consequently, long-term forecasts do not predict recessions, although they do project varying rates of growth over the forecast period.

FORECASTING ACCURACY

Evaluating the accuracy of macroeconomic forecasts is an economic discipline in its own right. The recognized authority in this area is Stephen McNees. In an analysis of forecasts over the 1976–87 period (which also includes reference to 1974), he finds that forecasting errors tend to increase as the time horizon of the forecast lengthens.[1] For example, as the forecast period extends from one quarter to eight quarters ahead, forecasts become less accurate for employment, unemployment, consumer prices, housing starts, interest rates, and the federal budget deficit. This general tendency has some exceptions, however. Forecast error declines over the eight quarters for projections of the GNP in current and constant dollars as well as of several GNP components. Based on the range of different forecasters' projections over the eleven-year period, errors measured in percentage points of annual growth rates rose from about 1.5 to 2.5 percentage points from the first to the eighth quarter for consumer prices but declined from about 2.5 to 1.3 percentage points for real GNP over the same period. For some GNP components, however, forecasting errors are much larger—10 to 30 percentage points.

The improved accuracy of longer forecasts in the case of the GNP reflects that surprise movements in one quarter tend to be followed by similar surprise movements in the opposite direction in the following quarter. This "canceling out" of forecasting errors in successive time periods is attributed to temporary, unpredicted shocks such as a strike or oil shortage affecting supply, or monetary consumer credit controls or auto price incentives affecting demand. In contrast, such surprises tend to increase the forecasting errors of the consumer price index and the GNP implicit price deflator over time. The reason for these differential impacts of economic shocks on the forecasting errors of GNP and inflation is not clear.

In comparisons of one-year forecasts derived from econometric models versus those based on non-modified autoregressive procedures, McNees finds that on average the econometric forecasts are significantly more accurate—about 20 percent more accurate for real GNP and GNP in current dollars and under 10 percent more accurate for the GNP implicit price deflator. Virtually all of the superiority of the econometric model forecasts occurs in the first quarter of the forecast period; forecasts of quarterly changes in the second to fourth quarters are just as accurate for the autoregressive procedure. Presumably, the greater accuracy during the first quarter reflects the short-term accuracy of the judgments associated with econometric model forecasts. In addition, econometric models typically forecast anywhere from several hundred to over a thousand macroeconomic variables while the autoregressive data reflect just three variables—GNP in current dollars, real GNP, and the GNP implicit price deflator (although the autoregressive procedure may be used for any number of variables).

McNees also found that the accuracy of annual forecasts of real GNP and inflation has generally improved over time. Striking exceptions occurred in 1974 and 1982, however. In 1974, forecasts tended to understate both inflation and real GNP substantially; in 1982, both real GNP and inflation were overstated substantially. The economic backdrop was quite different in these two periods. The 1974 aberration occurred during the supply shocks that followed an unanticipated event, that is, the Arab oil embargo and the accompanying sharp rise in oil prices. The 1982 aberration, on the other hand, occurred in an environment in which tight monetary policies had been pursued since 1979 to restrain demand and control inflation. Thus, the 1974 miscalculation resulted from the effects of unpredictable supply shocks, whereas the 1982 error appears due to miscalculating the effects of known monetary restraints on economic growth and inflation. McNees argues that major forecasting improvements will come from reducing such occasional egregious errors rather than from the small reduction possible to the normal forecasting error. Large forecasting errors are relatively infrequent, but deep recessions and high inflation are undesirable for the well-being of the nation, and better forecasts may lead to economic policies that can dampen such cyclical extremes.

McNees also analyzed how a forecaster's judgment affects the accuracy of the forecast.[2] As noted above, forecasters invariably modify forecasts derived from the equations of econometric models. McNees studied the effect of these judgments on the accuracy of econometric forecasts by analyzing records kept by a sample of four forecasters who reported their forecasts before and after the judgmental changes were made. Their records suggested that the judgmental modifications typically improved the forecasts, with the greatest improvement observed in the first quarter. The accuracy of the adjustments lessened as the forecasts extended to eight quarters ahead, occasionally worsening the forecasts by going in the wrong direction or by making too large a change, but overall the judgmental modifications improved the forecasts.

In considering the effect of subjective judgments on forecasting error, it is important not to lose sight of the fact that all forecasts contain underlying judgments regardless of how rigorously quantitative they are. A forecaster makes subjective judgments when determining whether to develop an autoregressive or an econometric forecast, as well as during the development of the mathematical specifications of these autoregressive or econometric forecasts.

There are inherent methodological limitations to forecasters' attempts to determine the complex interrelationships among the factors governing the economic future. In essence, a forecast is an extrapolation of past trends with allowances for expected continuities or discontinuities with the past. However, the complex nature of the economy as well as the limits of statistical data inhibit complete understanding of these trends. At an elementary level, many economic indicators that forecasters rely on are subject to substantial periodic revision, such as the GNP and the balance of trade. Any forecast is bound to be off if the indicators are revised after the forecast is made. Therefore, an analyst wishing to assess a forecast's accuracy must take into account the level of built-in "error" due to data revision. To do so requires data for the forecast period on the former, unrevised basis as well as on the revised basis, and such figures typically are not available. In this situation analysts typically attempt to approximate the unrevised data. One method of approximation is to determine the percent difference between the unrevised and revised data for a period when both data sets were published and then to use this ratio to estimate unrevised figures for the forecast period.

Many other methodological problems complicate the analysis of forecasting, but the more fundamental problem is that it is just not possible to predict accurately the relative importance and the significant interactions of the elements used in developing forecasts, such as the rate of economic growth, stage of the business cycle, income, consumption, investment, saving, productivity, inflation, interest rates, value of the dollar, and so forth. Forecasters can use statistical analysis of trends in past years and their own judgment to estimate these relationships, but these estimates are necessarily rough. For one thing, they represent an average of the experience of past years; this experience may not capture the unique characteristics of the forecast period. Secondly, statistical relationships and judgments can only describe a plausible behavior in terms of what would be expected according to current economic theory and experience. They cannot fully explain how each factor actually interacts with the others in the economic system as a whole.

The extent to which forecasts diverge from subsequent experience, however, provides lessons in the art and science of forecasting. When forecasting errors are large, they motivate analysts to discover what went wrong and why; that is, was the error due to a flaw in technical methodology or to intangible or new circumstances that were difficult to anticipate? Methodological flaws cover errors such as incorrectly specifying the relationships between unemployment and inflation or between the federal deficit and interest rates. Flaws in methodology can be improved for the next round of forecasts, but little can be done to prevent forecast error due to the unpredictability of the future. Examples of unanticipated events include the intangible psychologically driven waves of foreign inflows and outflows of money caused by speculation rather than observable changes in investment opportunities in the United States and abroad, or new events for which there is minimal previous experience, such as the political and economic upheavals in former Communist countries. Thus, even in a world of perfect data, perfect quantification of the future would be highly unlikely.

Even a forecast that seems accurate may contain hidden errors. Forecasts sometimes quite accurately project overall economic growth, employment, and inflation, but incorporate significant offsetting errors in the components of the forecasting methodology. For example, offsetting errors may occur in specifying the relationships between unemployment and inflation, and the federal deficit and interest rates. Consequently, the forecast is right for the wrong reasons. While an accurate forecast may be comforting, if it results from poor methodology it may give a false sense of security regarding future forecasts. Unfortunately, an accurate forecast can hamper impartial evaluations of the methodology. The accurate results and the euphoria resulting from a successful forecast may make it difficult for the forecaster to suspect a problem with the methodology at the time.

EFFECT OF FORECASTS ON ECONOMIC BEHAVIOR

There are contradictory ideas regarding how macroeconomic forecasts affect the behavior of households and businesses and thus affect the economy. Depending on how forecasts are translated into actions, they may function as a self-fulfilling prophecy or a self-correcting mechanism.

Forecasts become a self-fulfilling prophecy when households and businesses respond with actions that help the forecast come true. For example, a forecast of rising unemployment may cause households and businesses to cut back on spending because of insecurity about jobs and prospects for lower profits; thus, the forecast may bring on higher unemployment. A forecast of rising inflation may cause a spurt in current spending as consumers attempt to buy at current prices before expected price increases occur; this spurt in spending can itself bring on higher inflation. Indications of how the future is perceived are included in the stock price and consumer confidence components of the leading index of economic activity.

Forecasts function as a self-correcting mechanism when households and businesses take deliberate actions to help make the forecast inaccurate. For example, a forecast of higher unemployment may cause businesses to lower prices and banks to lower interest rates in order to bolster the quantity of sales and loans, thereby stimulating spending and lowering unemployment. A forecast of higher prices may cause households to restrain spending because consumers fear their income will not keep up with inflation; at the same time, businesses and banks may respond by raising prices and interest rates to ensure they do not fall behind in the upward spiral, but the increases may be to such high levels that they restrain spending. Both of these actions would tend to lower inflation, although the latter one would have a delayed effect until after the initial increases in prices and interest rates dampen spending.

At any rate, assessing the self-fulfilling versus self-correcting functions of forecasts is impossible because currently there is no information on how forecasts affect household and business behavior. Intuitively, it seems that the functions co-exist, but at the present time any estimates of their relative impact can only be conjectural.

REVIEW QUESTIONS

• How does an econometric model differ from an autoregressive methodology as a forecasting technique?

• How do short-term, medium-term, and long-term forecasts differ from each other?

• How can policymakers deal with the possibility of large errors in macroeconomic forecasts?

• What role does the forecaster's judgment play in macroeconomic forecasts?

• How may macroeconomic forecasts affect future economic trends?

NOTES

1. Stephen K. McNees, "How Accurate Are Macroeconomic Forecasts?" *New England Economic Review,* Federal Reserve Bank of Boston, July/August 1988.

2. Stephen K. McNees, "Man vs. Model? The Role of Judgment in Forecasting," *New England Economic Review,* Federal Reserve Bank of Boston, July/August 1990.

10
EPILOGUE: THE PRODUCTION OF ECONOMIC STATISTICS

This book has described how economic statistics are used to analyze trends in the economy and formulate fiscal and monetary policies to foster economic growth and lower unemployment and inflation. The lifeblood of such analyses are weekly, monthly, quarterly, annual, and less frequently provided statistical data such as the five-year economic censuses and the ten-year population census. Most of these statistics are produced by a few federal agencies: the Bureau of Labor Statistics in the U.S. Department of Labor, the Bureau of the Census and the Bureau of Economic Analysis in the U.S. Department of Commerce, the Economic Research Service and the National Agricultural Statistics Service in the U.S. Department of Agriculture, the Internal Revenue Service in the U.S. Department of the Treasury, and the Federal Reserve. Spending for the statistical programs of these agencies totaled $550 million in fiscal year 1990 (excluding the 1990 population census and the Federal Reserve programs).[1]

This figure may seem costly, but the expense cannot be evaluated without considering the importance of high-quality economic data to successful economic analysis. After all, the most sophisticated analytic techniques are only as good as the data they rely on. Indeed, one may easily conclude that the government invests too little rather than too much in economic data programs when the costs of developing economic data are compared to their importance. Economic data are central in the formulation of fiscal and monetary policies to attain steady economic growth and low unemployment and inflation. These policies affect billions of dollars in economic output and the lives of hundreds of millions of people.

Thus, recent cutbacks in federal spending that threaten the content, accuracy, and timeliness of economic statistics have troubling implications and merit serious consideration by economic analysts and government policymakers. Relevant, credible, and timely data that are readily available to the public are essential to the economic and social well-being of a democratic nation. As a professional economist, I have not only used federal statistics but have been involved in planning and evaluating the programs that produce them. In this epilogue, I present my own and others' views on how federal statistical programs must be changed to deal with major economic issues during the 1990s and into the twenty-first century. As the domestic and international economic environments daily become more complex, it is imperative that the quality of economic data used to interpret this world not only be maintained but also improved.

CONCERNS ABOUT ECONOMIC STATISTICS

During the 1980s and early 1990s, concern has grown about whether federal statistical programs have kept pace with the needs of the economy. Several studies have documented deficiencies. Most recently, the National Association of Business Economists (NABE) in 1988 and the Office of Technology Assessment (OTA) in the U.S. Congress in 1989 and 1990 have identified important weaknesses in the current statistical programs.[2]

The NABE study estimated that real resources spent on the statistical programs of the federal agencies identified above (i.e., spending in constant dollars) declined by 7 percent from 1979 to 1988. Several statistical programs were discontinued during this period, including family budget studies, quality of life and income-size measures of the national accounts, monthly surveys of selected service industries, measures of labor turnover, new hires and dismissals, the annual oil and gas survey, and research on developing price indexes for the construction of nonresidential buildings. Despite these cutbacks to accommodate the declining resources available for statistical programs, however, NABE found many problems in the current data that need to be addressed, as well as several omissions in data collection.

Among the weaknesses in the current data, NABE identified the following as most in need of attention:

• Response rates on some surveys (e.g., the Quarterly Financial Report and Manufacturers' Shipments, Inventories, and Orders) are declining;
• The consumer price index has not been assessed by an outside group of experts since 1960;
• The poverty standard, which is based on an income analysis method adopted in the early 1960s, is outdated;
• The Standard Industrial Classification system fails to reflect vast changes in the nation's industrial structure;
• Current data analysis methods do not consider effects of the underground economy;
• Nonresidential construction costs are poorly estimated.

In regard to omissions in the current programs, NABE identified the following as the most important kinds of data collection to pursue:

• Data on new international financial instruments that affect measures of the balance of payments;
• A unified, government wide effort to obtain information for analyzing industrial competitiveness; and

• A sampling frame of the names, addresses, and size of American businesses should be made freely available to all federal agencies for statistical purposes only, although previous attempts to amend confidentiality laws that restrict one agency from sharing its list of businesses with another agency have been unsuccessful.

The OTA analysis similarly noted several areas where undertaking new kinds of data would be useful. Specifically, OTA recommended collecting the following data:

• The value of plant and equipment assets in U.S. industries.
• Expenditures by business for employee training.
• Shipments of goods by different types of transportation (truck, rail, water, air).
• Data to analyze the effects of mergers and acquisitions.

OTA also advocated more cooperation between the Bureau of the Census and the Bureau of Economic Analysis to speed up preparation of the quinquennial and annual input–output tables.

STRATEGIES FOR IMPROVING ECONOMIC STATISTICS

Officials of the federal statistical agencies maintain that the cutback in resources for economic statistics in the 1980s did not diminish the quality of "core" data (such as the gross national product, unemployment, the consumer price index, and the balance of payments) but rather that the cutbacks led to eliminating less essential statistics or to providing them less frequently. Quantitative measures of the accuracy of economic statistics differ depending on the nature of the data: they include revisions to preliminary data, sampling errors of surveys, and the statistical discrepancy in the gross national product and the balance of payments. Based on these gauges, the accuracy of macroeconomic statistics has not declined, with one striking exception: there has been a startling rise in the statistical discrepancy of the balance of payments from a general level of $20 to $30 billion during the 1980s to $64 billion in 1990. This discrepancy means that $64 billion entering the U.S. are unaccounted for in the records of trade and money flows used in preparing the balance of payments estimates. Such a large discrepancy increases the tentative nature of analyses of the U.S. economy's international dimensions such as those in Chapter 3 under Exports and Imports.

Moreover, even though quantitative measures of statistical error do not show a decline (other than in the balance of payments), the view that most economic statistics have not declined in accuracy is questionable. Two qualitative factors, the lower response rates on some surveys and the cutbacks in small-scale research projects in statistical programs, suggest that a more general decline in accuracy has occurred. The lower response rate on surveys reflects a greater reluctance of companies and households to participate in surveys. This attitude may carry over to lessen the validity of the data reported by survey respondents. While there are no quantitative estimates of this reporting error, it is quite likely that carelessness in reporting accurate data has risen along with hostility toward surveys. If so, the diminished accuracy of the survey data adversely affects two types of economic indicators. The most clearly harmed indicators are those that are directly based on survey data such as the unemployment rate (derived from a survey of households) and the indicators on prices, employment, wages, sales, inventories, orders, profits, and plant and equipment expenditures (derived from surveys of businesses). However, inaccurate survey data also affect economic indicators like the gross national product and the balance of payments, which are prepared from data collected in many surveys. If statistical agencies are to counter the harmful effects resulting from a hostile mood toward surveys, they will need more resources to conduct outreach programs to raise participation rates in surveys as well as to encourage more careful reporting by survey respondents.

The budget stringency of the 1980s and early 1990s also led to cutbacks in the small-scale research projects conducted by analysts in statistical agencies which focus on how to improve the methodological procedures for producing economic statistics. These small projects are not shown as separate line items in agency budgets and thus are not visible in presidential and congressional budget reviews. But they are important, and their decline has probably led to a lower level of accuracy in economic data.

The president's 1992 budget submitted to Congress in February 1991 recognized the need to improve the quality of the core statistics. An initiative by Michael Boskin, chairman of the Council of Economic Advisers, requested additional funds of approximately $30 million in fiscal year 1992 as well as a series of multiyear increases totaling about $230 million over 1992–96.[3] The funds would be used to enhance a wide array of data and methodologies used in preparing economic statistics, with the following goals:

- Modernize and strengthen the national and international economic accounts.
- Increase the coverage of service industries.
- Distinguish between quality and inflation changes in price data.
- Improve the household and business surveys of employment and unemployment.
- Track changes across industries by (a) reconciling separate lists of business establishments maintained by the Bureau of Labor Statistics and the Bureau of the Census, and (b) modernizing the Standard Industrial Classification system to keep up with rapid changes occurring in all industries.
- Prepare for future statistical work force needs by establishing a graduate degree and nondegree program in survey statistics at a Washington area university.
- Improve the quality of federal statistical data by pursuing new legislation to allow limited sharing of confidential statistical data between agencies.

These improvements focus on strengthening the statistics that measure current macroeconomic trends and the infrastructure for collecting these statistics. The improvements are relatively comprehensive but fail to address two central omissions of the current programs. While these changes would provide better measures for developing fiscal and monetary policies to guide the economy toward steady growth and low unemployment and inflation, they would not provide sufficient data for analyzing basic policy questions related to U.S. competitiveness (such as how foreign investments affect U.S. production) and to the economic well-being of the population (such as the minimum subsistence income required for living in the 1990s).

In testimony before the Joint Economic Committee of Congress, the National Association of Business Economists supported the proposed multiyear improvements, but stated that the improvements focus on short-term deficiencies while neglecting a fundamental long-term organizational gap for establishing priorities to enhance various economic statistics.[4] Currently, the chief statistician of the U.S. government who oversees the planning and coordination of federal statistical programs in all agencies is part of the OMB Office of Information and Regulatory Affairs. The main objective of this agency is deregulation and paperwork reduction; thus, its statistical function has been widely criticized for being subordinated to these main activities and for showing little leadership in shaping government-wide priorities for statistical programs. In recommending a basic organizational change, NABE calls for new legislation to elevate the importance of statistics by creating an Office of the Chief Statistician which would report directly to the Director of the Office of Management and Budget and which would have budget review responsibility for economic statistics agencies.

The NABE testimony also supports a research program to update the poverty standard. Resistance to revising the poverty standard stems from two factors: (a) fears that a revised standard would lead to increased federal spending and thus raise the federal deficit, and (b) philosophic objections, such as those articulated by Thomas Sowell and Charles Murray, that antipoverty programs are undesirable forms of welfare that discourage work incentives and in fact hurt the poor more than they help them.[5] Regardless of views on the merits of antipoverty programs, however, it is shocking that public debate on poverty policy is guided by data based on 1960-era attitudes toward subsistence living standards (see Chapter 6 under The CPI and Measuring Poverty).

Obtaining increased funding to vitalize statistical data programs in the 1990s is likely to be difficult. Elected officials are generally reluctant to spend money for intangibles that are not readily perceived as making a difference in people's lives. Unlike spending for programs such as income maintenance, housing, education, health, the environment, and defense, the paybacks from increased spending for better economic measures are not very visible. Thus, even though the costs of statistical programs are relatively insignificant and even though accurate statistical data are necessary for effective implementation of civilian and defense programs, neither the public nor elected officials are easily convinced of the need to spend money to improve statistical measures.

Moreover, this general resistance to spending is heightened during periods of large federal deficits, such as are likely to prevail through most of the 1990s. Even if Congress were to authorize multiyear funding for the initiative introduced in the president's fiscal year 1992 budget, the multiyear proposals would have to be justified anew each year in the yearly budget requests for 1993–96 to have the funds appropriated for actual spending. These annual requests are likely to face increasingly strong opposition since they contain the bulk of the increased funding requested ($200 million of the $230 million planned during 1992–96). In the 1992 budget, Congress appropriated $18 million of the $30 million requested in increased funding.

The political prospects of such proposals could be enhanced if they were buttressed with tangible examples of how better statistical data improve analyses of economic trends and policies. Such a strategy is impractical, however. While it is easy to document instances of misleading information in preliminary data, and such events receive considerable media publicity, revisions have not been found to have noticeable policy effects in the past. Economic policymakers in the executive branch, the Federal Reserve, and Congress are well aware of the revision problem and the need to assess data trends over several quarters before determining the most appropriate course of action in any current period (see Chapter 1 for a discussion of revisions). The real policymaking problems of statistical deficiencies result not from differences in preliminary and revised figures but from intrinsic inaccuracies in both the preliminary and revised data. Unfortunately, documenting such data flaws is difficult. Thus, demonstrating inaccuracies in current economic data does not appear to be a promising strategy for convincing public officials to allocate more funds for statistical research.

An alternative strategy for persuading that better statistics lead to better governance is to focus on the policy issues of government data. If Congress and the president were persuaded that the economic statistics presently produced by federal agencies do not provide adequate tools for dealing with the increasing complexity and globalization of the U.S. economy and that the United States will be at a growing economic disadvantage until it revitalizes its information base, they would be more likely to support increased funding. One way of achieving this end would be to modify the multiyear statistical initiative to provide that more of the allocated resources go to data collection related to widely shared concerns about international competitiveness and domestic poverty policy. The advantage of this strategy is that payoffs of increased investment in statistical measures in these areas are more readily perceived. Results such as an improved ability to trace the effects of foreign investment in the United States and abroad on U.S. production, or a greater proportion of the population achieving minimum living conditions appropriate to the 1990s, are documentable. Thus, altering the budget initiative to focus on these concrete policy issues could not only achieve greater political support for increased statistical expenditures but also help remedy important deficiencies in the current program.

In summary, as resources for economic statistical programs have been cut in recent years, statistical measures have deteriorated in accuracy and content of coverage. Proposals to maintain or increase spending on statistical data have met with little support among public officials or their staffs because the value of statistical data is not widely appreciated. In the immediate future, the lack of support should be countered by appealing to widely held concerns about international competitiveness and domestic poverty policy. In the long run, greater attempts to demonstrate and publicize the relationship between good economic data and effective governance could increase general support for statistical programs among both policymakers and the public. Statistical agencies and economic analysts must convey the message that comprehensive and reliable economic data are not an expendable luxury in modern industrial societies, but a necessary investment if social and economic well-being are to be maintained and improved.

NOTES

1. Office of Management and Budget, Executive Office of the President, *Statistical Programs of the United States Government: Fiscal Year 1991.*

2. National Association of Business Economists, "Report of the Statistics Committee of the National Association of Business Economists," February 1988; and Office of Technology Assessment, U.S. Congress, "Statistical Needs for a Changing U.S. Economy," Background Paper, September 1989, and "A Comparison of OTA's and the Economic Policy Council's Recommendations for Improving Economic Statistics," Staff Paper, March 7, 1990.

3. U.S. Council of Economic Advisers, Executive Office of the President, "FY 1992 Economics Statistics Initiative: Improving the Quality of Economic Statistics," mimeo, February 14, 1991. This statement was summarized in the *Survey of Current Business,* March 1991, pp. 4–5.

4. Martin Fleming, "Improving the Quality of Economic Statistics," Statistics Committee, National Association of Business Economists, March 1, 1991; and "Testimony to the Joint Economic Committee, U.S. Congress," March 1, 1991.

5. Thomas Sowell, *The Economics and Politics of Race: An International Perspective* (William Morrow: 1983); and Charles Murray, *Losing Ground: American Social Policy, 1950–1980* (Basic Books: 1984).

REFERENCES

Abt Associates Inc. 1984. *Unreported Taxable Income from Selected Illegal Activities, March 31, 1983.* Report prepared for the Internal Revenue Service, and printed by the IRS in September 1984.

Adams, Larry T. 1985. "Changing employment patterns of organized workers." *Monthly Labor Review.* February.

Adams, Walter, and James L. Brock. 1988. *Dangerous Pursuits: Mergers and Acquisitions in the Age of Wall Street.* McGraw-Hill.

Alterman, William. 1989. "Price Trends in U.S. Trade: New Data, New Insights." National Bureau of Economic Research, Conference on Research in Income and Wealth, International Economic Transactions: Issues in Measurement and Empirical Research. Washington, D.C. November 3–4.

Anderson, Kay E., Philip M. Doyle, and Albert E. Schwenk. 1990. "Measuring Union-Nonunion Earnings Differences." *Monthly Labor Review.* June.

"Announcements." 1991. *Federal Reserve Bulletin.* February.

Armitage, Kenneth, and Dixon A. Tranum. 1990. "Industrial Production: 1989 Developments and Historical Revision." *Federal Reserve Bulletin.* April.

Aschauer, David Alan. 1989. "Is Public Expenditure Productive?" *Journal of Monetary Economics.* March.

———. 1989. "Public investment and productivity growth in the Group of Seven." *Economic Perspectives.* Federal Reserve Bank of Chicago. September/October.

Bach, Christopher L. 1991. "U.S. International Transactions, Fourth Quarter and Year 1990." *Survey of Current Business.* March.

Batra, Ravi. 1987. *The Great Depression of 1990.* Simon & Schuster.

Batten, Dallas S., and Courtenay C. Stone. 1983. "Are Monetarists an Endangered Species?" *Review.* Federal Reserve Bank of St. Louis. May.

Bauman, Alvin. 1990. "A new measure of compensation cost adjustments." *Monthly Labor Review.* August.

Baumol, William J., Sue Anne Batey Blackman, and Edward N. Wolff. 1989. *Productivity and American Leadership: The Long View.* The MIT Press.

Becker, Eugene H. 1984. "Self-employed workers: an update to 1983." *Monthly Labor Review.* July.

Bell, Linda A. 1989. "Union Concessions in the 1980s." *Quarterly Review.* Federal Reserve Bank of New York. Summer.

Bigman, David. 1984. "Exchange Rate Determination: Some Old Myths and New Paradigms." In *Floating Exchange Rates and the State of World Trade Payments,* eds. David Bigman and Teizo Taya. Ballinger.

Board of Governors of the Federal Reserve System. 1984. *Federal Reserve System: Purposes and Functions.*

———. 1986. *Industrial Production 1986 Edition: With a Description of the Methodology.* December.

————. 1986. *Monetary Policy Report to Congress Pursuant to the Full Employment and Balanced Growth Act of 1978.* February 19.

————. 1987. *Monetary Policy Report to Congress Pursuant to the Full Employment and Balanced Growth Act of 1978.* February 19.

————. 1990. *Monetary Policy Report to Congress Pursuant to the Full Employment and Balanced Growth Act of 1978.* February 20.

Boehm, Ernst A. 1990. "Understanding Business Cycles Today: A Critical Review of Theory and Fact." In *Analyzing Modern Business Cycles: Essays Honoring Geoffrey H. Moore*, ed. Philip A. Klein. M. E. Sharpe.

Bosworth, Barry P. 1985. "Taxes and the Investment Recovery." *Brookings Papers on Economic Activity*, 1.

————. 1989. Testimony before the Committee on Ways and Means, House of Representatives, United States Congress, April 19.

Bradley, Karen, and Avril Euba. 1977–78. "How Accurate Are Capital Spending Surveys?" *Quarterly Review*. Federal Reserve Bank of New York. Winter.

Bregger, John E. 1984. "The Current Population Survey: A historical perspective and BLS' role." *Monthly Labor Review*. June.

Bureau of the Census, U.S. Department of Commerce. 1989. "Survey of Plant Capacity, 1987." *Current Industrial Reports*. January.

Bureau of Economic Analysis, U.S. Department of Commerce. 1984. *Handbook of Cyclical Indicators: a supplement to the Business Conditions Digest.*

————. 1991. "Improving the Quality of Economic Statisics: The 1992 Economic Statistics Initiative." *Survey of Current Business*. March.

Bureau of Labor Statistics, U.S. Department of Labor. 1988. *BLS Handbook of Methods.* April.

Canner, Glenn B., Charles A. Luckett, and Thomas A. Durkin. 1990. "Mortgage Refinancing." *Federal Reserve Bulletin*. August.

Cantor, Richard. 1990. "Effects of Leverage on Corporate Investment and Hiring Decisions." *Quarterly Review*. Federal Reserve Bank of New York. Summer.

Carson, Carol S. 1984. "The Underground Economy: An Introduction." *Survey of Current Business*. May.

Carson, Carol S., and Bruce T. Grimm. 1991. "Satellite Accounts in a Modernized and Extended System of Economic Accounts." *Business Economics*. January.

Carson, Carol S., and Jeanette Honsa. 1990. "The United Nations System of National Accounts: An Introduction." *Survey of Current Business*. June.

Congressional Budget Office, U.S. Congress. 1991. *How Federal Spending for Infrastructure and Other Public Investments Affects the Economy*. July.

Cook, Timothy Q. 1986. "Treasury Bills." *Instruments of the Money Market*. Federal Reserve Bank of Richmond.

Cooper, Richard N. 1985. "Discussion Paper." *Brookings Papers on Economic Activity*, 1.

Copeland, Kennon R., and Jennifer M. Rothgeb. 1990. "Testing Alternative Questionnaires for the Current Population Survey." Proceedings of the Section on Survey Research Methods, American Statistical Association.

Corson, Walter, and Walter Nicholson. 1988. *An Examination of Declining UI Claims during the 1980s*. Prepared by Mathematica Policy Research for the U.S. Department of Labor, Unemployment Insurance Occasional Paper 88–3, Employment and Training Administration, U.S. Department of Labor. A condensed version of this report can be found in Employment and Training Administration, U.S. Department of Labor, *The Secretary's Seminars on Unemployment Insurance*, Unemployment Insurance Occasional Paper 89–1, 1989.

Coughlin, Cletus C., and Kees Koedijk. 1990. "What Do We Know About the Long-Run

Real Exchange Rate?" *Review*. Federal Reserve Bank of St. Louis. January/February.

Darby, Michael R. 1984. "The U.S. Productivity Slowdown: A Case of Statistical Myopia." *American Economic Review*. June.

de Leeuw, Frank, and Thomas M. Holloway. 1983. "Cyclical Adjustment of the Federal Budget and Federal Debt." *Survey of Current Business*. December.

————. 1985. "The Measurement and Significance of the Cyclically Adjusted Federal Budget and Debt." *Journal of Money, Credit and Banking*. May.

de Leeuw, Frank, Michael Mohr, and Robert P. Parker. 1991. "Gross Product by Industry. 1977–88: A Progress Report on Improving the Estimates." *Survey of Current Business*. January.

Denison, Edward F. 1985. *Trends in Economic Growth, 1929–1982*. The Brookings Institution.

Dertouzos, Michael L., Richard K. Lester, Robert M. Solow, and The MIT Commission on Industrial Productivity. 1989. *Made in America: Regaining the Productive Edge*. The MIT Press.

Duchin, Faye. 1990. "Technological Change and International Trade." *Economic Systems Research*, vol. 2, no. 1. New York University Institute for Economic Analysis.

Eisner, Robert. 1986. *How Real Is the Federal Deficit?* The Free Press.

Englander, A. Steven. 1991. "Optimal Monetary Design: Rules versus Discretion Again." *Quarterly Review*. Federal Reserve Bank of New York. Winter.

Eskenazi, Gerald. 1990. "Baseball Statistics: How Much Is Enough?" *New York Times*. April 30.

Estrella, Arturo, and Gikas Hardouvelis. 1990. "Possible Roles of the Yield Curve in Monetary Policy." *Intermediate Targets and Indicators for Monetary Policy: A Critical Survey*. Federal Reserve Bank of New York. July.

Feige, Edgar L., ed. 1989. *The underground economies: tax evasion and information distortion*. Cambridge University Press.

Fieleke, Norman S. 1989. "The Terms on Which Nations Trade." *New England Economic Review*. Federal Reserve Bank of Boston. November/December.

Flaim, Paul O. 1990. "Population changes, the baby boom, and the unemployment rate." *Monthly Labor Review*. August.

Fleming, Martin. 1991. "Improving the Quality of Economic Statistics." Statistics Committee, National Association of Business Economists. March 1.

————. 1991. Testimony to the Joint Economic Committee, U.S. Congress. March 1.

Friedman, Benjamin M. 1988. *Day of Reckoning: The Consequences of American Economic Policy Under Reagan and After*. Random House.

————. 1990. "Views on the Likelihood of Financial Crisis." Working Paper No. 3407. National Bureau of Economic Research.

Friedman, Benjamin M., and Kenneth N. Kuttner. 1989. "Money, Income and Prices after the 1980s." Working Paper No. 2852. National Bureau of Economic Research. February.

Friedman, Milton. 1968. "The Role of Monetary Policy." *American Economic Review*. March.

Fulco, Lawrence J. 1984. "Strong post-recession gain in productivity contributes to slow growth in labor costs." *Monthly Labor Review*. December.

Garner, C. Alan, and Richard E. Wurtz. 1990. "Is the Business Cycle Disappearing?" *Economic Review*. Federal Reserve Bank of Kansas City. May/June.

Getz, Patricia M. 1990. "Establishment Estimates Revised to March 1989 Benchmarks and 1987 SIC Codes." *Employment and Earnings*. Bureau of Labor Statistics, U.S. Department of Labor. September.

Goldstein, Morris, and Mohsin S. Khan. 1985. "Income and Price Effects in Foreign Trade." In *Handbook of International Economics*, vol. 2, ed. R. W. Jones and P. B. Kenen. Elsevier Science Publishing.

Goodfriend, Marvin, and William Whelpley. 1986. "Federal Funds." In *Instruments of the Money Market*. Federal Reserve Bank of Richmond.

Green, Gloria P. 1969. "Comparing employment estimates from household and payroll surveys." *Monthly Labor Review*. December.

Greenspan, Alan. 1991. "Economic Forecasting in the Private and Public Sectors." *Business Economics*. January.

Greider, William. 1987. *Secrets of the Temple: How the Federal Reserve Runs the Country*. Simon & Schuster.

Hamel, Harvey R. 1979. "Two-fifths of discouraged workers sought work during prior six-month period." *Monthly Labor Review*. March.

Healy, Paul, Krishna Palepu, and Richard Ruback. 1990. "Does Corporate Performance Improve After Mergers?" Working Paper No. 3348. National Bureau of Economic Research.

Hertzberg, Marie P., and Barry A. Beckman. 1989. "Business Cycle Indicators: Revised Composite Indexes." *Survey of Current Business*. January.

Hilton, Spence, and Vivek Moorthy. 1990. "Targeting Nominal GNP." In *Intermediate Targets and Indicators for Monetary Policy: A Critical Survey*. Federal Reserve Bank of New York. July.

Hirsch, Albert A. 1985. "An Analysis of Disinflation: 1980–83." *Business Economics*. January.

Hirtle, Beverly, and Jeanette Kelleher. 1990. "Financial Market Evolution and the Interest Sensitivity of Output." *Quarterly Review*. Federal Reserve Bank of New York. Summer.

Hooper, Peter, and Kathryn A. Larin. 1989. "International Comparisons of Labor Costs in Manufacturing." *Review of Income and Wealth*. December.

Hosley, Joan D., and James E. Kennedy. 1985. "A Revision of the Index of Industrial Production." *Federal Reserve Bulletin*. July.

Howenstine, Ned G. 1990. "U.S. Affiliates of Foreign Companies: Operations in 1988." *Survey of Current Business*. July.

Internal Revenue Service, U.S. Department of the Treasury. 1983. *Income Tax Compliance Research: Estimates for 1973–1981*. July.

———. 1990. *Income Tax Compliance Research: Net Tax Gap and Remittance Gap Estimates*. Publication 1415. April.

Isard, Peter, and Lois Stekler. 1985. "U.S. International Capital Flows and the Dollar." *Brookings Papers on Economic Activity*, 1.

Jablonski, Mary, Kent Kunze, and Phyllis Flohr Otto. 1990. "Hours at work: a new base for BLS productivity statistics." *Monthly Labor Review*. February.

Jackman, Patrick C. 1990. "The CPI as a Cost of Living Index." Paper presented at the 65th annual conference of the Western Economic Association. San Diego, California. June 29–July 3.

Joint Center for Housing Studies of Harvard University. 1990. *The State of the Nation's Housing 1990*.

Joint Economic Committee, Congress of the United States. 1980. *1980 Supplement to Economic Indicators*.

———. 1985. "Full Employment and Balanced Growth Act of 1978." *Employment Act of 1946, As Amended, with Related Laws*.

———. 1991. "The 1991 Joint Economic Report." March.

Kahn, George A. 1989. "The Changing Interest Sensitivity of the U.S. Economy." *Economic Review*. Federal Reserve Bank of Kansas City. November.

Kan, William, Reva Krieger, and P. A. Tinsley. 1989. "The Long and Short of Industrial Strength Pricing." Finance and Economic Discussion Series, Federal Reserve Board. November.

Kaufman, Henry. 1986. *Interest Rates, the Markets, and the New Financial World.* Times Books.

Kenessey, Zoltan E. 1979. "Capacity Utilization Statistics: Further Plans." *Measures of Capacity Utilization: Problems and Tasks.* Staff Studies 105. Board of Governors of the Federal Reserve System. July.

————. 1989. "The Development of a Monthly Service Output Index." In *The Service Economy.* Coalition of Services Industries. April.

Keynes, John Maynard. 1936. *The General Theory of Employment, Interest, and Money.* Harcourt Brace Jovanovich. Reprinted in 1964.

Klein, Philip A., ed. 1990. "What's Natural about Unemployment?" In *Analyzing Modern Business Cycles: Essays Honoring Geoffrey H. Moore.* M. E. Sharpe.

Koenig, Evan F., and Kenneth M. Emery. 1991. "Misleading Indicators? Using the Composite Leading Indicators to Predict Cyclical Turning Points." *Economic Review.* Federal Reserve Bank of Dallas. July.

Koopmans, Tjalling C. 1947. "Measurement without Theory." *Review of Economics and Statistics.* August.

Kutscher, Ronald E., and Richard W. Riche. 1990. "Impact of Technology on Employment and the Workforce—The U.S. Experience." World Bank Seminar on Employment and Social Dimension of Economic Adjustment. Washington, D.C. February 27–28.

Kuttner, Robert. 1984. *The Economic Illusion: False Choices between Prosperity and Social Justice.* Houghton Mifflin.

Laidler, David. 1990. "The Legacy of the Monetarist Controversy." *Review.* The Federal Reserve Bank of St. Louis. March/April.

Landefeld, J. Steven, and Eugene P. Seskin. 1983. "A Comparison of Anticipatory Surveys and Econometric Models in Forecasting U.S. Business Investment." Paper presented at 16th Centre for International Research on Economic Tendency Surveys (CIRET) Conference. Washington, D.C. September 21–24.

Landefeld, J. Steven, and Ann M. Lawson. 1991. "Valuation of the U.S. Net International Investment Position." *Survey of Current Business.* May.

Lebergott, Stanley. 1986. "Discussion," of paper by Romer, 1986. *Journal of Economic History.* June.

Leibenstein, Harvey. 1966. "Allocative Efficiency vs. 'X-Efficiency.' " *American Economic Review.* June.

Leon, Carol Boyd. 1981. "The employment-population ratio: its value in labor force analysis." *Monthly Labor Review.* February.

Lichtenberg, Frank. 1990. "Industrial Diversification and Its Consequences for Productivity." Working Paper No. 3231. National Bureau of Economic Research.

Liebling, Herman I., Peter T. Bidwell, and Karen E. Hall. 1976. "The Recent Performance of Anticipation Surveys and Econometric Model Projections of Investment Spending in the United States." *Journal of Business.* October.

Lipsey, Robert E., and Irving B. Kravis. 1987. *Saving and Economic Growth: Is the United States Really Falling Behind?* The Conference Board.

Lowe, Jeffrey H. 1990. "Gross Product of U.S. Affiliates of Foreign Companies, 1977–87." *Survey of Current Business.* June.

Luckett, Charles, A., and James D. August. 1985. "The Growth of Consumer Debt." *Federal Reserve Bulletin.* June.

McDonald, Richard J. 1984. "The 'underground economy' and BLS statistical data." *Monthly Labor Review.* January.

McIntyre, Robert S., and Dean C. Tipps. 1985. "The Failure of Corporate Tax Incentives." *Citizens for Tax Justice.* January.

McNees, Stephen K. 1988. "How Accurate Are Macroeconomic Forecasts?" *New En-*

gland Economic Review. Federal Reserve Bank of Boston. July/August.

————. 1990. "Man vs. Model? The Role of Judgment in Forecasting." *New England Economic Review*. Federal Reserve Bank of Boston. July/August.

Maisel, Sherman J. 1982. *Macroeconomics: Theories and Policies*. W. W. Norton.

Mansfield, Edwin. 1983. *Principles of Macroeconomics*. 4th ed. W. W. Norton.

Margasak, Larry. 1991. "Bird-Dogging Bureaucracy: Quayle-Led Council Watches Over Impact on U.S. Competitiveness." Associated Press Wire Release. May 20.

Mark, Jerome A. 1987. "Technological Change and Employment: Some Results from BLS Research." *Monthly Labor Review*. April.

Mark, Jerome A., William H. Waldorf, et al. 1983. *Trends in Multifactor Productivity*. Bureau of Labor Statistics. Bulletin 2178. September.

Marrinan, Jane. 1989. "Exchange Rate Determination: Sorting Out Theory and Evidence." *New England Economic Review*. Federal Reserve Bank of Boston. November/December.

Meulendyke, Ann-Marie. 1989. *U.S. Monetary Policy and Financial Markets*. Federal Reserve Bank of New York.

Mishel, Lawrence R. 1989. "The Late Great Debate on Deindustrialization." *Challenge*. January/February.

Mitchell, Wesley C. 1927. *Business Cycles: The Problem and Its Setting*. National Bureau of Economic Research.

Mitchell, Wesley C., and Arthur F. Burns. 1938. *Statistical Indicators of Cyclical Revivals*. Bulletin 69. National Bureau of Economic Research. Reprinted in 1961 in *Business Cycle Indicators*, ed. Geoffrey H. Moore.

Moore, Geoffrey H. 1950. *Statistical Indicators of Cyclical Revivals and Recessions*. Occasional Paper 31. National Bureau of Economic Research.

————. 1969. "Generating Leading Indicators from Lagging Indicators." *Western Economic Journal*. June.

————. 1983. *Business Cycles, Inflation, and Forecasting. 2d ed. No. 24. National Bureau of Economic Research Studies in Business Cycles*. Ballinger.

————, ed. 1961. *Business Cycle Indicators*. National Bureau of Economic Research.

Moorthy, Vivek. 1989–90. "Unemployment in Canada and the United States: The Role of Unemployment Insurance Benefits." *Quarterly Review*. Federal Reserve Bank of New York. Winter.

Morris, Charles S. 1984. "The Productivity 'Slowdown': A Sectoral Analysis." *Economic Review*. Federal Reserve Bank of Kansas City. April.

Mosimann, Thomas J. 1991. "Measures of Error for Changes in the Consumer Price Index January 1978–December 1986." *CPI Detailed Report*. Bureau of Labor Statistics, U.S. Department of Labor. February.

Munnell, Alicia H. 1990. "Why Has Productivity Growth Declined? Productivity and Public Investment." *New England Economic Review*. Federal Reserve Bank of Boston. January/February.

————. 1991. "Is There a Shortfall in Public Capital Investment? An Overview." *New England Economic Review*. Federal Reserve Bank of Boston. May/June.

Murray, Charles. 1984. *Losing Ground: American Social Policy, 1950–1980*. Basic Books.

National Association of Business Economists. 1988. "Report of the Statistics Committee of the National Association of Business Economists." February.

National Commission on Employment and Unemployment Statistics. 1979. *Counting the Labor Force*. U.S. Government Printing Office. Labor Day.

Niskanen, William A. 1988. *Reaganomics: An Insider's Account of the Policies and the People*. Oxford University Press.

Office of Management and Budget, Executive Office of the President. 1991. "Statistical Programs of the United States Government: Fiscal Year 1991."

Office of Technology Assessment, U.S. Congress. 1989. "Statistical Needs for a Changing U.S. Economy." Background paper. September.

———. 1990. "A Comparison of OTA's and the Economic Policy Council's Recommendations for Improving Economic Statistics." Staff Paper. March 7.

O'Leary, James J. 1990. "The U.S. Economy on the Edge of a Recession—How Serious Could It Be?" United States Trust Company. October 15.

Oliner, Stephen D. 1989. "Private Business Capital: Trends, Recent Developments, and Measurement Issues." *Federal Reserve Bulletin*. December.

Orr, James. 1991. "The Trade Balance Effects of Foreign Direct Investment in U.S. Manufacturing." *Quarterly Review*. Federal Reserve Bank of New York. Summer.

Parker, Robert P. 1984. "Improved Adjustments for Misreporting of Tax Return Information Used to Estimate the National Income and Product Accounts." *Survey of Current Business*. June.

Phillips, A. W. 1958. "The Relation between Unemployment and the Rate of Change of Money Wage Rates in the United Kingdom, 1861–1957." *Economica*. November.

Porter, Richard D., and Amanda S. Bayer. 1984. "A Monetary Perspective on Underground Economic Activity in the United States." *Federal Reserve Bulletin*. March.

———. 1989. "Monetary perspective on underground economic activity in the United States." In *The underground economies: tax evasion and information distortion*, ed. Edgar L. Feige. Cambridge University Press.

Pozdena, Randall J. 1990. "Do Interest Rates Still Affect Housing?" *Economic Review*. Federal Reserve Bank of San Francisco. Summer.

Raddock, Richard D. 1985. "Revised Federal Reserve Rates of Capacity Utilization." *Federal Reserve Bulletin*. October.

———. 1990. "Recent Developments in Industrial Capacity and Utilization." *Federal Reserve Bulletin*. June.

Ravenscraft, David, and F. M. Scherer. 1987. *Mergers, Sell-Offs, and Economic Efficiency*. The Brookings Institution.

Renshaw, Edward. 1991. "On Measuring Economic Recessions." *Challenge*. March/April.

Romer, Christina. 1986. "Spurious Volatility in Historical Unemployment Data." *Journal of Political Economy*. February.

———. 1986. "Is the Stabilization of the Postwar Economy a Figment of the Data?" *American Economic Review*. June.

———. 1986. "New Estimates of Prewar Gross National Product and Unemployment." *Journal of Economic History*. June.

Rosenbaum, David E. 1990. "Unemployment Insurance Aiding Fewer Workers." *New York Times*. December 1.

Ruggles, Patricia. 1990. *Drawing the Line: Alternative Poverty Measures and Their Implications for Public Policy*. The Urban Institute Press.

Ryding, John. 1990. "Housing Finance and the Transmission of Monetary Policy." *Quarterly Review*. Federal Reserve Bank of New York. Summer.

Safire, William. 1975. *Before the Fall: An Inside View of the Pre-Watergate White House*. Doubleday.

Sahling, Leonard, and M. A. Akhtar. 1984–85. "What Is Behind the Capital Spending Boom?" *Quarterly Review*. Federal Reserve Bank of New York. Winter.

Scherer, F. M. 1980. *Industrial Market Structure and Economic Performance.*, 2d ed. Rand McNally College Publishing.

Scholl, Russell B. 1991. "The International Investment Position of the United States in 1990." *Survey of Current Business*. June.

Seidman, Laurence S. 1989. *Saving for America's Economic Future: Parables and Policies.* M. E. Sharpe.

Seskin, Eugene P., and David F. Sullivan. 1985. "Revised Estimates of New Plant and Equipment Expenditures in the United States, 1947–83." *Survey of Current Business.* February.

Shiskin, Julius. 1961. *Signals of Recession and Recovery.* Occasional Paper 77. National Bureau of Economic Research.

————. 1973. Discussion of paper by Saul H. Hymans, "On the Use of Leading Indicators to Predict Cyclical Turning Points." *Brookings Papers on Economic Activity,* 2.

Smolensky, Eugene. 1965. "The Past and Present Poor." In *The Concept of Poverty.* Chamber of Commerce of the United States.

Sowell, Thomas. 1983. *The Economics and Politics of Race: An International Perspective.* William Morrow.

Steinberg, Edward. 1990. "What's in a Base Year? The Net Exports Paradox." *The Margin.* September/October.

Stiltner, Kenneth R., and David R. Barton. 1990. "Econometric Models and Construction Forecasting." *Construction Review.* March/April.

Stinson, John F., Jr. 1983. 1984. "Comparison of Nonagricultural Employment Estimates from Two Surveys." *Employment and Earnings.* Bureau of Labor Statistics, U.S. Department of Labor. March.

Stock, James H., and Mark W. Watson. 1989. "New Indexes of Coincident and Leading Economic Indicators." *NBER Macroeconomics Annual,* vol. 4. The MIT Press.

Stockman, David A. 1986. *The Triumph of Politics: The Inside Story of the Reagan Revolution.* Harper & Row.

Tamm, Feliks. 1984. "An Introduction to the System of Coincident, Leading and Lagging Indexes." unpublished. Bureau of Economic Analysis, U.S. Department of Commerce. October.

Tanzi, Vito. 1985. "Federal Deficits and Interest Rates in the United States: An Empirical Analysis." *International Monetary Fund Staff Papers.* December.

Tatom, John A. 1991. "Public Capital and Private Sector Performance." *Review.* The Federal Reserve Bank of St. Louis. May/June.

Thurow, Lester C. 1985. *The Zero-Sum Solution: Building a World-Class American Economy.* Simon & Schuster.

Tolchin, Susan J., and Martin Tolchin. 1983. *Dismantling America: The Rush to Deregulate.* Houghton Mifflin.

Tootell, Geoffrey M. B. 1991. "Regional Economic Conditions and the FOMC Votes of District Presidents." *New England Economic Review.* Federal Reserve Bank of Boston. March/April.

————. 1991. "Are District Presidents More Conservative than Board Governors?" *New England Economic Review.* Federal Reserve Bank of Boston. September/October.

U.S. Council of Economic Advisers. Various issues. "The Annual Report of the Council of Economic Advisers and Appendix Tables." *Economic Report of the President.*

————. 1991. "FY 1992 Economics Statistics Initiative: Improving the Quality of Economic Statistics." Mimeo. February 14.

Volcker, Paul A. 1985. "Statement to the Committee on Banking, Housing, and Urban Affairs, U.S. Senate." February 20.

Vroman, Wayne. 1990. "The Decline in Unemployment Insurance Claims Activity in the 1980s." The Urban Institute, Washington, D.C. December.

Watson, Mark W. 1991. "Using econometric models to predict recessions," *Economic Perspectives.* Federal Reserve Bank of Chicago.November/December.

Weir, David R. 1986. "The Reliability of Historical Macroeconomic Data for Comparing Cyclical Stability." *Journal of Economic History.* June.

Woodham, Douglas M. 1984. "Potential Output Growth and the Long-Term Inflation Outlook." *Quarterly Review*. Federal Reserve Bank of New York. Summer.

Yergin, Daniel. 1991. *The Prize: The Epic Quest for Oil, Money, and Power*. Simon & Schuster.

Young, Allan H. 1989. "Alternative Measures of Real GNP." *Survey of Current Business*. April.

Zarnowitz, Victor, and Charlotte Boschan. 1975. "Cyclical Indicators: An Evaluation and New Leading Indexes." *Business Conditions Digest*. May.

————. 1975. "New Composite Indexes of Coincident and Lagging Indicators." *Business Conditions Digest*. November.

INDEX

A

Abt Associates, 20
Adams, Larry, 230*n.29*
Adams, Walter, 131
Agriculture, Department of, 234, 312
Akhtar, M., 82
Alterman, William, 114
Anderson, Kay, 211
Armitage, Kenneth, 175*n.1*
Aschauer, David, 148*n.61*
August, James, 143*n.12*
Automatic stabilizers, 94–98

B

Bach, Christopher, 106
Balance of payments, 104–106
    and external debt, 116–121
    statistical discrepancy in, 106
Banking. *See* Federal Reserve.
Barton, David, 92
Baseball, 8–9
Batra, Ravi, 28–29
Batten, Dallas, 281*n.9*
Bauman, Alvin, 230*n.33*
Baumol, William, 223
Bayer, Amanda, 18
Becker, Eugene, 203
Beckman, Barry, 301*n.6*

Bell, Linda, 210
Benchmarks
    definition of, 11–12
Bidwell, Peter, 144*n.19*
Bigman, David, 146*n.42*
Blackman, Sue, 223
Boehm, Ernst, 31*n.1*
Boschan, Charlotte, 301*n.7*
Boskin, Michael, 315
Bosworth, Barry, 82, 133
Bradley, Karen, 144n.19
Bregger, John, 228*n.1*
Brock, James, 131
Budgets. *See* Government
    budgets.
Burns, Arthur, 264, 283
Bush, George, 30, 129
Business cycles
    data problem for long term
        comparisons, 27–28
    definition of, 22–23
    and depressions, 28–29
    designation of, 23–26
    and leading, coincident, lagging
        indexes, 283–285
    and National Bureau of Economic
        Research, 23
    in the United States since the 19th
        century, 26–28
Business optimism, 75, 284–285

Government budgets *(continued)*
  automatic stabilizers, 95–98
  cyclically-adjusted, 98–100
  full employment surplus, 98
  government and GNP, 40–41, 93–94
  high employment budget, 98
Government investment. *See*
  Investment and saving
Green, Gloria, 229*nn.21, 24*
Greenspan, Alan, 261
Greider, William, 264
Grimm, Bruce, 134
Gross domestic product (GDP)
  definition of, 43–44
  and foreign investment, 57–60
  and GNP, 33, 54
  primary measure of U. S.
    production, 33
  and productivity, 215–216
Gross national product (GNP). *See
  also* Consumer expenditures,
    Exports, Government budgets,
    Imports, Investment and saving,
    Plant and equipment investment,
    and Residential construction
  alternative measures of, 42–44
  cyclical movements of, 53–60
  definition of, 33–36
  and economic well-being, 35–36
  and employment, 203
  error range of, 45–47
  and industrial production, 153–156
  and inflation, 38–40
  and inventories, 42–43, 48–49,
    53–57
  long-term trends in, 52–53
  and money supply, 266–269
  and personal income, 63
  and prices, 38–40, 242–244, 266–269

Gross national product *(continued)*
  real GNP, 38–40
  seasonally adjusted annual rate,
    44–45
  statistical discrepancy in, 47
  system of national accounts, 36–38
  and underground economy, 18–19
  and unemployment (Okun's law),
    194–196

H

Hall, Karen, 144*n.19*
Hamel, Harvey, 180
Hamilton, Lee, 262, 263
Hardouvelis, Gikas, 278
Harvard University, 89
Healy, Paul, 131
Hertzberg, Marie, 301*n.6*
Hilton, Spence, 257
Hirsch, Albert, 241
Hirtle, Beverly, 274
Holloway, Thomas, 100
Honsa, Jeanette, 142*n.2*
Hooper, Peter, 223
Hours worked or paid for
  definition of, 206
  leading indicator, 206–207
  and productivity, 216
Households
  and demographic projections, 89
  and income measures, 208–209
  and survey data, 178–80, 234–235
Housing. *See* Residential construction
Howenstine, Ned, 146*n.37*
Humphrey-Hawkins Act. *See* Full
  Employment and Balanced
  Growth Act

T

U

Norman Frumkin is an economics writer and consultant, and teaches at the Graduate School, U.S. Department of Agriculture. He also authored the award-winning *Guide to Economic Indicators*.